AI-Driven Insights Into the Depths of Psychopathologies

Gorkem Derin
Istanbul University-Cerrahpaşa, Turkey

Kadir Uludag
https://orcid.org/0000-0003-3713-4670
Shanghai Jiao Tong University, China

IGI Global Scientific Publishing
Publishing Tomorrow's Research Today

Vice President of Editorial Melissa Wagner
Director of Acquisitions Mikaela Felty
Director of Book Development Jocelynn Hessler
Production Manager Mike Brehm
Cover Design Jose Rosado

Published in the United States of America by
IGI Global Scientific Publishing
701 East Chocolate Avenue
Hershey, PA, 17033, USA
Tel: 717-533-8845 | Fax: 717-533-7115
Website: https://www.igi-global.com E-mail: cust@igi-global.com

Library of Congress Cataloging-in-Publication Data

Names: Derin, Görkem, 1993- editor | Uludağ, Kadir, 1994- editor
Title: AI-driven insights into the depths of psychopathologies / edited by: Gorkem Derin, Kadir Uludag.
Description: Hershey PA : IGI Global Scientific Publishing, [2026] | Includes bibliographical references. | Summary: "This book aims to explore the intersection of artificial intelligence and mental health disorders, specifically focusing on conditions like schizophrenia, depression, bipolar disorder, eating disorder, and personality disorders"-- Provided by publisher.
Identifiers: LCCN 2025042310 (print) | LCCN 2025042311 (ebook) | ISBN 9798337313252 hardcover | ISBN 9798337313269 paperback | ISBN 9798337313276 ebook
Subjects: LCSH: Psychology, Pathological | Artificial intelligence--Medical applications
Classification: LCC RC454.4 .A388 2026 (print) | LCC RC454.4 (ebook)
LC record available at https://lccn.loc.gov/2025042310
LC ebook record available at https://lccn.loc.gov/2025042311

British Cataloguing in Publication Data
A Cataloguing in Publication record for this book is available from the British Library.

Table of Contents

Detailed Table of Contents

This chapter presents an integrative framework — predictive-personalized artificial intelligence (AI) — for digital mental health, combining real-time risk forecasting with dynamically adaptive therapeutic interventions. Unlike existing approaches that separate prediction and intervention, this framework utilizes machine learning, natural language processing, and mobile sensing to integrate behavioral, linguistic, and physiological data to anticipate episodes such as depressive relapses or suicidal ideation. The chapter details closed-loop system architecture linking prediction engines with intervention modules, highlighting personalization, adaptivity, and temporal sensitivity. Ethical and clinical issues including algorithmic bias, data privacy, false positives, and accountability are critically examined. The framework is positioned as a scalable augmentation to human-centered care, advancing a user-focused, anticipatory vision for AI in mental health.

Abstract Background: The Graduate Record Examination (GRE) in Psychology is a psychology test that assesses a student's general psychology knowledge. ChatGPT can assist students in preparing for the GRE psychology. Thus, we aimed to ask ChatGPT psychology questions related to GRE. Methods: This article explores the use of ChatGPT in responding to GRE psychology questions. The authors analyze the accuracy of ChatGPT's responses. Results: ChatGPT correctly answered ninety percent of the questions. Furthermore, there is a likelihood that ChatGPT can answer these questions because it already knows the answer since ChatGPT provided some of the answers without knowing the exact question. However, ChatGPT could not answer the unclear questions with 100 percent accuracy in this study. Therefore, future studies claim that ChatGPT can answer exam questions (e.g., law, biology, and

augments professional judgment, providing a path toward more effective, equitable, and accountable mental health care.

Substance use disorders (SUDs) pose a significant challenge in healthcare, marked by the compulsive use of substances despite negative consequences. Traditional methods of treatment and diagnosis, while somewhat effective, have limitations such as high costs, lengthy processes, and vulnerability to human error. This book chapter explores how integrating machine learning (ML) and artificial intelligence (AI) can address these issues and examines the transformative potential of advanced technologies in improving understanding, treatment, and prevention of SUDs and behavioral addictions. The chapter reviews recent research and developments, highlighting how these technologies enhance diagnosis, treatment prediction, outcomes, and risk assessment in SUDs. It merges insights from current studies with innovative AI tools like digital phenotyping, predictive modeling, and mobile health applications to demonstrate how AI can greatly improve outcomes for individuals with SUDs.

Artificial intelligence (AI) is rapidly progressing innovative technology to simulate the human brain. AI technology provides important classifications, predictions and therapeutic interventions in different psychopathologies. Neuroscience research offers a wealth of inspiration for novel kinds of algorithms and architectures for early diagnostics and development of the disorder. Recently, many studies and reviews have investigated the mutual relationship between AI and neuroscience. Complex deep neural networks inspired by neuroanatomical structures are utilized to create variable AI models including working memory, visual processing, speech and emotion recognition to manifest behavioral abnormalities in psychopathologies. This scoping review focuses on how neuroscience and AI are convergent to understand underlying mechanisms in mental health disorders and the development of new models for prevention.

This chapter explores the potential of Artificial Intelligence in mental health, with a special focus on psychopathologies. The researchers expand on AI's role in assisting clinicians' diagnosis, symptom tracking, predictive modelling, and therapy for psychiatric and neurodevelopmental disorders like Depression, Anxiety, Post-Traumatic Stress Disorder (PTSD), Substance Use Disorder, Autism Spectrum Disorder (ASD), and ADHD. Crucial interventions include wearables for anxiety, virtual reality exposure for PTSD, and robotic social companions for children with ASD. Despite these advancements, the use of AI chatbots as a replacement for therapy has been a subject of debate, largely due to issues around safety. The study highlights potential limitations, including risks in user interactions, limited therapeutic support, algorithmic biases, accessibility issues, and ethical concerns; advocating for "Human in the Loop" models where AI and clinicians work together, and calling for ethically designed AI systems that augment access without compromising on empathy, nuance and relational depth.

Preface

The rapid integration of artificial intelligence into mental health research and clinical practice is reshaping how psychopathologies are understood, detected, and treated. Advances in machine learning, natural language processing, digital phenotyping, and neuroscience-inspired computation have opened new pathways to identify psychological distress earlier, model its complexity more precisely, and deliver increasingly adaptive and personalized interventions. At the same time, these technological developments raise profound ethical, clinical, and epistemological questions regarding privacy, bias, accountability, and the evolving role of human judgment in mental health care.

AI-Driven Insights Into the Depths of Psychopathologies brings together interdisciplinary perspectives to examine how artificial intelligence is transforming the landscape of mental health assessment, diagnosis, education, and intervention. Rather than presenting AI as a replacement for clinicians or established therapeutic frameworks, this volume emphasizes augmentation: AI as a set of tools that can enhance human-centered care, support clinical decision-making, and expand access while remaining grounded in ethical responsibility and scientific rigor.

The chapters span predictive and personalized mental health systems, multimodal risk detection, precision psychiatry, educational applications of large language models, and disorder-specific domains, including mood disorders, eating disorders, substance use disorders, and neurodevelopmental and trauma-related conditions. Collectively, they highlight a shift from static, symptom-based models toward dynamic, data-informed approaches that capture the temporal, transdiagnostic, and individualized nature of psychopathology.

This volume is intended for researchers, clinicians, educators, and graduate students in psychology, psychiatry, neuroscience, data science, and digital health who seek a critical and forward-looking understanding of AI's role in mental health. By integrating technical innovation with clinical insight and ethical reflection, the book aims to contribute to a more responsive, equitable, and accountable future for mental health care in the age of artificial intelligence.

CHAPTER OVERVIEW

Chapter 1: From Prediction to Personalization: Adaptive AI Systems for Forecasting and Managing Mental Health Crises

The opening chapter introduces a predictive–personalized AI framework that integrates real-time risk forecasting with adaptive intervention delivery. By combining behavioral, linguistic, and physiological data within closed-loop systems, the chapter illustrates how AI can move beyond isolated prediction toward anticipatory and individualized care. Ethical considerations such as bias, privacy, and accountability are foregrounded, establishing key themes that resonate throughout the book.

Chapter 2: Can ChatGPT Answer GRE Psychology Questions?

This chapter examines the performance of large language models in educational assessment contexts, using GRE psychology questions as a case study. By evaluating accuracy and limitations, it raises broader questions about knowledge representation, test validity, and the implications of AI-assisted learning. The chapter also cautions against methodological pitfalls when evaluating AI systems on publicly available data.

Chapter 3: From Signals to Symptoms: Multimodal AI and Privacy-Preserving Approaches to Detecting Transdiagnostic Risk in Psychopathology

Focusing on transdiagnostic mental health risk, this chapter explores how multimodal AI systems integrate data from smartphones, wearables, and language-based platforms to detect early signs of distress. It critically reviews digital markers, foundation models, and privacy-preserving techniques, emphasizing the importance of clinician-led implementation and ethical safeguards.

Chapter 4: Precision Psychiatry in the Age of AI: Early Detection and Personalized Treatment of Mood Disorders

This chapter applies AI-driven approaches to mood disorders, highlighting how digital behavior, biomarkers, genomics, and neuroimaging can inform early detection and individualized treatment strategies. Through clinical vignettes and comparative analyses, it demonstrates how AI can enhance diagnostic precision while reinforcing the central role of professional judgment.

Chapter 5: Advanced Technologies in Substance Use Disorders: Artificial Intelligence and Machine Learning

This chapter explores how AI and machine learning can improve the diagnosis, risk assessment, and treatment prediction of substance use disorders and behavioral addictions. By examining digital phenotyping, predictive modeling, and mobile health applications, it highlights the potential of advanced technologies to enhance outcomes while acknowledging existing clinical and implementation challenges.

Chapter 6: Neuroscientific Approaches to Artificial Intelligence for Psychopathologies

Bridging neuroscience and AI, this chapter reviews brain-inspired computational models used to study and detect psychopathologies. It examines how neural architectures modeled on cognitive and neuroanatomical systems contribute to emotion recognition, working memory modeling, and early diagnosis, underscoring the reciprocal relationship between neuroscience and artificial intelligence.

Chapter 7: Advancements in Psychotherapy and Treatment: The Use of AI Interventions for Psychopathologies

The concluding chapter focuses on AI-assisted interventions across a range of psychiatric and neurodevelopmental disorders. From wearables and virtual reality to robotic companions and chatbots, it evaluates both therapeutic potential and limitations. Emphasizing "human-in-the-loop" models, the chapter argues for ethically designed AI systems that expand access without compromising empathy, relational depth, or clinical responsibility.

Chapter 1
From Prediction to Personalization:
Adaptive AI Systems for Forecasting and Managing Mental Health Crises

Hariz Aftab
https://orcid.org/0000-0002-8682-1621
Lovely Professional University, India

Mirza Jahanzeb Beg
https://orcid.org/0000-0002-6308-2678
Kumaraguru College of Liberal Arts and Science, India

ABSTRACT

This chapter presents an integrative framework — predictive-personalized artificial intelligence (AI) — for digital mental health, combining real-time risk forecasting with dynamically adaptive therapeutic interventions. Unlike existing approaches that separate prediction and intervention, this framework utilizes machine learning, natural language processing, and mobile sensing to integrate behavioral, linguistic, and physiological data to anticipate episodes such as depressive relapses or suicidal ideation. The chapter details closed-loop system architecture linking prediction engines with intervention modules, highlighting personalization, adaptivity, and temporal sensitivity. Ethical and clinical issues including algorithmic bias, data privacy, false positives, and accountability are critically examined. The framework is positioned as a scalable augmentation to human-centered care, advancing a user-focused, anticipatory vision for AI in mental health.

DOI: 10.4018/979-8-3373-1325-2.ch001

INTRODUCTION: THE PROMISE AND PERIL OF PREDICTIVE AI IN MENTAL HEALTH

In contemporary times, artificial intelligence (AI) is ubiquitous, infiltrating nearly every aspect of human life while molding daily lives and routines. Whether it is the digital world, such as the recommendations we receive on present-day entertainment platforms, or established industries, such as healthcare, education, finance, and transportation, AI systems increasingly mediate how people connect with technology and the world around them. AI has provided new age solutions that can process large quantities of data, more accurately recognize patterns, and quickly complete complicated tasks, which allows more rapid and focused decision-making and innovation. In addition to convenience, AI is being used in critical survival aspects related to climate change modelling, diagnosis in medicine, and mental health assessments (Beg & Verma, 2024; Beg, 2025; D'Alfonso, 2020; Kaack et al., 2022; Mitsala et al., 2021). AI is constantly evolving and, regarding the future reliance on it, we need to consider not just the pace of technological development, but what it means to exist in a world with intelligent machines in relation to ethics, culture, and their existence itself.

While much of the current discourse on AI and mental health centers around its predictive capabilities, this chapter goes further by examining the critical integration gap between forecasting risk and implementing effective, context-sensitive interventions. It interrogates not only how AI detects mental distress, but also how such technologies can ethically, practically, and culturally be woven into real-world care systems without displacing human agency or deepening systemic inequities. In the last several years, mental health has aligned with developments in artificial intelligence (AI), particularly in predictive technologies, representing a substantive evolution in the nature of behavioral psychological disorders. Traditionally, mental health care has operated on a reactive basis where intervention occurs post hoc when the individual recognition of psychological distress becomes clear with diagnostic criteria primarily relying on self-reports, clinical interviews, and observable behavior (Waldman & Terzic, 2019). Essentially, these existing diagnostic criteria have been guided by moments of behavior, which is limited by the dimensions of time, social stigma, and underreporting. Predictive AI concurrently is capable of reshaping the paradigm. Utilizing incredibly large and diverse data sets such as social media messages, biometric data, data from wearables, electronic health records, and even linguistic markers, AI systems are increasingly able to discern subtle patterns linked to mental illness prior to detectible and observable illness (Beg et al., 2024; Mansoor & Ansari, 2024). Such technologies aspire to predict risk and recommend timely intervention and treatment in advance of the condition presenting itself so that care could be shifted from "clinical treatment" to "psychosocial prevention," potentially sparing immense suffering and supporting mental well-being.

Although AI has the transformative potential in the field of mental health care, it also presents numerous ethical, epistemological, and practical challenges. The use of predictive systems in such highly personal and context-dependent realm raises important questions: Who determines risk thresholds, and what can "informed consent" mean with constant data collection? Can an algorithmic recommendation every truly capture the relational, cultural, and emotional dimensions of psychological distress? At what point should AI meaningfully influence clinical decision-making when that decision is of a human being's autonomy and vulnerability? Moreover, predictive systems run the risk of reinforcing already present hierarchies and structural inequities. Should this model rely on biased or missing data, the model would misrepresent entire groups of people, generating what could be termed as knowledge-based discrimination: systematic misrepresentation, exclusion, or erasure of whole communities from mental health care narratives. A complication in the problem of biases in AI is the opacity of many AI models. AI often operates within units, and evaluating the assumptions behind outputs is unapparent. Transparency assures accountability. To mitigate the reproduction of injustice, AI needs to be situated into a larger framework of equity, justice, and care, where people not algorithms remain the primary agents in the decision-making process.

This chapter seeks to provide a holistic and critically reflective consideration of the meanings and implications of predictive AI in mental health. It opens with contextualizing the shift from systems that are reactive to mental health ecosystems that can be proactive, suggesting positive possibilities of anticipatory technologies. After outlining the existing gaps and limitations of predictive mental health tools and technologies intended for use in practice, the chapter turns toward more complex issues of ethical implications, which are key concerns with early adoption and research use of AI and predictive tools. These dimensions related to ethics include but are not limited to surveillance, consent, privacy, algorithmic bias and discrimination, clinical accountability, and ethical tints involved in predicative interventions. The chapter aims to take the reader to think about the challenges of algorithmic and predictive futures and wade through the nuances of how we might think about how they are shaping better or worse sociotechnically conceived futures with predictive technologies in mental health, towards more ethically responsible, inclusive, human-centered futures. This chapter has not simply embraced the technological promises of AI, nor has it rejected the possibilities of AI through fear-based skepticism. Instead, it seeks to strike a balance in order to navigate a middle ground - acknowledging the great possibilities of predictive AI to improve mental health care, while also demanding the utmost ethical vigilance to ensure greater ethical oversight, maintaining the practice of interdisciplinary dialogue, and ensuring political oversight.

PREDICTING PSYCHOLOGICAL CRISES: MODELS AND MECHANISMS

The advent of predictive artificial intelligence (AI) in mental health care represents a significant advance in the development of mental health assessment and treatment. In the past, a reactive model has predominated the delivery of mental health services. In contrast, we have the ability to use AI to analyze large amounts of data from multiple different modalities such as language, behavior, and biometrics and we are able to move towards a more preventative model of care. This model prioritizes the ability to predict a psychological crisis before it is fully developed, therefore allowing for an intervention that is more timely, targeted, and potentially effective.

Embedded within the process of making predictive-limited or -capable actions, it is important to understand the important differences between forecasting and intervention. Specifically, forecasting means an AI system may identify patterns in individuals suggesting that they are at an increased probability for future decline of a mental condition (Reece et al., 2016). Intervention means the effort extended to mitigate or prevent that foreseen decline. Forecasting, while it may generate innovative ways of conceptualizing previously invisible psychological vulnerabilities, does not benefit clinical care without an intervention. A "prediction" that someone could likely suffer a depressive episode only provides clinical value if there is a preemptive, personalized, and contextually relevant intervention made. Therefore, predictive AI can only be beneficial when the value of that prediction (to the clinician or the patient) relates to the clinician's capacity to act upon that prediction by utilizing any aspect of the care that is being provided as an ethically consistent and human-centered strategy.

There are different methods under the heading of predictive models. Predictive models in mental health AI cover a spectrum of machine learning architectures that consider temporal, linguistic, physiological, and behavioral signals of distress. The types of predictive modelling techniques can be broken down into three main groups: time-series techniques that evaluate time ordered observations in order to find changes in data that occur over time (Hsu et al., 2024); natural language processing (NLP) techniques that focus on textual or spoken language and examine these mediums for indicators of mental health (Calvo et al., 2017); and participatory multimodal deep learning framework which considers data from -- for instance -- audio, text, video, and sensors into a single prediction (Tzirakis et al., 2017).

Time-series models, for example, can be used to assess fluctuations in mood, such as in patients with bipolar disorder, in order to early identify manic or depressive episodes (Pham et al., 2020). Deep learning architectures, and more specifically recurrent neural networks (RNN) and transformers, have improved extraction of value from aggregated and unstructured datasets from social media, wearable devices and smartphone apps (Bos et al., 2022). In this regard, predictive models can reveal relationships that offer insight as to how digital behavior can be related to mental health outcomes; for example, increased smartphone use late at night may correlate with increasing anxiety, and decreased linguistic complexity could indicate cognitive fatigue. Bayesian forecasting methods have some valuable features, including recognizing and managing uncertainty, and their ability to use prior knowledge to inform predictive judgements (Pavez & Allende, 2024; Popat & Ive, 2023). A Bayesian system is a statistical method that updates predictions based on new evidence, allowing for continuous learning and refinement of forecasts (Delgadillo et al, 2023). Bayesian models are adept at applying new data to update prior predictions, and as such, they are well suited to dynamic and personalized assessments of risk (Busk et al., 2020). The real strength of these approaches is their probabilistic nature, which allows clinicians to temper decisions in a climate of uncertainty—an unavoidable characteristic of diagnosis and treatment in mental health (Popat & Ive, 2023).

The predictive ability of Artificial Intelligence (AI) to monitor all of and help define aspects of mental health is contingent on the quality and diversity of data upon which it is trained. These datasets can generally be categorized into active and passive datasets. Passive datasets consist of data that has been collected from a person without active involvement from that individual, including data pertaining to smartphone usage, keystrokes, voice incline, geolocation, and measured physiological data from active wearables (e.g., heart rate variability, sleep patterns, movement) (Torous et al., 2019). These passive measures, for example, can act as antecedent markers of emotional dysregulation, social withdrawal and circadian rhythm (important for mental health) disturbance. Active data consists of willingly collected data resulting from active engagement from the person, and could consist of data from self-report questionnaires, ecological momentary assessments (EMAs) (Shiffman et al., 2008), or conversational data from chatbot AI conversations (Beg & Verma, 2025; Fitzpatrick et al., 2017). Data collected varies widely from self-report measures that examine suicidal ideation, hopelessness, and disorganization via the presentation of linguistic markers of mental illness. These AI features measure not only descriptive and predictive qualities (e.g., risk factors), but AI programmability includes the ability to triangulate passive measures with textual markers with accuracy comparable to a licensed professional. Syntactic complexity, topic modeling, and sentiment analysis are at the forefront of triangulating these risk factors. Incorporating all of this multimodal data stream provides a more trustworthy view of the individual's mental state for AI predictions. For instance, using linguistic data from text messages in conjunction with physiological data from wearables might provide context to differentiate between acute mood changes and chronic affective disorders.

A number of studies and clinical applications support the utility of predictive AI in mental health applications. One highly visible use case has been suicide risk prediction. Suicide research has found a number of predictive AI models that analyze electronic health records (EHR), emergency department visits, and patient notes to predict the likelihood of a patient attempting suicide. Some of these models can outperform clinical predictions. Moreover, predictive algorithms have been developed that monitor patients with bipolar disorder via mobile applications and wearable devices to anticipate the arrival of manic and depressive episodes through continuous observations of sleep, activity, and speech (Faurholt-Jepsen et al., 2015). Such methods for monitoring human behavior have produced findings utilizing physiological monitoring to make informed clinical decisions ahead of the manic or depressed event. Similarly, AI models conducted for PTSD have operated successfully based on language methodology in narratives that infer cognitive processing reflecting psychological deterioration (Son et al., 2020). Chatbot-type interventions also continue to provide relevant evidence (Beg & Verma, 2025; Fitzpatrick et al., 2017). AI systems like Woebot and Wysa that facilitate a therapeutic dialogue, have employed predictive analytics to adjust their responses in relation to the user's emotional state and risk profile, thus modeling users not only as support but also a vehicle to obtaining data toward further predictive models (Rządeczka et al., 2024).

Despite recent advancements in developing predictive models for mental health crises, challenges persist in achieving credible predictions. A primary concern is the sparsity and fragmentation of data, often inconsistent or poorly documented, which hinders the creation of meaningful, generalizable models. Additionally, models trained on population-level datasets may not account for individual variability, symptomology, or cultural context, leading to inaccurate predictions. False positives, where individuals are incorrectly flagged as at risk, can cause unnecessary interventions and anxiety (Christley, 2010). Conversely, false negatives can result in missed opportunities for timely care (Klinkman, 1998). Sensitivity and specificity are crucial when developing these models. Generalizability is another issue, as models developed in one demographic or cultural context may perform poorly in others due to differences in language, healthcare access, or mental health reporting. The interpretability of AI models is also critical, as many machine learning systems, particularly deep learning networks, operate as "black boxes," making it difficult to understand how conclusions are reached (Joyce, 2023). This opacity presents barriers to clinical trust and practical application in care strategies. Ongoing efforts to create explainable AI (XAI) aim to address these concerns and improve transparency and accountability in mental health predictions.

Overall, there is a clear and immediate need for an integrative model to integrate forecasting and interventions into one cohesive framework. This framework will need to ensure predictive accuracy, as but must also consider premise ethical considerations, and clinical judgement for patient-centered care. Predictions should not replace therapeutic decision making, but should help inform it, and AI-generated suggestions should not exist apart from our human nature, beyond the individual, and relationships. In addition, predictive AI technology should be incorporated with adequate safeguards that provide informed consent, privacy of data and fairness of the algorithms. Engaging a group of diverse professionals as a team of clinicians, data scientists, ethicists and patients is critical to keeping these technologies as tools of care, rather than control and surveillance.

Table 1. Strengths and Limitations of Key AI Approaches in Digital Mental Health Prediction

Model Type	Strengths	Limitations
Time-Series Models	- Good at finding patterns over time (like changes in mood or sleep). - Useful for early signs of mental health problems. - Works well for tracking someone's mental health regularly.	- Needs regular and complete data collected over time. - Doesn't work well if some data is missing or recorded at irregular times. - Not great at using outside or personal context.
Natural Language Processing (NLP)	- Can understand emotions and thoughts from text or speech. - Picks up on mood, language use, and tone. - Works on things like social media, chat messages, or therapy notes.	- May not work well with different languages or ways of speaking. - Depends a lot on the quality of the words people use. - Can't detect things outside of speech or text.
Multimodal Deep Learning	- Combines different types of data (like voice, sleep, text, facial expression) for better prediction. - Gives a full picture of someone's mental state. - Helps give more personalized results.	- Needs a lot of labeled data to learn from. - Takes a lot of computer power. - Can be hard to understand how it works, which may reduce trust from doctors or users.
Bayesian Forecasting Models	- Can update predictions when new data comes in. - Deals well with missing or uncertain information. - Gives clear risk estimates with confidence levels.	- Needs good starting assumptions to work well. - Can be slow or hard to use with complex or large data. - Often difficult to build and explain

ADAPTIVE INTERVENTIONS: PERSONALIZED RESPONSES TO FORECASTED RISK

Traditional clinical mental health care focuses on identifying and providing care for psychological conditions after there were noticeable indicators of concern that warranted clinical need. This approach is necessary in acute care, but the paradigm does not meet the growing need for early assessment, ongoing monitoring, and individualized preventive care for patients experiencing early warning signs of mental health challenges. Global mental health-related crises are becoming predominant due to compounded socio-economic stresses, excessive digital information, and perseverating post-pandemic malaise. In this context, a pivot toward a proactive ecosystem is imperative. Predictive artificial intelligence (AI) can help usher in this transition of care around mental health by turning the balance of care away from treating illness to promoting wellness. A proactive mental health ecosystem, consists of a system in which AI algorithms utilize behavioral, physiological, and contextual data in real-time to assess potential risks and intervene in a having effect or impact on prevention. Such predictive shifts toward an automated approach will reassign traditional mental health systems into living ecosystems that can be fluid and fallible within the qualities of care for individuals. This transition will have vast and challenging impacts that need to be evaluated in relation to workable frameworks for clinical practices, the ethics of mental health treatment, considerate bases of governing data, and perhaps an entirely redefined understanding of care.

At the center of this ecosystem are adaptive interventions, evolving therapeutic strategies that adapt to an individual therapeutic needs, behaviors, and mental state. Increasingly, adaptive interventions are relying on Just-in-Time Adaptive interventions (JITAIs) utilizing reinforcement learning and user modeling to targeted anticipated risk for mental health (Van Genugten et al., 2025). JITAIs have a potential to offer timing and the opportunity for therapeutic support exactly when an individual is at the highest risk or at the greatest chance of change, providing the best opportunity for success, and avoiding issue with user fatigue with the intervention or using too large a dose of intervention (Nahum-Shani et al., 2018). At the heart of adaptive interventions is reinforcement learning (RL), a subfield of machine learning in which systems learn optimal actions through trial-and-error learning, based on the input provided by the environment (Sutton & Barto, 2018). In mental health contexts, RL algorithms can be developed and trained using continuous streams of user data such as mood logs, sleep logs, voice intonation, digital activity, and physiological signals from wearable technology to identify distress signals and tailor system responses accordingly (Diaz-Ramos et al., 2023). These systems can ultimately refine and adapt over time, learning specifically what kinds of interventions (e.g., brief mindfulness exercises, motivational messages, behavioral challenges) have been most effective for the individual based on their reactions in prior contexts. Closely related to RL are JITAIs' scopes of action. The intent is to provide the right support at the right moment. While standard treatments provide the same content or the same schedule or frequency of treatment for each user, JITAIs embody a dynamic decision-making process where the system continuously scans the user's context, psychological state, and actions to determine if, when, and how to intervene (Nahum-Shani et al.,

2018). JITAIs are built around decisions points, where providing some intervention could lead to the highest gain, relying on passive measures (e.g. geolocation, phone activity), active inputs (e.g. self-reports), and historical outcomes (Nahum-Shani et al., 2018). JITAIs can be flexible interventions and are able to provide tailored interventions at multiple levels of granularity when considering mood, behavior, and environment changes associated with mental health.

Personalization in this area also comes in the form of user modelling, which is a process in which AI systems create and update an internal representation of an individual user's preferences, needs, vulnerabilities, and responsiveness (Purificato et al., 2024). As the user interacts with the system, the model of the user will change, allowing the algorithm to adjust its predictions and recommendations. For example, if a user in a system often skips the meditation prompts but completes the behavioral activation tasks, the system may focus on recommending the behavioral activation tasks instead of the meditation prompts, or phase out the meditation prompts altogether in their original format or change the format to align better with the user. User modelling not only enhances the appropriateness of the interventions received, but also increases the sense of individual recognition and autonomy which are the two most impactful elements on therapeutic engagement, as well as adherence. The intersection of reinforcement learning, user modeling, and adaptive delivery is already being implemented in real-world contexts. Digital mental health platforms like Woebot, Wysa, and Youper, for example, incorporate aspects of just-in-time adaptive interventions (JITAIs), harnessing natural language processing and predictive analytics to deliver personalized, AI-assisted cognitive behavioral therapy (CBT), mindfulness-based stress reduction (MBSR), or behavioral activation approaches (Inkster et al., 2018; Farzan et al., 2025; Mehta et al., 2021; Prochaska et al., 2021). Additionally, it connects users in a continual therapeutic relationship, interpreting distress from written emotional cues and generating requisite interventions responsively, as (or even before) they emerge. For some interventions, (if the system determines that someone is in a crisis, or that user is resistant to treatment, for example) they have the ability to escalate treatment to a human clinician.

Yet, shifting away from reactive systems and towards proactive ecosystems is more than technology; it requires radical structural changes in how mental health delivery is imagined and performed. Clinical workflows need to be rethought so that AI informs clinicians in a coherent way, with the appropriate form of human expertise and nuance. For instance, in a hospital integrating a Just-In-Time Adaptive Intervention (JITAI) system, a patient's mood, sleep, or speech patterns might be continuously monitored through wearable devices and mobile apps. If the AI model detects early signs of depressive relapse, it could alert the clinician dashboard in real time, prompting preemptive outreach such as scheduling an appointment, adjusting medication, or triggering a chatbot-based intervention. This means clinicians no longer wait for patients to report worsening symptoms, instead, their workflow involves interpreting AI-flagged signals and responding proactively. As such, new working definitions of professional roles need to be developed in which the clinician not only operates as a therapist and a human being, but as an interpreter of data, an agent of artificial intelligence (AI), and an ethical agent regarding digital concerns. We need new training opportunities that embrace these learning outcomes related to digital literacy, AI ethics, and algorithmic interpretation. Correspondingly, robust data governance to manage the tidal wave of sensitive user data acquired through apps, wearables, or digital waste must be designed to be transparent, secure, respectful of patient autonomy, and a part of a legitimate data governance strategy.

Proactive ecosystems have the distinct capacity to rethink care around mental health throughout the life-course. Predictive AI allows for longitudinal tracking to enable clinicians and systems to see how mental health shifts over developmental stages, life events, and environmental exposures (Chen et al., 2024). Instead of managing just isolated episodes, systems of care can recognize longer-term trends of vulnerability or resilience, initiating activities and pre-emptive interventions that may prevent relapse, episodic events, chronicity, or co-morbidity by conceptualizing their place in a continuum. This long view approach also cultivates continuity of care, supported by platforms regarded as companions beyond just service-based models of care. Moreover, proactive systems facilitate forecasting of mental health at the community and population level. Aggregated and anonymized data from digital mental health platforms can help policymakers and public health officials identify emerging trend forecasts (e.g., regional spikes in anxiety or depression) and vulnerable or targeted demographic compartments for intervention. Such forecasting can inform budgetary decisions about resource allocation, prevention campaigns, and monitoring mental health consequences associated with larger social impacts, such as economic downturns, pandemics, and climate pressures.

The human dimension must also remain central to this digital transformation. While predictive artificial intelligence (AI) offers unprecedented precision and scalability, mental health supports are uniquely relational, subjective, and affective. Emotions, empathy, cultural context, and the therapeutic alliance cannot be fully articulated by code (Ullrich, 2019). Therefore, a proactive system must be hybrid by design: productivity trickle-down technology that automates workloads and allows for the nuances of human care to be irreplaceable. The patient must be viewed as an active user, not just passively monitored and acted upon, or "data subjects." Patients can co-write their care journey, and digital platforms need to allow for feedback loops, user customizations, and meaningful consent to improve trust and motivation.

MindHelix is an innovative mental health program in India that integrates AI tools with human mental health providers in a hybrid model for individuals who may struggle with traditional forms of therapy as a result of location, cost, or stigma.

MindHelix uses an AI system to assess mental health conditions using chatbots or self-reporting tools. The AI system uses algorithms based on the input provided by the user to understand patterns of language, behavior and possible indications of depression, anxiety, or stress. MindHelix's AI system then employs NLP to provide real-time feedback, offering strategies for coping, such as mindfulness, breathing, or cognitive behavioral therapy, as well as suggesting a preferred route towards coping with mental health concerns. Once the user and AI have generated an assessment of mental health conditions, the user is connected with certified mental health providers, of which the most common are psychologists or counselors. Many consumer products which made use of AI powered solutions still required human oversight or control. It was important to note that the data gleaned from user interactions with the AI tools allowed practitioners to better understand the user's history and mental state. The practitioner also benefited from the application of human skills, expertise and intuition, contributing to a clearer presentation of assessment mental health. MindHelix was therefore able to provide clients with more directed mental health interventions. The program has had positive effects, especially in rural areas with little mental health resources. Because AI can be integrated into the first part of care, MindHelix is able to provide more access to more people and at a lower cost, thus providing larger populations access to mental health services. The hybrid model also decreases the load on human professionals, to spend more time focused on cases requiring deeper, personalized intervention.

There will be many ethical challenges when designing and implementing proactive ecosystems. Continuous audits, transparency about model design, and inclusion in data collection can help overcome some potential challenges regarding algorithmic bias, surveillance creep, or overemphasis on predictive metrics. Another equal concern is accessibility to AI tools for the mental health supports; ensuring that all tools are accessible and culturally adapted for the general public (given their proprietary nature and digitally literate populations). Furthermore, and as importantly, we should not only see digitally literate or upper-class populations benefitting from advanced AI-driven wellness tools; there is a challenge of making responsible AI mental health tools equitable to access across diverse populations. Also note the issue of emotional literacy that needs to be addressed in systems design. AI systems are able to intelligently model, not only cognitive states but with some success, emotional states and their interactions. We are witnessing the development of new research directions in affective computing that will enable AI systems to characterize and reason about not only basic emotional cues, but also complex situations that furnish cues of conflict, complex emotion—including irony, ambivalence, and suppressed distress for example—using multimodal data. Comprehensive recognition of subtle, complex and nuanced cues could significantly improve the appropriateness and sensitivity of JITAIs when used with populations who are known to under report symptoms due to various cultural norms or internalized stigma. In addition, the potential integration of new experiences offered by new technologies, particularly VR and AR, may augment the potential of proactive systems. For example, VR based exposure therapies, combined with adaptive algorithms and real-time monitoring, may deliver immersive therapeutic experiences tailored to the moment. These multisensory interventions, utilizing biosensors and AI informed feedback loops, may also approximate the affective richness of face-to-face (F2F) therapy to a greater degree than mobile apps.

SYSTEM ARCHITECTURE: BUILDING PREDICTIVE-PERSONALIZED FEEDBACK LOOPS

Although we have witnessed incredible potential for growth in mental health treatment with the advent of artificial intelligence, there remain vast limitations and challenges that inhibit AI's ability to fulfil its promise across the mental health care ecosystem. In order to leverage this capacity, it is crucial to recognize these insufficiencies in order to develop equitable, inclusive, and effective mental health technologies. One of the main issues is the lack of diversity within training datasets. Most AI mental health models are created using data derived from people in defined populations - usually, white, middle-class citizens residing in western countries. The datasets used to train algorithms do not encompass the psychological experience of all humans broadly. Context, culture, language, and social adversity all defines differential expressions of mental health and resulted pathways. Limitations of datasets trained on narrow data will misinterpret or underdiagnose mental health in people that are part of marginalized or underrepresented communities. Lack of diversity is not merely a technical issue designed to safeguard the public, it is an ethical matter and will reproduce systematic exclusions inequity thereof access to mental health treatment and outcomes. New methods like transfer learning and synthetic data generation are beginning to solve this bias, allowing models to generalize to groups that have been underrepresented. Furthermore, explicitly forming multilingual, culturally-sensitive datasets, from diverse geolocations, has begun to take precedence.

Alongside insistence on a human-centered perspective, AI-informed tools, assessments, and strategies can compound issues with reducing mental health to risk-status binary or categorically defined categories (i.e. high risk and low risk) particularly when enough context is not provided. Human psychological states are dynamic, contextual, and frequently cannot be reduced to fixed categories. The binary classification systems distort reality will prevent accessing anything other than remedial systems including defeating the nuance experience of an insomnia patient whose phenotype, expressed as self-reported sleep, fluctuates from positive to negative. A person identified as a "low risk," for example, manifests signs of slow deterioration while someone flagged as a "high risk" category may have had a temporary aberration of distress whether or not that distress disorder persists clinically, which is outside the binary classification. AI in restricted and established measurements that documents personal experience will produce innumerable false positives, and false negatives due to several social and community determinants that inhibit trusted beliefs and normative practice. In order to address this inflexibility, recent advancements in temporal and dynamic modeling, using personalized behavioral baselines, allow systems to track dynamic mental states across time and not rigidly through strict thresholds. Probabilistic and continuous risk estimation models have been used to start better capturing this complexity.

Equally significant, issues of explainability and transparency persist. In mental health, many of the algorithms used as AI are black boxes. When on the black boxes of algorithms are used, AI provides absolutely no explanation as to whether or how the implication to predict will be generated. The inability of black boxes to explain how predictions are established poses further barriers to clinical utility for a number of ethical concerns from governing patient, payer, and provider. Clinicians must understand, apply critique, and verify AI-driven predictions to make meaningful decisions that can be verified in practice. Without being transparent with AI is means absolutely trusting clinical AI will not gain support or built trust from practitioners or clients alike. Additionally, explainability and transparency are still significant issues (Iwaya et al., 2023). Many of the AI algorithms in mental health are black boxes that do not descriptively explain how the predictions are made. This lack of interpretability constitutes barriers to clinical integration, and poses ethical challenges to using automated systems in mental health, as no clinician can meaningfully critique, understand, or confirm an AI recommendation without knowledge about how it operates. Without any insight, trust can no longer be a meaningful part of the interaction for either practitioners or patients. Explainable artificial intelligence (XAI) approaches like attention maps and model-agnostic XAI techniques are becoming more widely researched to gain insight into AI-enabled mental health predictions. Hybrid models that include clinician-in-the-loop feedback loops are also being introduced to marry the autonomy of automated decision-making with human reflexivity.

Many of the AI mental health platforms that illustrate feedback loops or user interaction mechanisms are fairly simplistic in their functionality, often requiring only casual engagement from users with barely any space for correcting, customizing, or sharing the process with the AI system. While this may fit with the directive approach of T2D care, this does not accurately reflect the need for a therapeutic alliance or mutual understanding of the clinical approach taken in mental health care. In addition, neither patients nor clinicians are included in cycles of iterative feedback. The failure to incorporate these groups of people further limits the iterative capability of the AI tools. Participatory design methodologies and active learning systems are being evaluated to incorporate user and clinician feedback in a live setting so that AI tools adapt to patient experiences and don't remain static. Finally, privacy, data security and consent concerns are amplified by AI applications that make use of continuously and passively collected data. Mental health data is arguably one of the most sensitive types of personal data (Vredenburgh, 2024). It is very important to ensure that users provide ongoing, informed consent, understand how their data will be used and are involved in the entire lifecycle of their data. Not incorporating these practices not only creates serious ethical issues, but it can also cause users to avoid using digital tools altogether. Protocols such as federated learning and differential privacy are being adopted to provide assurance that private mental health data is preserved during multi-user model training on a massive scale. At the same time, edge computing is helping to increase the speed of AI processing, while preserving patient control over their data. To ensure a robust and effective AI-driven mental health system, a closed loop system designed for continuous data collection, predictive modeling and adaptive interventions will be required. This section describes the necessary architectural framework to execute such a system including technical considerations, design and implementation principles.

Figure 1.

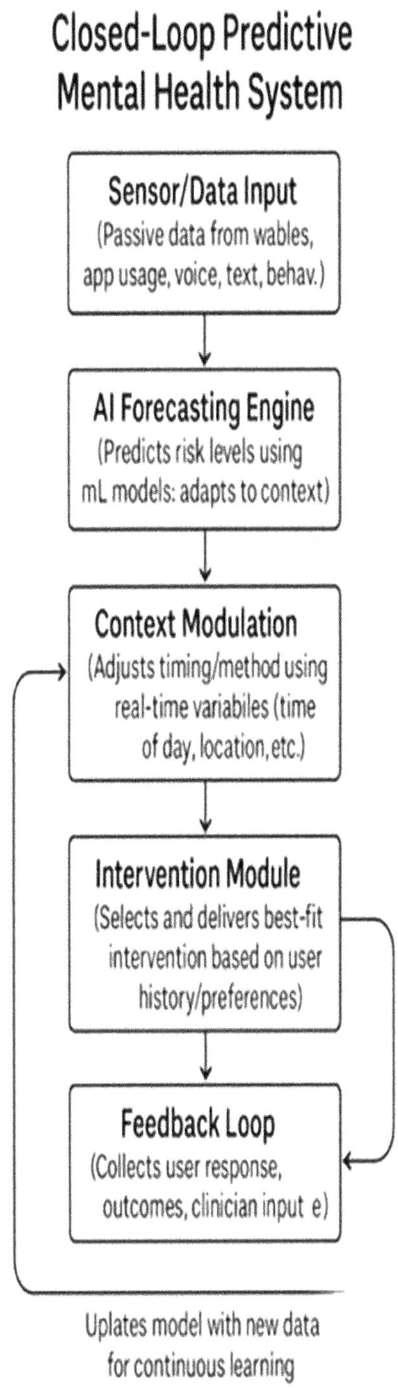
Closed-Loop Predictive
Mental Health System
Sensor/Data Input
(Passive data from wables,
app usage, voice, text, behav.)
AI Forecasting Engine
(Predicts risk levels using
mL models: adapts to context)
Context Modulation
(Adjusts timing/method using
real-time variabiles (time
of day, location, etc.)
Intervention Module
(Selects and delivers best-fit
intervention based on user
history/preferences)
Feedback Loop
(Collects user response,
outcomes, clinician input e)
Uplates model with new data
for continuous learning

Framework for Closed-Loop Mental Health Systems

In mental health, closed-loop systems refer to dynamic feedback loops where information is continually exchanged between the user and system, enabling real-time responsiveness and personalization of care (Liu, 2021). These systems require specialized data entry, processing, and feedback components that adjust in real-time. Closed-loop systems are defined by the way they take in information, interpret it relative to risk or need, decide on interventions or actions, implement them, and evaluate impacts so as to inform future actions. Closed-loop systems are predicated on sensor inputs. In mental health, sensors can be passive (e.g., smartphone usage-tracking, speech and tone analysis, GPS location, and wearables that monitor sleep data or heart rate) or active (e.g., mood logs, check lists assessing symptoms, self-reports, etc.). Sensors are important for "real-time" monitoring and discovering relevant trends in psychological dynamics. The predictive engine is generally powered by artificial intelligence, and will facilitate incoming streams of data, establish trajectories of mental health, predict levels of future risk, and recommend interventions when appropriate. Crucially, these models must appreciate historical data, user preferences, and social determinants of mental health to ensure ethically and reliably informed interventions. The types of intervention modules can be micro-level actions like motivational prompts, or serious escalation protocols like contacting mental health professionals. Intervention modules should be customizable to users and contexts, and should always consider user needs. A feedback interface that allows both users and clinicians to input qualitative data is essential, as it deepens system learning, enhances transparency, and offers users control over their mental health journey. Underpinning all packages is a robust data governance layer that adheres to ethical data collection and data processing, security encryption, and corresponding to laws and regulations including those outlined in GDPR, HIPAA and similar regulations.

Integration of the Forecasting and Intervention Modules

In order for a closed-loop mental health system to be effective, it is critical to facilitate smooth communication between the forecasting engine and the intervention module. A forecast without timely, smart intervention can seem intrusive and fail to carry any forward momentum; while intervention without forecasting is unlikely to make sense, and may result in inappropriate or wasted responses. Implementation requires three elements of integration: risk thresholding, which is establishing criteria for when to trigger an intervention (often by making a probabilistic evaluation of psychological distress); context modulation, which ensures that real-time contextual variables (e.g. time of day, user location, social interactions) are factored in to ensure that timely and sensitive support is offered; matching interventions, to ensure the response selected from the bank of treatment options is the best response to put in place based on the user's medical history, past ratings feedback, and user preferences; and escalation, which means having a clear and fast way for the system to alert the individual's clinician, or emergency services when the individual's risk level crosses into a significant threshold. Overall, these elements all work together so that a coherent, responsive and user-centered mental health system exists. For enhanced adoption, systems must incorporate a local context. Working with NGOs can give important insight as to what the community needs, and providing options in the local language in the app interface enables easier accessibility. Inclusion of local culturally relevant practices and support fosters trust as well as improved engagement.

To assess a closed-loop mental health system's effectiveness and impact requires strong, varied study designs. A mixed-methods approach using qualitative and quantitative data can permit an adequate evaluation to assess the effectiveness of the system. This quantitative data may consist of user uptake, symptom severity change, and treatment success, while the qualitative data may come from user based interviews or focus groups exploring the experiences of patients, clinicians, and caregivers. Longitudinal studies would also be an asset when examining longer-term effects of continuous, AI based retrieval or interventions for mental health support on an individual's psychological health. By following a user for longer time periods researchers could be able to observe how these systems influence mental health trends, the degree to which they promote resilience, and overall life outcomes. Longitudinal trials could also assist in iteratively resolving issues related to user engagement over time and adapting the intervention over time. Longitudinal studies could also examine cost-effectiveness and implementation at scale across disparate populations and contexts from rural to urban settings.

Challenges in Real-Time Responsiveness and Personalization

While the emergence of real-time, personalized mental health systems is exciting, it raises many complicated questions that need to be analyzed and discussed to support ethical, efficient, and scalable implementation. One of the most salient issues is latency and processing speed. Real-time intervention requires low-latency responses, which often necessitates edge computing (computational methodologies conducted at the edge of the network, closer to where it is being generated) to eliminate the time between the recognition of data (behavior) and the response (intervention), especially since mobile devices will most likely serve as the primary interface. Another key consideration is ignoring noise and ambiguity with data. Mental health data is nebulous, and behavioral variables, such as increased screen time during a given period, could point towards depressive symptoms or suggest binge-watching.

Distinguishing meaningful psychological patterns from incidental patterns will be challenging. Balancing scalability and individuality is also a critical consideration; to be effective, systems need to operate at scale (meaning generally serve millions of people) while providing deeply individualized interventions. This tension between wide-spread treatment and individualized treatment remains a key design consideration. The issue of ethics in personalization, specifically to avoid developing AI systems that limit decision-making for users and/or reinforce maladaptive behaviors under the label of "personalization," is an important consideration. AI systems should not constrain user agency, but they should be transparent and accountable. Interoperability is also extremely important; systems/concepts that facilitate integrated care (mental health, EHRs, clinical workflows, other digital systems, etc.) must work. While culturalization is also further complicated, generally speaking, if something works in one culture, there is a possibility it could be inappropriate or harmful in another culture requiring it to be "localized" in terms of language, content, and therapeutic models. Finally, attention must be given to various international regulations for software-based interventions that can fall under definitions of digital therapeutics, medical devices and therapeutic services for mental health, as it is important to measure compliance with legal and ethical norms.

Despite these barriers, AI-enhanced mental health systems have the potential to revolutionize care by shifting from static, reactive models to dynamic, predictive ecosystems. Yet, current tools are constrained by homogeneity in data, insufficient contextual sensitivity, weak feedback mechanisms, and ongoing privacy concerns. To overcome these limitations, a closed-loop systems architecture like integrating real-time sensing, adaptive forecasting, and contextually-aware interventions is essential. Addressing the technical, ethical, and cultural dimensions of AI personalization will be pivotal in achieving meaningful, long-term mental health support. Ultimately, the path to building clinically robust, socially-just, predictive feedback loops lies in inclusive design, participatory co-creation of technology, and rigorous evaluation of these systems in diverse, real-world settings.

ETHICAL AND CLINICAL CONSIDERATIONS

The deployment of predictive AI with respect to mental health contexts gives rise to serious ethical concerns that go beyond technology and evidenced effectiveness (Verma et al., 2025). These included, but are not limited to, data ownership, algorithmic accountability, informed consent, equity, autonomy, and the ethics of preemption. Predictive AI, like any medical system that contains algorithms and evidence, is affecting clinical decision-making, therapeutic alliances, and public health decisions, and there are emerging implications for the development of ethics that can adequately respond to these challenges with precision and breadth. What follows are some notable ethical and clinical considerations that inform the future building and use of AI-based mental health care.

Surveillance, Data Ownership, and Informed Consent

The constant, and often hidden, collection of user data through mobile apps, wearable tech, and digital tracking of behaviors creates a form of surveillance in mental health care. It is worth noting that predictive AI has a yearning for massive amounts of data, which we may not always think about in terms of diminishing autonomy and transparency. Users generally have little awareness or understanding of how much personal data, including keystroke dynamics to voice inflection, is harvested, processed, analyzed, and monetized by mental health processes. It is not as simple as whether we are informed or give consent to this; rather, the contract of informed consent is a fundamental component of health care ethics, and it diminishes its purpose.

In order to mitigate these risks, ethical models need to adopt principles of data sovereignty- whereby individuals have ownership over personal mental health data-and data minimalism, whereby only the most relevant data is collected and/or stored. Data governance should allow for transparency through mechanisms for explicit consent, regular audits, opt-outs, and decentralized storage for privacy and ownership. Additionally, one of the ways to improve individuals' transparency and ownership of their information would be to build blockchain technologies into these ethical models to offer access control and audit trails about who, when, and what information was accessed. This could ultimately provide not only ethical use but also legal use, as well as trustworthiness to the user. Furthermore, AI systems trained on data predominantly from WEIRD (Western, educated, industrialized, rich, and democratic) populations are likely to amplify systemic inequities in diagnostic and care in the mental health context. It is more than likely that these models will miss or misidentify non-normative forms of psychological distress in circumstances and cultural experiences outside of the researchers' and AI designers' own social and economic/cultural circumstances. This process can also be understood in terms of a form of epistemic injustice in the scholarship.

Inclusive and Culturally-Aware AI Development

Ethical AI design must include representational equity or the intentional inclusion of marginalized communities in data collection, model training, and evaluation. This indicates that developers must center the practice of inclusive epistemologies in which lived experience is valued alongside quantification. Working closely with communities, implementing annotators with cultural awareness and sensitivity, and utilizing participatory research principles can ensure that AI tools are more reflective of the multiplicity of mental health experiences globally. In addition, algorithmic audits should be performed regularly to identify any latent biases and to remediate them, making public or, at a minimum, share the results publicly (as a way to increase accountability). This promotes a systematic practice of responding to user feedback and learning/upgrading the model, especially communities that are often under-represented, potentially impacting user experience and their education or mental health externally.

Explainability and Clinical Accountability

One of the most frequent concerns raised relating to predictive AI is the "black box" dimension of more complex machine learning (ML) models, as they generally provide outputs without clear reasoning behind them. The risk here is that their lack of transparency threatens the trust of patients and leads to an erosion of clinical accountability. When clinicians create a dilemma around being more passive with decisions for diagnosing or beyond (due to reliance on an opaque system for recommendations), actions are not active, ethical decision-making based on experience, knowledge, and judgment, but rather actions based on machine recommendations without consideration. This leads to the need for this discipline to formally consider explainable AI (XAI). XAI means having models that have explainable outputs, or are provided with explanations of the decision. Clinicians need to be able to interrogate how a particular prediction comes about, and where it can fit into the broader decision-making process. Additionally, training programs for mental health professionals and students must now adapt to teaching equity in using AI systems in their work and what ethical data interpretation might entail. Trying to make more clear on what is being asked of the clinician to understand AI in their work, potentially allows for explainability to be more of a shared responsibility that can enhance patient-centered care and autonomy.

Risk, Autonomy, and Clinical Escalation Protocols

Predictive systems often generate alerts based on probabilistic models of harm such as multinational suicide risks or relapse predictions. These predictive systems can have significant life-saving potential, though they can also present serious moral dilemmas. Should interventions be implemented with an algorithmic prediction? If it is wrong? Intervening too early, or with coercive power could violate patient autonomy, further stigmatize or burden a clinician. The main issue is to balance risk and autonomy. Risk scores must be interpreted as input information, not as an endpoint. Informed consent must include useful information on what the predictions can initiate, and what interventions may result. Multi-disciplinary ethical boards should be engaged to create clinical escalation plans based on patients' rights and values. In addition, developers should allow for sensitivity-specificity thresholds that can be modified in real-time based on individual patient preferences and clinical context. If the sensitive-specificity thresholds are opaque, patients' rights are violated and therapeutic boundaries are destroyed creating false opportunities for patients when they are distressed, in pain, or scared, as opposed to violated agency. This will reduce false positive opportunity and enhance recognition of boundaries and agency.

Cultural, Moral, and Interdisciplinary Responsibilities

The emergence of predictive AI in mental health is not just technocentric. The technologies that underpin predictive AI in mental health are sociotechnical; they emerge from particular cultural stories, institutional frameworks, and public policies. We must watch out for the tendency to flatten complex mental phenomena into computable categories. This threatens to reduce the multiplicities that make aspects of care meaningful which cannot be quantitatively represented. Our experience of caring relationships, empathy, relationality, and meaning-making help us re-conceptualize care through a holistic lens. Careful attention to our collective responsibility will undergird the future development of AI technologies in this space. It is incumbent upon developers, clinicians, ethicists, policymakers, and the public to act with shared responsibility to ensure that the goals underlying the use of these technologies center upon equity, justice, and human thriving. Deliberant engagement between diverse disciplines will be important, as will public deliberation about what values ought to underpin the development of predictive AI in mental health. The creation of open-access ethical standards, similar to the Helsinki Declaration in medical research, could the foundation for all stakeholders in the development of ethical AI. All stakeholders should contribute to the evolution of ethical guidelines in this space via public consultation. We should openly recognize that improving mental health is not simply a clinical enterprise; it is a cultural and moral endeavor.

Avoiding Clinical Deskilling and Promoting Human-Centered AI

The increasing role of AI in influencing clinical practice involves a potential clinical trend of deskilling and dependence on AI. AI may have the potential to produce clinical decision-making at the expense of rational clinical reasoning on the part of clinicians. Clinicians may disengage from critical reflection, compassion, traditional critical judgement, and clinical intuition that permeates quality mental health care. To mitigate this, a techno-social approach to designing in human-in-the-loop, so that AI enhances clinician expertise, would help to ensure that AI remains meaningful as a workplace tool. At the same time, the ethical use of AI will need to mean that AI should strengthen a productive engagement in process, primarily for human engagement, thinking, evaluation and clinical rationale, while reminding clinicians that AI is a tool, and it has to pass through a human judgement, and contextual need for engagement and intervention.

IMPLEMENTATION AND FUTURE DIRECTIONS

The power to catalyze change with predictive AI in mental health care will depend not only on its technological capacity, but also on the broad equitable and context-sensitive implementations, or configurations it affords. As the field begins to gather momentum, it is crucial for the academic and community stakeholders to redirect their attention to priority issues in the implementation of the tools across varied contexts, the scalability available to them across diverse populations, and a prospective research agenda that emphasizes relevance, inclusivity, and engagement across fields of study. This section will outline a few options for the sustainable and ethical implementation of predictive AI tools in mental health care.

Scalability in Low Resource Settings, Marginalized Populations

In spite of the rapid emergence of digital mental health technologies, we are still seeing significant variability in their roll out across geographic, socio-economic contexts etc. One of the most urgent implications of the potential of predictive AI lies in the adaptation of them within low-resources contexts, where access to traditional mental health resources is limited. AI enabled tools could be a vehicle to offer scalable, mobile-ready, and nuanced adaptable interventions that do not require an expansive clinical work force or infrastructure. Nevertheless, the successful deployment of such systems in low-resourced settings entails careful consideration of culturally appropriate design, low-cost technology infrastructure, and community buy-in. Language localization, respect for indigenous epistemologies, and sensitivity to social stigma are critical. Likewise, developers should understand the barriers faced by individuals with low digital literacy and infrastructural issues like intermittent internet access or outdated devices. Working alongside community health workers, NGOs, and governmental stakeholders can foster trust, build support, and ensure these systems do not merely replicate those developed in high-resourced settings without meaningful regard for contextual factors.

Hybrid Approaches: AI + Human Support

While AI systems provide timely predictions and scalable interventions, they cannot replace the care and lived experience provided by human practitioners. A potentially fruitful avenue for implementation is through hybrid approaches, blending the predictive capacities of AI with the relational capabilities of therapists, counselors, and peer supporters. In these approaches, the AI system serves a triage system, or early warning system, or behavioral coach for users, while human clinicians deliver personalized, contextualized, and emotionally attuned care.

Hybrid systems provide solutions or lessen many of the primary ethical and practical challenges associated with AI-only solutions. For example, clinicians may disregard recommendations from algorithms based on their clinical intuition or the preference of the patient, helping protect the notion of human judgment in the delivery of care. Also, in many cases, hybrid models promote heightened trust with users as they may be more likely to engage with a digital platform if they recognize that there is a human therapist involved. Further, hybrid models are only successful when adequately integrated into existing health systems. For instance, this may entail interoperating with electronic health records, clinician training related to AI literacy, and establishing adequate communication protocols between digital and human actors involved in care delivery. Demonstration programs in various countries (e.g., India and Kenya), integrating mobile-based mental health platforms into community health systems provide valuable case studies for hybrid implementation at scale.

Pathways for Clinical Integration and Therapist-AI Collaboration

To transition past pilots and app-based deployment, predictive AI needs to be situated within the clinical workflow. This will entail the creation of decision-support systems that are usable, interpretable, and provide support in ways that align with the way clinicians think. We will require collaboration between AI developers and mental health professionals to maximize the usability, clinical relevance, and ethically conceptualized tools provided by predictive AI. Therapist-AI collaboration provides opportunities for a more individualized treatment planning process. For example, predictive-based systems could assess a patient's engagement with prescribed therapeutic exercises, provide real-time feedback to the patient regarding mood trends, and suggest ways to personalize CBT (Cognitive-Behavioural Therapy) protocols as they unfold. The therapist would then think about and interpret these insights in relation to the patient's lived experience, creating a feedback loop with good insight and quality of care. Implementation will also require readiness of institutions. Health systems must think about the training of staff on AI usage, data governance systems, and training on the legal aspects of using AI responsibly. Institutional commitment to standardized approaches for escalation, auditing, and ethical review for patient safety and liability.

Research Priorities: Longitudinal Validation, Diversity, and Interdisciplinarity

The transformative potential of predictive AI in mental health depends on a solid, inclusive research framework. Present predictive AI models do not utilize longitudinal validation. Although we may be aware of trends in the specific short-term outcomes we study with AI (e.g. whether an AI-assisted intervention outputs short-term improvement in anxiety), we cannot know how the engagement of AI may alter real-world mental health trajectories over time. Longitudinal studies are important to our efforts to realize AI-based interventions in meaningful ways, especially in real-world contexts and among diverse populations. There continues to be a lack of diversity among the training datasets used to create predictive AI systems. Models trained on datasets that do not represent a diversity of populations and health systems run the risk of reinforcing disparities and biases in whatever outcome and often create biased recommendations. In addition, we must prioritize ethical recruitment and collection of data that reflects a greater diversity of cultural, demographic, and clinical contexts. Utilizing community based participatory research (CBPR) methods where possible to engage underrepresented groups in collaboratively developing and evaluating contextualized digital approaches is suggested. Interdisciplinary collaboration is the foundation of sustainable innovation in the field. Computer scientists, clinicians, ethicists, social workers, and public health practitioners must work together to imagine, implement, and evaluate predictive systems that are technically robust and socially responsive. Public engagement is equally important: the people who these systems will ultimately affect must have a say in shaping them.

Future Directions: Responsible Innovation and Policy-Theory Provisions

With predictive AI using at a rapid rate, planning is going to need to be proactive. Policy and regulatory frameworks need to extend beyond biomedical-based provisions, and expand the framework to reflect the complexities of unfamiliar regulatory challenges fallacious to AI algorithmic systems like errors and accountability, privacy to our data, and the limits of autonomy when utilizing AI for decision making. Future studies will also need to consider how predictive AI can fit within interdisciplinary systems like digital phenotyping approaches, neurofeedback, and biosensor models. These systems offer a higher ability to assess the nuances of mental health states than using predictive AI on its own, but can also offer ethical and technological issues. The intent of predictive AI is not to imagine a circumstance of being able to predict and ultimately control human behavior, it is to magnify the capabilities of people and communities to be enabled to flourish. Moving beyond technological deterministic approaches to imagining frameworks to those that are built on an ethical foundation of care; respect for human rights; and principles of social justice. Assuming larger valuative hypothesizes, the intention for the field to imagine a path forward for implementation of predictive AI could encompass inclusive, evidence-informed, ethically robust contexts.

CONCLUSION

Predictive AI has the potential to transform how we perceive, understand, diagnose, and support mental health. Its capabilities from continuous risk estimation to population-specific interventions signal a shift towards a future that is anticipatory, adaptive, and contextualized, rather than reactive. With this potential comes ethical responsibility wherein these tools must uphold the core aims of mental health care that are dignity, empathy, justice, and flourishing. Mental health is not solely a matter of symptoms and diagnoses; it is deeply embedded in experience, culture, and social context. Therefore, predictive AI must be designed around ethical principles that center people over data. Transparency, explainability, and fairness are not optional but foundational.

The development of predictive mental health ecosystems sits at the intersection of human and technological considerations. These systems must not only detect patterns of crisis but also acknowledge moments of ambiguity, uncertainty, and autonomy. The balance between automation and human interpretation will be central to the future of such tools. A responsible vision for AI in mental health must embrace complexity and include clinicians, patients, designers, ethicists, and policymakers. Hybrid models that combine AI's data-processing abilities with human empathy can deliver timely and personalized care but they must also be socially and culturally sensitive. This vision must extend beyond affluent or urban populations. In low-resource and vulnerable communities, predictive AI should enable inclusion and empowerment, not deepen inequality. This means investing in infrastructure, designing for linguistic and cultural diversity, and incorporating feedback from those most affected.

Ethical innovation requires creativity grounded in dignity and accountability. It demands interdisciplinary collaboration, responsible governance, and a long-term perspective. Real-world validation through longitudinal studies, sociocultural diversity, and participatory research is essential to ensure these systems are effective in everyday life. We are not merely creating new tools but shaping new paradigms of care and responsibility in an age of intelligent machines. The decisions we make today about who builds these systems, who they serve, and how they are governed will echo for generations. In essence, predictive AI is not the endpoint of innovation in mental health. It opens deeper questions about care, listening, and healing. Grounding technological advancement in human values ensures that the future of mental health care is not only more efficient, but also more just, humane, and transformative.

It will take global partnerships and strategic funding initiatives to make our aspirations a reality. Governments, research entities, NGOs, and technology companies will need to collaborate and fund efforts aimed at designing culturally adaptive AI tools. Each initiative that receives support should be prioritizing the design of mental health systems inclusive of each community, especially those in lower resource, rural, or marginalized areas. Action will also be needed to support infrastructure for multiple languages, cultural contexts, and locale-specific needs in order for the tools to be effective to a wide diversity of populations.

REFERENCES

Beg, M. J. (2025). Responsible AI integration in mental health research: Issues, guidelines, and best practices. *Indian Journal of Psychological Medicine*, *47*(1), 5–8. DOI: 10.1177/02537176241302898 PMID: 39650770

Beg, M. J., & Verma, M. VCKM, M., & Verma, M. K. (2024). Artificial intelligence for psychotherapy: A review of the current state and future directions. *Indian Journal of Psychological Medicine*. Advance online publication. DOI: 10.1177/02537176241260819 PMID: 40831472

Beg, M. J., & Verma, M. K. (2024). Exploring the potential and challenges of digital and AI-driven psychotherapy for ADHD, OCD, schizophrenia, and substance use disorders: A comprehensive narrative review. *Indian Journal of Psychological Medicine*. Advance online publication. DOI: 10.1177/02537176241300569 PMID: 39677516

Beg, M. J., & Verma, M. K. (2025). Revolutionizing mental healthcare through artificial intelligence. In Uludag, K., & Ahmad, N. (Eds.), *Chatbots and mental healthcare in psychology and psychiatry* (pp. 21–54). IGI Global., DOI: 10.4018/979-8-3693-3112-5.ch002

Bos, F. M., Schreuder, M. J., George, S. V., Doornbos, B., Bruggeman, R., van der Krieke, L., Haarman, B. C. M., Wichers, M., & Snippe, E. (2022). Anticipating manic and depressive transitions in patients with bipolar disorder using early warning signals. *International Journal of Bipolar Disorders*, *10*(1), 12. DOI: 10.1186/s40345-022-00258-4 PMID: 35397076

Busk, J., Faurholt-Jepsen, M., Frost, M., Bardram, J., Vedel Kessing, L., & Winther, O. (2020). Forecasting mood in bipolar disorder from smartphone self-assessments: Hierarchical Bayesian approach. *JMIR mHealth and uHealth*, *8*(4), e15028. https://mhealth.jmir.org/2020/4/e15028 PMID: 32234702

Calvo, R. A., Milne, D. N., Hussain, M. S., & Christensen, H. (2017). Natural language processing in mental health applications using non-clinical texts. *Natural Language Engineering*, *23*(5), 649–685. DOI: 10.1017/S1351324916000383

Chen, S., Yu, J., & Chamouni, S.. (2024). Integrating machine learning and artificial intelligence in life-course epidemiology: Pathways to innovative public health solutions. *BMC Medicine*, *22*(1), 1–10. DOI: 10.1186/s12916-024-03566-x PMID: 39218895

Christley, R. M. (2010). Power and error: Increased risk of false positive results in underpowered studies. *The Open Epidemiology Journal*, *3*(1), 16–19.

D'Alfonso, S. (2020). AI in Mental Health. *Current Opinion in Psychology*, *36*, 112–117. DOI: 10.1016/j.copsyc.2020.04.005 PMID: 32604065

Delgadillo, J., Budimir, S., Barkham, M., Humer, E., Pieh, C., & Probst, T. (2023). A Bayesian network analysis of psychosocial risk and protective factors for suicidal ideation. *Frontiers in Public Health*, *11*, 1010264. DOI: 10.3389/fpubh.2023.1010264 PMID: 36935710

Diaz-Ramos, R. E., Noriega, I., Trejo, L. A., Stroulia, E., & Cao, B. (2023). Using Wearable Devices and Speech Data for Personalized Machine Learning in Early Detection of Mental Disorders: Protocol for a Participatory Research Study. *JMIR Research Protocols*, *12*, e48210. DOI: 10.2196/48210 PMID: 37955959

Farzan, M., Ebrahimi, H., Pourali, M., & Sabeti, F. (2025). Artificial Intelligence-Powered Cognitive Behavioral Therapy Chatbots: A Systematic Review. *Iranian Journal of Psychiatry*, *20*(1), 102–110. DOI: 10.18502/ijps.v20i1.17395 PMID: 40093525

Faurholt-Jepsen, M., Vinberg, M., Frost, M., Debel, S., Margrethe Christensen, E., Bardram, J. E., & Kessing, L. V. (2015). Daily electronic self-monitoring in bipolar disorder using smartphones–the MONARCA I trial: A randomized, placebo-controlled, single-blind, parallel group trial. *Psychological Medicine*, *45*(13), 2691–2704. DOI: 10.1017/S0033291715000410 PMID: 26220802

Fitzpatrick, K. K., Darcy, A., & Vierhile, M. (2017). Delivering cognitive behavior therapy to young adults with symptoms of depression and anxiety using a fully automated conversational agent (Woebot): A randomized controlled trial. *JMIR Mental Health*, *4*(2), e19. DOI: 10.2196/mental.7785 PMID: 28588005

Hsu, F. M., Chen, H. C., Wang, K. C., Ling, W. L., & Chen, N. C. (2024). Application of time series analysis in predicting postpartum depression: Integrating data from the hospitalization period and early postpartum weeks. *Archives of Women's Mental Health*. Advance online publication. DOI: 10.1007/s00737-024-01521-6 PMID: 39367991

Inkster, B., Sarda, S., & Subramanian, V. (2018). An empathy-driven, conversational artificial intelligence agent (Wysa) for digital mental well-being: Real-world data evaluation mixed-methods study. *JMIR mHealth and uHealth*, *6*(11), e12106. PMID: 30470676

Iwaya, L. H.. (2023). On the privacy of mental health apps: An empirical investigation and its implications for app development. *Empirical Software Engineering*, *28*(1), 2. DOI: 10.1007/s10664-022-10236-0 PMID: 36407814

Joyce, D. W., Kormilitzin, A., Smith, K. A., & Cipriani, A. (2023). Explainable artificial intelligence for mental health through transparency and interpretability for understandability. *NPJ Digital Medicine*, *6*, 6. DOI: 10.1038/s41746-023-00751-9 PMID: 36653524

Kaack, L. H., Donti, P. L., Strubell, E., Kamiya, G., Creutzig, F., & Rolnick, D. (2022). Aligning artificial intelligence with climate change mitigation. *Nature Climate Change*, *12*(6), 518–527.

Klinkman, M. S., Coyne, J. C., Gallo, S., & Schwenk, T. L. (1998). False positives, false negatives, and the validity of the diagnosis of major depression in primary care. *Archives of Family Medicine*, *7*(5), 451. PMID: 9755738

Liu, Y., Liu, Y., Tang, Y., Jiang, D., & Yu, H. (2021). A closed-loop healthcare processing approach based on deep reinforcement learning. *Multimedia Tools and Applications*, *80*(12), 18691–18708. DOI: 10.1007/s11042-020-08896-5

Mansoor, M. A., & Ansari, K. H. (2024). Early detection of mental health crises through artificial-intelligence-powered social media analysis: A prospective observational study. *Journal of Personalized Medicine*, *14*(9), 958. DOI: 10.3390/jpm14090958 PMID: 39338211

Mehta, A., Niles, A. N., Vargas, J. H., Marafon, T., Couto, D. D., & Gross, J. J. (2021). Acceptability and effectiveness of artificial intelligence therapy for anxiety and depression (Youper): Longitudinal observational study. *Journal of Medical Internet Research*, *23*(6), e26771. PMID: 34155984

Mitsala, A., Tsalikidis, C., Pitiakoudis, M., Simopoulos, C., & Tsaroucha, A. K. (2021). Artificial Intelligence in Colorectal Cancer Screening, Diagnosis and Treatment. A New Era. *Current Oncology (Toronto, Ont.)*, *28*(3), 1581–1607. DOI: 10.3390/curroncol28030149 PMID: 33922402

Nahum-Shani, I., Smith, S. N., Spring, B. J., Collins, L. M., Witkiewitz, K., Tewari, A., & Murphy, S. A. (2018). Just-in-Time Adaptive Interventions (JITAIs) in Mobile Health: Key Components and Design Principles for Ongoing Health Behavior Support. *Annals of Behavioral Medicine*, *52*(6), 446–462. DOI: 10.1007/s12160-016-9830-8 PMID: 27663578

Pavez, J., & Allende, H. (2024). A Hybrid System Based on Bayesian Networks and Deep Learning for Explainable Mental Health Diagnosis. *Applied Sciences (Basel, Switzerland)*, *14*(18), 8283. DOI: 10.3390/app14188283

Pham, T., Tran, T., Luo, W., & Venkatesh, S. (2020). Deepcare: A deep dynamic memory model for predictive medicine. *arXiv*. https://arxiv.org/abs/2007.02064

Popat, R., & Ive, J. (2023). Embracing the uncertainty in human-machine collaboration to support clinical decision-making for mental health conditions. *Frontiers in Digital Health, 5*, 1188338. DOI: 10.3389/fdgth.2023.1188338 PMID: 37731823

Prochaska, J. J., Vogel, E. A., Chieng, A., Kendra, M., Baiocchi, M., Pajarito, S., & Robinson, A. (2021). A therapeutic relational agent for reducing problematic substance use (Woebot): Development and usability study. *Journal of Medical Internet Research, 23*(3), e24850. PMID: 33755028

Purificato, E., Boratto, L., & De Luca, E. W. (2024). User modeling and user profiling: A comprehensive survey. *arXiv*. https://doi.org//arXiv.2402.09660DOI: 10.48550

Reece, A. G., Reagan, A. J., Lix, K. L. M., Dodds, P. S., Danforth, C. M., & Langer, E. J. (2016). *Forecasting the onset and course of mental illness with Twitter data.* arXiv. https://arxiv.org/abs/1608.07740

Rządeczka, M., Sterna, A., Stolińska, J., Kaczyńska, P., & Moskalewicz, M. (2024). The efficacy of conversational artificial intelligence in rectifying the theory of mind and autonomy biases: Comparative analysis. *arXiv preprint arXiv:2406.13813.* https://arxiv.org/abs/2406.13813

Shiffman, S., Stone, A. A., & Hufford, M. R. (2008). Ecological momentary assessment. *Annual Review of Clinical Psychology, 4*, 1–32. DOI: 10.1146/annurev.clinpsy.3.022806.091415 PMID: 18509902

Son, Y., Clouston, S. A. P., Kotov, R., Eichstaedt, J. C., Bromet, E. J., Luft, B. J., & Schwartz, H. A. (2020). World Trade Center responders in their own words: Predicting PTSD symptom trajectories with AI-based language analyses of interviews. arXiv preprint arXiv:2011.06457. https://arxiv.org/abs/2011.06457

Sutton, R. S., & Barto, A. G. (2018). *Reinforcement Learning: An Introduction* (2nd ed.). MIT Press., https://www.andrew.cmu.edu/course/10-703/textbook/BartoSutton.pdf

Torous, J., Lipschitz, J., Ng, M., & Firth, J. (2019). The potential of digital phenotyping to advance the contributions of nutritional psychiatry. *Nutrition (Burbank, Los Angeles County, Calif.), 66*, 110554. DOI: 10.1016/j.outlook.2020.03.007

Tzirakis, P., Trigeorgis, G., Nicolaou, M. A., Schuller, B. W., & Zafeiriou, S. (2017). End-to-end multimodal emotion recognition using deep neural networks. *IEEE Journal of Selected Topics in Signal Processing, 11*(8), 1301–1309.

Ullrich, H. E. (2019). Culture, Empathy, and the Therapeutic Alliance. *Psychodynamic Psychiatry, 47*(4), 425–440. DOI: 10.1521/pdps.2019.47.4.425 PMID: 31913784

Van Genugten, C., Thong, M. S. Y., van Ballegooijen, W., Kleiboer, A., Spruijt-Metz, D., Smit, J. H., Sprangers, M. A. G., Terhorst, Y., & Riper, H. (2025). Beyond the current state of just-in-time adaptive interventions in mental health: A systematic review. *Frontiers in Digital Health*, *7*, 1460167. DOI: 10.3389/fdgth.2025.1460167 PMID: 39935463

Verma, M., Chanthar, K. M., & Beg, M. J. (2025). Ethical considerations surrounding the use of AI-interventions in the application of mental healthcare. In Uludag, K., & Ahmad, N. (Eds.), *Chatbots and mental healthcare in psychology and psychiatry* (pp. 193–222). IGI Global., DOI: 10.4018/979-8-3693-3112-5.ch009

Vredenburgh, K. (2024). Transparency and Explainability for Public Policy. *LSE Public Policy Review*, *3*(3).

Waldman, S. A., & Terzic, A. (2019). Healthcare evolves from reactive to proactive. *Clinical Pharmacology and Therapeutics*, *105*(1), 10. PMID: 30597564

Chapter 2
Can ChatGPT Answer GRE Psychology Questions?

Kadir Uludag
https://orcid.org/0000-0003-3713-4670
Shanghai Jiao Tong University Mental Health Center, China

ABSTRACT

Abstract Background: The Graduate Record Examination (GRE) in Psychology is a psychology test that assesses a student's general psychology knowledge. ChatGPT can assist students in preparing for the GRE psychology. Thus, we aimed to ask ChatGPT psychology questions related to GRE. Methods: This article explores the use of ChatGPT in responding to GRE psychology questions. The authors analyze the accuracy of ChatGPT's responses. Results: ChatGPT correctly answered ninety percent of the questions. Furthermore, there is a likelihood that ChatGPT can answer these questions because it already knows the answer since ChatGPT provided some of the answers without knowing the exact question. However, ChatGPT could not answer the unclear questions with 100 percent accuracy in this study. Therefore, future studies claim that ChatGPT can answer exam questions (e.g., law, biology, and mathematics) have to be sure that questions are not publicly available. Conclusion: The use of ChatGPT in responding to GRE psychology questions can enhance students' studying experience.

1. INTRODUCTION

The Graduate Record Examination (GRE) in Psychology is a multiple choice test widely used for graduate school admissions in psychology, while the most popular chatbot, called ChatGPT, has been used in psychology (Uludag, 2023a) and medical education (Kung et al., 2023; Sallam, 2023). GRE scores may be related

DOI: 10.4018/979-8-3373-1325-2.ch002

to academic performance of individuals. Through an extensive analysis of nearly 100 studies involving 10,000 students, this research discovered a strong predictive relationship between GRE scores and various academic indicators. Specifically, GRE scores were found to effectively forecast first year grade point average (GPA), graduate GPA, and faculty ratings for both master's and doctoral students (Kuncel et al., 2010). The research findings indicate that GRE scores serve as a reliable predictor for several indicators, including the first year grade point average (GPA), graduate GPA, and faculty ratings.

Chatbots can be used in various areas such as psychiatry, psychology, coding (Farah et al., 2022), and education (Kuhail et al., 2023). Furthermore, previous studies analyzed whether chatbots can be used to analyze texts psychologically (Uludag, 2023b; Uludag, 2024). Moreover, ChatGPT can be used in psychology education by providing extensive information. Chatbots can potentially revolutionize GRE psychology preparation by providing expert responses. Using ChatGPT to answer GRE psychology questions, students can receive customized feedback and explanations, allowing them to identify areas of strength.

This manuscript explores the use of ChatGPT in responding to GRE psychology questions, analyzing its accuracy and effectiveness, as well as the potential benefits and concerns associated with ChatGPT use. By exploring this topic, we aim to contribute to a better understanding of the potential impact of artificial intelligence (AI) models on GRE psychology preparation. This analysis involves assessing how well ChatGPT can provide accurate responses, its overall effectiveness in aiding with GRE preparation, as well as the broader implications of relying on AI tools in the field of psychology education and test preparation.

2. METHODS

The first version of ChatGPT was used (2023). We have asked questions to analyze whether ChatGPT can answer GRE questions. We utilized the URL "https://poe.com/" to access the ChatGPT interface.

The questions publically shared on the following website were used to test ChatGPTs' efficacy.

https://www.ets.org/pdfs/gre/practice-book-psychology.pdf

ChatGPT (2023) was partially used to improve writing quality of this article.

3. RESULTS

ChatGPT correctly answered ninety percent of the questions. In addition, it provided detailed answers to some of the questions. We have compiled a collection of inquiries and corresponding responses.

Anwer 1: The correct answer is (C) The presence of receptors on the postsynaptic neuron that have an affinity for that particular neurotransmitter. The ability of a postsynaptic neuron to respond to a neurotransmitter depends on the presence of receptors on the postsynaptic neuron that can bind to the neurotransmitter. When a neurotransmitter binds to its receptor, it can cause a change in the postsynaptic neuron's membrane potential, leading to an excitatory or inhibitory response. The other answer choices are not correct because they do not directly relate to the ability of a postsynaptic neuron to respond to a neurotransmitter.

Answer 2: The correct answer is (E) subjective. Critics have argued that projective tests, such as the Rorschach inkblot test or the Thematic Apperception Test (TAT), are too subjective. These tests rely on the interpretation of ambiguous stimuli, such as inkblots or pictures, and responses are open to interpretation by the examiner. Critics argue that the interpretation of responses is too subjective and can be influenced by the examiner's biases, leading to unreliable or invalid results. The other answer choices are not correct because they do not relate to the specific criticism of projective tests as being too subjective.

Answer 3: The correct answer is (D) chunking. Chunking is the process of grouping information into smaller, more meaningful units. In this example, the string of letters B-F-J-T-A-V-K-C has been chunked into three groups: JFK, TV, and CAB. This makes the information easier to remember and recall. The other answer choices are not correct because they do not accurately describe the process used in this example. Simplifying involves reducing complex information to its essential components, clustering involves grouping related items together, seriating involves arranging items in a specific order, and paraphrasing involves restating information in different words.

Answer 4: When persuasive communications follow the peripheral route, they focus on (D) emotions. The peripheral route to persuasion involves using superficial or secondary cues, such as emotions, to influence attitudes or behavior. In this approach, the content of the message may not be as important as the emotional appeals used to convey the message. The other answer choices do not accurately describe the focus of persuasive communications that follow the peripheral route.

Answer 5: The correct answer is (A) It can have more than one surface structure. The sentence "The dishwasher is running" can have more than one surface structure, meaning it can be expressed in different ways while still conveying the same meaning. For example, it could be rephrased as "The running dishwasher" or "The dishwasher is currently in operation." The other answer choices are not correct because they do not accurately describe the characteristics of this sentence.

6. The correct answer is (A) Excessive concern about the safety and well-being of attachment figures. Children with separation anxiety disorder often experience excessive fear or anxiety over separation from attachment figures, as well as excessive concern about their safety and well-being. They may worry about things like illness, injury, or death of the attachment figure while they are apart. The other answer choices are not correct because they do not accurately describe the symptoms of separation anxiety disorder as outlined in the DSM-5.

Answer 6: The correct answer is (A) It can have more than one surface structure. The sentence "The dishwasher is running" can have more than one surface structure, meaning it can be expressed in different ways while still conveying the same meaning. For example, it could be rephrased as "The running dishwasher" or "The dishwasher is currently in operation." The other answer choices are not correct because they do not accurately describe the characteristics of this sentence.

6. The correct answer is (A) Excessive concern about the safety and well-being of attachment figures. Children with separation anxiety disorder often experience excessive fear or anxiety over separation from attachment figures, as well as excessive concern about their safety and well-being. They may worry about things like illness, injury, or death of the attachment figure while they are apart. The other answer choices are not correct because they do not accurately describe the symptoms of separation anxiety disorder as outlined in the DSM-5.

Answer 7: The correct answer is (C) Although procedural memory may not rely on normal hippocampal functioning, declarative memory does. Patients with bilateral damage to the hippocampal formation are still able to improve their performance on motor learning tasks, such as the Tower of Hanoi, even though they cannot consciously remember having seen the task before. This suggests that procedural memory, which is involved in motor learning and other non-conscious tasks, may not rely on normal hippocampal functioning. However, their lack of conscious awareness of the task suggests that declarative memory, which involves conscious recall of facts and events, does rely on the hippocampus.

Answer 8: The correct answer is (D) Endorphin. Endorphins are chemicals produced in the brain and nervous system that are similar in structure to opiates and can reduce pain. They are also involved in reward and pleasure pathways in the brain. The action of naloxone, which is an opioid antagonist, can block the effects of endorphins.

Answer 9: The correct answer is (A) generalized weakening of the immune system. Prolonged stress can have a negative impact on the immune system, leading to a weakening of the overall immune response. This can increase the risk of infectious diseases and other health problems.

Answer 10: The correct answer is (E) substantia nigra. Parkinson's disease is characterized by the degeneration of dopaminergic cells in the substantia nigra, which is a region of the midbrain that plays a key role in movement control.

Answer 11: The correct answer is (E) The infant understands objects to be solid bounded entities that take up space and move on continuous paths. By six months of age, infants have developed an object concept that includes an understanding of objects as solid, bounded entities that take up space and move on continuous paths. They are able to track moving objects in the visual field and are surprised when two objects occupy the same space at the same time.

Answer 12: The correct answer is (A) Test-retest. Test-retest reliability refers to the consistency of scores on the same test given to the same group of people on two different occasions. In this example, the researcher administered a vocabulary test to a group of students and then administered a similar test to the same group of students one week later. The high correlation between the two test scores ($r = .90$) suggests that the test has good test-retest reliability.

Answer 13: Answer: (A) Men who heard the jazz piece and women who heard the operatic piece scored higher on the mood inventory than those in the other two groups.

The graph shows two bars for each gender, one for their response to the jazz piece and one for their response to the operatic piece. For both men and women, the bar representing their response to the jazz piece is lower than the bar representing their response to the operatic piece. Therefore, people who heard the operatic piece scored higher on the mood inventory than those who heard the jazz piece. However, within each gender, the bar representing the response to the operatic piece is higher than the bar representing the response to the jazz piece. Therefore, men who heard the jazz piece and women who heard the operatic piece scored higher on the mood inventory than those in the other two groups.

Answer 14:(D) Previous studies have shown that men are less emotional than women.

This invalidates the conclusion because it suggests that the observed differences in mood between men and women may be due to pre-existing differences in emotional reactivity, rather than differences in the effects of jazz and opera.

Answer 15: (C) The sample size was too small to draw a valid conclusion.

This is the most serious problem with the methodology because a small sample size may not be representative of the population as a whole, and the results may not be reliable or generalizable. A larger sample size would increase the confidence in the findings and reduce the likelihood of chance effects or biases influencing the results.

Answer 16: The correct answer is (B) individualism. Individualism refers to a preference for a loosely knit social framework in which individuals are expected to take care of themselves and their immediate families, rather than relying on a larger social group. In contrast, collectivism emphasizes the interdependence and interconnectedness of individuals within a larger social group or community.

Answer 17. The correct answer is (A) overshadowing. Overshadowing occurs when the presence of a more salient stimulus, such as a loud noise, interferes with the conditioning of a less salient stimulus, such as a subtle smell. In this example, the loud noise is more salient and therefore becomes the conditioned stimulus that elicits the conditioned eye blink response, while the subtle smell does not.

Answer 18. The correct answer is (C) Karen Horney. Karen Horney proposed that people cope with basic anxiety by moving toward people, away from people, or against people. Moving toward people involves seeking out love and affection from others, while moving away from people involves withdrawing from others and seeking self-sufficiency. Moving against people involves adopting a hostile or aggressive stance toward others in an attempt to gain control and power.

Answer 19. The correct answer is (C) When a sound is presented that is intermediate between the phonemes /b/ and /p/, listeners report that they heard either a distinct /b/ or a distinct /p/. This phenomenon is known as categorical perception, which refers to the tendency to perceive speech sounds as belonging to discrete, non-overlapping categories, even when the sounds are physically similar.

Answer 20. The correct answer is (D) temperament. Alexander Thomas and Stella Chess identified three categories of infants based on their temperament: easy, difficult, and slow to warm up. Easy infants are generally relaxed and adaptable, difficult infants are fussy and easily upset, and slow to warm up infants are initially hesitant but eventually become more comfortable with new experiences.

Answer 21. The correct answer is (D) Semantic memory. Semantic memory refers to the knowledge and understanding of concepts and factual information, such as vocabulary and general knowledge. It is considered to be a more stable and enduring form of memory than episodic memory, which involves the recall of specific events and experiences. Therefore, semantic memory is the least likely to show a decline in late life.

Answer 22. The correct answer is (B) temporal summation. Temporal summation refers to the cumulative effect on a postsynaptic neuron produced by the rapid and repeated firing of a presynaptic neuron. This can result in the generation of an action potential in the postsynaptic neuron.

Answer 23. The correct answer is (B) Autism spectrum disorder. Autism spectrum disorder is a neurodevelopmental disorder characterized by atypical developmental patterns, including stereotyped motor responses and poor communication skills. Tardive dyskinesia is a movement disorder caused by long-term use of certain medications, Down syndrome is a genetic disorder caused by the presence of an extra copy of chromosome 21, and Williams syndrome is a genetic disorder characterized by developmental and cognitive delays.

Answer 24. The correct answer is (D) self-disclosure. Self-disclosure refers to the sharing of personal information about oneself with another person. It is an important component of social interaction and can help to build trust and intimacy between individuals.

Answer 25. The correct answer is (D) Relational. Research suggests that young adolescent girls exhibit more relational aggression than young adolescent boys. Relational aggression involves behaviors that harm others through damage to social relationships, such as spreading rumors or excluding others from social groups.

Answer 26. The correct answer is (C) overregularization. Overregularization is the application of grammatical rules to exceptions or irregular forms, resulting in errors such as "runned" instead of "ran". Telegraphic speech refers to the use of short, simple phrases to convey meaning, while fast mapping refers to the rapid learning of new words through context and association. Overextension refers to the application of a word to a broader range of objects or situations than is appropriate, while holophrasing refers to the use of a single word to convey a complete thought or idea.

Answer 27. The correct answer is (D) dorsal stream. The visual system is composed of two major pathways: the dorsal stream and the ventral stream. The dorsal stream, also known as the "where" pathway, is responsible for processing visual information related to the location and movement of objects in space. In contrast, the ventral stream, or "what" pathway, is responsible for processing visual information related to the identity and characteristics of objects.

Answer 28. The correct answer is (B) Erik Erikson. Erik Erikson revised Sigmund Freud's stages of development by replacing Freud's psychosexual stages with psychosocial stages. Erikson's theory emphasizes the role of social and cultural factors in shaping development, and his stages focus on the development of identity and the resolution of psychosocial conflicts.

Answer 29. The correct answer is (C) formal operational. Jean Piaget proposed that cognitive development progresses through four stages: sensorimotor, preoperational, concrete operational, and formal operational. The pendulum task described in the question involves the manipulation of variables and the use of systematic experimentation, which is characteristic of formal operational thinking.

Answer 30. The correct answer is (A) knowledge about mental representations. The ability to lie with the intention of deceiving another person involves an understanding of mental states, such as beliefs and intentions, and the ability to manipulate and represent these mental states. This development is based on a change in the child's knowledge about mental representations, rather than on other cognitive skills or abilities.

Answer 31. The correct answer is (B) variability of individual scores. The standard deviation is a measure of the variability or spread of individual scores around the mean. It provides information about how much the individual scores differ from each other and from the mean score.

Answer 32. The correct answer is (C) dreaming. Rapid eye movements (REM) are a characteristic feature of the sleep stage associated with dreaming. During REM sleep, the eyes move rapidly back and forth under closed eyelids, and brain activity is similar to that during wakefulness.

Answer 33. The correct answer is (D) cross-sectional. The investigator's research design involves comparing the attitudes of different age groups at one point in time. This is a cross-sectional design, which allows for the examination of age-related differences in attitudes, but does not follow the same individuals over time.

Answer 34. The correct answer is (C) identical twins. Concordance rates refer to the degree of similarity in a trait or disorder between individuals who share a particular relationship. If a psychological disorder has a genetic basis, the highest concordance rate would be expected between identical twins, who share 100% of their genes.

Answer 35. The correct answer is (A) the id. According to Sigmund Freud's theory of personality, the id is the primitive and instinctual part of the psyche that is driven by basic needs and desires, such as hunger and thirst. In the scenario described in the question, the child is driven by the need for food, which is a basic biological drive associated with the id.

Answer 36. The correct answer is (C) Carl Jung identified two components of the unconscious: the preconscious and the formal unconscious. Carl Jung actually identified two different components of the unconscious: the personal unconscious, which contains repressed or forgotten memories and experiences, and the collective unconscious, which contains inherited archetypes and universal symbols.

Answer 37. The correct answer is (B) extroverted stable. Eysenck's personality theory includes two basic dimensions: extraversion/introversion and emotional stability/neuroticism. Juanita's sociable, easygoing, and lively personality traits suggest high extraversion and emotional stability.

Answer 38. The correct answer is (D) early life relationships. Object relations theory emphasizes the impact of early life relationships and experiences on the development of personality and the formation of interpersonal relationships. It focuses on the way individuals internalize and represent their relationships with important others.

Answer 39. The correct answer is (C) Hypersomnolence. Hypersomnolence refers to excessive daytime sleepiness or prolonged nighttime sleep, typically lasting 10 or more hours per day. This can be a symptom of various sleep disorders, including sleep apnea, narcolepsy, or other medical conditions.

Answer 40. The correct answer is (B) blue wavelengths and yellow wavelengths add together to make green wavelengths. Mixing blue and yellow pigments together results in the perception of green because blue and yellow wavelengths of light are absorbed by the pigments and the remaining wavelengths that are reflected or transmitted to the eye combine to produce the sensation of green.

Answer 41. The correct answer is (D) Yoked control < normal sleep control < depressed. If sleeplessness leads to depression, one would expect to see higher scores on the depression questionnaire for the depressed-insomniac group compared to both the normal-sleep control and the yoked control groups.

Answer 42. The correct answer is (C) Normal sleep control = yoked control < depressed. If depression arises for reasons other than sleeplessness, one would expect to see higher scores on the depression questionnaire for the depressed-insomniac group compared to both the normal-sleep control and the yoked control groups, but no significant difference between the normal-sleep control and yoked control groups.

Answer 43. The correct answer is (B) The study failed to examine other factors that might also contribute to depression. If the results were consistent with the hypothesis that sleeplessness does not lead to depression, a criticism of the study and its conclusion would be that it did not examine or control for other factors that might contribute to depression, such as stress or other psychological or physiological factors.

Answer 44. The correct answer is (B) If two tasks using the same component are done concurrently, performance will be impaired on one or both. Baddeley and Hitch's theory of working memory includes the concept of limited capacity and the idea that performing two tasks that use the same component of working memory simultaneously will result in competition for that limited capacity, leading to impaired performance on one or both tasks.

Answer 45. The correct answer is (A) Hermann Ebbinghaus. Hermann Ebbinghaus was a German psychologist who conducted pioneering research on memory and forgetting. He developed the method of using nonsense syllables (consonant-vowel-consonant combinations) to study memory and forgetting, and his work laid the foundation for the study of experimental psychology.

Answer 46. The correct answer is (B) Lights flickering. The conditioned stimulus is the lights flickering, because it is the neutral stimulus that became associated with the fearful response (conditioned response) due to its repeated pairing with the unconditioned stimulus (the storms).

Answer 47. The correct answer is (B) Ivan Pavlov. Ivan Pavlov is best known for his classical conditioning experiments with dogs, in which he demonstrated that a neutral stimulus (such as a bell) could acquire the ability to evoke a response (such as salivation) originally attributed to another stimulus (such as food).

Answer 48. The correct answer is (C) The long-term store. The long-term store is believed to have the largest capacity of the three memory stores (sensory store, short-term store, and long-term store) and can hold vast amounts of information for extended periods of time, potentially indefinitely.

Answer 49. The correct answer is (D) Pragmatics. Pragmatics is the study of how context contributes to meaning in language, including the use of polite words such as "please" and "thank you" in everyday speech.

Answer 50. The correct answer is (D) Non-shared environments. Non-shared environments, including differences in experiences and social interactions, can contribute to individual differences in personality even among monozygotic twins who share the same genetic material and many aspects of their environment.

Answer 51. The correct answer is (D) A black-and-white pattern. Newborns are most attracted to high-contrast visual stimuli, such as black-and-white patterns or other highly contrasting visual patterns.

Answer 52. The correct answer is (A) Excitation transfer. Excitation transfer theory suggests that residual arousal from one situation can amplify the emotional response to a subsequent situation, leading to an overreaction or exaggerated response.

Answer 53. The correct answer is (C) Self-affirmation. Cleotha is engaging in self-affirmation, a process in which an individual focuses on and reinforces their positive self-attributes or achievements to boost self-esteem and maintain a positive self-concept.
Answer 54. The correct answer is (B) With adults and advanced peers. According to Vygotsky's sociocultural theory, children learn best when working with more knowledgeable others, such as adults or advanced peers, who can provide guidance, support, and scaffolding for their learning.
Answer 55. The correct answer is (D) Sensorimotor. According to Piaget's theory of cognitive development, the sensorimotor stage occurs from birth to about two years old and is characterized by the development of object permanence and the coordination of sensory experiences with motor actions.
Answer 56. (C)
Answer 57. (C)
Answer 58. (B)
Answer 59. (D)
Answer 60. (A)
Answer 61. (A)
Answer 62. (B)
Answer 63. (E)
Answer 64. (A)
Answer 65. (D)
Answer 66. (C)
Answer 67. (E)
Answer 68. (D)
Answer 69. (E)
Answer 70. (A)
Answer 71. (C)
Answer 72. (A)
Answer 73. (C)
Answer 74. (C)
Answer 75. (C)
Answer 76. (A)
Answer 77. (C) Morpheme
Answer 78. (D) Both talking and driving require attentional resources, and adequate attentional resources may not be allocated to driving.
Answer 79. (B) transduction
Answer 80. (C) Public conformity
Answer 81. (D) Axon hillock
Answer 82. (C) It increases the speed of the electrical impulses.

Answer 83. (D) Individuation
Answer 84. (D) organizational
Answer 85. (A) Psychodynamic
Answer 86. (B) motor neuron
Answer 87. (C) prosopagnosia
Answer 88. (E) decenter
Answer 89. (D) Damage to different areas of the brain
Answer 90. (A) crystallized intelligence
Answer 91. (D) is influenced by the historical context in which it occurs
Answer 92. (E) Edward Thorndike
Answer 93. (A) Genetic history of schizophrenia
Answer 94. (B) a delusion
Answer 95 (D) a command hallucination
Answer 96. (E) Psychosocial history
Answer 97. (A) Hearing voices is a positive symptom.
Answer 98. (E) Increasing the emphasis on measuring specific abilities rather than g
Answer 99. (C) Long-term maladaptive traits and behavior patterns
Answer 100. (B) Trichromatic versus opponent-process
Answer 101. give reference to the questions mentioned above.

I apologize, as an AI language model, I do not have access to the specific content or material that the questions are referencing. The questions appear to be from a practice exam or study guide for a psychology course or exam.

4. DISCUSSION

The use of ChatGPT in answering GRE psychology questions can revolutionize how students prepare for the exam. ChatGPT can provide students with personalized feedback, allowing them to identify areas of strength.

One potential benefit of using ChatGPT in GRE preparation is the ability to adapt to each student's individual needs. For example, ChatGPT can analyze a student's responses and provide personalized feedback, which can help them to identify areas of weakness and focus their studying efforts effectively. Additionally, ChatGPT can provide students with expert responses and explanations, which can help them to understand complex concepts better and improve their performance on the exam.

CONCLUSION

It is possible for ChatGPT to respond accurately to past GRE questions due to its existing knowledge. Consequently, researchers in the field suggest that in order to determine ChatGPT's ability to answer exam questions, such as those in law, biology, and mathematics, it is essential to ensure that the questions are not accessible to the public.

Suggestions for Further Studies

Further studies should investigate the use of ChatGPT in psychology education. Additionally, chatbots can be employed to generate novel GRE questions. Subsequent research endeavors can delve into the ethical considerations associated with the utilization of language models such as ChatGPT in standardized testing.

Assessing the impact of ChatGPT on user trust and satisfaction: Studies could focus on understanding how users perceive and trust the responses generated by ChatGPT. This could involve exploring the factors that influence user satisfaction, trust-building strategies, and ways to address potential concerns or misunderstandings.

Future research can explore the potential of ChatGPT as a tool for stimulating creativity and generating novel ideas across various domains, such as art, design, or problem-solving. This could involve evaluating its ability to inspire and assist users in creative endeavors. Moreover, additional research can focus on comparing different chatbot versions. Moreover, video-generating chatbots can enhance the education of young people, and future studies can investigate related topics.

Limitations

ChatGPT versions may differ, and ChatGPT answers may be personal.

REFERENCES

Farah, J. C., Spaenlehauer, B., Bergram, K., Holzer, A., & Gillet, D. (2022). Challenges and opportunities in integrating interactive chatbots into code review exercises: A pilot case study. In *Proceedings of the IATED Conference* (pp. 3816–3825). IATED.

Kuhail, M. A., Alturki, N., Alramlawi, S., & Alhejori, K. (2023). Interacting with educational chatbots: A systematic review. *Education and Information Technologies*, *28*(1), 973–1018.

Kuncel, N. R., Wee, S., Serafin, L., & Hezlett, S. A. (2010). The validity of the Graduate Record Examination for master's and doctoral programs: A meta-analytic investigation. *Educational and Psychological Measurement*, *70*(2), 340–352. DOI: 10.1177/0013164409344508

Kung, T. H., Cheatham, M., Medenilla, A., Sillos, C., De Leon, L., Elepaño, C., Madriaga, M., Aggabao, R., Diaz-Candido, G., Maningo, J., & Tseng, V. (2023). Performance of ChatGPT on USMLE: Potential for AI-assisted medical education using large language models. *PLOS Digital Health*, *2*(2), e0000198. DOI: 10.1371/journal.pdig.0000198 PMID: 36812645

Sallam, M. (2023). ChatGPT utility in health care education, research, and practice: Systematic review on the promising perspectives and valid concerns. *Health Care*, *11*(6), 887. DOI: 10.3390/healthcare11060887 PMID: 36981544

Uludag, K. (2023a). *The use of AI-supported chatbot in psychology*. *SSRN*. https://doi.org/DOI: 10.2139/ssrn.4331367

Uludag, K. (2023b). *ChatGPT can distinguish grandiose delusional thoughts from non-grandiose thoughts* (SSRN Scholarly Paper No. 4392582). SSRN Electronic Journal. https://doi.org/DOI: 10.2139/ssrn.4392582

Uludag, K. (2024). Exploring the association between textual parameters and psychological and cognitive factors. *Psychology Research and Behavior Management*, *17*, 1139–1150. https://pubmed.ncbi.nlm.nih.gov/38505355/ PMID: 38505355

SUPPLEMENTARY MATERIALS

Table 1. Responses of ChatGPT

Answer 1: (C) (✓)	Answer 26. (C) (✓)	Answer 51. (D) (✓)	Answer 76. (A) (✓)
Answer 2:(E) (✓)	Answer 27. (D) (✗)	Answer 52. (A) (✓)	Answer 77. (C) (✓)
Answer 3: (D) (✓)	Answer 28 (B) (✓)	Answer 53. (C) (✓)	Answer 78. (D) (✓)
Answer 4: (D) (✓)	Answer 29. (C) (✓)	Answer 54. (B) (✓)	Answer 79. (B) (✓)
Answer 5:(A) (✗)	Answer 30. (A) (✓)	Answer 55. (D) (✓)	Answer 80. (C) (✓)
Answer 6: (A) (✓)	Answer 31. (B). (✓)	Answer 56. (C) (✓)	Answer 81. (D) (✓)
Answer 7: (C) (✓)	Answer 32. (C). (✓)	Answer 57. (C) (✗)	Answer 82. (C) (✓)
Answer 8: (D) (✓)	Answer 33. (D). (✓)	Answer 58. (B) (✓)	Answer 83. (D) (✓)
Answer 9: (A) (✓)	Answer 34. (C). (✓)	Answer 59. (D) (✓)	Answer 84. (D) (✓)
Answer 10: (E) (✓)	Answer 35. (A) (✓)	Answer 60. (A) (✗)	Answer 85. (A) (✓)
Answer 11: (E) (✓)	Answer 36. (C) (✓)	Answer 61. (A) (✓)	Answer 86. (B) (✓)
Answer 12: (A) (✗)	Answer 37. (B) (✓)	Answer 62. (B) (✓)	Answer 87. (C) (✓)
Answer 13: (A) (✓)	Answer 38. (D). (✓)	Answer 63. (E) (✓)	Answer 88. (E) (✓)
Answer 14:(D) (✗)	Answer 39. (C) (✓)	Answer 64. (A) (✓)	Answer 89. (D) (✓)
Answer 15: (C) (✗)	Answer 40. (B) (✗)	Answer 65. (D) (✓)	Answer 90. (A) (✓)
Answer 16: (B) (✓)	Answer 41. (D) (✗)	Answer 66. (C) (✓)	Answer 91. (D) (✓)
Answer 17. (A). (✓)	Answer 42. (C) (✓)	Answer 67. (E) (✓)	Answer 92. (E) (✓)
Answer 18. (C) (✓)	Answer 43. (B) (✗)	Answer 68. (D) (✓)	Answer 93. (A) (✓)
Answer 19. (C) (✓)	Answer 44. (B) (✓)	Answer 69. (E) (✓)	Answer 94. (B) (✓)
Answer 20. (D) (✓)	Answer 45. (A) (✓)	Answer 70. (A) (✓)	Answer 95 (D) (✓)
Answer 21. (D) (✓)	Answer 46. (B) (✓)	Answer 71. (C) (✓)	Answer 96. (E) (✓)
Answer 22. (B) (✓)	Answer 47. (B) (✓)	Answer 72. (A) (✓)	Answer 97. (A) (✓)
Answer 23. (B) (✓)	Answer 48. (C) (✓)	Answer 73. (C) (✓)	Answer 98. (E) (✓)
Answer 24. (D) (✓)	Answer 49. (D) (✓)	Answer 74. (C) (✓)	Answer 99. (C) (✓)
Answer 25. (D) (✓)	Answer 50. (D) (✓)	Answer 75. (C) (✓)	Answer 100. (B) (✓)

Table 2. Responses from the textbook

1 C	26 C	51 D	76 A
2 E	27 E	52 A	77 C
3 D	28 B	53 C	78 D
4 D	29 C	54 B	79 B
5 B	30 A	55 D	80 C
6 A	31 B	56 C	81 D
7 C	32 C	57 E	82 C
8 D	33 D	58 B	83 D
9 A	34 C	59 D	84 D
10 E	35 A	60 B	85 A
11 E	36 C	61 A	86 B
12 C	37 B	62 B	87 C
13 A	38 D	63 E	88 E
14 E	39 C	64 A	89 D
15 B	40 C	65 D	90 A
16 B	41 A	66 C	91 D
17 A	42 C	67 E	92 E
18 C	43 D	68 D	93 A
19 C	44 B	69 E	94 B
20 D	45 A	70 A	95 D
21 D	46 B	71 C	96 E
22 B	47 B	72 A	97 A
23 B	48 C	73 C	98 E
24 D	49 D	74 C	99 C
25 D	50 D	75 C	100 B

Chapter 3
From Signals to Symptoms:
Multimodal AI and Privacy-Preserving Approaches to Detecting Transdiagnostic Risk in Psychopathology

Mohit Verma
https://orcid.org/0009-0004-4032-2458
Lovely Professional University, India

Mirza Jahanzeb Beg
https://orcid.org/0000-0002-6308-2678
Kumaraguru College of Liberal Arts and Science, Coimbatore, India

ABSTRACT

Mental health disorders often cross diagnostic boundaries, creating overlapping risk patterns that are difficult to capture with conventional tools. Digital technologies such as smartphones, wearables, and language-based platforms now offer opportunities to detect early signs of distress through continuous and ecologically valid measures. This chapter examines how multimodal artificial intelligence builds upon these signals to identify transdiagnostic risk states by integrating behavioral, physiological, and linguistic data. It reviews current evidence on digital markers, highlighting strengths, limitations, and the potential of foundation models that combine multiple modalities for improved accuracy. Ethical and practical challenges, including privacy, data scarcity, and clinical translation, are also discussed. The

DOI: 10.4018/979-8-3373-1325-2.ch003

chapter concludes that multimodal AI, when developed with privacy-preserving safeguards and embedded in clinician-led care, could advance more personalized and responsive approaches to mental health.

INTRODUCTION

The classification of psychiatric disorders has long been dominated by categorical frameworks such as the DSM and ICD. These systems have offered consistency and reliability in clinical communication, research design, and healthcare delivery. However, they face persistent limitations that have become increasingly apparent with advances in neuroscience, genetics, and clinical research. Threshold-based definitions often lack precision and risk inflating diagnoses by pathologizing normal variations in behavior and emotion (Wakefield, 2016; Young, 2013). The categorical approach also struggles to account for the high rates of comorbidity and symptom overlap observed across populations, leading to diagnostic heterogeneity and limited clinical validity (Clark et al., 2017; Park & Kim, 2020). These challenges extend into applied contexts, where arbitrary boundaries complicate both epidemiological studies and individualized treatment planning. Although updates in ICD-11 and DSM-5 introduced dimensional elements, such as severity ratings and cultural adaptability, their reliance on consensus-driven revisions and limited integration of biological markers highlight the constraints of existing nosological systems (Clark et al., 2017).

Against this backdrop, transdiagnostic perspectives have gained traction as a way to address the shortcomings of categorical diagnosis. These approaches move beyond disorder-specific models to investigate common mechanisms that cut across multiple conditions, reflecting the shared etiology and symptomatology found in many psychiatric disorders (Dalgleish et al., 2020; Nasrallah, 2021). For example, large-scale studies have identified internalizing and externalizing dimensions as broad latent factors underlying comorbidity across anxiety, mood, and substance-related conditions (Krueger & Eaton, 2015). Neuroimaging and meta-analytic evidence further supports the existence of overlapping neural dysfunctions, such as impairments in the insula, thalamus, and prefrontal cortex, although findings also caution against prematurely labeling all phenomena as transdiagnostic without rigorous evidence (Barch, 2020). Despite conceptual and methodological challenges, the transdiagnostic framework provides an empirically grounded alternative to categorical systems by aligning psychiatric nosology with the dimensional nature of symptoms and mechanisms.

The Research Domain Criteria project represents one institutionalized effort to operationalize this shift. By prioritizing domains of functioning such as cognition, emotion regulation, and social processes, the RDoC framework encourages a dimensional and neuroscience-informed understanding of psychopathology (Cuthbert, 2014). Its integration into psychiatric training has already demonstrated utility in linking clinical cases to underlying neurobehavioral systems, thus improving the translational potential of research in patient care (Etkin & Cuthbert, 2014). Other transdiagnostic models, such as the Hierarchical Taxonomy of Psychopathology, attempt to systematize this knowledge into clinically useful structures, although debates remain about thresholds, clinical cutoffs, and trial methodology (Dalgleish et al., 2020). Together, these efforts illustrate the movement toward reconceptualizing psychiatric disorders as complex, interconnected phenomena that require dimensional assessment rather than categorical classification.

Recent developments in artificial intelligence (AI) provide a promising avenue for advancing these transdiagnostic approaches. Machine learning methods allow for the integration of multimodal data including genetic, neuroimaging, behavioral, and clinical information, enabling the detection of patterns that transcend traditional diagnostic boundaries (Lin et al., 2020). Risk prediction models have already been applied to electronic health records, demonstrating feasibility in identifying individuals at elevated risk for psychosis and other outcomes across diverse healthcare settings (Ford et al., 2025). Large language models also offer new opportunities to capture dimensional symptom profiles from clinical notes, aligning with RDoC constructs and demonstrating predictive validity for real-world outcomes such as hospitalization and readmission (McCoy & Perlis, 2024). These approaches illustrate how AI can facilitate early and dynamic detection of risk states in psychiatry, complementing existing frameworks while addressing their methodological and clinical limitations.

Central to this emerging field is the notion of transdiagnostic risk states. These are conditions of heightened vulnerability that cut across diagnostic categories, often preceding the onset of specific syndromes and reflecting pluripotent trajectories of psychopathology (McGorry et al., 2018). Identifying such states allows for preventive interventions before full disorders emerge, but requires methodological tools capable of disentangling shared and disorder-specific features. Foundation models, including large language models and multimodal neural architectures, offer a potential solution by integrating diverse data streams while adapting to new contexts. Their scalability, combined with growing emphasis on privacy-preserving approaches, positions them as central to the next generation of psychiatric research and clinical care (Na et al., 2025).

This chapter will build on these developments by reviewing empirical studies that investigate digital markers of mental health derived from smartphones, wearable devices, voice, and text data, with close attention to study quality, sample characteristics, and generalizability. It will then examine how multimodal foundation models integrate such diverse signals to detect risk states with greater accuracy than single-modal approaches, while also considering their limitations and evidence gaps. The discussion will extend to privacy-preserving techniques such as federated learning, anonymization, and secure aggregation, emphasizing their practical applications in clinical and research contexts. In addition, the role of synthetic data in addressing the scarcity of clinical datasets will be analyzed, alongside risks of bias amplification and strategies for mitigation. Finally, the chapter will consider the clinical realities of embedding AI tools into stepped-care models, highlighting the necessity of keeping human clinicians central to interpretation and decision-making.

EVIDENCE REVIEW: WHAT WE KNOW SO FAR

Smartphones and wearable devices have transformed the capacity to capture behavioral and physiological signals associated with mental health. Studies using these tools have demonstrated potential for monitoring depression, anxiety, bipolar disorder, and suicidality, though methodological heterogeneity and translational challenges persist. Research on bipolar disorder has shown that smartphone-based systems can detect illness phase transitions by analyzing behavioral and physiological signals, with predictive accuracies ranging from 67 to 97 percent (Antosik-Wójcińska et al., 2020). Similarly, prognostic models incorporating digital data to guide relapse prevention strategies demonstrated incremental benefits over baseline severity measures, although external validation and data completeness remain significant limitations (Cohen et al., 2023). Digital interventions such as smartphone-based programs for depression and anxiety have achieved modestly above-chance prediction of treatment response, yet dependence on self-report data and missing information constrained robustness (Hornstein et al., 2021). Broader systematic reviews echo these limitations, noting that many prognostic models lack adequate calibration and rarely undergo external validation (Moriarty et al., 2022).

Wearable sensing has further extended opportunities for continuous monitoring. The e-Prevention project, which combined wearable, speech, and facial expression data, successfully predicted relapse in schizophrenia and bipolar disorder, though modest sample sizes and reliance on commercial devices constrained its conclusions (Zlatintsi et al., 2022). Reviews of digital phenotyping similarly report that mobility, communication, and physiological signals consistently correlate with symptom exacerbation, yet study heterogeneity in design and data handling continues to hinder comparability and replication (Bufano et al., 2023). Nonclinical samples also provide preliminary evidence that smartphone-based sensing can detect behavioral correlates of stress and mild depression, though variability in sensor platforms and high attrition rates limit reliability (Choi et al., 2024). Clinical samples have shown consistent associations between reduced mobility, decreased social interaction, and disrupted circadian rhythms with depressive symptom severity, but predictive accuracy is often moderate and constrained by missing data and insufficient external validation (Leaning et al., 2024). Personalized models applied to wearable data have achieved promising accuracy for bipolar mood episode prediction (Lipschitz et al., 2025), suggesting that individualized approaches may overcome some field-wide limitations.

Parallel work has focused on speech and language features as potential markers of mental health. Acoustic and linguistic signals provide unobtrusive, ecologically valid indicators of symptom states, yet findings remain variable across disorders. For schizophrenia, a meta-analysis of 46 studies revealed robust associations between pause duration and negative symptoms such as alogia, while pitch variability and speech rate showed weaker but significant differences between patients and controls. Multivariate models achieved higher classification accuracy (76–88 percent) than univariate analyses, yet high between-study variability, small samples, and methodological inconsistency undermined generalizability (Alberto et al., 2019). In bipolar disorder, both cross-sectional and longitudinal studies have demonstrated feasibility of smartphone-based voice monitoring, with depressive states associated with increased latency and vocal perturbations, and manic states linked to pressured or louder speech. Predictive accuracies across studies ranged between 70 and 89 percent, but sex differences, medication effects, and sample limitations complicate interpretations (Crocamo et al., 2025; Faurholt-Jepsen et al., 2016; Kaczmarek-Majer et al., 2025).

Automated speech analysis has also been applied to autism spectrum disorder, where meta-analytic results reveal small but reliable differences in pitch mean and range (Cohen's d 0.4–0.5, accuracy 61–64 percent), while multivariate models outperform univariate approaches with classification accuracies as high as 96 percent. Nevertheless, replication is rare, predictive features vary, and models often fail to generalize across populations (Fusaroli et al., 2016). In depression, speech-based models integrating acoustic and linguistic features achieve accuracies up to 91 percent, particularly when multimodal approaches are employed (Koops et al., 2023). Similarly, a machine learning classifier trained on speech from combat veterans distinguished posttraumatic stress disorder from controls with AUC 0.95 and nearly 90 percent classification accuracy, though restricted samples and lack of external validation constrain clinical application (Marmar et al., 2019). Studies in nonclinical populations have also demonstrated that acoustic features predict schizotypy, depression, and anxiety symptoms with moderate accuracy (R^2 up to 0.44), though generalizability to clinical populations remains uncertain (Olah et al., 2023). Reviews of psychosis risk emphasize that abnormalities in semantic coherence, syntactic complexity, and prosody can be quantified with advanced natural language processing and machine learning techniques, yet methodological inconsistency and cultural variability remain significant barriers to establishing robust, transdiagnostic markers (Olah et al., 2024).

Multimodal approaches that integrate text, audio, and video signals show particular promise. For example, combining linguistic, prosodic, facial, and movement features predicted provisional diagnoses of posttraumatic stress disorder and major depressive disorder with AUCs of 0.90 and 0.86, respectively, with speech content features contributing most strongly (Schultebraucks et al., 2022). Similarly, in the DAIC-WOZ dataset, text features outperformed audio in distinguishing mental health conditions (accuracy up to 87.8 percent vs. 71.8 percent), though multimodal integration achieved the most robust performance across classifiers (Drougkas et al., 2024). These findings underscore the potential of multimodal digital phenotyping to enhance predictive accuracy beyond unimodal approaches, while also highlighting the methodological and interpretive challenges posed by feature dominance and small datasets.

Synthesizing across studies, systematic reviews and meta-analyses converge on several conclusions. First, digital markers derived from smartphones, wearables, and speech consistently associate with mood, anxiety, and psychotic symptoms, yet effect sizes are often modest and highly heterogeneous. Reported accuracies range from near chance to above 90 percent, with larger effects observed in controlled laboratory contexts and smaller, less consistent effects in real-world data. Second, most models are developed in small, convenience samples, often without external validation, limiting generalizability across populations, cultures, and clinical settings. Third, the diversity of elicitation tasks, sensor platforms, and analytic strategies impedes cumulative knowledge building, with a lack of standardized protocols and open datasets slowing progress. Finally, while multimodal integration enhances predictive performance, challenges of interpretability, bias, and scalability remain unresolved.

While these findings highlight the promise of digital markers, the evidence remains uneven, with substantial variation in effect sizes, methodological rigor, and sample diversity. Voice and smartphone-based features demonstrate potential for identifying risk states across depression, anxiety, suicidality, and related conditions, yet most studies remain constrained by small cohorts, limited follow-up, and a lack of replication across cultural and clinical settings. These limitations underscore the need for analytic approaches that can move beyond narrow, single-modality investigations and instead integrate diverse data streams into coherent models of mental health. The next section turns to foundation models, which provide a framework for combining signals across modalities and hold the potential to improve accuracy, generalizability, and clinical relevance in psychiatry and psychotherapy.

FOUNDATION MODELS IN MENTAL HEALTH

Foundation models are large-scale machine learning architectures that are pre-trained on vast datasets and then adapted for a range of downstream tasks. Unlike earlier single-task models, they are designed to capture complex patterns across diverse modalities such as language, voice, imaging, and behavioral signals, which makes them particularly promising for psychiatry and psychotherapy. Their ability to generalize across domains has drawn attention to their potential in detecting risk states, supporting clinical decision-making, and advancing research.

Language-based models have shown considerable progress. For example, research evaluating pre-trained language models for Arabic mental health care found that fine-tuned models such as MARBERT outperformed classical machine learning approaches and non-fine-tuned models, achieving strong classification performance in question-answer tasks. However, limitations included the small dataset size and challenges in capturing emotional nuance, underscoring the need for more extensive and culturally sensitive datasets (Alhuzali & Alasmari, 2024). Similarly, large-scale studies in English-speaking contexts illustrate the capacity of large language models to classify unstructured electronic health record text. GPT-4 demonstrated high agreement with clinicians in broad classification tasks but variable accuracy in fine-grained categories, suggesting potential for reducing coding workload while highlighting the importance of improved training strategies and more diverse clinical input (Cardamone et al., 2025).

Beyond text, foundation models are increasingly being applied to neuroimaging data. BrainLM, for instance, was pretrained on thousands of hours of functional MRI recordings and demonstrated strong generalization to unseen datasets. It was able to predict clinical variables, forecast brain states, and identify functional networks without supervision, surpassing traditional modeling techniques. Yet, reliance on adult cohorts and the inherent complexity of fMRI signals limit the scope of current findings (Caro et al., 2023). Similar developments include NeuroSTORM, a model trained on tens of millions of frames of fMRI data across multiple countries, which outperformed existing approaches in diverse tasks ranging from emotion phenotype prediction to disease classification. Despite its success, the model reflects demographic imbalances and the need for broader representation in training datasets (Wang et al., 2025).

Multimodal approaches have also demonstrated value. AudiFace integrated facial, audio, and linguistic features to detect depression, outperforming unimodal baselines and reaching F1 scores as high as 0.93. While this highlights the promise of multimodal fusion, the study was limited by small sample sizes and lack of external validation, raising concerns about generalizability (Flores et al., 2022). Similarly, research comparing speech and text foundation models across English and

Spanish datasets showed that multimodal models consistently performed better than unimodal approaches, though they exhibited gender bias in detection performance and emphasized the need for fairness and larger, more diverse datasets. Other work, such as ContextVecNet, applied multimodal fusion of text and image data from social media, achieving very high accuracy and recall in detecting depression, but limitations related to demographic bias and reliance on self-reported data point to important caveats (Tahir et al., 2025).

The utility of foundation models extends beyond clinical diagnosis to research itself. Large language models have been employed in psychiatric research to assist with literature review, participant selection, statistical analysis, and manuscript preparation. While these applications improve efficiency, concerns remain regarding bias, validity, and reliability, reminding us that human oversight is indispensable (Hua et al., 2025). Benchmarking initiatives such as PsychBench further highlight both the potential and current limitations of these systems. Although some large language models performed well in clinical text understanding, their diagnostic accuracy and medication recommendations remained insufficient for complex psychiatric cases, indicating the necessity of targeted fine-tuning and improved evaluation metrics (Liu et al., 2025).

Applications of foundation models to structured health records and behavioral sensing data have further expanded possibilities. For instance, vector quantized models trained on smartphone and wearable data demonstrated strong performance in detecting behavioral shifts predictive of suicidality, while Pretrained Actigraphy Transformer models successfully predicted medication use and depression from accelerometer data (Oliver et al., 2025; Ruan et al., 2025). These approaches show scalability and interpretability, yet they also illustrate the technical and ethical challenges of handling large-scale personal data.

Together, these studies demonstrate that foundation models can integrate signals across multiple modalities and achieve performance that often surpasses traditional approaches. However, their reliance on massive datasets raises important issues regarding data access, computational costs, fairness, and clinical validity. The next step is to consider how such models can be embedded into systems that respect privacy and autonomy, ensuring that their deployment in mental health care remains both effective and ethically grounded.

PROTECTING PRIVACY AND AUTONOMY

The collection of sensitive data in mental health research raises pressing ethical concerns. Unlike other health domains, psychiatric information often carries profound implications for stigma, discrimination, and personal autonomy. Continuous data streams from smartphones, wearables, or electronic health records can reveal not only symptoms but also intimate aspects of daily life, making the risks of misuse or unauthorized access especially consequential. Scholars and stakeholders have repeatedly emphasized that while artificial intelligence holds potential to improve mental health prediction and treatment, its adoption must be guided by strong safeguards that protect privacy, maintain trust, and ensure patient participation in decision-making (Carr, 2020; Karimian et al., 2022).

Federated learning has emerged as one of the most promising approaches to achieve this balance. Instead of pooling sensitive data in centralized servers, federated learning allows models to be trained across distributed devices or institutions, with only model parameters shared. Studies demonstrate that federated frameworks can match or even exceed the accuracy of centralized methods while keeping raw data local. For instance, comparative evaluations of centralized and federated approaches for predicting depression and anxiety showed similar predictive performance, with federated models also providing stronger privacy guarantees through differential privacy and secure aggregation (Bohra et al., 2024). Other work integrating multimodal signals into federated architectures achieved high accuracy in predicting mental health conditions, suggesting that privacy-preserving frameworks do not necessarily entail a trade-off with clinical utility (Dubey et al., 2025). Nonetheless, federated systems are not immune to challenges. They face vulnerabilities to inference or poisoning attacks, suffer from communication overhead, and must contend with heterogeneous data distributions across clients (Liu et al., 2021; Xu et al., 2021).

Recent innovations attempt to address these limitations. Hybrid federated learning frameworks, such as clustered and quantum approaches, reduce communication burdens and improve performance on stress detection from wearable data by enabling local aggregation and encryption (Gupta et al., 2024). Similarly, personalized federated models that incorporate contextual cues from mobile devices have been shown to enhance the detection of depression, anxiety, and stress while remaining lightweight enough for smartphone deployment (Shin et al., 2023). Alternative architectures like FedStack allow heterogeneous local models to be combined into a global system, preserving privacy while enabling personalization in mental health monitoring (Shaik et al., 2022). Despite these advances, scalability and regulatory compliance remain significant barriers, especially in cross-jurisdictional contexts where legal frameworks diverge (Yadav et al., 2023).

Beyond federated learning, anonymization and de-identification strategies have also been employed, though their effectiveness is limited. As data streams become increasingly multimodal, re-identification risks grow, and current anonymization techniques often lack theoretical guarantees, especially for audio and video collected in therapy sessions (Mandal et al., 2025; Martinez-Martin et al., 2021). Encryption methods, including homomorphic encryption, offer stronger safeguards but add considerable computational burden, which can limit deployment in resource-constrained settings. These challenges underscore the importance of combining technical measures with ethical governance frameworks, participatory consent processes, and transparency to ensure public trust (Idowu & Idowu, 2025; McCradden et al., 2020).

What becomes clear from this evidence is that privacy-preserving methods must not only safeguard data but also respect the autonomy and voices of those most affected. Patient and public involvement remains underdeveloped in many AI projects, raising the risk that systems reproduce existing inequities or overlook cultural sensitivities (Carr, 2020). Technical innovation must therefore go hand in hand with inclusive design and robust governance to ensure that mental health AI is both effective and just. The next section considers synthetic data as a complementary strategy to reduce reliance on sensitive real-world datasets while introducing its own set of opportunities and risks.

THE ROLE OF SYNTHETIC DATA

The development of reliable artificial intelligence systems for mental health care is limited by the scarcity of high-quality clinical datasets. Traditional approaches to data collection are hindered by privacy regulations, fragmented health records, and cultural differences in diagnosis and reporting. Synthetic data has emerged as a possible solution, offering a way to expand training sets without compromising patient confidentiality. By generating simulated but realistic clinical information, synthetic data can supplement limited real-world samples and enhance model robustness in detecting and predicting mental health concerns (Mendes et al., 2022; Vedanta & Rao, 2024). This potential is especially critical in psychiatry, where diverse and representative data remain limited.

Synthetic datasets have demonstrated promise in improving classification accuracy, especially in low-resource contexts. For example, models trained with hybrid datasets that combine real-world data with synthetically generated samples have achieved higher accuracy and greater generalizability than those trained on natural data alone (Vedanta & Rao, 2024). Similarly, synthetic dialogues annotated for motivational interviewing have improved model performance in identifying psychological features such as empathy and coherence, while maintaining strong semantic fidelity (Kumar et al., 2024). These findings suggest that synthetic data can help bridge gaps where real-world datasets are insufficient, particularly in supporting culturally specific or linguistically nuanced psychiatric research.

However, synthetic data also raises significant challenges related to bias amplification and fairness. Studies have shown that large-scale generative models, such as GPT-3 and GPT-4, can reproduce and even exaggerate demographic biases, particularly in psychiatric diagnosis and treatment recommendations (Hastings, 2024; Heinz et al., 2023). These concerns are not merely technical but deeply ethical, as fairness in healthcare machine learning requires recognition of patients as both moral equals and individuals with distinct contexts and needs (Giovanola & Tiribelli, 2023). Algorithmic bias has been shown to disproportionately affect marginalized groups, reinforcing inequities rather than reducing them (Lloyd, 2018; Norori et al., 2021). Without careful design, synthetic data generation risks embedding systemic inequalities into clinical tools, thereby undermining their clinical and ethical value.

To mitigate these risks, researchers have begun exploring strategies that integrate fairness into synthetic data pipelines. Differentially private generative models, such as DP-CGANS, offer one pathway by balancing privacy preservation with data utility while reducing risks of identity disclosure (Sun et al., 2023). Reinforcement learning methods that reward equitable performance across demographic groups also show potential for minimizing residual biases during model training (Yang et al., 2023). Beyond technical innovations, calls have been made for transparent governance structures, inclusive participatory design, and regulatory safeguards to ensure that synthetic data does not become a vehicle for exploitation or surveillance (Kim, 2023; Tomičić & Gjorgjioska, 2024).

In mental health, where stigma and cultural sensitivity are central concerns, the ethical stakes of synthetic data are particularly high. Data poverty disproportionately affects communities in the Global South, minority groups, and socioeconomically disadvantaged populations, who are often excluded from large-scale datasets (Ibrahim et al., 2021; Timmons et al., 2023). Synthetic data, if developed inclusively, could help redress these inequities by providing balanced inputs for models and ensuring that diagnostic and therapeutic recommendations are not biased toward dominant populations. At the same time, researchers must remain vigilant about how these datasets are constructed, annotated, and deployed to avoid reproducing colonial or Western-centric frameworks that marginalize alternative epistemologies (Tomičić & Gjorgjioska, 2024).

The role of synthetic data in mental health therefore extends beyond technical problem solving. It represents an opportunity to address scarcity while foregrounding fairness, privacy, and cultural validity. Its success depends not only on innovation in data generation but also on embedding ethical and sociocultural awareness in design and application. As synthetic data becomes increasingly integrated into model training pipelines, its interplay with multimodal learning requires further attention, particularly in ensuring that generated signals preserve both clinical reliability and patient dignity. This naturally leads to the question of how multimodal data streams themselves can be integrated to provide richer, context-sensitive insights into psychopathology.

FROM MODELS TO CLINICAL REALITY

The integration of artificial intelligence into mental health care has progressed from experimental models to tools that are increasingly tested in clinical contexts. A central area of development has been conversational agents and chatbots, which are designed to deliver therapeutic interactions at scale. For example, Abubakar et al. (2024) demonstrated that a reinforcement learning–trained chatbot was capable of producing context-aware, coherent, and emotionally attuned responses that resemble supportive dialogue. These findings underscore the potential of AI to extend therapeutic reach, but they also highlight gaps such as limited multimodal input and insufficient benchmarking against standardized clinical measures. Similarly, reviews of AI-based chatbots show that while interventions grounded in cognitive behavioral therapy and generative systems like GPT-3.5 improve short-term outcomes in depression and anxiety, they remain constrained by issues of cultural adaptation, data privacy, and lack of longitudinal validation (Algumaei et al., 2025). These developments illustrate that AI is unlikely to function as a replacement for therapists but instead as a component that supports stepped-care approaches.

Stepped-care frameworks provide a structured model in which interventions are matched to symptom severity and individual needs, offering an effective way to integrate AI into existing health systems. Studies of stratified care platforms such as TourHeart+ and WHO-guided interventions indicate that digital systems can increase accessibility and flexibility, particularly in diverse and resource-constrained populations (Mak et al., 2023; Purgato et al., 2025). Evidence suggests that these tools can reduce symptoms of distress, promote engagement, and support early intervention, although success depends heavily on careful design, usability, and integration with clinician oversight. Without such alignment, digital tools risk overburdening users or producing disengagement due to poorly tailored content or inadequate crisis protocols (Tsoi et al., 2022).

A persistent theme across the literature is the necessity of clinician involvement in the deployment of AI. AI systems that forecast risk or propose treatment pathways can inform decision-making, but clinicians remain central in interpreting outputs and applying them in context (Auf et al., 2025; Higgins et al., 2024). This emphasis on human oversight addresses not only accuracy and accountability but also the ethical requirement that vulnerable individuals receive care guided by professional judgment. Ethical analyses further caution against over-reliance on chatbots, warning that therapeutic misconception may arise when patients perceive AI systems as substitutes for trained professionals (Khawaja & Bélisle-Pipon, 2023). Such misconceptions can compromise safety and autonomy, particularly in settings where human support is limited.

Another important consideration is how patients perceive and respond to AI-based systems. Research shows that willingness to engage with conversational agents is shaped by trust, attachment, and interpersonal vulnerabilities (Guglielmucci & Di Basilio, 2025). While some users value anonymity and accessibility, others remain cautious due to concerns about privacy, limited therapeutic depth, or the absence of authentic empathy (Meadi et al., 2025). The concept of a digital therapeutic alliance has been proposed to capture the relational qualities that can emerge in AI-mediated therapy, though studies consistently find that emotional depth and personalization remain weaker compared to human interactions (Malouin-Lachance et al., 2025). Moreover, patient trust in AI is often lower when they are aware that recommendations originate from algorithms rather than clinicians, which further highlights the enduring centrality of human oversight (Maslej et al., 2023).

Despite these challenges, evidence suggests that clinician-AI partnerships may optimize outcomes. Hybrid models that combine AI tools with human support have shown improvements in adherence and reduced dropout, especially in large-scale deployments across diverse populations. Yet significant concerns persist regarding algorithmic bias, insufficient cultural adaptation, and unclear ethical responsibilities. Reviews consistently call for patient and public involvement in design processes to ensure that systems are not only technically robust but also equitable, inclusive, and trustworthy (Putica et al., 2025; Zidaru et al., 2021).

Taken together, these findings suggest that AI is best understood as an augmentative technology in mental health care, capable of supporting stepped-care delivery, extending reach, and informing clinical decisions when guided by human oversight. The ongoing task lies in balancing innovation with ethical responsibility, patient safety, and sustained clinician involvement. This raises further questions about how privacy-preserving approaches can be integrated into these emerging systems, an issue that will be addressed in the following section.

PROPOSED FRAMEWORK FOR ETHICAL TRIALS

Designing ethical trials for artificial intelligence in mental health requires more than technical precision. Trials must protect the rights of participants, ensure inclusivity, and build trust in research practices that often rely on sensitive personal data. These responsibilities begin with how participants are recruited, which populations are included or excluded, and how consent is secured. Decisions in these areas determine not only who benefits from innovation but also who may be left out of it. Evidence from recent reviews shows that while AI-based tools are being tested across varied populations, ethical safeguards remain inconsistently applied, and inclusion of marginalized groups is often inadequate. Addressing these gaps is essential for ensuring that AI research in mental health is both clinically meaningful and socially responsible. The following subsection examines recruitment, inclusion, and consent procedures as the foundation for ethically sound trials.

Recruitment, Inclusion, and Consent in Ethical AI Trials

Recruitment, inclusion, and consent procedures form the ethical foundation of trials that evaluate artificial intelligence in mental health. Evidence from recent reviews shows that current practices are inconsistent and often lack transparency. For example, Algumaei et al. (2025) found that although AI chatbots demonstrated strong short-term outcomes in populations ranging from students to health workers across diverse cultural contexts, inclusion practices frequently excluded individuals in low-resource settings, and reporting of ethical safeguards was inconsistent. Similarly, Budler & Stiglic (2025) noted that fewer than half of reviewed studies explicitly documented both ethical approval and informed consent, with smaller studies and those published in lower-impact journals being most likely to omit them. Such variability raises concerns about participant protection and reinforces the need for standardized frameworks.

Broader reviews of algorithmic applications in mental health also suggest that ethical practices are uneven. Gooding & Kariotis (2021) reported that only a minority of studies explicitly addressed issues such as consent and anonymization, with legal considerations and patient involvement often absent. This neglect of service user perspectives not only undermines transparency but also reduces the legitimacy of research outcomes. Skorburg et al. (2024) further argue that trials which treat participants primarily as sources of data neglect lived experience and risk marginalizing service user voices. In contrast, frameworks such as CONSORT-AI and SPIRIT-AI offer guidance on improving methodological clarity, ensuring that trial protocols specify how AI systems handle input and output data, human interaction, and error management (Liu et al., 2020; Rivera et al., 2020).

Beyond formal reporting standards, efforts to embed ethical reflection within trial design have also been undertaken. The Canada Protocol – MHSP, for instance, proposes a structured checklist that addresses privacy, transparency, security, and health-related risks in AI mental health research (Mörch et al., 2020). These tools highlight the importance of moving beyond minimal compliance and toward proactive ethical engagement. Zidaru et al. (2021) similarly emphasized the importance of public and patient involvement in designing AI systems, noting that inclusive recruitment and transparent consent procedures are vital for building trust and ensuring that interventions are aligned with user needs.

Taken together, the evidence indicates that ethical trials of AI in mental health must go beyond securing approval from review boards. Recruitment should prioritize diversity and inclusion across cultural, socioeconomic, and clinical backgrounds. Consent must be informed, transparent, and adapted to the complexities of data-driven systems, including disclosures about how data will be processed, stored, and potentially reused. Such practices lay the groundwork for subsequent considerations of privacy safeguards in the selection of sensing methods, which will be the focus of the next section.

Recommended Sensing Methods and Privacy Safeguards

The growing use of GPS, speech, and text-based sensing methods offers promising avenues for understanding mental health in everyday contexts. These technologies allow researchers and clinicians to capture subtle behavioral and social markers that might otherwise go unnoticed in traditional clinical assessments. When combined with wearable devices that measure physiological activity such as heart rate or movement, these methods provide a more comprehensive picture of individual functioning. However, their use must be carefully balanced against significant ethical challenges concerning privacy, autonomy, and the risk of unintended harms.

Evidence demonstrates that passive sensing methods can yield clinically relevant markers of psychological well-being. Ben-Zeev et al. (2015) showed that data from geospatial activity, speech duration, and sleep monitoring were associated with changes in stress, depression, and loneliness among young adults, suggesting that such data can capture day-to-day variability in mental states. Boonstra et al. (2018) similarly demonstrated the potential of Bluetooth and GPS data to identify movement patterns and social contexts, with participants expressing moderate comfort provided that data use was transparent and securely managed. Extending this line of research, wearable devices have been investigated for their ability to monitor child and adolescent populations, with findings indicating promising accuracy in detecting early signs of anxiety and depression when measures such as movement and heart rate variability are included (O'Leary et al., 2024). Together, these studies highlight the potential for multimodal sensing to provide ecological and continuous markers of mental health.

Despite these benefits, there are considerable risks linked to the collection and interpretation of sensor-based data. Bauer et al. (2017) warned that behavioral data derived from smartphones can be easily repurposed for surveillance or profiling, often without informed consent, raising concerns about autonomy and stigma. Martinez-Martin et al. (2018) further cautioned that the spread of digital phenotyping beyond clinical settings into consumer markets heightens risks of data misuse, lack of oversight, and erosion of trust. Jacobson et al. (2020) underscored that these challenges extend to fundamental ethical questions about informed consent, fairness, and algorithmic transparency.

User perspectives also reveal important differences in willingness to share various types of data. Di Matteo et al. (2018) found that participants were more comfortable sharing screen state data but highly reluctant to allow constant audio monitoring, reflecting fears of intrusive surveillance. Rooksby et al. (2019) echoed this sentiment, noting that while students recognized the potential benefits of passive sensing, many were concerned about autonomy, institutional trust, and the emotional strain of being continuously monitored. These findings suggest that sensing methods must be adapted to respect user preferences and to provide clear privacy protections.

Ethical critiques have also drawn attention to deeper risks beyond data protection. Faissner et al. (2024) argued that digital phenotyping apps risk undermining epistemic agency by privileging algorithmic predictions over the lived accounts of users, particularly when predictive outputs fail to align with personal experiences of distress. Valentine et al. (2023) highlighted the potential tension between personalization and privacy when recommender systems in mental health apps rely on ecological data to generate interventions, often at the expense of user control.

The evidence therefore suggests that sensing methods such as GPS, speech analysis, text prompts, and wearable data can enrich psychiatric assessment, but their utility is inseparable from questions of privacy, transparency, and agency. Future developments in this area must prioritize robust safeguards, including informed consent processes that are meaningful rather than perfunctory, user-centered design that respects individual preferences, and governance structures that prevent misuse of sensitive data. Only when these conditions are met can multimodal sensing contribute responsibly to the identification of risk in psychopathology. This naturally leads to the next concern, which is how artificial intelligence models process and interpret these diverse data streams in ways that remain reliable, fair, and clinically meaningful.

Evaluating Effectiveness and Interpretability of AI in Mental Health

Evaluating artificial intelligence models in mental health requires attention not only to statistical performance but also to clinical relevance, patient well-being, and interpretability. Traditional benchmarks such as accuracy, sensitivity, and area under the curve provide important insights but they do not fully capture how these systems perform in real-world therapeutic contexts. Measures that reflect patient-centred outcomes, therapeutic alliance, and trust in technology are increasingly recognized as essential. These dimensions ensure that models are not only technically reliable but also clinically meaningful and ethically responsible.

Research on conversational agents offers useful evidence in this regard. A meta-analysis of 32 randomized controlled trials demonstrated that such agents produce measurable improvements in symptoms of depression, anxiety, stress, and general distress, though long-term outcomes remain less consistent (He et al., 2023). Similarly, digital interventions guided by non-clinicians have been shown to be nearly as effective as clinician-supported approaches, with notable advantages in accessibility and scalability (Leung et al., 2022). Yet feasibility trials illustrate that engagement barriers, particularly concerns about privacy and relevance, can substantially limit their utility in practice (Fujita et al., 2025). These findings suggest that while outcomes can be improved in controlled conditions, adoption in naturalistic settings requires design choices that reduce complexity and promote trust.

Predictive modelling studies also highlight the potential and limits of AI. Machine learning algorithms applied to digital mental health programs have achieved moderate success in forecasting treatment outcomes, identifying key predictors such as baseline symptom severity, motivation, and work impairment (Hornstein et al., 2021). However, moderate accuracy rates and difficulties with external validation indicate that further development is needed before these tools can be relied upon for personalized treatment planning. Broader evaluations confirm that predictive accuracy often declines when applied to new populations, emphasizing the importance of rigorous validation and replication efforts (Rutledge et al., 2019).

Alongside clinical outcomes, interpretability plays a central role in determining the acceptability of AI in psychiatry. Studies of explainable AI methods show that clinicians prefer interpretations that align with clinical reasoning, such as free-text rationales or patient similarity comparisons, over more abstract features like attention highlights (Hou & Wang, 2025). Benchmarking frameworks such as CausalGym also advance the evaluation of model interpretability by assessing whether internal representations capture meaningful causal relationships, although current approaches are limited in scope and generalizability (Arora et al., 2024). This growing emphasis on interpretability reflects the need for AI tools that clinicians and patients can understand and trust, rather than systems that deliver predictions without explanation.

Another key factor concerns patient experience and engagement. Reviews of therapeutic alliance in digital mental health show that while digital interventions can foster supportive relationships, the nature of this alliance differs from traditional settings, with engagement often serving as a mediator of outcomes (Tremain et al., 2020). Studies of mobile health applications further show that users value features that combine education, symptom tracking, and social support, which can reduce unmet care needs and enhance quality of life (Wang et al., 2020). Taken together, these findings highlight that evaluation frameworks must move beyond technical performance toward measures that integrate well-being, engagement, and clinical interpretability.

Ultimately, the effectiveness of AI in mental health care will depend on how well evaluation strategies integrate patient-centred outcomes, rigorous validation, and explainability. These dimensions not only determine clinical utility but also shape trust and long-term adoption in therapeutic contexts. As AI models evolve, the challenge lies in balancing predictive accuracy with meaningful interpretability, paving the way for discussion on how foundation models can advance these aims in psychiatry and psychotherapy.

FUTURE DIRECTIONS AND OPEN QUESTIONS

The next decade of research on artificial intelligence in mental health will likely be defined not by questions of feasibility but by questions of personalization, fairness, and trust. A rapidly growing body of literature demonstrates that smartphone sensors, digital phenotyping, and machine learning models can predict stress, mood fluctuations, and other mental health outcomes with varying degrees of success. Yet these findings remain fragmented and inconsistently generalizable, leaving significant gaps between technological promise and clinical utility. The task ahead is not only to refine existing methods but also to confront unresolved conceptual, methodological, and ethical dilemmas that determine whether these systems can be responsibly integrated into healthcare.

One of the most pressing challenges concerns personalization. Across studies, there is consistent evidence that idiographic models tend to outperform nomothetic ones in predicting stress, mood, or anxiety. In other words, when algorithms are tuned to the baseline of a single individual, their predictive accuracy improves (Aalbers et al., 2023; Jacobson & Bhattacharya, 2022). Yet even within this domain, the magnitude of improvement is modest and often fails to surpass naïve baselines such as predicting the average affective state of a given person. This paradox reflects a deeper tension. On the one hand, individuals vary significantly in their digital behaviors, physiological responses, and contextual patterns, making personalization necessary. On the other hand, the data sparsity inherent to individual-level modeling makes robust learning difficult. Jaques et al. (2017) illustrate this by showing that personalized models require at least 15 days of labeled data to achieve meaningful prediction accuracy. Li & Washington (2024) further demonstrate that personalized deep learning models can reach very high accuracy for emotion recognition, yet their scalability is questionable. These findings suggest that future research must move beyond a binary opposition between nomothetic and idiographic approaches and instead develop hybrid strategies. Multitask learning, transfer learning, and zero-shot modeling may provide viable solutions that leverage population-level data to bootstrap personalization while minimizing data burden on individual users.

The problem of personalization also raises a more conceptual issue. Current research typically assumes that personalization refers to technical optimization of model fit to an individual's baseline. Yet this perspective risks narrowing personalization to algorithmic fine-tuning. True personalization in clinical care requires more than predictive accuracy; it must also integrate the values, goals, and lived experiences of individuals. Beg & Verma (2025) highlight that users of AI-based psychotherapy apps often describe frustrations with scripted empathy and fragmented therapeutic narratives. Such findings imply that personalization must be reconceptualized not only as a statistical endeavor but as a relational and cultural process. Systems that adapt only to behavioral baselines without accommodating user preferences, cultural background, or therapeutic context may achieve technical accuracy while still failing to meet the needs of those they are designed to serve. In this sense, personalization in digital mental health should be treated as a multidimensional construct encompassing predictive modeling, therapeutic responsiveness, cultural sensitivity, and co-design with end users.

Equally important is the question of fairness. Several reviews provide strong evidence that AI in healthcare and beyond is shaped by structural inequities (Cary et al., 2023; Jain et al., 2023; Kostick-Quenet et al., 2022; Leavy, 2018; Turner Lee, 2018; Livingston, 2020; Nadeem et al., 2020; O'Connor & Liu, 2024; Park et al., 2022). Underrepresentation of minoritized populations in training datasets leads to algorithmic misclassification, while lack of diversity among AI developers perpetuates implicit bias. These findings underscore that fairness cannot be reduced to technical fixes such as bias correction algorithms, although such techniques (e.g., disparate impact removal, as shown by Park et al., 2022) have value. True fairness requires systemic changes: diversified datasets, inclusive research practices, and accountability mechanisms that extend across the AI development pipeline. Without these, digital phenotyping risks amplifying the very inequities it aims to mitigate.

The literature also reveals that fairness is not uniform across dimensions of identity. Gender bias and racial bias operate differently, and both intersect with socioeconomic status, geographic location, and cultural context. For example, Beg & Verma (2025) document cultural microaggressions embedded in AI psychotherapy apps, suggesting that systems trained primarily on Western populations may inadvertently alienate users in non-Western contexts. Similarly, Kostick-Quenet et al. (2022) show that even when race is not directly predictive of health outcomes, structural disparities in access and referral patterns distort the composition of training datasets. These observations highlight a critical future direction: fairness research must adopt an intersectional lens that accounts for the multiplicative effects of race, gender, class, and geography. Moreover, global perspectives are essential. Alberto et al. (2023) show that the overwhelming majority of published AI health research comes from high-income countries. As Mensah emphasizes in the Ghanaian context, regulatory frameworks in low- and middle-income countries remain underdeveloped, yet these are precisely the settings where AI could either narrow or widen health disparities.

Ensuring fairness therefore requires not only technical innovation but also global collaboration, policy reform, and capacity building in underrepresented regions.

Building trust is another critical priority. Baron (2025) argues that explainability may not be necessary for all forms of trust in AI, since some models of trust are not interpersonal but reliance based. However, empirical studies by Duarte et al. (2023), Schmidt et al. (2020), and Shabankareh et al. (2025) complicate this picture. They show that explainability can sometimes enhance trust but at other times undermine it, leading to overtrust in low-performing systems or diminished confidence in accurate ones. The implication is that trust cannot be engineered solely through technical explainability. Instead, it emerges from a constellation of factors including predictive accuracy, fairness, user autonomy, privacy protections, and cultural alignment. Cutillo et al. (2020) and Sasikala & Sachan (2024) stress that transparency and user-centered design are vital for trustworthiness. Yet transparency is not monolithic: different stakeholders require different forms of explanation. Patients may need understandable accounts of why a system recommended a particular intervention, while clinicians may require detailed model diagnostics, and regulators may demand audit trails. Designing explainability with this pluralism in mind remains an open challenge (Verma et al., 2025).

Another underexplored dimension of trust concerns temporal continuity. Beg & Verma (2025) note that users often experience AI psychotherapy apps as fragmented, with limited capacity to sustain therapeutic narratives over time. Trust is not built in a single interaction but through consistent, reliable engagement. Systems that fail to recognize users' past experiences or adapt to their evolving contexts risk eroding trust even if they are technically accurate. Future research should therefore explore how AI systems can cultivate therapeutic continuity through memory architectures, longitudinal learning, and integration with human providers.

Taken together, these issues point toward several broader gaps in the current literature. First, there is a lack of consensus on evaluation metrics. Studies vary widely in whether they report predictive accuracy, explained variance, area under the curve, or user trust measures, making it difficult to compare findings. Moreover, many studies still rely on self-reported data for ground truth, which may not accurately reflect clinical states. Second, few studies conduct longitudinal validation in real-world clinical settings. As Torous et al. (2025) note, most evidence comes from pilot trials with limited engagement and high attrition, leaving open the question of how these systems perform at scale. Third, there is insufficient integration between technological and clinical frameworks. For instance, while Jacobson & Bhattacharya (2022) achieve robust prediction of anxiety symptoms using LSTM models, the clinical implications of these predictions remain uncertain. Do they meaningfully inform treatment, reduce symptom burden, or improve quality of life? Without such outcome-oriented evaluations, predictive success risks remaining a technical curiosity rather than a clinical contribution.

A further gap lies in the lack of attention to human–AI collaboration. Most current research treats AI as either a replacement or a stand-alone tool. Yet the future may lie in hybrid systems where AI augments human clinicians by providing early detection, continuous monitoring, or decision support, while humans provide therapeutic depth, contextual interpretation, and ethical oversight. Such hybrid models raise new questions: how should responsibilities be distributed between humans and AI? How can accountability be maintained? What training do clinicians need to effectively integrate AI insights into practice? Addressing these questions requires not only technical research but also interdisciplinary dialogue across psychology, medicine, ethics, law, and computer science.

Finally, there is an emerging opportunity to move beyond prediction to intervention. Many studies demonstrate that digital phenotyping can forecast stress, mood, or anxiety with moderate accuracy. The next step is to translate these predictions into just-in-time adaptive interventions (JITAIs) that deliver personalized, context-aware support. Gönül's reinforcement learning framework and Surendra's integration of AI with neural interface technologies offer early glimpses of such possibilities. Yet these remain experimental and face barriers of scalability, ethical governance, and user adherence. To realize their potential, future work must develop interventions that are not only technically adaptive but also clinically validated, ethically grounded, and acceptable to users.

In sum, the future of AI in mental health hinges on its ability to balance personalization, fairness, and trust. This requires moving beyond narrow technical definitions toward multidimensional frameworks that integrate statistical performance with human values, cultural contexts, and clinical relevance. It also requires identifying and addressing the gaps that currently limit progress, from inconsistent evaluation metrics to lack of longitudinal trials and insufficient attention to human–AI collaboration. Emerging opportunities, from hybrid models to just-in-time adaptive interventions, hold promise for transforming mental health care, but only if pursued with methodological rigor and ethical vigilance. The field stands at a critical juncture: whether AI becomes a tool that exacerbates inequities or one that expands access to personalized, trustworthy care will depend on the research choices made in the years to come.

CONCLUSION

The convergence of multimodal artificial intelligence and psychiatry offers both promise and complexity. By drawing on signals from voice, language, physiology, and behavior, these approaches move beyond narrow symptom checklists and begin to capture the layered nature of human experience. This capacity to integrate diverse forms of data raises the possibility of detecting risk states before they become clinically entrenched and of supporting more individualized pathways of care. Yet this potential must be viewed not as a replacement for human understanding but as an extension of it, where computational tools complement the interpretive expertise of clinicians and researchers.

At the same time, the field is confronted with challenges that go beyond technical accuracy. Questions of data ownership, informed consent, and privacy are central to any application of these methods. The sensitivity of mental health information makes the stakes particularly high, demanding safeguards that protect not only individuals but also communities whose voices may be marginalized in data-driven research. Ethical reflection must therefore run in parallel with technological innovation, ensuring that advances do not inadvertently reproduce biases or amplify disparities in access to care.

A second challenge lies in the generalizability of findings. Much of the current evidence arises from limited samples, often drawn from university populations or specific cultural contexts. For multimodal models to achieve their potential, they must be tested across diverse groups and settings, acknowledging that mental health risk does not manifest uniformly. This calls for methodological rigor as well as an openness to collaboration across disciplines, institutions, and societies. Only then can findings be translated responsibly into real-world practice.

Taken together, these reflections point toward a future in which multimodal AI contributes meaningfully to psychiatry and psychology while remaining grounded in ethical responsibility. The ultimate aim is not to automate care but to enrich the ways in which we understand and respond to psychological suffering. As research advances, the field will need to continually balance innovation with respect for the human subjects at its core. It is in this balance that the enduring value of multimodal approaches will be realized.

REFERENCES

Aalbers, G., Hendrickson, A. T., Vanden Abeele, M. M., & Keijsers, L. (2023). Smartphone-Tracked Digital Markers of Momentary Subjective Stress in College Students: Idiographic Machine Learning Analysis. *JMIR mHealth and uHealth, 11*, e37469. DOI: 10.2196/37469 PMID: 36951924

Abubakar, A. M., Gupta, D., & Parida, S. (2024). A Reinforcement Learning Approach for Intelligent Conversational Chatbot For Enhancing Mental Health Therapy. *Procedia Computer Science, 235*, 916–925. DOI: 10.1016/j.procs.2024.04.087

Alberto, I. R. I., Alberto, N. R. I., Altinel, Y., Blacker, S., Binotti, W. W., Celi, L. A., Chua, T., Fiske, A., Griffin, M., Karaca, G., Mokolo, N., Naawu, D. K. N., Patscheider, J., Petushkov, A., Quion, J., Senteio, C., Taisbak, S., Tırnova, İ., Tokashiki, H., & Yap, K. (2023). Who does the fairness in health AI community represent? https://doi.org/DOI: 10.1101/2023.03.20.23287471

Alberto, P., Arndis, S., Vibeke, B., & Riccardo, F. (2019). *Voice Patterns in Schizophrenia: A systematic Review and Bayesian Meta-Analysis*. https://doi.org/DOI: 10.1101/583815

Algumaei, A., Yaacob, N. M., Doheir, M., Al-Andoli, M. N., & Algumaie, M. (2025). Symmetric Therapeutic Frameworks and Ethical Dimensions in AI-Based Mental Health Chatbots (2020–2025): A Systematic Review of Design Patterns, Cultural Balance, and Structural Symmetry. *Symmetry, 17*(7), 1082. DOI: 10.3390/sym17071082

Alhuzali, H., & Alasmari, A. (2024). *Evaluating the Effectiveness of the Foundational Models for Q&A Classification in Mental Health care.*

Antosik-Wójcińska, A. Z., Dominiak, M., Chojnacka, M., Kaczmarek-Majer, K., Opara, K. R., Radziszewska, W., Olwert, A., & Święcicki, Ł. (2020). Smartphone as a monitoring tool for bipolar disorder: A systematic review including data analysis, machine learning algorithms and predictive modelling. *International Journal of Medical Informatics, 138*, 104131. DOI: 10.1016/j.ijmedinf.2020.104131 PMID: 32305023

Arora, A., Jurafsky, D., & Potts, C. (2024). *CausalGym: Benchmarking causal interpretability methods on linguistic tasks.*

Auf, H., Svedberg, P., Nygren, J., Nair, M., & Lundgren, L. E. (2025). The Use of AI in Mental Health Services to Support Decision-Making: Scoping Review. *Journal of Medical Internet Research, 27*, e63548. DOI: 10.2196/63548 PMID: 39854710

Barch, D. M. (2020). What Does It Mean to Be Transdiagnostic and How Would We Know? *The American Journal of Psychiatry*, *177*(5), 370–372. DOI: 10.1176/appi.ajp.2020.20030243 PMID: 32354269

Baron, S. (2025). Trust, Explainability and AI. *Philosophy & Technology*, *38*(1), 4. DOI: 10.1007/s13347-024-00837-6

Bauer, M., Glenn, T., Monteith, S., Bauer, R., Whybrow, P. C., & Geddes, J. (2017). Ethical perspectives on recommending digital technology for patients with mental illness. *International Journal of Bipolar Disorders*, *5*(1), 6. DOI: 10.1186/s40345-017-0073-9 PMID: 28155206

Beg, M. J., & Verma, M. K. (2025). Artificial Intelligence-based Psychotherapy: A Qualitative Exploration of Usability, Personalization, and the Perception of Therapeutic Progress. *Indian Journal of Psychological Medicine*. Advance online publication. DOI: 10.1177/02537176251357477 PMID: 40686925

Ben-Zeev, D., Scherer, E. A., Wang, R., Xie, H., & Campbell, A. T. (2015). Next-generation psychiatric assessment: Using smartphone sensors to monitor behavior and mental health. *Psychiatric Rehabilitation Journal*, *38*(3), 218–226. DOI: 10.1037/prj0000130 PMID: 25844912

Bohra, A., Vadodaria, K., Desai, V., Sawant, V., & Tawde, P. (2024). Enhancing Privacy in Mental Health Prediction Using Centralized and Federated Learning Models. *2024 International Conference on Artificial Intelligence and Emerging Technology (Global AI Summit)*, 1141–1146. https://doi.org/DOI: 10.1109/GlobalAISummit62156.2024.10947768

Boonstra, T. W., Nicholas, J., Wong, Q. J., Shaw, F., Townsend, S., & Christensen, H. (2018). Using Mobile Phone Sensor Technology for Mental Health Research: Integrated Analysis to Identify Hidden Challenges and Potential Solutions. *Journal of Medical Internet Research*, *20*(7), e10131. DOI: 10.2196/10131 PMID: 30061092

Bufano, P., Laurino, M., Said, S., Tognetti, A., & Menicucci, D. (2023). Digital Phenotyping for Monitoring Mental Disorders: Systematic Review. *Journal of Medical Internet Research*, *25*, e46778. DOI: 10.2196/46778 PMID: 38090800

Cardamone, N. C., Olfson, M., Schmutte, T., Ungar, L., Liu, T., Cullen, S. W., Williams, N. J., & Marcus, S. C. (2025). Classifying Unstructured Text in Electronic Health Records for Mental Health Prediction Models: Large Language Model Evaluation Study. *JMIR Medical Informatics*, *13*, e65454–e65454. DOI: 10.2196/65454 PMID: 39864953

Caro, J. O., Fonseca, A. H. de O., Averill, C., Rizvi, S. A., Rosati, M., Cross, J. L., Mittal, P., Zappala, E., Levine, D., Dhodapkar, R. M., Han, I., Karbasi, A., Abdallah, C. G., & van Dijk, D. (2023). *BrainLM: A foundation model for brain activity recordings*. https://doi.org/DOI: 10.1101/2023.09.12.557460

Carr, S. (2020). 'AI gone mental': Engagement and ethics in data-driven technology for mental health. *Journal of Mental Health (Abingdon, England)*, *29*(2), 125–130. DOI: 10.1080/09638237.2020.1714011 PMID: 32000544

Cary, M. P., Zink, A., Wei, S., Olson, A., Yan, M., Senior, R., Bessias, S., Gadhoumi, K., Jean-Pierre, G., Wang, D., Ledbetter, L. S., Economou-Zavlanos, N. J., Obermeyer, Z., & Pencina, M. J. (2023). Mitigating Racial And Ethnic Bias And Advancing Health Equity In Clinical Algorithms: A Scoping Review. *Health Affairs*, *42*(10), 1359–1368. DOI: 10.1377/hlthaff.2023.00553 PMID: 37782868

Choi, A., Ooi, A., & Lottridge, D. (2024). Digital Phenotyping for Stress, Anxiety, and Mild Depression: Systematic Literature Review. *JMIR mHealth and uHealth*, *12*, e40689. DOI: 10.2196/40689 PMID: 38780995

Cilar Budler, L., & Stiglic, G. (2025). Ethical approval and informed consent in mental health research: A scoping review. *AI & Society*. Advance online publication. DOI: 10.1007/s00146-025-02364-0

Clark, L. A., Cuthbert, B., Lewis-Fernández, R., Narrow, W. E., & Reed, G. M. (2017). Three Approaches to Understanding and Classifying Mental Disorder: *ICD-11, DSM-5*, and the National Institute of Mental Health's Research Domain Criteria (RDoC). *Psychological Science in the Public Interest*, *18*(2), 72–145. DOI: 10.1177/1529100617727266 PMID: 29211974

Cohen, Z. D., DeRubeis, R. J., Hayes, R., Watkins, E. R., Lewis, G., Byng, R., Byford, S., Crane, C., Kuyken, W., Dalgleish, T., & Schweizer, S. (2023). The Development and Internal Evaluation of a Predictive Model to Identify for Whom Mindfulness-Based Cognitive Therapy Offers Superior Relapse Prevention for Recurrent Depression Versus Maintenance Antidepressant Medication. *Clinical Psychological Science*, *11*(1), 59–76. DOI: 10.1177/21677026221076832 PMID: 36698442

Crocamo, C., Cioni, R. M., Canestro, A., Nasti, C., Palpella, D., Piacenti, S., Bartoccetti, A., Re, M., Simonetti, V., Barattieri di San Pietro, C., Bulgheroni, M., Bartoli, F., & Carrà, G. (2025). Acoustic and Natural Language Markers for Bipolar Disorder: A Pilot, mHealth Cross-Sectional Study. *JMIR Formative Research*, *9*, e65555–e65555. DOI: 10.2196/65555 PMID: 40239203

Cruz Rivera, S., Liu, X., Chan, A.-W., Denniston, A. K., Calvert, M. J., Ashrafian, H., Beam, A. L., Collins, G. S., Darzi, A., Deeks, J. J., ElZarrad, M. K., Espinoza, C., Esteva, A., Faes, L., Ferrante di Ruffano, L., Fletcher, J., Golub, R., Harvey, H., Haug, C., & Yau, C. (2020). Guidelines for clinical trial protocols for interventions involving artificial intelligence: The SPIRIT-AI extension. *The Lancet. Digital Health*, *2*(10), e549–e560. DOI: 10.1016/S2589-7500(20)30219-3 PMID: 33328049

Cuthbert, B. N. (2014). The RDoC framework: Facilitating transition from ICD/ DSM to dimensional approaches that integrate neuroscience and psychopathology. *World Psychiatry; Official Journal of the World Psychiatric Association (WPA)*, *13*(1), 28–35. DOI: 10.1002/wps.20087 PMID: 24497240

Cutillo, C. M., Sharma, K. R., Foschini, L., Kundu, S., Mackintosh, M., Mandl, K. D., Beck, T., Collier, E., Colvis, C., Gersing, K., Gordon, V., Jensen, R., Shabestari, B., & Southall, N. (2020). Machine intelligence in healthcare—Perspectives on trustworthiness, explainability, usability, and transparency. *NPJ Digital Medicine*, *3*(1), 47. DOI: 10.1038/s41746-020-0254-2 PMID: 32258429

Dalgleish, T., Black, M., Johnston, D., & Bevan, A. (2020). Transdiagnostic approaches to mental health problems: Current status and future directions. *Journal of Consulting and Clinical Psychology*, *88*(3), 179–195. DOI: 10.1037/ccp0000482 PMID: 32068421

Di Matteo, D., Fine, A., Fotinos, K., Rose, J., & Katzman, M. (2018). Patient Willingness to Consent to Mobile Phone Data Collection for Mental Health Apps: Structured Questionnaire. *JMIR Mental Health*, *5*(3), e56. DOI: 10.2196/mental.9539 PMID: 30158102

Drougkas, G., Bakker, E. M., & Spruit, M. (2024). Multimodal machine learning for language and speech markers identification in mental health. *BMC Medical Informatics and Decision Making*, *24*(1), 354. DOI: 10.1186/s12911-024-02772-0 PMID: 39578814

Duarte, R. de B., Correia, F., Arriaga, P., & Paiva, A. (2023). AI Trust: Can Explainable AI Enhance Warranted Trust? *Human Behavior and Emerging Technologies*, *2023*, 1–12. DOI: 10.1155/2023/4637678

Dubey, P., Dubey, P., & Bokoro, P. N. (2025). Federated learning for privacy-enhanced mental health prediction with multimodal data integration. *Computer Methods in Biomechanics and Biomedical Engineering. Imaging & Visualization*, *13*(1). Advance online publication. DOI: 10.1080/21681163.2025.2509672

Etkin, A., & Cuthbert, B. (2014). Beyond the DSM: Development of a Transdiagnostic Psychiatric Neuroscience Course. *Academic Psychiatry*, *38*(2), 145–150. DOI: 10.1007/s40596-013-0032-4 PMID: 24493358

Faissner, M., Kuhn, E., Müller, R., & Laacke, S. (2024). Detecting your depression with your smartphone? – An ethical analysis of epistemic injustice in passive self-tracking apps. *Ethics and Information Technology*, *26*(2), 28. DOI: 10.1007/s10676-024-09765-7

Faurholt-Jepsen, M., Busk, J., Frost, M., Vinberg, M., Christensen, E. M., Winther, O., Bardram, J. E., & Kessing, L. V. (2016). Voice analysis as an objective state marker in bipolar disorder. *Translational Psychiatry*, *6*(7), e856–e856. DOI: 10.1038/tp.2016.123 PMID: 27434490

Flores, R., Tlachac, M. L., Toto, E., & Rundensteiner, E. (2022, December). Audiface: Multimodal deep learning for depression screening. In *Machine Learning for Healthcare Conference* (pp. 609-630). PMLR.

Ford, E., Stone, J., Oliver, D., Fell, B., Roque, G., Robertson, S., Fusar-Poli, P., & Greenwood, K. (2025). Local adaptation and validation of a transdiagnostic risk calculator for first episode psychosis using mental health patient records. *Frontiers in Psychiatry*, *16*. Advance online publication. DOI: 10.3389/fpsyt.2025.1584719 PMID: 40766924

Fujita, J., Yano, Y., Shinoda, S., Sho, N., Otsuki, M., Suda, A., Takayama, M., Moroga, T., Yamaguchi, H., Ishii, M., & Miyazaki, T. (2025). Challenges in Implementing a Mobile AI Chatbot Intervention for Depression Among Youth on Psychiatric Waiting Lists: Randomized Controlled Study Termination Report. *JMIRx Med*, *6*, e70960–e70960. DOI: 10.2196/70960 PMID: 41055096

Fusaroli, R., Lambrechts, A., Bang, D., Bowler, D. M., & Gaigg, S. B. (2016). *"Is Voice A Marker for Autism Spectrum Disorder? A Systematic Review And Meta-Analysis"*. https://doi.org/DOI: 10.1101/046565

Giovanola, B., & Tiribelli, S. (2023). Beyond bias and discrimination: Redefining the AI ethics principle of fairness in healthcare machine-learning algorithms. *AI & Society*, *38*(2), 549–563. DOI: 10.1007/s00146-022-01455-6 PMID: 35615443

Gooding, P., & Kariotis, T. (2021). Ethics and Law in Research on Algorithmic and Data-Driven Technology in Mental Health Care: Scoping Review. *JMIR Mental Health*, *8*(6), e24668. DOI: 10.2196/24668 PMID: 34110297

Guglielmucci, F., & Di Basilio, D. (2025). Predicting Engagement With Conversational Agents in Mental Health Therapy by Examining the Role of Epistemic Trust, Personality, and Fear of Intimacy: Cross-Sectional Web-Based Survey Study. *JMIR Human Factors*, *12*, e70698–e70698. DOI: 10.2196/70698 PMID: 40737594

Gupta, A., Kumar Maurya, M., Dhere, K., & Kumar Chaurasiya, V. (2024). Privacy-Preserving Hybrid Federated Learning Framework for Mental Healthcare Applications: Clustered and Quantum Approaches. *IEEE Access : Practical Innovations, Open Solutions*, *12*, 145054–145068. DOI: 10.1109/ACCESS.2024.3464240

Hastings, J. (2024). Preventing harm from non-conscious bias in medical generative AI. *The Lancet. Digital Health*, *6*(1), e2–e3. DOI: 10.1016/S2589-7500(23)00246-7 PMID: 38123253

He, Y., Yang, L., Qian, C., Li, T., Su, Z., Zhang, Q., & Hou, X. (2023). Conversational Agent Interventions for Mental Health Problems: Systematic Review and Meta-analysis of Randomized Controlled Trials. *Journal of Medical Internet Research*, *25*, e43862. DOI: 10.2196/43862 PMID: 37115595

Heinz, M. V., Bhattacharya, S., Trudeau, B., Quist, R., Song, S. H., Lee, C. M., & Jacobson, N. C. (2023). Testing domain knowledge and risk of bias of a large-scale general artificial intelligence model in mental health. *Digital Health*, *9*. Advance online publication. DOI: 10.1177/20552076231170499 PMID: 37101589

Higgins, O., Wilson, R. L., & Chalup, S. K. (2024). Using machine learning to assist decision making in the assessment of mental health patients presenting to emergency departments. *Digital Health*, *10*. Advance online publication. DOI: 10.1177/20552076241287364 PMID: 39534524

Hornstein, S., Forman-Hoffman, V., Nazander, A., Ranta, K., & Hilbert, K. (2021). Predicting therapy outcome in a digital mental health intervention for depression and anxiety: A machine learning approach. *Digital Health*, *7*. Advance online publication. DOI: 10.1177/20552076211060659 PMID: 34868624

Hou, J., & Wang, L. L. (2025). Explainable AI for Clinical Outcome Prediction: A Survey of Clinician Perceptions and Preferences. *AMIA Joint Summits on Translational Science Proceedings. AMIA Joint Summits on Translational Science*, *2025*, 215–224. PMID: 40502256

Hua, Y., Beam, A., Chibnik, L. B., & Torous, J. (2025). From statistics to deep learning: Using large language models in psychiatric research. *International Journal of Methods in Psychiatric Research*, *34*(1). Advance online publication. DOI: 10.1002/mpr.70007 PMID: 39777756

Ibrahim, H., Liu, X., Zariffa, N., Morris, A. D., & Denniston, A. K. (2021). Health data poverty: An assailable barrier to equitable digital health care. *The Lancet. Digital Health, 3*(4), e260–e265. DOI: 10.1016/S2589-7500(20)30317-4 PMID: 33678589

Idowu, O. F., & Idowu, S. (2025). Artificial Intelligence Applications in Mental Health Crisis Prediction: Navigating Privacy, Consent, and Fairness in Clinical Decision-Making. *International Journal of Computer Applications Technology and Research*. https://doi.org/DOI: 10.7753/IJCATR1408.1009

Jacobson, N. C., Bentley, K. H., Walton, A., Wang, S. B., Fortgang, R. G., Millner, A. J., Coombs, G., Rodman, A. M., & Coppersmith, D. D. L. (2020). Ethical dilemmas posed by mobile health and machine learning in psychiatry research. *Bulletin of the World Health Organization, 98*(4), 270–276. DOI: 10.2471/BLT.19.237107 PMID: 32284651

Jacobson, N. C., & Bhattacharya, S. (2022). Digital biomarkers of anxiety disorder symptom changes: Personalized deep learning models using smartphone sensors accurately predict anxiety symptoms from ecological momentary assessments. *Behaviour Research and Therapy, 149*, 104013. DOI: 10.1016/j.brat.2021.104013 PMID: 35030442

Jain, A., Brooks, J. R., Alford, C. C., Chang, C. S., Mueller, N. M., Umscheid, C. A., & Bierman, A. S. (2023). Awareness of Racial and Ethnic Bias and Potential Solutions to Address Bias With Use of Health Care Algorithms. *JAMA Health Forum, 4*(6), e231197. DOI: 10.1001/jamahealthforum.2023.1197 PMID: 37266959

Jaques, N., Taylor, S., Sano, A., & Picard, R. (2017, September). Predicting tomorrow's mood, health, and stress level using personalized multitask learning and domain adaptation. In *IJCAI 2017 Workshop on artificial intelligence in affective computing* (pp. 17-33). PMLR.

Kaczmarek-Majer, K., Dominiak, M., Antosik, A. Z., Hryniewicz, O., Kamińska, O., Opara, K., Owsiński, J., Radziszewska, W., Sochacka, M., & Święcicki, Ł. (2025). Acoustic features from speech as markers of depressive and manic symptoms in bipolar disorder: A prospective study. *Acta Psychiatrica Scandinavica, 151*(3), 358–374. DOI: 10.1111/acps.13735 PMID: 39118422

Karimian, G., Petelos, E., & Evers, S. M. A. A. (2022). The ethical issues of the application of artificial intelligence in healthcare: A systematic scoping review. *AI and Ethics, 2*(4), 539–551. DOI: 10.1007/s43681-021-00131-7

Khawaja, Z., & Bélisle-Pipon, J.-C. (2023). Your robot therapist is not your therapist: Understanding the role of AI-powered mental health chatbots. *Frontiers in Digital Health, 5*. Advance online publication. DOI: 10.3389/fdgth.2023.1278186 PMID: 38026836

Kim, J. (2023). *Data brokers and the sale of Americans' mental health data*. Duke Sanford School of Public Policy.

Koops, S., Brederoo, S. G., de Boer, J. N., Nadema, F. G., Voppel, A. E., & Sommer, I. E. (2023). Speech as a Biomarker for Depression. *CNS & Neurological Disorders - Drug Targets, 22*(2), 152–160. DOI: 10.2174/1871527320666211213125847 PMID: 34961469

Kostick-Quenet, K. M., Cohen, I. G., Gerke, S., Lo, B., Antaki, J., Movahedi, F., Njah, H., Schoen, L., Estep, J. E., & Blumenthal-Barby, J. S. (2022). Mitigating Racial Bias in Machine Learning. *The Journal of Law, Medicine & Ethics, 50*(1), 92–100. DOI: 10.1017/jme.2022.13 PMID: 35243993

Krueger, R. F., & Eaton, N. R. (2015). Transdiagnostic factors of mental disorders. *World Psychiatry; Official Journal of the World Psychiatric Association (WPA), 14*(1), 27–29. DOI: 10.1002/wps.20175 PMID: 25655146

Kumar, V., Ntoutsi, E., Rajawat, P. S., Medda, G., & Recupero, D. R. (2024). *Unlocking LLMs: Addressing Scarce Data and Bias Challenges in Mental Health.*

Leaning, I. E., Ikani, N., Savage, H. S., Leow, A., Beckmann, C., Ruhé, H. G., & Marquand, A. F. (2024). From smartphone data to clinically relevant predictions: A systematic review of digital phenotyping methods in depression. *Neuroscience and Biobehavioral Reviews, 158*, 105541. DOI: 10.1016/j.neubiorev.2024.105541 PMID: 38215802

Leavy, S. (2018). Gender bias in artificial intelligence. *Proceedings of the 1st International Workshop on Gender Equality in Software Engineering*, 14–16. https://doi.org/DOI: 10.1145/3195570.3195580

Leung, C., Pei, J., Hudec, K., Shams, F., Munthali, R., & Vigo, D. (2022). The Effects of Nonclinician Guidance on Effectiveness and Process Outcomes in Digital Mental Health Interventions: Systematic Review and Meta-analysis. *Journal of Medical Internet Research, 24*(6), e36004. DOI: 10.2196/36004 PMID: 35511463

Li, J., & Washington, P. (2024). A Comparison of Personalized and Generalized Approaches to Emotion Recognition Using Consumer Wearable Devices: Machine Learning Study. *JMIR AI, 3*, e52171. DOI: 10.2196/52171 PMID: 38875573

Lin, E., Lin, C.-H., & Lane, H.-Y. (2020). Precision Psychiatry Applications with Pharmacogenomics: Artificial Intelligence and Machine Learning Approaches. *International Journal of Molecular Sciences*, *21*(3), 969. DOI: 10.3390/ijms21030969 PMID: 32024055

Lipschitz, J. M., Lin, S., Saghafian, S., Pike, C. K., & Burdick, K. E. (2025). Digital phenotyping in bipolar disorder: Using longitudinal Fitbit data and personalized machine learning to predict mood symptomatology. *Acta Psychiatrica Scandinavica*, *151*(3), 434–447. DOI: 10.1111/acps.13765 PMID: 39397313

Liu, J. C., Goetz, J., Sen, S., & Tewari, A. (2021). Learning From Others Without Sacrificing Privacy: Simulation Comparing Centralized and Federated Machine Learning on Mobile Health Data. *JMIR mHealth and uHealth*, *9*(3), e23728. DOI: 10.2196/23728 PMID: 33783362

Liu, S., Wang, R., Zhang, L., Zhu, X., Yang, R., Zhou, X., Wu, F., Yang, Z., Jin, C., & Wang, G. (2025). *PsychBench: A comprehensive and professional benchmark for evaluating the performance of LLM-assisted psychiatric clinical practice*.

Liu, X., Cruz Rivera, S., Moher, D., Calvert, M. J., Denniston, A. K., Ashrafian, H., Beam, A. L., Chan, A.-W., Collins, G. S., Deeks, A. D. J., ElZarrad, M. K., Espinoza, C., Esteva, A., Faes, L., Ferrante di Ruffano, L., Fletcher, J., Golub, R., Harvey, H., Haug, C., & Yau, C. (2020). Reporting guidelines for clinical trial reports for interventions involving artificial intelligence: The CONSORT-AI extension. *The Lancet. Digital Health*, *2*(10), e537–e548. DOI: 10.1016/S2589-7500(20)30218-1 PMID: 33328048

Livingston, M. (2020). Preventing Racial Bias in Federal AI. *Journal of Science Policy & Governance*, *16*(02). Advance online publication. DOI: 10.38126/JSPG160205

Lloyd, K. (2018). *Bias Amplification in Artificial Intelligence Systems*.

Mak, W. W. S., Ng, S. M., & Leung, F. H. T. (2023). A Web-Based Stratified Stepped Care Platform for Mental Well-being (TourHeart+): User-Centered Research and Design. *JMIR Formative Research*, *7*, e38504. DOI: 10.2196/38504 PMID: 36947112

Malouin-Lachance, A., Capolupo, J., Laplante, C., & Hudon, A. (2025). Does the Digital Therapeutic Alliance Exist? Integrative Review. *JMIR Mental Health*, *12*, e69294–e69294. DOI: 10.2196/69294 PMID: 39924298

Mandal, A., Chakraborty, T., & Gurevych, I. (2025). *Towards Privacy-aware Mental Health AI Models: Advances*. Challenges, and Opportunities.

Marmar, C. R., Brown, A. D., Qian, M., Laska, E., Siegel, C., Li, M., Abu-Amara, D., Tsiartas, A., Richey, C., Smith, J., Knoth, B., & Vergyri, D. (2019). Speech-based markers for posttraumatic stress disorder in US veterans. *Depression and Anxiety, 36*(7), 607–616. DOI: 10.1002/da.22890 PMID: 31006959

Martinez-Martin, N., Insel, T. R., Dagum, P., Greely, H. T., & Cho, M. K. (2018). Data mining for health: Staking out the ethical territory of digital phenotyping. *NPJ Digital Medicine, 1*(1), 68. DOI: 10.1038/s41746-018-0075-8 PMID: 31211249

Martinez-Martin, N., Luo, Z., Kaushal, A., Adeli, E., Haque, A., Kelly, S. S., Wieten, S., Cho, M. K., Magnus, D., Fei-Fei, L., Schulman, K., & Milstein, A. (2021). Ethical issues in using ambient intelligence in health-care settings. *The Lancet. Digital Health, 3*(2), e115–e123. DOI: 10.1016/S2589-7500(20)30275-2 PMID: 33358138

Maslej, M. M., Kloiber, S., Ghassemi, M., Yu, J., & Hill, S. L. (2023). Out with AI, in with the psychiatrist: A preference for human-derived clinical decision support in depression care. *Translational Psychiatry, 13*(1), 210. DOI: 10.1038/s41398-023-02509-z PMID: 37328465

McCoy, T. H., & Perlis, R. H. (2024). Characterizing research domain criteria symptoms among psychiatric inpatients using large language models. *Journal of Mood and Anxiety Disorders, 8*, 100079. DOI: 10.1016/j.xjmad.2024.100079 PMID: 40655912

McCradden, M. D., Baba, A., Saha, A., Ahmad, S., Boparai, K., Fadaiefard, P., & Cusimano, M. D. (2020). Ethical concerns around use of artificial intelligence in health care research from the perspective of patients with meningioma, caregivers and health care providers: A qualitative study. *CMAJ Open, 8*(1), E90–E95. DOI: 10.9778/cmajo.20190151 PMID: 32071143

McGorry, P. D., Hartmann, J. A., Spooner, R., & Nelson, B. (2018). Beyond the "at risk mental state" concept: Transitioning to transdiagnostic psychiatry. *World Psychiatry; Official Journal of the World Psychiatric Association (WPA), 17*(2), 133–142. DOI: 10.1002/wps.20514 PMID: 29856558

Mendes, J. P. M., Moura, I. R., Van de Ven, P., Viana, D., Silva, F. J. S., Coutinho, L. R., Teixeira, S., Rodrigues, J. J. P. C., & Teles, A. S. (2022). Sensing Apps and Public Data Sets for Digital Phenotyping of Mental Health: Systematic Review. *Journal of Medical Internet Research, 24*(2), e28735. DOI: 10.2196/28735 PMID: 35175202

Mörch, C.-M., Gupta, A., & Mishara, B. L. (2020). Canada protocol: An ethical checklist for the use of artificial Intelligence in suicide prevention and mental health. *Artificial Intelligence in Medicine, 108,* 101934. DOI: 10.1016/j.artmed.2020.101934 PMID: 32972663

Moriarty, A. S., Meader, N., Snell, K. I. E., Riley, R. D., Paton, L. W., Dawson, S., Hendon, J., Chew-Graham, C. A., Gilbody, S., Churchill, R., Phillips, R. S., Ali, S., & McMillan, D. (2022). Predicting relapse or recurrence of depression: Systematic review of prognostic models. *The British Journal of Psychiatry, 221*(2), 448–458. DOI: 10.1192/bjp.2021.218 PMID: 35048843

Na, H., Hua, Y., Wang, Z., Shen, T., Yu, B., Wang, L., Wang, W., Torous, J., & Chen, L. (2025). *A Survey of Large Language Models in Psychotherapy: Current Landscape and Future Directions.*

Nadeem, A., Abedin, B., & Marjanovic, O. (2020). Gender bias in AI: A review of contributing factors and mitigating strategies. *ACIS 2020 Proceedings*. 27.

Nasrallah, H. A. (2021). Re-Inventing the Dsm as A Transdiagnostic Model: Psychiatric Disorders Are Extensively Interconnected. *Annals of Clinical Psychiatry, 33*(3), 148–150. DOI: 10.12788/acp.0037 PMID: 34398730

Norori, N., Hu, Q., Aellen, F. M., Faraci, F. D., & Tzovara, A. (2021). Addressing bias in big data and AI for health care: A call for open science. *Patterns (New York, N.Y.), 2*(10), 100347. DOI: 10.1016/j.patter.2021.100347 PMID: 34693373

O'Connor, S., & Liu, H. (2024). Gender bias perpetuation and mitigation in AI technologies: Challenges and opportunities. *AI & Society, 39*(4), 2045–2057. DOI: 10.1007/s00146-023-01675-4

O'Leary, A., Lahey, T., Lovato, J., Loftness, B., Douglas, A., Skelton, J., Cohen, J. G., Copeland, W. E., McGinnis, R. S., & McGinnis, E. W. (2024). Using Wearable Digital Devices to Screen Children for Mental Health Conditions: Ethical Promises and Challenges. *Sensors (Basel), 24*(10), 3214. DOI: 10.3390/s24103214 PMID: 38794067

Olah, J., Diederen, K., Gibbs-Dean, T., Kempton, M. J., Dobson, R., Spencer, T., & Cummins, N. (2023). Online speech assessment of the psychotic spectrum: Exploring the relationship between overlapping acoustic markers of schizotypy, depression and anxiety. *Schizophrenia Research, 259,* 11–19. DOI: 10.1016/j.schres.2023.03.044 PMID: 37080802

Olah, J., Spencer, T., Cummins, N., & Diederen, K. (2024). Automated analysis of speech as a marker of sub-clinical psychotic experiences. *Frontiers in Psychiatry, 14*. Advance online publication. DOI: 10.3389/fpsyt.2023.1265880 PMID: 38361830

Oliver, R., Pérez-Sabater, J., Paz-Arbaizar, L., Herrero-Quevedo, D., Artés-Rodríguez, A., Lancho, A., & Olmos, P. M. (2025). *A Vector-Quantized Foundation Model for Patient Behavior Monitoring*.

Park, J., Arunachalam, R., Silenzio, V., & Singh, V. K. (2022). Fairness in Mobile Phone–Based Mental Health Assessment Algorithms: Exploratory Study. *JMIR Formative Research, 6*(6), e34366. DOI: 10.2196/34366 PMID: 35699997

Park, S.-C., & Kim, Y.-K. (2020). *Anxiety Disorders in the DSM-5: Changes*. Controversies, and Future Directions., DOI: 10.1007/978-981-32-9705-0_12

Purgato, M., Tedeschi, F., Turrini, G., Cadorin, C., Compri, B., Muriago, G., Ostuzzi, G., Pinucci, I., Prina, E., Serra, R., Tarsitani, L., Witteveen, A. B., Roversi, A., Melchior, M., McDaid, D., Park, A., Petri-Romão, P., Kalisch, R., Underhill, J., & Barbui, C. (2025). Effectiveness of a stepped-care programme of WHO psychological interventions in a population of migrants: Results from the RESPOND randomized controlled trial. *World Psychiatry; Official Journal of the World Psychiatric Association (WPA), 24*(1), 120–130. DOI: 10.1002/wps.21281 PMID: 39810692

Putica, A., Khanna, R., Bosl, W., Saraf, S., & Edgcomb, J. (2025). Ethical decision-making for AI in mental health: The Integrated Ethical Approach for Computational Psychiatry (IEACP) framework. *Psychological Medicine, 55*, e213. DOI: 10.1017/S0033291725101311 PMID: 40702980

Rahsepar Meadi, M., Sillekens, T., Metselaar, S., van Balkom, A., Bernstein, J., & Batelaan, N. (2025). Exploring the Ethical Challenges of Conversational AI in Mental Health Care: Scoping Review. *JMIR Mental Health, 12*, e60432. DOI: 10.2196/60432 PMID: 39983102

Rooksby, J., Morrison, A., & Murray-Rust, D. (2019). Student Perspectives on Digital Phenotyping. *Proceedings of the 2019 CHI Conference on Human Factors in Computing Systems*, 1–14. https://doi.org/DOI: 10.1145/3290605.3300655

Ruan, F. Y., Zhang, A., Oh, J. Y., Jin, S., & Jacobson, N. C. (2025). *Foundation Models for Wearable Movement Data in Mental Health Research*.

Rutledge, R. B., Chekroud, A. M., & Huys, Q. J. (2019). Machine learning and big data in psychiatry: Toward clinical applications. *Current Opinion in Neurobiology, 55*, 152–159. DOI: 10.1016/j.conb.2019.02.006 PMID: 30999271

Sasikala, D. B., & Sachan, S. (2024). Decoding Decision-making: Embracing Explainable AI for Trust and Transparency. In *Exploring the Frontiers of Artificial Intelligence and Machine Learning Technologies*. San International Scientific Publications. https://doi.org/DOI: 10.59646/efaimltC3/133

Schmidt, P., Biessmann, F., & Teubner, T. (2020). Transparency and trust in artificial intelligence systems. *Journal of Decision Systems*, *29*(4), 260–278. DOI: 10.1080/12460125.2020.1819094

Schultebraucks, K., Yadav, V., Shalev, A. Y., Bonanno, G. A., & Galatzer-Levy, I. R. (2022). Deep learning-based classification of posttraumatic stress disorder and depression following trauma utilizing visual and auditory markers of arousal and mood. *Psychological Medicine*, *52*(5), 957–967. DOI: 10.1017/S0033291720002718 PMID: 32744201

Shabankareh, M., Khamoushi Sahne, S. S., Nazarian, A., & Foroudi, P. (2025). The impact of AI perceived transparency on trust in AI recommendations in healthcare applications. *Asia-Pacific Journal of Business Administration*. Advance online publication. DOI: 10.1108/APJBA-12-2024-0690

Shaik, T., Tao, X., Higgins, N., Gururajan, R., Li, Y., Zhou, X., & Acharya, U. R. (2022). *FedStack: Personalized activity monitoring using stacked federated learning*. https://doi.org/DOI: 10.1016/j.knosys.2022.109929

Shin, J., Yoon, H., Lee, S., Park, S., Liu, Y., Choi, J. D., & Lee, S.-J. (2023). *FedTherapist: Mental Health Monitoring with User-Generated Linguistic Expressions on Smartphones via Federated Learning*.

Skorburg, J. A., O'Doherty, K., & Friesen, P. (2024). Persons or data points? Ethics, artificial intelligence, and the participatory turn in mental health research. *The American Psychologist*, *79*(1), 137–149. DOI: 10.1037/amp0001168 PMID: 38236221

Sun, C., van Soest, J., & Dumontier, M. (2023). Generating synthetic personal health data using conditional generative adversarial networks combining with differential privacy. *Journal of Biomedical Informatics*, *143*, 104404. DOI: 10.1016/j.jbi.2023.104404 PMID: 37268168

Tahir, W. Bin, Khalid, S., Alshahrani, S., Alharbi, S. S., & Alhasson, H. F. (2025). ContextVecNet: A Context-Driven Multimodal Learning Framework for Depression Detection. *IEEE Journal of Biomedical and Health Informatics*, •••, 1–12. DOI: 10.1109/JBHI.2025.3602719 PMID: 40864577

Timmons, A. C., Duong, J. B., Simo Fiallo, N., Lee, T., Vo, H. P. Q., Ahle, M. W., Comer, J. S., Brewer, L. C., Frazier, S. L., & Chaspari, T. (2023). A Call to Action on Assessing and Mitigating Bias in Artificial Intelligence Applications for Mental Health. *Perspectives on Psychological Science*, *18*(5), 1062–1096. DOI: 10.1177/17456916221134490 PMID: 36490369

Tomičić, A., & Gjorgjioska, M. A. (2024). Epistemic inequality in the digital era: Unpacking biases in digital mental health. *Theory & Psychology*, *34*(6), 777–797. DOI: 10.1177/09593543241279131

Torous, J., Linardon, J., Goldberg, S. B., Sun, S., Bell, I., Nicholas, J., Hassan, L., Hua, Y., Milton, A., & Firth, J. (2025). The evolving field of digital mental health: Current evidence and implementation issues for smartphone apps, generative artificial intelligence, and virtual reality. *World Psychiatry; Official Journal of the World Psychiatric Association (WPA)*, *24*(2), 156–174. DOI: 10.1002/wps.21299 PMID: 40371757

Tremain, H., McEnery, C., Fletcher, K., & Murray, G. (2020). The Therapeutic Alliance in Digital Mental Health Interventions for Serious Mental Illnesses: Narrative Review. *JMIR Mental Health*, *7*(8), e17204. DOI: 10.2196/17204 PMID: 32763881

Tsoi, E. W. S., Mak, W. W. S., Ho, C. Y. Y., & Yeung, G. T. Y. (2022). A Web-Based Stratified Stepped Care Mental Health Platform (TourHeart): Semistructured Interviews With Stakeholders. *JMIR Human Factors*, *9*(2), e35057. DOI: 10.2196/35057 PMID: 35560109

Turner Lee, N. (2018). Detecting racial bias in algorithms and machine learning. *Journal of Information. Communication and Ethics in Society*, *16*(3), 252–260. DOI: 10.1108/JICES-06-2018-0056

Valentine, L., D'Alfonso, S., & Lederman, R. (2023). Recommender systems for mental health apps: Advantages and ethical challenges. *AI & Society*, *38*(4), 1627–1638. DOI: 10.1007/s00146-021-01322-w PMID: 35068708

Vedanta, S. P., & Rao, M. (2024). PsychSynth: Advancing Mental Health AI Through Synthetic Data Generation and Curriculum Training. *2024 9th International Conference on Computer Science and Engineering (UBMK)*, 1–6. https://doi.org/DOI: 10.1109/UBMK63289.2024.10773545

Verma, M., Chanthar, K. M. M. V., & Beg, M. J. (2025). *Ethical Considerations Surrounding the Use of AI-Interventions in Application of Mental Healthcare.*, DOI: 10.4018/979-8-3693-3112-5.ch009

Wakefield, J. C. (2016). Diagnostic Issues and Controversies in DSM-5: Return of the False Positives Problem. *Annual Review of Clinical Psychology*, *12*(1), 105–132. DOI: 10.1146/annurev-clinpsy-032814-112800 PMID: 26772207

Wang, C., Jiang, Y., Peng, Z., Li, C., Bang, C., Zhao, L., Lv, J., Sepulcre, J., Yang, C., He, L., Liu, T., Barron, D., Li, Q., Hirschtick, R., Kim, B.-H., Li, X., & Yuan, Y. (2025). *Towards a general-purpose foundation model for fMRI analysis.*

Wang, T.-F., Huang, R.-C., Yang, S.-C., Chou, C., & Chen, L.-C. (2020). Evaluating the Effects of a Mobile Health App on Reducing Patient Care Needs and Improving Quality of Life After Oral Cancer Surgery: Quasiexperimental Study. *JMIR mHealth and uHealth*, *8*(7), e18132. DOI: 10.2196/18132 PMID: 32716303

Xu, X., Peng, H., Sun, L., Bhuiyan, M. Z. A., Liu, L., & He, L. (2021). *FedMood: Federated Learning on Mobile Health Data for Mood Detection.* https://doi.org/ DOI: 10.1109/TII.2021.3113708

Yadav, N., Pandey, S., Gupta, A., Dudani, P., Gupta, S., & Rangarajan, K. (2023). Data Privacy in Healthcare: In the Era of Artificial Intelligence. *Indian Dermatology Online Journal*, *14*(6), 788–792. DOI: 10.4103/idoj.idoj_543_23 PMID: 38099022

Yang, J., Soltan, A. A. S., Eyre, D. W., & Clifton, D. A. (2023). Algorithmic fairness and bias mitigation for clinical machine learning with deep reinforcement learning. *Nature Machine Intelligence*, *5*(8), 884–894. DOI: 10.1038/s42256-023-00697-3 PMID: 37615031

Young, G. (2013). Breaking Bad: DSM-5 Description, Criticisms, and Recommendations. *Psychological Injury and Law*, *6*(4), 345–348. DOI: 10.1007/s12207-013-9181-8

Zidaru, T., Morrow, E. M., & Stockley, R. (2021). Ensuring patient and public involvement in the transition to AI-assisted mental health care: A systematic scoping review and agenda for design justice. *Health Expectations*, *24*(4), 1072–1124. DOI: 10.1111/hex.13299 PMID: 34118185

Zlatintsi, A., Filntisis, P. P., Garoufis, C., Efthymiou, N., Maragos, P., Menychtas, A., Maglogiannis, I., Tsanakas, P., Sounapoglou, T., Kalisperakis, E., Karantinos, T., Lazaridi, M., Garyfalli, V., Mantas, A., Mantonakis, L., & Smyrnis, N. (2022). E-Prevention: Advanced Support System for Monitoring and Relapse Prevention in Patients with Psychotic Disorders Analyzing Long-Term Multimodal Data from Wearables and Video Captures. *Sensors (Basel)*, *22*(19), 7544. DOI: 10.3390/s22197544 PMID: 36236643

Chapter 4
Precision Psychiatry in the Age of AI: Early Detection and Personalized Treatment of Mood Disorders

Mohit Verma
https://orcid.org/0009-0004-4032-2458
Lovely Professional University, India

Mirza Jahanzeb Beg
https://orcid.org/0000-0002-6308-2678
Kumaraguru College of Liberal Arts and Science, Coimbatore, India

ABSTRACT

This chapter examines the role of artificial intelligence in precision psychiatry with a focus on mood disorders. It considers how AI can address the limitations of symptom-based diagnostic systems by integrating digital behavior, genomic data, biomarkers, and neuroimaging. The discussion highlights the potential of AI to detect early signs of mood dysregulation through passive and active monitoring, while also informing treatment approaches tailored to individual biological and psychological profiles. Ethical and practical issues are critically assessed, including concerns about privacy, algorithmic bias, and the demand for transparency in decision-making systems. Clinical vignettes and comparative analyses are used to illustrate how AI can support, rather than replace, clinical expertise by strengthening decision-making and personalizing care. The chapter argues for a hybrid model in which technology augments professional judgment, providing a path toward more effective, equitable, and accountable mental health care.

DOI: 10.4018/979-8-3373-1325-2.ch004

INTRODUCTION

Precision psychiatry represents a transformative approach in mental health care that aims to stratify individuals based on a constellation of biological, psychological, and digital markers to inform diagnosis, prognosis, and treatment. Rooted in the broader framework of precision medicine, it seeks to move beyond categorical diagnoses and instead utilize biomarkers, neuroimaging, genetic data, digital phenotyping, and real-world behavioral indicators to inform clinical decisions. Distinct from the broader concept of personalized psychiatry; which typically tailors treatment to individual characteristics based on clinical judgment; precision psychiatry seeks to use measurable, often computationally derived indicators to guide decision-making. This model offers the potential to identify subtypes within heterogeneous disorders, track disease trajectories, and predict treatment responses with higher accuracy. The ultimate goal is to improve outcomes by identifying which interventions are most effective for which individuals at specific points in time.

Traditional psychiatric diagnostic systems such as the Diagnostic and Statistical Manual of Mental Disorders (DSM) and the International Classification of Diseases (ICD) have long served as the backbone of clinical practice. However, they are increasingly critiqued for their categorical nature, which may obscure the dimensional and heterogeneous reality of mental disorders (First & Wakefield, 2010). While these systems have offered a shared language for clinicians and researchers, their reliance on symptom-based criteria has contributed to significant heterogeneity within diagnostic categories. As a result, individuals with the same diagnosis often exhibit vastly different underlying pathophysiology and treatment responses, thereby complicating both clinical management and the search for robust biomarkers. For instance, studies have shown that inter-rater reliability for several DSM-5 diagnoses, including major depressive disorder, is only moderate (Regier et al., 2013). Moreover, these frameworks are limited in their ability to integrate neurobiological findings, leading to poor alignment between diagnostic categories and underlying pathophysiology (Insel et al., 2010). This disconnect hampers efforts to develop objective biomarkers and contributes to a reliance on trial-and-error approaches in treatment.

The shortcomings of current diagnostic systems are particularly consequential in mood disorders, where misdiagnosis and suboptimal treatment are common. The impact of these limitations manifests in real-world as delayed diagnoses, ineffective treatments, and poor long-term outcomes for many individuals with psychiatric disorders. Major depressive disorder and bipolar disorder frequently overlap in symptom presentation yet require vastly different management strategies and their misdiagnosis or delayed intervention can exacerbate symptom severity, increase chronicity, and heighten the risk of functional impairment, suicide, and treatment resistance. Additionally, response rates to first-line antidepressants remain low, with the Sequenced Treatment Alternatives to Relieve Depression (STAR*D) trial revealing remission in only about one-third of patients after initial treatment (Rush et al., 2006). These disorders are not only highly prevalent but also deeply disabling, contributing substantially to the global burden of disease. Despite the availability of various pharmacological and psychotherapeutic treatments, many individuals experience partial remission or chronic symptomatology, highlighting the urgent need for more precise and individualized care models.

Mood disorders are inherently heterogeneous in their etiology, symptomatology, and treatment response. Genetic predispositions, neurobiological alterations, trauma histories, psychosocial stressors, and lifestyle factors interact dynamically to influence onset, progression, and recovery. These influences not only shape symptom expression but also impact treatment responsiveness and relapse vulnerability. Therefore, a one-size-fits-all approach is unlikely to capture this complexity. Within such a context, individualized care must be informed by a comprehensive assessment of risk profiles and underlying mechanisms rather than solely by presenting symptoms. Precision psychiatry offers a pathway toward such care, emphasizing stratification based on quantifiable data and predictive modeling.

Within this evolving landscape, artificial intelligence (AI) has emerged as a powerful ally in the pursuit of precision mental health care. Artificial intelligence, encompassing a range of computational techniques that enable machines to mimic human intelligence, offers unprecedented opportunities to analyze large, multimodal datasets with speed and depth beyond human capacity. Within mental health research and practice, artificial intelligence has shown considerable promise in identifying latent patterns within high-dimensional datasets, enabling the discovery of novel phenotypes, risk signatures, and intervention targets. Subfields such as machine learning and deep learning have been utilized to predict treatment response, detect suicidal ideation from speech and text, classify diagnostic categories based on neuroimaging data, and monitor behavioral changes through passive sensing technologies. These approaches offer distinct advantages over traditional statistical methods by accommodating complex interactions, non-linearity, and dynamic temporal patterns (Beg et al., 2025).

The convergence of artificial intelligence with psychiatry has given rise to a new era of data-driven mental health, where insights from neuroimaging, genomics, digital phenotyping, and electronic health records can be synthesized to inform clinical decision-making. By facilitating early detection of symptom trajectories and enabling real-time monitoring of mental health states, data-driven approaches offer the possibility of timely and adaptive interventions. From natural language processing of clinical notes and social media posts to wearable sensors tracking sleep and activity, data-driven tools are being developed to detect early warning signs, monitor treatment progress, and predict relapse. Although these technologies remain in early stages of clinical integration, they exemplify the potential of artificial intelligence to augment traditional psychiatric assessment and intervention. When embedded within the broader framework of precision psychiatry, such innovations offer a compelling vision for a future in which care is not only more accurate but also more responsive to the evolving needs of individuals with mood disorders.

AI-DRIVEN EARLY DETECTION OF MOOD DISORDERS

The early detection of mood disorders has traditionally relied on self-reported symptoms and intermittent clinical interviews, both of which are limited by subjectivity, recall bias, and the episodic nature of care. Recent advances in artificial intelligence have fundamentally expanded this diagnostic horizon by enabling the synthesis of vast and multidimensional datasets that were previously inaccessible to standard psychiatric practice. This shift moves beyond simple symptom tracking to a more holistic computational approach where AI algorithms integrate distinct streams of evidence ranging from ecological behavioral data and biological markers to longitudinal risk trajectories. By triangulating these disparate sources, AI systems offer the potential to construct a continuous and objective picture of mental health while identifying subtle patterns of dysregulation that precede clinical deterioration. The following sections explore how this technological evolution is being realized across three critical frontiers which include the passive sensing of digital phenotypes, the machine learning analysis of biological substrates, and the development of predictive models for relapse prevention (Verma et al., 2025).

Digital Phenotyping

Digital phenotyping, also known as personal sensing, involves the systematic collection and analysis of data generated by personal digital devices such as smartphones to infer psychological states and mental health conditions. This method offers an advancement over traditional psychiatric practices by enabling more precise and continuous monitoring, which can enhance user engagement and reduce the likelihood of negative side effects. Ongoing clinical research increasingly incorporates digital phenotyping as a means of identifying early indicators of conditions such as depression, schizophrenia, and post-traumatic stress disorder. Rather than relying solely on conventional assessments, researchers are exploring the potential of data drawn from smartphones and wearable devices to offer more timely and sensitive insights into mental health. These efforts extend beyond diagnosis, aiming to uncover behavioral and cognitive patterns that may serve as predictors of treatment response. The integration of digital phenotyping with the broader goals of precision medicine emphasizes both its promise and its limitations. By aligning real-time data collection with individualized care strategies, this approach not only refines clinical decision-making but also encourages a shift toward anticipatory and patient-specific interventions. In doing so, it contributes to the evolution of medical knowledge and the development of more effective, tailored healthcare solutions (Verma et al., 2025).

Digital phenotyping has emerged as a powerful frontier in the early detection of mood disorders, capitalizing on the ubiquity of smartphones and wearable technologies to capture high-resolution, real-time behavioral data. This approach entails the continuous collection and analysis of both passive and active data streams that reflect how individuals move, communicate, sleep, and interact with their environments. By grounding psychiatric evaluation in objective, ecologically valid indicators, digital phenotyping enables a more nuanced, temporally rich characterization of mental health trajectories than traditional assessments confined to clinical settings.

Among its most promising applications is the detection of depressive and manic episodes in bipolar disorder and major depressive disorder. Behavioral data such as reduced physical activity, altered sleep patterns, and disrupted social interactions have shown consistent associations with shifts in mood states. These features, when processed through machine learning algorithms, allow for the identification of early warning signs that often precede symptomatic relapse (Leaning et al., 2024). The integration of heart rate, sleep, and activity data from wearable sensors further refines this predictive capacity, offering clinicians a passive yet personalized view into an individual's daily fluctuations (Lipschitz et al., 2025).

In nonclinical populations, smartphone-based sensing has demonstrated the capacity to detect subtle deviations in behavior associated with stress, anxiety, and mild depressive symptoms. Lower mobility, increased screen time, and irregular sleep emerged as reliable indicators, although the interpretation of these signals often depends on contextual variables such as employment demands or lifestyle preferences (Choi et al., 2024). These findings underscore the importance of incorporating individualized baselines and contextual awareness into algorithmic models to avoid overgeneralization.

Feasibility studies across diverse clinical populations, including schizophrenia, anxiety disorders, and substance use, have also affirmed the utility of digital phenotyping in remote monitoring. Predictive features commonly identified include mobility, phone usage, and physiological signals, with vocal and facial behaviors contributing valuable cues (Bufano et al., 2023). Despite methodological heterogeneity across studies, the convergence of results points to digital phenotyping as a scalable strategy for augmenting traditional care with continuous feedback loops.

Some of the most compelling insights have been derived from national health cohorts, where wearable data combined with machine learning yielded robust predictions of anxiety symptom severity. In one such study, irritability, worry, and restlessness emerged as key predictors, offering a fine-grained portrait of generalized anxiety distinct from depressive symptoms (Jacobson & Feng, 2022). These approaches hold particular promise for populations with limited access to care or for whom stigma may inhibit help-seeking behaviors.

What sets digital phenotyping apart is its potential for integration across multiple data streams. Behavioral signatures, physiological metrics, and ecological momentary assessments, when fused with biological or genomic markers, enable a comprehensive, layered approach to mental health profiling (Brietzke et al., 2019). This richness opens doors to individualized treatment pathways, moving psychiatry closer to the goals of precision medicine.

However, this promise is tempered by a host of challenges that warrant critical appraisal. Chief among them is the lack of standardized protocols for data collection, interpretation, and validation. Heterogeneity in sensor types, sampling frequencies, and analytical models undermines the generalizability of findings (Mendes et al., 2022). A pervasive methodological concern is the reliance on small, often homogenous sample sizes, which limits the statistical power of predictive models (Welch et al., 2022; Zhong et al., 2025). Furthermore, the lack of rigorous external validation increases the risk of overfitting, where algorithms perform exceptionally well on training data but fail to replicate in independent cohorts (Parra et al., 2022; Lipschitz et al., 2025). Issues with data sparsity also persist; high rates of sample attrition and missing data often necessitate complex imputation strategies that can obscure true behavioral signals or introduce systematic bias (Leaning et al., 2024). Efforts to refine ecological validity and address these methodological deficits are critical for transitioning these tools from exploratory research to routine clinical application.

Ethical concerns loom large as well. The pervasive nature of data collection raises urgent questions about privacy, informed consent, algorithmic bias, and data governance. Individuals from marginalized groups may face disproportionate risks due to the lack of diversity in training datasets and the opacity of algorithmic decisions (Martinez-Martin et al., 2021). Ensuring that digital phenotyping technologies align with principles of transparency, accountability, and equity requires not only technical safeguards but also robust regulatory frameworks and inclusive design practices.

The conceptual foundation of digital phenotyping suggests that its true value lies in its granularity. Continuous monitoring enables the detection of minute fluctuations that are often imperceptible in episodic clinical encounters (Onnela & Rauch, 2016). When applied thoughtfully, this capacity can transform mental health care from reactive to proactive, identifying emergent patterns before they crystalize into full-blown crises.

Advances in deep learning have begun to expand the frontiers of digital phenotyping even further. Multimodal approaches that synthesize speech, facial expression, gaze, and heart rate variability are now capable of estimating psychological constructs such as emotion dysregulation with considerable precision (Parra et al., 2022). These models not only enhance predictive accuracy but also allow for the capture of affective states that are otherwise difficult to quantify.

Machine Learning Applications in Biological Data

The early detection of mood disorders increasingly relies on the integration of machine learning techniques with biological data streams that reflect the underlying physiological and neurological complexity of these conditions. Among these, genomics, peripheral biomarkers, and neuroimaging data have emerged as powerful, albeit challenging, sources of insight into individual vulnerability and pathophysiological trajectories.

In the field of genomics, machine learning offers a means to distill meaningful patterns from high-dimensional gene expression data. One compelling example involves the identification of diagnostic genes through weighted gene co-expression network analysis and feature selection algorithms. From peripheral blood gene expression profiles, researchers have isolated immune-related and inflammation-associated genes such as *S100A12* and *SERPINB2* that differentiate individuals with major depressive disorder (MDD) from healthy controls. These genes not only reflect altered biological states but also provide a foundation for constructing interpretable ML models with moderate diagnostic accuracy, demonstrating the value of transcriptomic data in screening for mood disorders (Wang et al., 2022). However, as with many high-dimensional omics studies, these findings must be interpreted with caution due to the pervasive multiple comparisons problem. When thousands of genes are tested simultaneously, the risk of false positives increases substantially; without rigorous experimental validation and replication in independent cohorts, the clinical utility of such "diagnostic" panels remains uncertain (Wang et al., 2022).

Biomarkers beyond the genome, especially those circulating in blood and urine, have also been extensively studied through supervised learning methods. Large biobank datasets have enabled the exploration of multiple biomarkers simultaneously, revealing distinct biochemical signatures associated with anxiety subtypes. Features such as neutrophil counts, hemoglobin levels, and creatinine emerged as discriminative variables for generalized anxiety, social anxiety, and panic disorder. While these findings offer a preliminary map of biological heterogeneity, the field is often hindered by a replicability crisis. Biomarker rankings frequently fluctuate across studies due to differences in sample demographics and assay methods, and as noted by Sharma & Verbeke (2021), such exploratory models often lack prospective validation. Without tracking individuals over time to see if these markers truly predict onset, their role remains limited to hypothesis generation rather than clinical prediction.

Expanding upon this, predictive modelling of depressive states using routine biomarkers has shown remarkable promise when augmented with resampling strategies to address class imbalance. Models trained on balanced datasets, particularly using ensemble methods like XGBoost, have demonstrated high accuracy in identifying depression from common lab values. These results support the feasibility of incorporating cost-effective, non-invasive biomarkers into AI-enabled mental health screening pipelines, particularly in resource-constrained settings. However, the reliance on self-reported diagnoses and the omission of demographic confounders limit the interpretability of these outcomes beyond the context of exploratory research (Sharma & Verbeke, 2020). Furthermore, the lack of prospective designs means that the temporal relationship between these physiological markers and the onset of depression remains ambiguous.

Neuroimaging data represents another critical frontier in AI-driven psychiatric research. Machine learning methods have been employed to identify structural and functional brain markers associated with affective disorders. Studies involving large neuroimaging cohorts have attempted to detect multivariate signatures of depression by combining modalities such as resting-state fMRI, structural MRI, and diffusion tensor imaging. Despite considerable effort and methodological rigor, diagnostic accuracies remain modest. Even the most predictive unimodal imaging features have struggled to surpass a ceiling of 62% accuracy (Winter et al., 2024). This ceiling effect is partly attributable to the immense dimensionality of neuroimaging data, which exacerbates the multiple comparisons problem, often leading to overfitting in smaller samples and a failure to replicate findings across different scanners and sites (Winter et al., 2024; Halkiopoulos et al., 2025).

Nonetheless, more narrowly defined psychiatric conditions such as borderline personality disorder (BPD) have yielded higher classification accuracies through structural imaging. Machine learning models applied to brain morphometry data have successfully differentiated BPD from both healthy individuals and bipolar patients, implicating a cortico-subcortical network involved in emotional regulation and affective instability. This suggests that in conditions with more distinct neuroanatomical alterations, machine learning may indeed capture clinically relevant features, especially when paired with carefully matched comparison groups (Grecucci et al., 2022).

Recent advancements in emotion recognition using neuroimaging add another dimension to the conversation. Deep learning architectures trained on fMRI, EEG, and PET data have shown potential in classifying emotional states and detecting affective abnormalities. While CNNs have excelled in visual pattern recognition, generative models such as GANs have been instrumental in expanding limited datasets, thereby improving model robustness. These technologies are especially promising in augmenting emotion-aware systems for real-time mental health monitoring, although challenges related to standardization, model interpretability, and ethical safeguards remain significant (Halkiopoulos et al., 2025).

Taken together, machine learning applications across genomics, biomarker profiling, and neuroimaging highlight the promise and complexity of leveraging biological data for early mood disorder detection. Each domain contributes uniquely to our understanding, yet no single data type or modelling strategy offers a definitive solution. Instead, it is through the thoughtful integration of multimodal biological inputs, validated across diverse populations and clinical endpoints, that AI can begin to support precise, personalized, and ethically sound mental health interventions.

Predictive Modelling and Relapse Prevention

The advent of artificial intelligence in psychiatry has heralded a critical shift from retrospective symptom assessment to prospective, individualized risk estimation. Nowhere is this transformation more visible than in the arena of relapse prevention for mood disorders. By leveraging predictive modelling, researchers and clinicians can anticipate deterioration in clinical status before the emergence of overt symptoms, allowing timely, targeted intervention.

Among the earliest efforts to harness predictive models in real-world settings are those using smartphone-based data to monitor mood fluctuations in bipolar disorder. These models incorporate both passive and active data streams, such as speech patterns, geolocation, physical activity, and self-reported mood, to construct dynamic, temporally sensitive profiles of an individual's mental state. Algorithms trained on such data have demonstrated remarkable variability in predictive accuracy, ranging from moderate to near-clinical utility, often depending on the quality and granularity of the input data (Antosik-Wójcińska et al. 2020). Voice modulation and usage frequency, for example, have emerged as subtle yet reliable markers of impending manic or depressive episodes, suggesting that relapse may be detectable in the fine contours of everyday behavior.

Yet, the reliability of such models is only as robust as the contexts in which they are developed. As highlighted by Antosik-Wójcińska et al. (2020), widespread adoption is currently hindered by heterogeneous study designs and small sample sizes that limit statistical power. Many predictive models suffer from a lack of standardization in features and inconsistent algorithmic frameworks, which, combined with limited population diversity, leads to a high risk of overfitting—where models perform well on training data but fail to generalize to new individuals. Consequently, the need for longitudinal datasets and rigorous external validation remains pressing to ensure clinical utility. Still, the foundational proof-of-concept has been established:

machine learning can identify relapse signals that are not readily visible to clinicians or patients themselves.

In the treatment of unipolar depression, predictive modelling has taken a more intervention-specific turn. Cohen et al. (2023) demonstrated how prognostic models could inform personalized treatment selection between antidepressant maintenance and mindfulness-based cognitive therapy. By incorporating a diverse array of predictors, ranging from baseline clinical severity to psychological traits, their model outperformed standard clinical judgment in forecasting relapse risk. Notably, individuals deemed poor candidates for pharmacological continuation had significantly better outcomes when shifted to mindfulness-based therapy. This finding illustrates the potential for AI to move beyond generalized prediction toward the tailoring of preventive interventions, transforming relapse management from a reactive to a precision-oriented process.

However, predictive accuracy remains variable across platforms and populations. In a large-scale study of a therapist-supported digital mental health intervention, Hornstein et al. (2021) showed that models trained to forecast treatment responsiveness reached only modest performance levels. The discrepancy between training and test populations, coupled with the limited use of imputation strategies for handling substantial missing data, weakened the models' ability to generalize. These methodological hurdles emphasize that while integrating AI into digital health interventions holds promise for identifying individuals requiring additional support, rigorous attention to data completeness and model robustness is essential.

The issue of generalizability is echoed in systematic evaluations of relapse prediction models for depression. Moriarty et al. (2022) found that most prognostic tools lacked rigorous methodological standards, with very few achieving low risk of bias or demonstrating sufficient predictive calibration. The review identified pervasive flaws, including inadequate sample sizes, opaque handling of missing data, and a critical lack of external validation. The field is still evolving, and without methodological integrity to address these deficits, predictive models risk becoming elegant but ultimately unreliable artifacts.

Despite these limitations, hybrid models that integrate diverse data types offer one of the most promising frontiers in relapse prevention. For instance, the e-Prevention project has illustrated how wearable sensors, facial expression analysis, and voice data can be fused within deep learning architectures to predict relapse in schizophrenia and bipolar disorder (Zlatintsi et al. 2022). These multimodal systems capture fluctuations in physiology and behavior with a resolution that far exceeds what is possible in traditional clinical visits. Crucially, such systems operate continuously in naturalistic settings, allowing for detection of subtle, preclinical shifts in mental state, though questions regarding generalizability due to localized sampling remain (Zlatintsi et al., 2022).

Even genetic and behavioral process features are now being explored as components of predictive models. Wallert et al. (2022) incorporated polygenic risk scores alongside clinical and demographic variables in predicting remission outcomes for individuals undergoing Internet-based cognitive behavioral therapy. Though the genetic contribution to predictive power was limited, the study revealed how AI can integrate traditionally siloed domains; genetics, symptomatology, and treatment history; into cohesive, individualized forecasts.

Relapse is not a binary outcome but rather a complex, dynamic progression marked by multiple interacting variables. Effective prediction must therefore move beyond linear associations and instead accommodate temporal fluctuations, intra-individual variability, and contextual nuances. AI-based modelling offers this capability, but the field must move deliberately to overcome its current limitations. Methodological rigor, population diversity, transparent reporting, and clinical integration are not ancillary concerns but essential preconditions for models that can guide treatment decisions with confidence.

In sum, predictive modelling stands as a crucial pillar in the architecture of AI-driven psychiatry. It offers a vision of mental healthcare that is proactive rather than reactive, personalized rather than generalized. While challenges remain, the integration of machine learning into relapse prevention strategies signals a profound evolution in how mood disorders are monitored, managed, and ultimately mitigated.

Current Limitations and Population Biases

AI-driven early detection of mental health disorders continues to face critical limitations, particularly regarding population biases that undermine diagnostic accuracy and ethical integrity. Algorithms trained on datasets that heavily feature Western, educated, industrialized, rich, and democratic populations lack sufficient cultural and socioeconomic diversity, resulting in predictive models that do not generalize well to underrepresented groups. This creates a significant gap in diagnostic performance, as individuals from non-Western or marginalized backgrounds may exhibit different behavioral, linguistic, or symptomatic markers that are misinterpreted or entirely overlooked. In healthcare settings, population bias compromises the reliability of AI-generated assessments, often leading to reduced sensitivity, inflated false positives, or skewed clinical recommendations for minority populations. Such disparities perpetuate existing inequities and erode trust in digital interventions. Additionally, the reliance on digital phenotyping data, such as smartphone behavior and social media usage, raises concerns about ecological validity, as these proxies may not reflect meaningful indicators of psychological distress across varying cultural or economic contexts. The absence of longitudinal validation further impairs the robustness of prediction, leaving clinicians without clear guidance on how to interpret AI-generated outputs across heterogeneous populations. To address these limitations, there is an urgent need to enhance data inclusivity, refine algorithmic transparency, and embed equity considerations throughout the lifecycle of AI tool development and deployment (Verma et al., 2025).

PERSONALIZED TREATMENT APPROACHES FOR MOOD DISORDERS

Personalized treatment in psychiatry is increasingly conceptualized not as a single intervention but as a tiered ecosystem where artificial intelligence aligns the intensity of care with individual clinical needs. This framework operates on a stepped care model where adaptive digital psychotherapies provide scalable and first line support for mild to moderate presentations while pharmacogenomic algorithms optimize medication selection for those requiring pharmacological management. At the highest level of acuity closed loop neuromodulation offers precise and biologically driven interventions for treatment resistant cases. The following subsections examine these three distinct yet complementary tiers demonstrating how data driven tools are reshaping the therapeutic landscape from broad accessibility to deep biological targeting.

Figure 1. The Integrated Precision Psychiatry Care Model

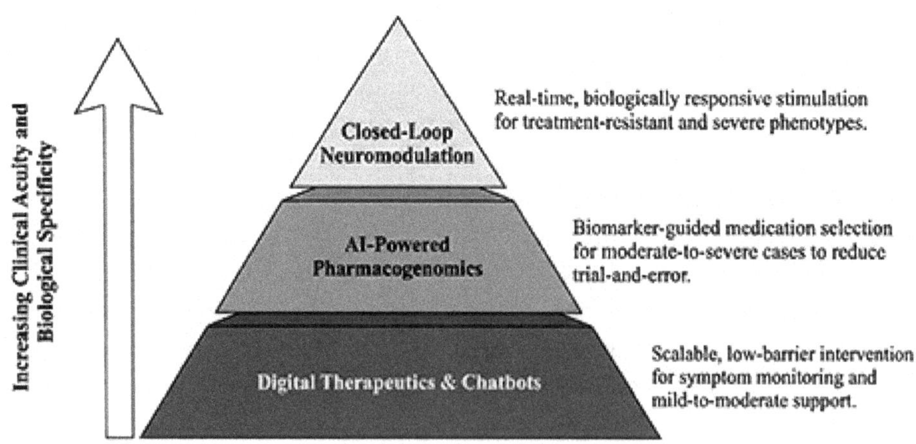

AI-Powered Pharmacogenomic Decision Tools

Pharmacogenomics, the study of how genetic variations influence individual responses to medications, represents a cornerstone in the shift toward personalized psychiatric care. In the treatment of mood disorders, where therapeutic response is notoriously unpredictable, pharmacogenomics offers a framework to refine medication selection, minimize adverse drug reactions, and optimize dosing. Psychiatric pharmacogenomics has long recognized the impact of polymorphisms in genes such as *CYP2D6* and *CYP2C19*, which modulate the metabolism of commonly prescribed antidepressants. Despite this, the routine implementation of pharmacogenomic insights into clinical psychiatry has remained limited, largely due to challenges in interpreting complex genetic data and integrating it into treatment algorithms. Recent advances in artificial intelligence are poised to change this landscape, offering powerful tools to translate genomic complexity into clinically actionable decisions.

Artificial intelligence, particularly machine learning and deep learning, enables the analysis of vast, high-dimensional genomic datasets alongside clinical variables to produce predictive models of treatment response. Unlike conventional statistical approaches, these algorithms can uncover non-linear interactions among genetic variants and between genetic and clinical factors, offering a more nuanced understanding of drug efficacy and tolerability in individuals with mood disorders. Several studies have demonstrated the capacity of AI-enhanced pharmacogenomic tools to outperform traditional models that rely on demographic or clinical data alone. For instance, models incorporating validated single nucleotide polymorphisms in genes such as *TSPAN5*, *ERICH3*, *DEFB1*, and *AHR* have shown significant improvements in predicting remission and response to selective serotonin reuptake inhibitors in major depressive disorder, with accuracy metrics frequently exceeding seventy percent (Athreya et al., 2019a; Athreya et al., 2019b).

The integration of AI with pharmacogenomics is not merely theoretical but increasingly operationalized through clinical decision support systems. These systems, often embedded within electronic health records, provide prescribing clinicians with real-time recommendations based on a patient's genomic profile. By synthesizing genomic, clinical, and demographic data, these tools can inform drug selection and dosing strategies that are tailored to individual risk-benefit profiles. For example, a clinician presented with a patient's AI-processed pharmacogenomic report might be alerted to avoid certain antidepressants in poor metabolizers of *CYP2C19*, or may be guided toward an SSRI with higher likelihood of remission based on polygenic risk patterns and baseline symptom clusters. Such decision support systems exemplify how AI facilitates the clinical translation of pharmacogenomic data, transforming raw genomic information into meaningful treatment guidance (Okpete & Byeon, 2024).

In more advanced applications, AI-powered pharmacogenomic models are increasingly incorporating multi-omics data, including gene expression, methylation profiles, and neuroimaging-derived endophenotypes. These approaches, while still largely experimental, demonstrate markedly higher predictive performance. In some cases, ensemble and deep learning models have achieved area under the curve values above 0.8, suggesting near-clinical utility when used to stratify patients into responders and non-responders across various treatment modalities (Lin et al., 2021). Moreover, the combination of clinical and pharmacogenomic data has been shown to significantly increase the explained variance in treatment outcomes compared to either data type alone, further underscoring the additive value of multimodal integration (Bobo et al., 2022; Sharew et al., 2024).

An instructive example of AI-driven pharmacogenomic support in psychiatry is found in Sherpa Rx, a clinical assistant developed to aid healthcare providers in interpreting complex pharmacogenomic information by embedding standardized resources such as CPIC guidelines and PharmGKB data. This system was evaluated using a retrieval-augmented generation framework, which enabled it to address real-world clinical queries with greater accuracy, completeness, and clinical relevance than baseline models. While the results were favorable, the study faced important limitations, including restricted validation sample sizes, single-expert evaluations, and difficulties in resolving genotypic distinctions with overlapping phenotypic implications (Rector et al., 2025). Beyond clinical decision aids, AI has also been applied to prioritize and interpret pharmacogenomic variants through machine learning models trained on curated functional datasets. One such study utilized classifiers including random forests and XGBoost to evaluate pharmacogenomic single nucleotide variants associated with drug metabolism and transport, identifying both known and novel variants in psychiatric populations. Although the classifiers achieved high performance in distinguishing functional effects, the analysis was constrained by the exclusion of non-coding and structural variants, a limited and imbalanced training dataset, and population-specific allele frequencies that restrict broader applicability (Pandi et al., 2021). Complementary efforts have focused on improving the efficiency of pharmacogenomic knowledge curation. For example, a machine learning-based text mining system was developed to extract variant-drug associations from large volumes of biomedical literature. Using entity recognition tools and logistic regression classifiers, the system identified thousands of associations, including many that were absent from existing curated databases. Despite this contribution, the tool was hindered by reliance on sentence-level co-occurrence, limited full-text access, and a high-precision approach that reduced recall, thereby omitting potentially relevant associations (Lever et al., 2020). Together, these examples demonstrate how AI can assist at multiple points along the pharmacogenomic pipeline, from the functional interpretation of variants to the clinical application of structured recommendations. However, their utility in psychiatric settings will depend on continued validation in diverse populations, improved model transparency, and integration into clinically meaningful workflows to ensure safe and effective translation of genomic insights into psychiatric practice.

Nonetheless, these models are not without their limitations. Their predictive accuracy often declines when applied to diverse populations, as many datasets remain predominantly composed of individuals of European ancestry. Additionally, the interpretability of complex AI algorithms remains a significant barrier to widespread clinical adoption. Clinicians may be hesitant to act on recommendations derived from opaque models, especially when the underlying rationale is not transparent. Furthermore, existing studies frequently rely on retrospective data, and prospective validations in real-world clinical settings are rare. As such, despite their promise, AI-driven pharmacogenomic tools must navigate substantial translational challenges before becoming routine components of psychiatric practice (Kam & Jeong, 2020; Pardiñas et al., 2021).

The future of AI-powered pharmacogenomic tools in psychiatry depends on addressing several critical issues. Methodologically, the field requires standardized phenotyping and benchmarking practices to facilitate reproducibility and cross-study comparisons. Ethically, data privacy and informed consent must be rigorously upheld, especially as models draw upon increasingly complex and sensitive data sources. Practically, integration into clinical workflows demands user-friendly interfaces, clinician education, and alignment with regulatory standards. Encouragingly, interdisciplinary collaborations and multi-institutional consortia are beginning to address these gaps, laying the groundwork for robust, equitable, and interpretable AI applications in precision psychiatry (Okpete & Byeon, 2024).

Adaptive Digital Psychotherapies and CBT-Based Chatbots

The emergence of adaptive digital psychotherapies represents a meaningful advancement in expanding access to mental health care, particularly for individuals experiencing mood disorders who are unable or unwilling to engage with traditional therapeutic services. AI-powered chatbots, grounded in principles of cognitive behavioral therapy, have been developed to address psychological distress across both clinical and nonclinical populations. These tools provide structured psychoeducation, mood monitoring, cognitive restructuring exercises, and motivational support through conversational interfaces designed to be accessible, affordable, and continuously available. By preserving user anonymity and eliminating logistical barriers such as scheduling and cost, they offer an alternative form of support for those deterred by stigma or constrained by limited access to human clinicians (Beg & Verma, 2025).

Evidence from pilot studies and randomized controlled trials has begun to characterize the therapeutic potential of these interventions. Woebot, a widely studied CBT-based chatbot, has demonstrated efficacy in reducing depressive symptoms in young adults following brief engagement periods, suggesting that conversational agents can deliver targeted therapeutic content with measurable outcomes. While effects on anxiety were less conclusive, reductions in depressive symptom severity were statistically significant when compared to digital psychoeducational controls. Despite the brevity of interventions and limited follow-up, the data indicate that short-term chatbot interactions can positively influence mood-related outcomes in self-referred populations (Fitzpatrick et al., 2017).

Similar findings have been reported in broader contexts. The chatbot Wysa, deployed among adults receiving orthopedic care, was associated with improvements in depressive symptoms and reductions in pain interference. While the absence of a control group and adjustment for confounders limits causal interpretation, the study supports the feasibility of integrating digital mental health tools into general medical care environments. The ability of such tools to supplement treatment in non-psychiatric clinical contexts underlines their flexibility and potential for scalability (Leo et al., 2022). Additional studies, including randomized evaluations of chatbot-supported mobile health applications for adolescents, have reported favorable outcomes in symptom reduction. These interventions, implemented during the COVID-19 pandemic, have demonstrated acceptability and usability in primary care settings, particularly among youth experiencing moderate depressive symptoms (Nicol et al., 2022).

Moreover, comparative studies examining chatbots against more traditional interventions, such as bibliotherapy, suggest that conversational agents may provide equal or superior benefits in symptom reduction and user engagement. In trials with university students, chatbot-based interventions led to measurable improvements in depressive symptoms. Although attrition and limited methodological detail constrain the interpretability of these findings, they suggest that digital agents can serve as viable alternatives to text-based self-help materials, especially when therapeutic interaction and responsiveness are prioritized (Liu et al., 2022).

Blended care models that combine traditional therapy with AI support have also been explored. In a study conducted during the COVID-19 pandemic, the integration of a CBT chatbot with therapist-guided sessions yielded significant reductions in psychological distress among adults experiencing pandemic-related stress. Although some outcomes lacked statistical significance and the sample size was modest, the results support the premise that AI agents can enhance conventional psychotherapy by maintaining therapeutic engagement between sessions and reinforcing skill practice (Danieli et al., 2022).

Despite these promising findings, important limitations remain. Current chatbots often operate using pre-scripted dialogue or semi-autonomous frameworks, which restrict their ability to detect and respond to emotional nuance or complex clinical needs. Misinterpretation of user input remains a persistent concern, especially in high-risk contexts where diagnostic precision and clinical sensitivity are critical. Ethical challenges, particularly around data privacy, informed consent, and the scope of AI autonomy, require sustained attention. Additionally, few interventions have undergone long-term validation, and most studies remain underpowered to detect subtle but clinically relevant changes in mood and functioning. These challenges highlight the need for continued interdisciplinary collaboration among clinicians, engineers, and researchers to improve algorithmic refinement, ensure ethical compliance, and facilitate responsible clinical integration (Beg & Verma, 2025).

Closed-Loop Brain Stimulation and Biofeedback Systems

The field of neuromodulation has undergone a profound shift with the advent of closed-loop brain stimulation systems that offer a compelling alternative to static, open-loop approaches. These systems represent a significant step toward precision psychiatry, particularly in the management of mood disorders. Unlike conventional neuromodulation methods that deliver stimulation at fixed parameters regardless of the patient's neural state, closed-loop systems incorporate real-time feedback mechanisms. These mechanisms allow dynamic adjustment of stimulation in accordance with neurophysiological or behavioral markers, thus enabling context-sensitive and patient-specific interventions (Chandrabhatla et al., 2023).

A core advantage of closed-loop stimulation lies in its capacity to respond to the fluctuating nature of mood states, which often resist stabilization through uniform treatment modalities. For instance, in treatment-resistant depression and obsessive-compulsive disorder, early clinical trials have shown that adaptive deep brain stimulation (DBS) systems can outperform traditional models by identifying and modulating biomarkers that correlate with pathological affective states (Groppa et al., 2024; Widge, 2023). Although mood disorders present a more complex neural architecture than movement disorders, which benefit from well-characterized biomarkers like beta oscillations in Parkinson's disease, exploratory efforts using stereo-electroencephalography (SEEG) and neuroimaging-guided targeting have begun to uncover idiosyncratic circuits that can be engaged for therapeutic benefit (Sheth et al., 2022).

Machine learning models are foundational to these systems. They process vast streams of multimodal data to detect patterns, predict neural shifts, and determine optimal stimulation parameters. Algorithms such as support vector machines, convolutional neural networks, and ensemble methods have been employed to decode pathological states and guide closed-loop responses in real time (Chandrabhatla et al., 2023; Talati, 2025). Despite impressive algorithmic performance in controlled environments, real-world implementation remains limited by small sample sizes, individual heterogeneity, and insufficient biomarker generalizability. These constraints underscore the urgency of multicenter trials and comprehensive data-sharing to build robust predictive frameworks.

A striking development in this domain has been the incorporation of nanotechnology to refine the interface between neural tissue and stimulation hardware. Smart neural electrodes made from carbon nanotubes and graphene offer improved biocompatibility, flexibility, and spatial precision. These advancements are particularly salient in anxiety disorders, where regions such as the amygdala and prefrontal cortex must be targeted with high specificity to avoid undesirable effects (Fahmawi & Dalu, 2025). These innovations not only enhance the precision of neuromodulation but also facilitate integration with wearable brain-computer interfaces, allowing for minimally invasive, continuous therapeutic interaction.

Further expanding the scope of personalization, recent studies have employed graph theory and control-theoretic models to design mathematically optimized stimulation strategies. Using resting-state EEG data, researchers have developed algorithms that localize control nodes in the cortical network and identify frequency-amplitude combinations that can restore functional connectivity in major depressive disorder (Wang & Sun, 2025). While such models remain largely theoretical and await clinical validation, their potential to move beyond trial-and-error programming into empirically grounded stimulation planning is promising.

Biofeedback systems represent another critical arm of closed-loop care. These systems provide patients with real-time information about their physiological states, often via wearables that monitor heart rate variability, galvanic skin response, or EEG signals. When integrated with artificial intelligence platforms, such feedback mechanisms can become predictive rather than merely reactive, guiding behavioral or neurostimulation interventions before maladaptive states escalate (Pavlopoulos et al., 2024). In this context, large language models and virtual agents serve not only as therapeutic interlocutors but also as data aggregators that inform individualized treatment plans based on continuous physiological monitoring.

Despite the technological promise, several barriers impede widespread clinical adoption. Technical limitations in sensing fidelity, the complexity of device implantation, and the unresolved ethical concerns surrounding autonomy, privacy, and equity remain significant. Moreover, most closed-loop systems are validated in brief perioperative windows or small case series, with little known about their long-term effects or scalability (Groppa et al., 2024; Widge, 2023).

Nonetheless, the trajectory is clear. Closed-loop brain stimulation and biofeedback systems are laying the groundwork for a new paradigm in the treatment of mood disorders—one that is not only adaptive and personalized but also deeply integrative. These systems are beginning to merge neurobiology, artificial intelligence, materials science, and clinical psychiatry into cohesive frameworks capable of addressing the multifaceted nature of affective dysregulation. As foundational research continues and ethical infrastructures evolve, their role in routine psychiatric care is poised to expand significantly.

Comparative Evaluation of Treatment Modalities

The evaluation of treatment options for mood disorders has long relied on randomized controlled trials, yet these are often limited in scope and feasibility. Artificial intelligence has begun to transform this landscape by enabling data-driven comparative effectiveness research that integrates evidence from diverse sources. Clinical trial data, electronic health records, real-world evidence, and even social media streams can now be synthesized into unified models that evaluate pharmacotherapy, psychotherapy, neuromodulation, and digital interventions within a single analytic framework (Bokolo & Liu, 2023; Horwitz et al., 2024; Wu et al., 2018). In doing so, AI provides a form of head-to-head comparison when direct randomized studies are impractical or unavailable, allowing clinicians to weigh treatment options with a level of granularity previously unattainable.

One of the most promising contributions of AI lies in personalized outcome prediction. Models trained on heterogeneous patient data can generate individualized estimates of remission likelihood or relapse risk across different treatment modalities. Deep learning systems, for instance, have identified subgroups of patients more likely to benefit from specific antidepressants, while ensemble approaches have refined predictions of success with internet-based therapy (Mehltretter et al., 2020; Pearson et al., 2019). Similarly, decision support systems such as Aifred provide physicians with patient-specific probabilities of remission under different antidepressant regimens, supporting shared decision-making and expanding consideration of treatment alternatives (Tanguay-Sela et al., 2021). These advances move beyond population-level averages to produce clinically actionable insights tailored to the unique biological and psychosocial profile of each patient.

A further shift has been the integration of multimodal measures of success. Comparative frameworks no longer assess treatments solely by symptom reduction but also by their effects on functional recovery, quality of life, and treatment adherence. Trials incorporating technology-facilitated care have demonstrated not only reductions in depressive severity but also improvements in patient satisfaction and management of comorbid conditions (Wu et al., 2018). Wearable devices enhance this approach by contributing continuous physiological and behavioral data, enriching assessments with real-world measures of sleep, activity, and heart rate variability (Abd-Alrazaq et al., 2023). These multidimensional outcomes are crucial in understanding the true impact of interventions, as a therapy that alleviates symptoms but imposes burdensome side effects or poor adherence cannot be considered superior.

Comparative evaluation also extends to sequencing and augmentation strategies, where AI-driven models simulate the clinical decision process over time. Reinforcement learning approaches have already been tested to adapt psychotherapy for chronic pain, tailoring delivery and intensity based on daily feedback to optimize outcomes with reduced clinician burden (Piette et al., 2022). Predictive modelling of antidepressant response offers similar possibilities for dynamically switching or augmenting treatments when progress stalls, with some frameworks even incorporating cost-benefit calculations to anticipate long-term treatment trajectories (Squarcina et al., 2021). Such tools could eventually guide clinicians through complex therapeutic pathways, helping to determine not just which intervention is best, but when and how it should be introduced in a patient's care plan.

Despite these advances, important limitations remain. Many predictive models are trained on small or demographically narrow samples, raising concerns about generalizability to more diverse populations (Ermers et al., 2020). Risks of overfitting, biased data representation, and opaque model architectures pose challenges for clinical trust and adoption. Moreover, there are profound ethical questions about the extent to which algorithmic recommendations should guide or potentially override clinical judgment. While AI can augment decision-making, reliance on automated predictions must be balanced with the clinician's nuanced understanding of the patient's lived experience, values, and preferences.

Taken together, AI-driven comparative evaluation of treatment modalities is not merely a technological advance but a conceptual reorientation. By integrating diverse datasets, generating individualized predictions, and expanding definitions of treatment success, these systems provide a more holistic picture of therapeutic efficacy. If developed responsibly and implemented with ethical safeguards, they hold the potential to reshape the clinical landscape of mood disorders, making treatment decisions more precise, dynamic, and responsive to the complexity of human experience.

CLINICAL VIGNETTES AND COMPARATIVE ANALYSES

The practical value of artificial intelligence in mental health becomes most apparent when applied to real or simulated cases that mirror the complexity of clinical decision making. Clinical vignettes serve as an essential bridge between abstract algorithmic outputs and their practical implications, offering a controlled environment to stress test how AI tools handle the nuance of patient history, demographics, and treatment trajectories before clinical deployment. Comparative analyses across these studies reveal important insights into diagnostic precision and therapeutic personalization, while simultaneously exposing the stark methodological limitations, specifically regarding racial bias and dataset homogeneity, that currently hinder broad implementation.

One instructive example comes from the evaluation of the Ada Health chatbot, tested against psychiatric case vignettes representing both adult and pediatric presentations. The system performed most consistently when guided by psychotherapists, achieving good diagnostic agreement for adult disorders (Cohen's kappa = 0.64). However, performance dropped precipitously in child and adolescent cases (Cohen's kappa = 0.40$) and when used by laypersons (Jungmann et al., 2019). This discrepancy illustrates a critical barrier in AI deployment: tools often falter when applied to developmental populations or when removed from expert oversight, underscoring that current algorithms function best as clinician extenders rather than standalone diagnostic agents.

In psychopharmacology, vignette-based investigations have quantified how large language models (LLMs) behave when confronted with complex treatment decisions. When supplied with prompts based on guidelines, augmented models such as GPT-4 and Qwen achieved higher accuracy in identifying treatments preferred by experts for bipolar and treatment resistant depression than unaugmented models. For instance, augmented GPT-4 correctly identified optimal treatments in 50.8% of cases, significantly outperforming community clinicians (23.1%). However, agreement with expert consensus remained only fair (Cohen's kappa = 0.31), and while models displayed comparable performance across gender and race in this specific study, broader field data suggests this is an exception rather than the rule (Perlis et al., 2024; Perlis et al., 2025).A major methodological critique of such comparative analyses is the persistent lack of diversity in training and validation datasets. Recent meta-analyses of mental health trials indicate that only 39.2% of studies report participant ethnicity, with representation dropping to as low as 12.4% in studies from Asia and the Middle East (Bellato et al., 2025). This "data invisibility" has tangible consequences: LLMs have been found to produce bias scores of 1.93 when diagnosing African American patients compared to 1.37 for race neutral cases, often recommending inferior treatments or guardianship at disproportionate rates (Bouguettaya et al., 2025). Without addressing these underlying dataset imbalances, vignette studies may present an overly optimistic view of AI fairness that fails to hold up in diverse real-world settings.

Patient stratification frameworks broaden the scope of vignettes by moving beyond static descriptions. The ALMOND model, for example, integrated pharmacogenomic biomarkers and symptom trajectories across diverse populations (N > 3,000), producing individualized treatment predictions that reflected the biological underpinnings of antidepressant response (AUC ≈ 0.70) (Athreya, 2019). Similarly, observational studies using causal inference and imitation learning have attempted to model physician decision making in treatment resistant depression. While these approaches identified meaningful treatment clusters, they ultimately lacked sufficient predictive accuracy for deployment, highlighting the difficulty of modeling complex care trajectories using retrospective data alone (Cousineau, 2020). Wearable technologies bring yet another dimension to vignette generation. A randomized controlled trial that integrated Fitbit data into predictive models created dynamic vignettes rooted in real time physiological and behavioral signals. These multitask learning models anticipated remission outcomes with greater accuracy than traditional single task approaches, demonstrating how continuous data streams can transform vignettes from static summaries into dynamic portraits of risk (Dai et al., 2022). However, such studies frequently suffer from small sample sizes (e.g., n=89) and high attrition, which raises concerns about the risk of overfitting and whether these "digital phenotypes" are robust enough to generalize to broader clinical populations.

Linguistic analyses of clinical interviews have also been used to craft vignettes from the "bottom up." Features such as speech speed, sentiment, and verbal complexity have been shown to classify depressive states with high accuracy. Random Forest models achieved 84% accuracy in one study, significantly outperforming Support Vector Machines (65%) (Lorenzoni et al., 2025). Yet, the reliance on specific datasets (like DAIC-WOZ) and the lack of cross-cultural validation means these models may struggle with linguistic variation. Research indicates that screening tools based on speech often perform less accurately for women and non-White speakers due to training data bias, further emphasizing the need for inclusive validation protocols.

Taken together, these clinical vignettes and comparative analyses show that while AI is reshaping psychiatric reasoning, its reliability is uneven. Structured chatbots and LLMs show promise for adult populations and pharmacological decision support but struggle with pediatric cases and complex clinical nuance. Moreover, the field is constrained by significant methodological flaws: small sample sizes, a lack of external validation, and systemic biases in training data that leave racial and ethnic minorities underrepresented. The future lies not just in refining algorithms, but in ensuring they are trained on representative datasets to create multidimensional vignettes that truly reflect the diversity of patient complexity (Higgins & Wilson, 2025; Kamra et al., 2020; Levkovich, 2025).

Table 1. Evidence Levels and Methodological Limitations Across AI Modalities

AI Application Area	Predominant Evidence Level	Key Methodological Limitations
Digital Phenotyping ***(Smartphone/Wearable Sensing)***	**Prospective Observational** Studies monitor patients over time to detect state changes, but do not yet routinely drive clinical interventions in RCTs.	• **Small, Homogeneous Samples:** Limits generalizability • **Data Sparsity:** High rates of missing data due to battery/sensor failure • **Lack of Standardization:** Sensor types vary between devices (Android vs. iOS).
Genomics & Biomarkers ***(Diagnostic Prediction)***	**Retrospective / Cross-Sectional** Analysis of existing biobank data rather than prospective clinical prediction.	• **Multiple Comparisons Problem:** High risk of false positives when testing thousands of genes • **Replicability Crisis:** Biomarker panels often fail to validate in new cohorts • **Lack of Prospective Validation:** Few studies track patients forward in time.
Neuroimaging ***(fMRI, EEG Diagnosis)***	**Retrospective Case-Control** Comparing scans of diagnosed patients vs. healthy controls.	• **Ceiling Effect:** Diagnostic accuracy rarely exceeds ~62% due to disorder heterogeneity • **Overfitting:** Small sample sizes relative to the number of voxels/ features • **Site Effects:** Difficulty replicating results across different MRI scanners.
Pharmacogenomic Decision Tools ***(Predicting Drug Response)***	**Retrospective Validation on RCT Data** Models are trained on data from *past* trials rather than tested in new, live clinical trials.	• **European Ancestry Bias:** Major datasets are predominantly White • **Low Variance Explained:** Polygenic scores often explain <6% of treatment outcome variance • **Retrospective Nature:** Reliance on completed trial data limits real-world applicability
Chatbots & Digital Therapeutics ***(CBT-based Agents)***	**Pilot Randomized Controlled Trials (RCTs)** Unlike other areas, this field has RCTs, but they are consistently small or exploratory.	• **Small Sample Sizes:** Many trials have N < 100 • **High Attrition:** Users frequently stop engaging after short periods • **Control Group Issues:** Waitlist controls are common, potentially inflating effect sizes.

continued on following page

Table 1. Continued

AI Application Area	Predominant Evidence Level	Key Methodological Limitations
Closed-Loop Brain Stimulation ***(DBS / Biofeedback)***	**Case Studies / Proof-of-Concept** Primarily single-subject cases or simulation studies.	• **Lack of Neural Targets:** Reliable biomarkers for mood states are not yet fully defined • **Invasiveness:** High cost and surgical risk limit large-scale data collection. • **Simulation Reliance:** Some models are validated on math models (Kuramoto) rather than patients
Clinical Vignettes & LLMs ***(Decision Support)***	**Simulation / Comparative Analysis** Testing models against "textbook" cases or expert consensus.	• **Racial/Demographic Bias:** Models show higher bias scores for minority groups • **Pediatric Failure:** Performance drops significantly for child/adolescent cases • **Lack of Real-World Noise:** Simulated vignettes lack the messiness of real EHRs.

ETHICAL, LEGAL, AND SOCIAL CONSIDERATIONS

The proliferation of artificial intelligence in mental health care has amplified longstanding concerns about privacy, surveillance, and the validity of digital consent. Mental health data, often deeply personal and sensitive, forms the backbone of many AI-driven interventions, whether through electronic health records, passive sensing devices, wearable technologies, or mobile applications. Unlike conventional clinical encounters where disclosure is guided by trust and interpersonal negotiation, digital systems continuously capture and process information, frequently without the user's full awareness of the scope of collection or the ways in which the data may be repurposed. This raises a central question: how much control do individuals truly retain over their own mental health information in an era where data fuels both clinical innovation and commercial interests (Verma et al., 2025).

Data Privacy, Surveillance, and Digital Consent

Privacy concerns are magnified when mental health technologies engage in forms of surveillance that blur therapeutic care with monitoring. Passive sensing tools, for example, can infer mood states or risk of crisis by tracking sleep, mobility, speech, or physiological activity. While such systems offer the promise of timely intervention, they also risk intruding into the intimate rhythms of everyday life. Service users have expressed ambivalence about these technologies, recognizing their potential for safety while also fearing misinterpretation, overreach, or coercion. The therapeutic alliance may be strained if patients perceive themselves as objects of observation rather than partners in care (Rogan et al., 2024). When surveillance extends beyond clinical contexts into consumer apps, the risks multiply, particularly because many applications lack transparent privacy standards, do not comply with medical regulations, and may share or sell user data to third parties (Gamble, 2020).

Digital consent, intended as the safeguard for autonomy, often functions more as a legal formality than as a meaningful process. Consent agreements are frequently presented through lengthy documents written in inaccessible language, discouraging careful review. Moreover, traditional consent assumes a discrete moment of decision, yet digital systems collect data dynamically and adaptively, creating a need for consent mechanisms that are ongoing, flexible, and revisable. Without such innovations, individuals are unlikely to grasp the extent to which their data is analyzed, stored, or even combined with external datasets for purposes far removed from the original context of care (Idowu & Idowu, 2025). This disconnect undermines the ethical principle of informed choice, reducing patient autonomy to a checkbox rather than a sustained right.

There are models of good practice that signal a more responsible path forward. Studies in extended reality therapies, for instance, have demonstrated how rigorous compliance with established data protection frameworks such as GDPR and HIPAA can be integrated into design without impeding clinical efficacy. By embedding privacy protections into the system's architecture from the outset, developers can foster trust and demonstrate that safeguarding information is not an afterthought but a structural commitment (Radanliev, 2025). Yet such examples remain the exception rather than the norm, with many AI-based tools still lacking robust legal oversight or clear accountability when breaches occur.

The challenge is not only technical but also relational and social. Vulnerable groups, including young people, migrants, and sexual or gender minorities, are disproportionately exposed to the risks of digital surveillance. Their data, if misused, may reinforce stigma, discrimination, or even legal jeopardy. At the same time, these populations often stand to benefit the most from accessible and innovative mental health supports. Thus, the stakes of balancing protection with empowerment are particularly acute (Gamble, 2020; Wies et al., 2021). Consent, in this light, cannot be conceived solely as an individual transaction but must be situated within broader structures of equity and justice.

Ultimately, the governance of data privacy and consent in AI-mediated mental health care requires more than compliance with technical standards. It demands participatory approaches that bring service users, carers, and clinicians into the design process as active partners. Only by embedding transparency, shared accountability, and cultural sensitivity into digital infrastructures can trust be maintained and the promise of AI realized without eroding the dignity and rights of those it seeks to support (Carr, 2020; Gooding & Kariotis, 2021; Saeidnia et al., 2024).

Algorithmic Bias and Health Disparities

The promise of artificial intelligence in healthcare and mental health is often framed as one of objectivity and neutrality, yet closer inspection reveals that these technologies are deeply vulnerable to reproducing and even amplifying social inequalities. Algorithms are only as fair as the data from which they learn, and health data itself is already shaped by histories of exclusion, unequal access to care, and cultural blind spots. When such biases are encoded into predictive systems, they do not remain neutral technical flaws but instead become mechanisms that distribute benefits unequally and impose harms disproportionately.

The influence of sex and gender on biomedical outcomes provides a striking example of this inequity. When algorithmic systems are trained on data that fail to capture the realities of intersex, transgender, or nonbinary individuals, the resulting models misclassify or ignore their health needs, further marginalizing groups that already face systemic disadvantages in medical settings (Cirillo et al., 2020). These errors are not simply technical mistakes; they reinforce a biomedical culture that privileges the health experiences of some populations while rendering others invisible.

Racial and ethnic disparities in algorithmic performance are equally consequential. Suicide prediction models, which hold potential as life-saving tools, have been shown to achieve high accuracy for White, Hispanic, and Asian patients but perform poorly for Black and American Indian patients (Coley et al., 2021). The consequence is stark: a system intended to identify those most at risk ends up providing fewer benefits to the very groups most burdened by inequities in mental health care. Such failures illustrate that unequal representation in training data can directly translate into life-and-death disparities.

Attempts to address these biases through technical mitigation strategies have shown promise but also revealed complexity. Machine learning models used for depression prediction demonstrate that bias is rarely uniform, as predictions may advantage women in one context and wealthier groups in another (Dang et al., 2024). Efforts to correct such imbalances often involve trade-offs, improving fairness for one group while inadvertently worsening outcomes for another. This dynamic makes clear that algorithmic justice cannot be achieved by a single adjustment or universal technique, but requires continuous monitoring and context-specific solutions.

Beyond individual studies, broader examinations of clinical machine learning have confirmed that bias is widespread, especially in diagnostic and prognostic models. Preprocessing strategies such as reweighing data or generating synthetic minority samples can reduce disparities, yet inconsistent use of fairness metrics and limited transparency continue to hinder progress (Huang et al., 2022). The absence of standardized approaches means that each deployment risks perpetuating inequities unless developers adopt a deliberate, ethically grounded framework.

The implications extend beyond technical domains into the realm of lived human experience. Digital mental health applications such as chatbots promise greater accessibility, but their design often fails to account for cultural nuance or the unique barriers faced by marginalized populations (Hamdoun et al., 2023). In these cases, the risk is not only that bias remains hidden in the background code, but that individuals from disadvantaged groups will experience these technologies as alienating, ineffective, or even harmful.

The deeper concern is that algorithmic bias can entrench systemic disparities in ways that are difficult to detect or contest. From the earliest stages of data collection to final deployment, choices about what to measure, how to categorize identities, and which outcomes to optimize are shaped by cultural assumptions and institutional priorities (Timmons et al., 2023). Without intervention, these decisions lock existing inequalities into the logic of technology itself. Scholars have warned that this cycle of reinforcement may render populations already underrepresented in care further excluded from its technological future (Walsh et al., 2020).

Addressing algorithmic disparities therefore demands more than technical fixes. It requires intentional inclusion of marginalized groups in research design, careful attention to sociocultural factors, and the establishment of governance structures that make fairness not an afterthought but a foundational criterion. Only through such measures can artificial intelligence in mental health and healthcare fulfill its promise of expanding equity rather than amplifying injustice.

Explainability and Accountability in AI Models

The integration of artificial intelligence into mental health care inevitably raises the question of how these systems can be rendered transparent and accountable to both professionals and patients. Explainability is not merely a technical aspiration but an ethical and clinical necessity. Models that provide predictions without intelligible reasoning risk undermining trust, limiting adoption, and exacerbating the very power imbalances they aim to address. The challenge lies in translating highly complex algorithmic processes into forms of reasoning that clinicians, patients, and regulators can comprehend and evaluate. Without such clarity, AI becomes a black box whose outputs may be perceived as authoritative yet remain inscrutable, creating risks of misplaced reliance and eroded responsibility (Joyce et al., 2023).

Efforts to enhance explainability have yielded a growing repertoire of techniques, ranging from model-agnostic strategies such as LIME and SHAP to more model-specific approaches like gradient-based attribution and attention analysis. These methods provide complementary insights into which features drive predictions and how models behave under different conditions. In clinical contexts, this capacity allows for a clearer alignment between algorithmic decision-making and established modes of psychiatric reasoning. However, there remains no universal consensus on what constitutes an adequate explanation, and explanations that satisfy one stakeholder group may fail to serve another. For instance, patients may desire accessible narratives that clarify why a system has flagged them at risk, while clinicians may require more granular indicators that map onto diagnostic categories or treatment guidelines (Joyce et al., 2023; Uban et al., 2021).

Accountability builds upon explainability by defining who bears responsibility for the consequences of AI-driven decisions. In mental health, this issue is particularly fraught given the probabilistic and interpretive nature of psychiatric data. Explanations alone are insufficient if there is no clear framework for tracing errors, correcting biases, and attributing responsibility. Recent studies emphasize that accountability is not only a matter of technical validation but also of ethical governance. The introduction of explainability frameworks and usability scales for clinicians illustrates an effort to operationalize accountability by providing systematic ways to assess and document transparency, trustworthiness, and usability (Kibria et al., 2025). This movement underscores the need for structures where accountability is distributed across developers, institutions, and practitioners, ensuring that responsibility does not collapse onto end users or remain unclaimed when errors occur.

Hybrid approaches that integrate human oversight with AI predictions offer one pathway to balancing explainability and accountability. Evidence suggests that while standalone AI systems can reduce perceived judgment and stigma, they risk being perceived as less accountable. Conversely, human–AI hybrids preserve a degree of human responsibility while leveraging computational precision, thereby fostering greater trust and intention to use such services (Tong et al., 2024). This dynamic illustrates that accountability in practice is not only about identifying who is liable in cases of harm but also about designing socio-technical systems that distribute responsibility in ways that align with human values and clinical expectations.

Accountability also requires robust governance beyond the clinic. Legal and organizational structures must address how AI models are validated, monitored, and sanctioned when they fail. Emerging frameworks informed by Kantian ethics and agency theory advocate for embedding principles of transparency, inclusivity, and fairness within AI governance structures, thereby grounding accountability in moral as well as procedural commitments (Tabaghdehi & Ayaz, 2025). Such approaches underscore that accountability is not reducible to technical explainability but must be anchored in the broader ethical commitments of institutions deploying these systems.

Ultimately, explainability and accountability operate in tandem, shaping how AI is received, trusted, and integrated within mental health practice. Explainability equips stakeholders with the tools to interrogate and understand algorithmic reasoning, while accountability ensures that decisions are owned, consequences are addressed, and ethical commitments are upheld. Together, they form the foundation upon which responsible AI in psychiatry and mental health care can be built, ensuring that the pursuit of innovation does not compromise the dignity, autonomy, and well-being of those it seeks to serve (Knowles et al., 2022; Singhal et al., 2024; Sentinella-Jerbić, 2024; Squires et al., 2023; Zogan et al., 2022).

Regulatory Frameworks and Clinician Responsibility

The rapid diffusion of artificial intelligence into psychiatry and mental health care has outpaced the legal and regulatory structures that would ordinarily safeguard clinical practice. Mental health, being one of the most sensitive domains of medicine, raises profound questions about how AI systems can be deployed without compromising patient rights, professional standards, and public trust. Regulatory frameworks exist to provide boundaries within which innovation may thrive responsibly, but they remain fragmented and uneven across national and international contexts. Some jurisdictions have advanced comprehensive data protection laws and stringent device regulations, while others operate within gaps marked by weak oversight, insufficient enforcement, or outdated legislation that fails to anticipate the complexity of adaptive learning systems (Pesapane et al., 2021; Jain, 2023).

The urgency for robust regulation is underscored by the ethical challenges inherent in psychiatric contexts. Unlike other medical fields, mental health practice involves vulnerable populations whose autonomy may fluctuate, whose privacy demands heightened protection, and whose data often carry intense social stigma. Existing laws concerning data protection, informed consent, and medical device certification are insufficient to account for AI's continuous learning capabilities and the opacity of many predictive models. In the absence of clear frameworks, liability becomes ambiguous, leaving clinicians exposed to legal risk while patients remain vulnerable to harm. Recent international efforts, such as the FUTURE-AI framework, represent attempts to harmonize guiding principles like fairness, usability, and traceability into best practices, but translation into enforceable law and clinical protocols remains incomplete (Lekadir et al., 2025).

Clinician responsibility in this context becomes a central ethical and legal question. While AI tools may suggest diagnoses, predict risks, or recommend interventions, the ultimate accountability for patient care still resides with the clinician. This creates a dual burden: professionals must not only exercise their clinical judgment but also evaluate the reliability, appropriateness, and limitations of AI-generated outputs. Failure to do so risks reducing clinicians to passive recipients of machine recommendations, eroding professional agency and potentially compromising the therapeutic alliance. The Integrated Ethical Approach for Computational Psychiatry emphasizes that clinicians must remain active arbiters, integrating AI insights with human-centered care, while respecting autonomy, beneficence, and justice (Putica et al., 2025).

Regulatory structures can support clinicians in fulfilling this role by setting standards for validation, mandating transparency requirements, and clarifying liability in cases of adverse outcomes. Yet regulation alone cannot resolve the clinical responsibility dilemma. It must be paired with professional training, guidelines issued by medical associations, and interdisciplinary oversight to ensure that clinicians are equipped to interrogate AI systems rather than defer uncritically to them. In psychiatric inpatient settings, where consent may be limited and surveillance technologies intensify ethical risks, clinicians must remain especially vigilant. They are tasked with safeguarding patients from intrusive monitoring or biased risk assessments while ensuring that innovations do not erode fundamental rights to dignity and privacy (Solaiman et al., 2023).

The situation in low- and middle-income countries highlights further complexity. Regulatory frameworks are often underdeveloped, digital literacy uneven, and infrastructural barriers acute. In such contexts, the clinician's responsibility expands beyond individual patient care to include advocacy for equitable and culturally sensitive deployment of AI systems. The use of telepsychiatry augmented by AI in India illustrates both the promise of extending mental health services to underserved populations and the risks of inadequate oversight in contexts of fragile data protection regimes and sociocultural diversity. Clinicians become mediators, ensuring that AI-driven care does not exacerbate inequalities or compromise trust in health systems (Thenral & Annamalai, 2020; Jain, 2023).

Ultimately, regulatory frameworks and clinician responsibility must evolve together. Regulations provide the structural safeguards for accountability and ethical governance, while clinicians embody the human element that ensures technology remains in service of care rather than control. A dynamic partnership between policymakers, professional bodies, and clinicians is therefore essential. Only through such collaboration can AI in mental health care be governed in a manner that respects both the promise of innovation and the vulnerabilities of those it seeks to help (Hoose & Králiková, 2024).

IMPLEMENTATION CHALLENGES AND FUTURE DIRECTIONS

The successful adoption of artificial intelligence in mental health is not limited by predictive accuracy alone but by the complexities of embedding such tools into the lived realities of clinical practice. Implementation is shaped by the capacity of health systems to integrate technology into existing structures, by the readiness of clinicians and patients to engage with it, by the rigor of validation processes across settings, and by the policy and infrastructural frameworks that govern its use. Only by addressing these dimensions in tandem can AI move from experimental promise to meaningful transformation in care.

The first challenge lies in the integration of predictive algorithms into electronic health records and clinical workflows. Most studies demonstrate predictive value in retrospective analyses, but few have moved beyond the research setting into real-world applications. The lack of interoperability across EHR systems further complicates implementation, as data standards and infrastructure vary widely across institutions and countries. Integration is not simply a matter of embedding algorithms into existing records; it requires careful re-engineering of workflows so that clinicians receive insights in ways that are timely, interpretable, and actionable. Without seamless integration, even the most sophisticated models risk becoming background tools that never inform actual patient care (Nickson et al., 2023; Al-Juhani et al., 2025). Recent work on learning health systems highlights the importance of iterative, feedback-driven design, where predictive tools continuously adapt to real-world data and clinical feedback loops (Rahimi et al., 2024). Equally, machine-readable SMART guidelines are being advanced as a mechanism to translate evidence and AI outputs directly into adaptable clinical pathways, ensuring that insights align with patient-care processes rather than disrupt them (World Health Organization, 2019).

Training clinicians and engaging patients represent equally critical frontiers. Predictive systems can only be effective if clinicians understand their limitations, interpret their outputs responsibly, and communicate them in ways that maintain trust with patients. Studies suggest that many clinicians feel underprepared to adopt digital tools into practice, with gaps in both digital literacy and confidence in AI-driven recommendations (Le et al., 2025; Mullerpattan et al., 2025). This absence of structured preparation can contribute to inappropriate reliance on AI outputs or, conversely, resistance to adoption. To address this, scholars argue for AI training to become part of medical curricula, covering technical logic, interpretability, ethical implications, and the relational aspects of communicating AI-informed decisions (Arvai et al., 2025). Patients, in turn, express ambivalence when AI tools are introduced without transparency or explanation, highlighting the risk that automation may erode rather than enhance therapeutic alliance. A sustainable future for AI in psychiatry requires re-imagining training not only in terms of technical knowledge but also in terms of the relational skills necessary to integrate AI into shared decision-making with patients. Studies show that when individuals are included in co-design processes, particularly in sensitive domains such as suicide prevention, they report greater trust and engagement, reinforcing the therapeutic alliance rather than undermining it (Jeyakumar et al., 2023).

Another barrier is the lack of robust multi-site validation and co-design approaches. Most predictive models rely on single-site data or homogenous populations, restricting their generalizability across diverse clinical and demographic settings (Chowdhury et al., 2021; Bhadra & Kumar, 2024). Without multi-site validation, there is a danger that AI models perpetuate biases that disproportionately disadvantage underrepresented groups. Co-design with patients, families, and frontline clinicians is equally crucial, ensuring that tools reflect real-world needs and values rather than technological possibilities alone. Collaborative design processes can also help surface concerns around fairness, privacy, and usability, all of which are central to trust and uptake (Jeyakumar et al., 2023; Haider et al., 2025).

Policy frameworks and sustainable AI infrastructure form the final pillar of successful implementation. The absence of consistent governance standards leaves institutions vulnerable to fragmented practices and ethical lapses, particularly with regard to data privacy, equity, and accountability. Current healthcare policies often lag behind technological capabilities, resulting in a regulatory vacuum in which models are developed and tested without clear pathways for safe clinical adoption. Building sustainable AI infrastructure requires investment in interoperable data systems, long-term mechanisms for monitoring and updating models, and explicit policies for post-market surveillance (Nemesure et al., 2021; Haider et al., 2025). Policies must also ensure equitable access, avoiding a scenario in which AI becomes a tool that amplifies disparities between well-resourced health systems and those with fewer resources.

Looking forward, the trajectory of AI in mental health will depend on bridging these gaps. Integration into EHR systems must be accompanied by redesigns of clinical workflows that prioritize interpretability and utility. Training programs must prepare clinicians not only to use AI tools but to integrate them into therapeutic relationships. Research must shift toward multi-site collaborations and co-design processes that foreground equity and patient voice. Finally, policymakers and health leaders must invest in governance structures and technical infrastructure that ensure AI systems remain transparent, equitable, and adaptable as clinical practices evolve. If these elements converge, the field may move beyond proof-of-concept models toward tools that genuinely transform mental health care.

CONCLUSION

The future of psychiatry is likely to be shaped by a model in which artificial intelligence complements rather than replaces human clinicians. AI has demonstrated the ability to detect complex and subtle signals across biological, behavioral, and digital domains, offering predictions and treatment recommendations that extend beyond what traditional methods provide (Iniesta et al., 2016). Yet the full meaning of these findings only emerges when interpreted within the therapeutic relationship, where empathy, judgment, and ethical reasoning remain indispensable (Doraiswamy et al., 2020).

This vision of hybrid care rests on the idea that neither technology nor clinician is sufficient alone. An AI system may suggest a treatment regimen guided by pharmacogenomic markers or neuroimaging signatures (Perlis, 2016), but the decision to apply these insights requires contextual understanding of the patient's lived experience. Human AI collaboration has already demonstrated benefits in settings such as peer-to-peer digital mental health support, where AI-assisted prompting improved empathetic dialogue without reducing human agency (Sharma et al., 2023). The task ahead is to scale such complementary models into mainstream practice.

At the same time, caution is warranted. Reports have shown that unsupervised chatbot use can lead to unintended consequences, including emotional dependence, overreliance on automated responses, and exacerbation of psychiatric symptoms in vulnerable individuals. Such concerns reinforce the need for clinician oversight, transparent protocols, and clearly defined ethical boundaries. AI should be deployed as an aid to care rather than an unmonitored substitute for professional involvement.

Moving forward, four areas will be central to building clinically responsible AI psychiatry. First, datasets must be expanded in size and diversity to avoid bias and ensure broad applicability. Evidence suggests that single-site models often fail to generalize, while multi-modal data integration improves prediction across populations (Dinga et al., 2019). Second, interpretability is critical. Models that provide explanations for their outputs build trust among clinicians and patients alike, whereas opaque algorithms undermine safe adoption (Doshi-Velez & Kim, 2017). Third, effective governance is needed. Regulatory proposals, such as the European Union's AI Act, represent important steps toward establishing oversight and accountability for algorithmic systems in medicine (Floridi, 2021). Finally, clinician training is essential. Physicians will require new competencies in integrating algorithmic outputs into patient care, ensuring that these tools enhance rather than complicate clinical workflows (Doraiswamy et al., 2020).

If these efforts are realized, psychiatry may advance toward a model that is both precise and humane. Artificial intelligence can identify relapse risk earlier than clinical observation, suggest treatment strategies tailored to genetic and behavioural signatures, and extend mental health care into settings with limited resources (Chekroud et al., 2016). However, these tools only reach their potential when embedded within a system that respects the primacy of human connection and professional responsibility. The most promising future lies in partnership: technology providing scale and sensitivity, and clinicians providing wisdom, empathy, and ethical grounding. In such a model, precision psychiatry becomes not only more scientifically informed but also more attuned to the individual who seeks care.

REFERENCES

Abd-Alrazaq, A., AlSaad, R., Shuwcihdi, F., Ahmed, A., Aziz, S., & Sheikh, J. (2023). Systematic review and meta-analysis of performance of wearable artificial intelligence in detecting and predicting depression. *NPJ Digital Medicine*, *6*(1), 84. DOI: 10.1038/s41746-023-00828-5

Al-Juhani, A., Desoky, R., Iskander, Z., Alotaibi, R. M., Alzain, N. N., Aljohani, N., Alrefaai, M. M., Alhasanat, R. A., AlMehaimeed, M. A., & Alharthi, A. S. (2025). Machine Learning Models for Predicting Mental Health Crises in Adolescents Using Electronic Health Records: A Systematic Review. *Cureus*. Advance online publication. DOI: 10.7759/cureus.89873

Antosik-Wójcińska, A. Z., Dominiak, M., Chojnacka, M., Kaczmarek-Majer, K., Opara, K. R., Radziszewska, W., Olwert, A., & Święcicki, Ł. (2020). Smartphone as a monitoring tool for bipolar disorder: A systematic review including data analysis, machine learning algorithms and predictive modelling. *International Journal of Medical Informatics*, *138*, 104131. DOI: 10.1016/j.ijmedinf.2020.104131

Arvai, N., Katonai, G., & Mesko, B. (2025). Health Care Professionals' Concerns About Medical AI and Psychological Barriers and Strategies for Successful Implementation: Scoping Review. *Journal of Medical Internet Research*, *27*, e66986.

Athreya, A. P. (2019). *Making augmented human intelligence in medicine practical: A case study of treating major depressive* disorder [Doctoral dissertation, University of Illinois at Urbana-Champaign]. IDEALS. http://hdl.handle.net/2142/105013

Athreya, A. P., Iyer, R., Wang, L., Weinshilboum, R. M., & Bobo, W. V. (2019a). Integration of machine learning and pharmacogenomic biomarkers for predicting response to antidepressant treatment: Can computational intelligence be used to augment clinical assessments? *Pharmacogenomics*, *20*(14), 983–988.

Athreya, A. P., Neavin, D., Carrillo-Roa, T., Skime, M., Biernacka, J., Frye, M. A., Rush, A. J., Wang, L., Binder, E. B., Iyer, R. K., Weinshilboum, R. M., & Bobo, W. V. (2019b). Pharmacogenomics-Driven Prediction of Antidepressant Treatment Outcomes: A Machine-Learning Approach With Multi-trial Replication. *Clinical Pharmacology and Therapeutics*, *106*(4), 855–865. DOI: 10.1002/cpt.1482

Beg, M. J., & Verma, M., M., V. C. K. M., & Verma, M. K. (2025). Artificial Intelligence for Psychotherapy: A Review of the Current State and Future Directions. *Indian Journal of Psychological Medicine*, *47*(4), 314–325.

Bellato, A., Raduà, J., Stocker, A., Lockman, M. S., Lall, A., Ravisankar, V., & Cortese, S. (2025). Reporting and Representation of Race and Ethnicity in Clinical Trials of Pharmacotherapy for Mental Disorders: A Meta-Analysis. *JAMA Psychiatry*.

Bhadra, S., & Kumar, C. J. (2024). Enhancing the efficacy of depression detection system using optimal feature selection from EHR. *Computer Methods in Biomechanics and Biomedical Engineering*, *27*(2), 222–236. DOI: 10.1080/10255842.2023.2181660

Bobo, W. V., Van Ommeren, B., & Athreya, A. P. (2022). Machine learning, pharmacogenomics, and clinical psychiatry: Predicting antidepressant response in patients with major depressive disorder. *Expert Review of Clinical Pharmacology*, *15*(8), 927–944. DOI: 10.1080/17512433.2022.2112949

Bokolo, B. G., & Liu, Q. (2023). Deep Learning-Based Depression Detection from Social Media: Comparative Evaluation of ML and Transformer Techniques. *Electronics (Basel)*, *12*(21), 4396.

Bouguettaya, A., Stuart, E. M., & Aboujaoude, E. (2025). Racial bias in AI-mediated psychiatric diagnosis and treatment: A qualitative comparison of four large language models. npj. *Digital Medicine*, *8*(1), 332.

Brictzke, E., Hawken, E. R., Idzikowski, M., Pong, J., Kennedy, S. H., & Soares, C. N. (2019). Integrating digital phenotyping in clinical characterization of individuals with mood disorders. *Neuroscience and Biobehavioral Reviews*, *104*, 223–230. DOI: 10.1016/j.neubiorev.2019.07.009

Bufano, P., Laurino, M., Said, S., Tognetti, A., & Menicucci, D. (2023). Digital Phenotyping for Monitoring Mental Disorders: Systematic Review. *Journal of Medical Internet Research*, *25*, e46778. DOI: 10.2196/46778

Carr, S. (2020). 'AI gone mental': Engagement and ethics in data-driven technology for mental health. *Journal of Mental Health (Abingdon, England)*, *29*(2), 125–130. DOI: 10.1080/09638237.2020.1714011

Chandrabhatla, A. S., Pomeraniec, I. J., Horgan, T. M., Wat, E. K., & Ksendzovsky, A. (2023). Landscape and future directions of machine learning applications in closed-loop brain stimulation. *NPJ Digital Medicine*, *6*(1), 79. DOI: 10.1038/s41746-023-00779-x

Chekroud, A. M., Zotti, R. J., Shehzad, Z., Gueorguieva, R., Johnson, M. K., Trivedi, M. H., Cannon, T. D., Krystal, J. H., & Corlett, P. R. (2016). Cross-trial prediction of treatment outcome in depression: A machine learning approach. *The Lancet. Psychiatry*, *3*(3), 243–250. DOI: 10.1016/S2215-0366(15)00471-X

Choi, A., Ooi, A., & Lottridge, D. (2024). Digital Phenotyping for Stress, Anxiety, and Mild Depression: Systematic Literature Review. *JMIR mHealth and uHealth, 12*, e40689. DOI: 10.2196/40689

Chowdhury, M., Cervantes, E. G., Chan, W.-Y., & Seitz, D. P. (2021). Use of Machine Learning and Artificial Intelligence Methods in Geriatric Mental Health Research Involving Electronic Health Record or Administrative Claims Data: A Systematic Review. *Frontiers in Psychiatry, 12*. Advance online publication. DOI: 10.3389/fpsyt.2021.738466

Cirillo, D., Catuara-Solarz, S., Morey, C., Guney, E., Subirats, L., Mellino, S., Gigante, A., Valencia, A., Rementeria, M. J., Chadha, A. S., & Mavridis, N. (2020). Sex and gender differences and biases in artificial intelligence for biomedicine and healthcare. *NPJ Digital Medicine, 3*(1), 81. DOI: 10.1038/s41746-020-0288-5

Cohen, Z. D., DeRubeis, R. J., Hayes, R., Watkins, E. R., Lewis, G., Byng, R., Byford, S., Crane, C., Kuyken, W., Dalgleish, T., & Schweizer, S. (2023). The Development and Internal Evaluation of a Predictive Model to Identify for Whom Mindfulness-Based Cognitive Therapy Offers Superior Relapse Prevention for Recurrent Depression Versus Maintenance Antidepressant Medication. *Clinical Psychological Science, 11*(1), 59–76. DOI: 10.1177/21677026221076832

Coley, R. Y., Johnson, E., Simon, G. E., Cruz, M., & Shortreed, S. M. (2021). Racial/Ethnic Disparities in the Performance of Prediction Models for Death by Suicide After Mental Health Visits. *JAMA Psychiatry, 78*(7), 726.

Cousineau, M. (2020). *Analytics for medical decision making: Applications to the management of treatment-resistant depression* [Doctoral Dissertation, McGill University]. eScholarship@McGill. https://escholarship.mcgill.ca/concern/theses/st74cw06n

Dai, R., Kannampallil, T., Zhang, J., Lv, N., Ma, J., & Lu, C. (2022). Multi-Task Learning for Randomized Controlled Trials. *Proceedings of the ACM on Interactive, Mobile, Wearable and Ubiquitous Technologies, 6*(2), 1–23. DOI: 10.1145/3534591

Dang, V. N., Cascarano, A., Mulder, R. H., Cecil, C., Zuluaga, M. A., Hernández-González, J., & Lekadir, K. (2024). Fairness and bias correction in machine learning for depression prediction across four study populations. *Scientific Reports, 14*(1), 7848. DOI: 10.1038/s41598-024-58427-7

Danieli, M., Ciulli, T., Mousavi, S. M., Silvestri, G., Barbato, S., Di Natale, L., & Riccardi, G. (2022). Assessing the Impact of Conversational Artificial Intelligence in the Treatment of Stress and Anxiety in Aging Adults: Randomized Controlled Trial. *JMIR Mental Health, 9*(9), e38067. DOI: 10.2196/38067

Dinga, R., Schmaal, L., Penninx, B. W. J. H., van Tol, M. J., Veltman, D. J., van Velzen, L., Mennes, M., van der Wee, N. J. A., & Marquand, A. F. (2019). Evaluating the evidence for biotypes of depression: Methodological replication and extension of. *NeuroImage. Clinical, 22*, 101796. DOI: 10.1016/j.nicl.2019.101796

Doraiswamy, P. M., Blease, C., & Bodner, K. (2020). Artificial intelligence and the future of psychiatry: Insights from a global physician survey. *Artificial Intelligence in Medicine, 102*, 101753. DOI: 10.1016/j.artmed.2019.101753

Doshi-Velez, F., & Kim, B. (2017). *Towards A Rigorous Science of Interpretable Machine Learning.*

Ermers, N. J., Hagoort, K., & Scheepers, F. E. (2020). The Predictive Validity of Machine Learning Models in the Classification and Treatment of Major Depressive Disorder: State of the Art and Future Directions. *Frontiers in Psychiatry, 11.* Advance online publication. DOI: 10.3389/fpsyt.2020.00472

Fahmawi, S., & Dalu, A. E. A. (2025). Nanotechnology in the Design of Smart Neural Electrodes for Treating Chronic Anxiety Disorders in Adults: An Innovative Approach to Precision Brain Stimulation. *International Journal of Innovative Science and Research Technology*, 2407–2413. https://doi.org/DOI: 10.38124/ijisrt/25jun1768

First, M. B., & Wakefield, J. C. (2010). Defining 'mental disorder' in DSM-V. *Psychological Medicine, 40*(11), 1779–1782. DOI: 10.1017/S0033291709992339

Fitzpatrick, K. K., Darcy, A., & Vierhile, M. (2017). Delivering Cognitive Behavior Therapy to Young Adults With Symptoms of Depression and Anxiety Using a Fully Automated Conversational Agent (Woebot): A Randomized Controlled Trial. *JMIR Mental Health, 4*(2), e19. DOI: 10.2196/mental.7785

Floridi, L. (2021). The European Legislation on AI: A Brief Analysis of its Philosophical Approach. *Philosophy & Technology, 34*(2), 215–222. DOI: 10.1007/s13347-021-00460-9

Gamble, A. (2020). Artificial intelligence and mobile apps for mental healthcare: A social informatics perspective. *Aslib Journal of Information Management, 72*(4), 509–523. DOI: 10.1108/AJIM-11-2019-0316

Gooding, P., & Kariotis, T. (2021). Ethics and Law in Research on Algorithmic and Data-Driven Technology in Mental Health Care: Scoping Review. *JMIR Mental Health, 8*(6), e24668. DOI: 10.2196/24668

Grecucci, A., Lapomarda, G., Messina, I., Monachesi, B., Sorella, S., & Siugzdaite, R. (2022). Structural Features Related to Affective Instability Correctly Classify Patients With Borderline Personality Disorder. A Supervised Machine Learning Approach. *Frontiers in Psychiatry, 13*. Advance online publication. DOI: 10.3389/fpsyt.2022.804440

Groppa, S., Gonzalez-Escamilla, G., Tinkhauser, G., Baqapuri, H. I., Sajonz, B., Wiest, C., Pereira, J., Herz, D. M., Dold, M. R., Bange, M., Ciolac, D., Almeida, V., Neuber, J., Mirzac, D., Martín-Rodríguez, J. F., Dresel, C., Muthuraman, M., Adarmes Gomez, A. D., Navas, M., & Coenen, V. A. (2024). Perspectives of Implementation of Closed-Loop Deep Brain Stimulation: From Neurological to Psychiatric Disorders. *Stereotactic and Functional Neurosurgery*, *102*(1), 40–54. DOI: 10.1159/000535114

Haider, R., Megha, W. A., Juba, J. T., Alamgir, A., & Ahmad, L. (2025). The conversational revolution in health promotion: Investigating chatbot impact on healthcare marketing, patient engagement, and service reach. *International Journal of Science and Research Archive*, *15*(3), 1585–1592.

Halkiopoulos, C., Gkintoni, E., Aroutzidis, A., & Antonopoulou, H. (2025). Advances in Neuroimaging and Deep Learning for Emotion Detection: A Systematic Review of Cognitive Neuroscience and Algorithmic Innovations. *Diagnostics (Basel)*, *15*(4), 456. DOI: 10.3390/diagnostics15040456

Hamdoun, S., Monteleone, R., Bookman, T., & Michael, K. (2023). AI-Based and Digital Mental Health Apps: Balancing Need and Risk. *IEEE Technology and Society Magazine*, *42*(1), 25–36. DOI: 10.1109/MTS.2023.3241309

Higgins, O., & Wilson, R. L. (2025). Integrating Artificial Intelligence (<scp>AI</scp>) With Workforce Solutions for Sustainable Care: A Follow Up to Artificial Intelligence and Machine Learning (<scp>ML</scp>) Based Decision Support Systems in Mental Health. *International Journal of Mental Health Nursing*, *34*(2). Advance online publication. DOI: 10.1111/inm.70019

Hoose, S., & Králiková, K. (2024). Artificial Intelligence in Mental Health Care: Management Implications, Ethical Challenges, and Policy Considerations. *Administrative Sciences*, *14*(9), 227. DOI: 10.3390/admsci14090227

Hornstein, S., Forman-Hoffman, V., Nazander, A., Ranta, K., & Hilbert, K. (2021). Predicting therapy outcome in a digital mental health intervention for depression and anxiety: A machine learning approach. *Digital Health*, *7*. Advance online publication. DOI: 10.1177/20552076211060659

Horwitz, A. G., Mills, E. D., Sen, S., & Bohnert, A. S. B. (2024). Comparative Effectiveness of Three Digital Interventions for Adults Seeking Psychiatric Services. *JAMA Network Open*, *7*(7), e2422115. DOI: 10.1001/jamanetworkopen.2024.22115

Hosseini Tabaghdehi, S. A., & Ayaz, Ö. (2025). AI ethics in action: A circular model for transparency, accountability and inclusivity. *Journal of Managerial Psychology*. Advance online publication. DOI: 10.1108/JMP-03-2024-0177

Huang, J., Galal, G., Etemadi, M., & Vaidyanathan, M. (2022). Evaluation and Mitigation of Racial Bias in Clinical Machine Learning Models: Scoping Review. *JMIR Medical Informatics*, *10*(5), e36388. DOI: 10.2196/36388

Idowu, O. F., & Idowu, S. (2025). Artificial Intelligence Applications in Mental Health Crisis Prediction: Navigating Privacy, Consent, and Fairness in Clinical Decision-Making. *International Journal of Computer Applications Technology and Research*, *14*(08), 97–111. DOI: 10.7753/IJCATR1408.1009

Iniesta, R., Stahl, D., & McGuffin, P. (2016). Machine learning, statistical learning and the future of biological research in psychiatry. *Psychological Medicine*, *46*(12), 2455–2465. DOI: 10.1017/S0033291716001367

Insel, T., Cuthbert, B., Garvey, M., Heinssen, R., Pine, D. S., Quinn, K., Sanislow, C., & Wang, P. (2010). Research Domain Criteria (RDoC): Toward a New Classification Framework for Research on Mental Disorders. *The American Journal of Psychiatry*, *167*(7), 748–751. DOI: 10.1176/appi.ajp.2010.09091379

Jacobson, N. C., & Feng, B. (2022). Digital phenotyping of generalized anxiety disorder: Using artificial intelligence to accurately predict symptom severity using wearable sensors in daily life. *Translational Psychiatry*, *12*(1), 336. DOI: 10.1038/s41398-022-02038-1

Jain, D. (2023). Regulation of Digital Healthcare in India: Ethical and Legal Challenges. *Health Care*, *11*(6), 911. DOI: 10.3390/healthcare11060911

Jeyakumar, T., Younus, S., Zhang, M., Clare, M., Charow, R., Karsan, I., Dhalla, A., Al-Mouaswas, D., Scandiffio, J., Aling, J., Salhia, M., Lalani, N., Overholt, S., & Wiljer, D. (2023). Preparing for an Artificial Intelligence–Enabled Future: Patient Perspectives on Engagement and Health Care Professional Training for Adopting Artificial Intelligence Technologies in Health Care Settings. *JMIR AI*, *2*, e40973. DOI: 10.2196/40973

Joyce, D. W., Kormilitzin, A., Smith, K. A., & Cipriani, A. (2023). Explainable artificial intelligence for mental health through transparency and interpretability for understandability. *NPJ Digital Medicine*, *6*(1), 6. DOI: 10.1038/s41746-023-00751-9

Jungmann, S. M., Klan, T., Kuhn, S., & Jungmann, F. (2019). Accuracy of a Chatbot (Ada) in the Diagnosis of Mental Disorders: Comparative Case Study With Lay and Expert Users. *JMIR Formative Research, 3*(4), e13863. DOI: 10.2196/13863

Kam, H., & Jeong, H. (2020). Pharmacogenomic Biomarkers and Their Applications in Psychiatry. *Genes, 11*(12), 1445. DOI: 10.3390/genes11121445

Kamel Rahimi, A., Pienaar, O., Ghadimi, M., Canfell, O. J., Pole, J. D., Shrapnel, S., van der Vegt, A. H., & Sullivan, C. (2024). Implementing AI in Hospitals to Achieve a Learning Health System: Systematic Review of Current Enablers and Barriers. *Journal of Medical Internet Research, 26*, e49655. DOI: 10.2196/49655

Kamra, V., Kumar, P., & Mohammadian, M. (2020). Machine Learning Based Psychological Disease Support Model Assisting Psychoanalysts and Individuals in Clinical Decision Ministration. *International Journal of Computing and Digital Systems, 9*(4), 665–675. DOI: 10.12785/ijcds/090414

Kibria, M. G., Kucirka, L., & Mostafa, J. (2025). Assessing AI Explainability: A Usability Study Using a Novel Framework Involving Clinicians. *2025 IEEE 13th International Conference on Healthcare Informatics (ICHI)*, 553–564. https://doi .org/DOI: 10.1109/ICHI64645.2025.00069

Knowles, B., Richards, J. T., & Kroeger, F. (2022). *The Many Facets of Trust in AI: Formalizing the Relation Between Trust and Fairness*. Accountability, and Transparency.

Le, J. T., Mahoney, A. E. J., Court, J. L., & Shiner, C. T. (2025). Barriers and Facilitators of Digital Mental Health Use in Regional, Rural, and Remote Australia: A Comparison of Clinician and Consumer Perspectives. *The Australian Journal of Rural Health, 33*(2). Advance online publication. DOI: 10.1111/ajr.70011

Leaning, I. E., Ikani, N., Savage, H. S., Leow, A., Beckmann, C., Ruhé, H. G., & Marquand, A. F. (2024). From smartphone data to clinically relevant predictions: A systematic review of digital phenotyping methods in depression. *Neuroscience and Biobehavioral Reviews, 158*, 105541. DOI: 10.1016/j.neubiorev.2024.105541

Lekadir, K., Frangi, A. F., Porras, A. R., Glocker, B., Cintas, C., Langlotz, C. P., Weicken, E., Asselbergs, F. W., Prior, F., Collins, G. S., Kaissis, G., Tsakou, G., Buvat, I., Kalpathy-Cramer, J., Mongan, J., Schnabel, J. A., Kushibar, K., Riklund, K., Marias, K., & Starmans, M. P. A. (2025). FUTURE-AI: International consensus guideline for trustworthy and deployable artificial intelligence in healthcare. *BMJ (Clinical Research Ed.), 081554*. Advance online publication. DOI: 10.1136/bmj-2024-081554

Leo, A. J., Schuelke, M. J., Hunt, D. M., Metzler, J. P., Miller, J. P., Areán, P. A., Armbrecht, M. A., & Cheng, A. L. (2022). A Digital Mental Health Intervention in an Orthopedic Setting for Patients With Symptoms of Depression and/or Anxiety: Feasibility Prospective Cohort Study. *JMIR Formative Research*, *6*(2), e34889. DOI: 10.2196/34889

Lever, J., Barbarino, J. M., Gong, L., Huddart, R., Sangkuhl, K., Whaley, R., Whirl-Carrillo, M., Woon, M., Klein, T. E., & Altman, R. B. (2020). PGxMine: Text mining for curation of PharmGKB. *Pacific Symposium on Biocomputing. Pacific Symposium on Biocomputing*, *25*, 611–622.

Levkovich, I. (2025). Is Artificial Intelligence the Next Co-Pilot for Primary Care in Diagnosing and Recommending Treatments for Depression? *Medical Science*, *13*(1), 8. DOI: 10.3390/medsci13010008

Lin, E., Lin, C.-H., & Lane, H.-Y. (2021). Machine Learning and Deep Learning for the Pharmacogenomics of Antidepressant Treatments. *Clinical Psychopharmacology and Neuroscience : the Official Scientific Journal of the Korean College of Neuropsychopharmacology*, *19*(4), 577–588. DOI: 10.9758/cpn.2021.19.4.577

Lipschitz, J. M., Lin, S., Saghafian, S., Pike, C. K., & Burdick, K. E. (2025). Digital phenotyping in bipolar disorder: Using longitudinal Fitbit data and personalized machine learning to predict mood symptomatology. *Acta Psychiatrica Scandinavica*, *151*(3), 434–447. DOI: 10.1111/acps.13765

Liu, H., Peng, H., Song, X., Xu, C., & Zhang, M. (2022). Using AI chatbots to provide self-help depression interventions for university students: A randomized trial of effectiveness. *Internet Interventions : the Application of Information Technology in Mental and Behavioural Health*, *27*, 100495. DOI: 10.1016/j.invent.2022.100495

Lorenzoni, G., Tavares, C., Nascimento, N., Alencar, P., & Cowan, D. (2025). Assessing ML classification algorithms and NLP techniques for depression detection: An experimental case study. *PLoS One*, *20*(5), e0322299. DOI: 10.1371/journal.pone.0322299

Martinez-Martin, N., Greely, H. T., & Cho, M. K. (2021). Ethical Development of Digital Phenotyping Tools for Mental Health Applications: Delphi Study. *JMIR mHealth and uHealth*, *9*(7), e27343. DOI: 10.2196/27343

Mehltretter, J., Rollins, C., Benrimoh, D., Fratila, R., Perlman, K., Israel, S., Miresco, M., Wakid, M., & Turecki, G. (2020). Analysis of Features Selected by a Deep Learning Model for Differential Treatment Selection in Depression. *Frontiers in Artificial Intelligence*, *2*. Advance online publication. DOI: 10.3389/frai.2019.00031

Mendes, J. P. M., Moura, I. R., Van de Ven, P., Viana, D., Silva, F. J. S., Coutinho, L. R., Teixeira, S., Rodrigues, J. J. P. C., & Teles, A. S. (2022). Sensing Apps and Public Data Sets for Digital Phenotyping of Mental Health: Systematic Review. *Journal of Medical Internet Research, 24*(2), e28735. DOI: 10.2196/28735

Moriarty, A. S., Meader, N., Snell, K. I. E., Riley, R. D., Paton, L. W., Dawson, S., Hendon, J., Chew-Graham, C. A., Gilbody, S., Churchill, R., Phillips, R. S., Ali, S., & McMillan, D. (2022). Predicting relapse or recurrence of depression: Systematic review of prognostic models. *The British Journal of Psychiatry, 221*(2), 448–458. DOI: 10.1192/bjp.2021.218

Mullerpattan, G. S., Pearala, N., Shetty, T., Hegde, P. R., Patley, R., Manjunatha, N., Math, S. B., & Kumar, C. N. (2025). Trainers' Perspectives Towards Digital Mental Health Training for Primary Care Providers: Insights from Focused Group Discussion. *Indian Journal of Psychological Medicine*. Advance online publication. DOI: 10.1177/02537176251360938

Nemesure, M. D., Heinz, M. V., Huang, R., & Jacobson, N. C. (2021). Predictive modeling of depression and anxiety using electronic health records and a novel machine learning approach with artificial intelligence. *Scientific Reports, 11*(1), 1980. DOI: 10.1038/s41598-021-81368-4

Nickson, D., Meyer, C., Walasek, L., & Toro, C. (2023). Prediction and diagnosis of depression using machine learning with electronic health records data: A systematic review. *BMC Medical Informatics and Decision Making, 23*(1), 271. DOI: 10.1186/s12911-023-02341-x

Nicol, G., Wang, R., Graham, S., Dodd, S., & Garbutt, J. (2022). Chatbot-Delivered Cognitive Behavioral Therapy in Adolescents With Depression and Anxiety During the COVID-19 Pandemic: Feasibility and Acceptability Study. *JMIR Formative Research, 6*(11), e40242. DOI: 10.2196/40242

Okpete, U. E., & Byeon, H. (2024). Challenges and prospects in bridging precision medicine and artificial intelligence in genomic psychiatric treatment. *World Journal of Psychiatry, 14*(8), 1148–1164. DOI: 10.5498/wjp.v14.i8.1148

Onnela, J.-P., & Rauch, S. L. (2016). Harnessing Smartphone-Based Digital Phenotyping to Enhance Behavioral and Mental Health. *Neuropsychopharmacology : Official Publication of the American College of Neuropsychopharmacology, 41*(7), 1691–1696. DOI: 10.1038/npp.2016.7

Pandi, M.-T., Koromina, M., Tsafaridis, I., Patsilinakos, S., Christoforou, E., van der Spek, P. J., & Patrinos, G. P. (2021). A novel machine learning-based approach for the computational functional assessment of pharmacogenomic variants. *Human Genomics*, *15*(1), 51. DOI: 10.1186/s40246-021-00352-1

Pardiñas, A. F., Owen, M. J., & Walters, J. T. R. (2021). Pharmacogenomics: A road ahead for precision medicine in psychiatry. *Neuron*, *109*(24), 3914–3929. DOI: 10.1016/j.neuron.2021.09.011

Parra, F., Benezeth, Y., & Yang, F. (2022). Automatic Assessment of Emotion Dysregulation in American, French, and Tunisian Adults and New Developments in Deep Multimodal Fusion: Cross-sectional Study. *JMIR Mental Health*, *9*(1), e34333. DOI: 10.2196/34333

Pavlopoulos, A., Rachiotis, T., & Maglogiannis, I. (2024). An Overview of Tools and Technologies for Anxiety and Depression Management Using AI. *Applied Sciences (Basel, Switzerland)*, *14*(19), 9068. DOI: 10.3390/app14199068

Pearson, R., Pisner, D., Meyer, B., Shumake, J., & Beevers, C. G. (2019). A machine learning ensemble to predict treatment outcomes following an Internet intervention for depression. *Psychological Medicine*, *49*(14), 2330–2341. DOI: 10.1017/S003329171800315X

Perlis, R. H. (2016). Abandoning personalization to get to precision in the pharmacotherapy of depression. *World Psychiatry; Official Journal of the World Psychiatric Association (WPA)*, *15*(3), 228–235. DOI: 10.1002/wps.20345

Perlis, R. H., Goldberg, J. F., Ostacher, M. J., & Schneck, C. D. (2024). Clinical decision support for bipolar depression using large language models. *Neuropsychopharmacology : Official Publication of the American College of Neuropsychopharmacology*, *49*(9), 1412–1416. DOI: 10.1038/s41386-024-01841-2

Perlis, R. H., Verhaak, P. F., Goldberg, J., Cusin, C., Ostacher, M., Malhi, G. S., Zarate, C. A., Shelton, R. C., Iosifescu, D. V., Tohen, M., Jha, M. K., Sajatovic, M., & Berk, M. (2025). Clinical decision support for pharmacologic management of treatment-resistant depression with augmented large language models. *Journal of Mood and Anxiety Disorders*, *12*, 100142. DOI: 10.1016/j.xjmad.2025.100142

Pesapane, F., Bracchi, D. A., Mulligan, J. F., Linnikov, A., Maslennikov, O., Lanzavecchia, M. B., Tantrige, P., Stasolla, A., Biondetti, P., Giuggioli, P. F., Cassano, E., & Carrafiello, G. (2021). Legal and Regulatory Framework for AI Solutions in Healthcare in EU, US, China, and Russia: New Scenarios after a Pandemic. *Radiation*, *1*(4), 261–276. DOI: 10.3390/radiation1040022

Piette, J. D., Newman, S., Krein, S. L., Marinec, N., Chen, J., Williams, D. A., Edmond, S. N., Driscoll, M., LaChappelle, K. M., Kerns, R. D., Maly, M., Kim, H. M., Farris, K. B., Higgins, D. M., Buta, E., & Heapy, A. A. (2022). Patient-Centered Pain Care Using Artificial Intelligence and Mobile Health Tools. *JAMA Internal Medicine*, *182*(9), 975. DOI: 10.1001/jamainternmed.2022.3178

Putica, A., Khanna, R., Bosl, W., Saraf, S., & Edgcomb, J. (2025). Ethical decision-making for AI in mental health: The Integrated Ethical Approach for Computational Psychiatry (IEACP) framework. *Psychological Medicine*, *55*, e213. DOI: 10.1017/S0033291725101311

Radanliev, P. (2025). Ethical methodologies for digital identity privacy in AI-driven dance movement therapy as a preventative mental health mechanism in the extended reality. *Frontiers in Virtual Reality*, *6*. Advance online publication. DOI: 10.3389/frvir.2025.1589744

Rector, A., Minor, K., Minor, K., McCormack, J., Breeden, B., Nowers, R., & Dorris, J. (2025). *Validating Pharmacogenomics Generative Artificial Intelligence Query Prompts Using Retrieval-Augmented Generation*. RAG.

Regier, D. A., Narrow, W. E., Clarke, D. E., Kraemer, H. C., Kuramoto, S. J., Kuhl, E. A., & Kupfer, D. J. (2013). DSM-5 Field Trials in the United States and Canada, Part II: Test-Retest Reliability of Selected Categorical Diagnoses. *The American Journal of Psychiatry*, *170*(1), 59–70. DOI: 10.1176/appi.ajp.2012.12070999

Rogan, J., Bucci, S., & Firth, J. (2024). Health Care Professionals' Views on the Use of Passive Sensing, AI, and Machine Learning in Mental Health Care: Systematic Review With Meta-Synthesis. *JMIR Mental Health*, *11*, e49577. DOI: 10.2196/49577

Rush, A. J., Trivedi, M. H., Wisniewski, S. R., Nierenberg, A. A., Stewart, J. W., Warden, D., Niederehe, G., Thase, M. E., Lavori, P. W., Lebowitz, B. D., McGrath, P. J., Rosenbaum, J. F., Sackeim, H. A., Kupfer, D. J., Luther, J., & Fava, M. (2006). Acute and Longer-Term Outcomes in Depressed Outpatients Requiring One or Several Treatment Steps: A STAR*D Report. *The American Journal of Psychiatry*, *163*(11), 1905–1917. DOI: 10.1176/ajp.2006.163.11.1905

Saeidnia, H. R., Hashemi Fotami, S. G., Lund, B., & Ghiasi, N. (2024). Ethical Considerations in Artificial Intelligence Interventions for Mental Health and Well-Being: Ensuring Responsible Implementation and Impact. *Social Sciences*, *13*(7), 381.

Sentinella-Jerbić, F. (2024). *EXPLAINABILITY OF MACHINE LEARNING MODELS IN PREDICTION OF AFFECTIVEDISORDERS* (Doctoral dissertation, Fakultet elektrotehnike i računarstva). https://repozitorij.fer.unizg.hr/en/islandora/object/fer%3A12717/datastream/PDF/view

Sharew, N. T., Clark, S. R., Schubert, K. O., & Amare, A. T. (2024). Pharmacogenomic scores in psychiatry: Systematic review of current evidence. *Translational Psychiatry*, *14*(1), 322. DOI: 10.1038/s41398-024-02998-6

Sharma, A., Lin, I. W., Miner, A. S., Atkins, D. C., & Althoff, T. (2023). Human–AI collaboration enables more empathic conversations in text-based peer-to-peer mental health support. *Nature Machine Intelligence*, *5*(1), 46–57. DOI: 10.1038/s42256-022-00593-2

Sharma, A., & Verbeke, W. J. M. I. (2020). Improving Diagnosis of Depression With XGBOOST Machine Learning Model and a Large Biomarkers Dutch Dataset (n = 11,081). *Frontiers in Big Data*, *3*. Advance online publication. DOI: 10.3389/fdata.2020.00015

Sharma, A., & Verbeke, W. J. M. I. (2021). Understanding importance of clinical biomarkers for diagnosis of anxiety disorders using machine learning models. *PLoS One*, *16*(5), e0251365. DOI: 10.1371/journal.pone.0251365

Sheth, S. A., Bijanki, K. R., Metzger, B., Allawala, A., Pirtle, V., Adkinson, J. A., Myers, J., Mathura, R. K., Oswalt, D., Tsolaki, E., Xiao, J., Noecker, A., Strutt, A. M., Cohn, J. F., McIntyre, C. C., Mathew, S. J., Borton, D., Goodman, W., & Pouratian, N. (2022). Deep Brain Stimulation for Depression Informed by Intracranial Recordings. *Biological Psychiatry*, *92*(3), 246–251. DOI: 10.1016/j.biopsych.2021.11.007

Singhal, A., Neveditsin, N., Tanveer, H., & Mago, V. (2024). Toward Fairness, Accountability, Transparency, and Ethics in AI for Social Media and Health Care: Scoping Review. *JMIR Medical Informatics*, *12*, e50048. DOI: 10.2196/50048

Solaiman, B., Malik, A., & Ghuloum, S. (2023). Monitoring Mental Health: Legal and Ethical Considerations of Using Artificial Intelligence in Psychiatric Wards. *American Journal of Law & Medicine*, *49*(2–3), 250–266. DOI: 10.1017/amj.2023.30

Squarcina, L., Villa, F. M., Nobile, M., Grisan, E., & Brambilla, P. (2021). Deep learning for the prediction of treatment response in depression. *Journal of Affective Disorders*, *281*, 618–622. DOI: 10.1016/j.jad.2020.11.104

Squires, M., Tao, X., Elangovan, S., Gururajan, R., Zhou, X., Li, Y., & Acharya, U. R. (2023). Identifying predictive biomarkers for repetitive transcranial magnetic stimulation response in depression patients with explainability. *Computer Methods and Programs in Biomedicine*, *242*, 107771. DOI: 10.1016/j.cmpb.2023.107771

Talati, D. V. (2025). Machine Learning for Personalized Brain Stimulation: AI-Optimized Neuromodulation Treatments. *International Journal of Science and Research Archive*, *14*(3), 331–338. DOI: 10.30574/ijsra.2025.14.3.0607

Tanguay-Sela, M., Benrimoh, D., Popescu, C., Perez, T., Rollins, C., Snook, E., Lundrigan, E., Armstrong, C., Perlman, K., Fratila, R., Mehltretter, J., Israel, S., Champagne, M., Williams, J., Simard, J., Parikh, S. V., Karp, J. F., Heller, K., Linnaranta, O., & Margolese, H. (2021). *Evaluating the Perceived Utility of an Artificial Intelligence-Powered Clinical Decision Support System for Depression Treatment Using a Simulation Centre*. https://doi.org/DOI: 10.1101/2021.04.21.21255899

Thenral, M., & Annamalai, A. (2020). Telepsychiatry and the Role of Artificial Intelligence in Mental Health in Post-COVID-19 India: A Scoping Review on Opportunities. *Indian Journal of Psychological Medicine*, *42*(5), 428–434. DOI: 10.1177/0253717620952160

Timmons, A. C., Duong, J. B., Simo Fiallo, N., Lee, T., Vo, H. P. Q., Ahle, M. W., Comer, J. S., Brewer, L. C., Frazier, S. L., & Chaspari, T. (2023). A Call to Action on Assessing and Mitigating Bias in Artificial Intelligence Applications for Mental Health. *Perspectives on Psychological Science*, *18*(5), 1062–1096.

Tong, J., Xu, D. J., Yan, A., & Li, Z. (2024). Leveraging Artificial Intelligence to Address the Paradox of Judgment and Accountability in Depression Treatment.

Uban, A. S., Chulvi, B., & Rosso, P. (2021). *On the Explainability of Automatic Predictions of Mental Disorders from Social Media Data.*, DOI: 10.1007/978-3-030-80599-9_27

Verma, M., Chanthar, K. M., & Beg, M. J. (2025). Ethical Considerations Surrounding the Use of AI-Interventions in Application of Mental Healthcare. In Uludag, K., & Ahmad, N. (Eds.), *Chatbots and Mental Healthcare in Psychology and Psychiatry* (pp. 193–222). IGI Global Scientific Publishing.,

Wallert, J., Boberg, J., Kaldo, V., Mataix-Cols, D., Flygare, O., Crowley, J. J., Halvorsen, M., Ben Abdesslem, F., Boman, M., Andersson, E., Hentati Isacsson, N., Ivanova, E., & Rück, C. (2022). Predicting remission after internet-delivered psychotherapy in patients with depression using machine learning and multi-modal data. *Translational Psychiatry*, *12*(1), 357. DOI: 10.1038/s41398-022-02133-3

Walsh, C. G., Chaudhry, B., Dua, P., Goodman, K. W., Kaplan, B., Kavuluru, R., Solomonides, A., & Subbian, V. (2020). Stigma, biomarkers, and algorithmic bias: Recommendations for precision behavioral health with artificial intelligence. *JAMIA Open*, *3*(1), 9–15. DOI: 10.1093/jamiaopen/ooz054

Wang, A., & Sun, J. (2025). Personalized EEG-guided brain stimulation targeting in major depression via network controllability and multi-objective optimization. *BMC Psychiatry*, *25*(1), 723. DOI: 10.1186/s12888-025-07171-x

Wang, Z., Meng, Z., & Chen, C. (2022). Screening of potential biomarkers in peripheral blood of patients with depression based on weighted gene co-expression network analysis and machine learning algorithms. *Frontiers in Psychiatry, 13*. Advance online publication. DOI: 10.3389/fpsyt.2022.1009911

Welch, V., Wy, T. J., Ligezka, A., Hassett, L. C., Croarkin, P. E., Athreya, A. P., & Romanowicz, M. (2022). Use of mobile and wearable artificial intelligence in child and adolescent psychiatry: Scoping review. *Journal of Medical Internet Research, 24*(3), e33560.

Widge, A. S. (2023). Closed-Loop Deep Brain Stimulation for Psychiatric Disorders. *Harvard Review of Psychiatry, 31*(3), 162–171. DOI: 10.1097/HRP.0000000000000367

Wies, B., Landers, C., & Ienca, M. (2021). Digital Mental Health for Young People: A Scoping Review of Ethical Promises and Challenges. *Frontiers in Digital Health, 3*. Advance online publication. DOI: 10.3389/fdgth.2021.697072

Winter, N. R., Blanke, J., Leenings, R., Ernsting, J., Fisch, L., Sarink, K., Barkhau, C., Emden, D., Thiel, K., Flinkenflügel, K., Winter, A., Goltermann, J., Meinert, S., Dohm, K., Repple, J., Gruber, M., Leehr, E. J., Opel, N., Grotegerd, D., & Hahn, T. (2024). A Systematic Evaluation of Machine Learning–Based Biomarkers for Major Depressive Disorder. *JAMA Psychiatry, 81*(4), 386.

World Health Organization. (2019). WHO guideline: recommendations on digital interventions for health system strengthening.

Wu, S., Ell, K., Jin, H., Vidyanti, I., Chou, C.-P., Lee, P.-J., Gross-Schulman, S., Sklaroff, L. M., Belson, D., Nezu, A. M., Hay, J., Wang, C.-J., Scheib, G., Di Capua, P., Hawkins, C., Liu, P., Ramirez, M., Wu, B. W., Richman, M., & Guterman, J. (2018). Comparative Effectiveness of a Technology-Facilitated Depression Care Management Model in Safety-Net Primary Care Patients With Type 2 Diabetes: 6-Month Outcomes of a Large Clinical Trial. *Journal of Medical Internet Research, 20*(4), e147. DOI: 10.2196/jmir.7692

Zhong, R., Wu, X., Chen, J., & Fang, Y. (2025). Using Digital Phenotyping to Discriminate Unipolar Depression and Bipolar Disorder: Systematic Review. *Journal of Medical Internet Research, 27*, e72229.

Zlatintsi, A., Filntisis, P. P., Garoufis, C., Efthymiou, N., Maragos, P., Menychtas, A., Maglogiannis, I., Tsanakas, P., Sounapoglou, T., Kalisperakis, E., Karantinos, T., Lazaridi, M., Garyfalli, V., Mantas, A., Mantonakis, L., & Smyrnis, N. (2022). E-Prevention: Advanced Support System for Monitoring and Relapse Prevention in Patients with Psychotic Disorders Analyzing Long-Term Multimodal Data from Wearables and Video Captures. *Sensors (Basel)*, *22*(19), 7544.

Zogan, H., Razzak, I., Wang, X., Jameel, S., & Xu, G. (2022). Explainable depression detection with multi-aspect features using a hybrid deep learning model on social media. *World Wide Web (Bussum)*, *25*(1), 281–304.

Chapter 5

Advanced Technologies in Substance Use Disorders (SUDs):

Artificial Intelligence (AI) and Machine Learning (ML)

Aslı Dila Akiş
https://orcid.org/0000-0002-2827-8106
Halic University, Turkey

ABSTRACT

Substance use disorders (SUDs) pose a significant challenge in healthcare, marked by the compulsive use of substances despite negative consequences. Traditional methods of treatment and diagnosis, while somewhat effective, have limitations such as high costs, lengthy processes, and vulnerability to human error. This book chapter explores how integrating machine learning (ML) and artificial intelligence (AI) can address these issues and examines the transformative potential of advanced technologies in improving understanding, treatment, and prevention of SUDs and behavioral addictions. The chapter reviews recent research and developments, highlighting how these technologies enhance diagnosis, treatment prediction, outcomes, and risk assessment in SUDs. It merges insights from current studies with innovative AI tools like digital phenotyping, predictive modeling, and mobile health applications to demonstrate how AI can greatly improve outcomes for individuals with SUDs.

DOI: 10.4018/979-8-3373-1325-2.ch005

1. INTRODUCTION

Substance use disorder (SUD) is a complex, chronic brain disorder that is characterized by compulsive drug-seeking behaviors despite adverse consequences to one's health and social relations. Like other chronic diseases such as diabetes or heart disease, drug addiction can be managed but presents unique challenges due to its psychological and neurobiological challenges (Ceceli et al., 2022; Heilig et al., 2021). Environmental and social factors highly influence the recovery process for individuals suffering from SUD. Research emphasizes the need for individuals to protect themselves from the environmental triggers that promote addictive behaviors. Establishing a new, supportive environment is essential for effective rehabilitation (Vafaie & Kober, 2022; Venniro et al., 2020). Traditional clinical assessment of SUD often relies on observations and psychometric tools, which can lack scalability and accuracy, resulting in costly and time-consuming procedures. Additionally, stigma and financial barriers may limit access to necessary medical services for many individuals struggling with addiction.

Recent advances in Artificial intelligence (AI) and Machine learning (ML) technologies have demonstrated potential in transforming the diagnosis, treatment prediction, and outcome/risk assessment of drug addiction. AI technologies can improve the accuracy of clinical assessments, personalize treatment plans by analyzing extensive patient data, and detect early signs of relapse or ongoing abuse (Quintanilla et al., 2023). AI's capabilities extend to monitoring patient behaviors and predicting those at higher risk of developing addiction, providing a proactive approach to treatment. AI offers an opportunity to overcome these limitations by enabling data-driven insights and personalized interventions that account for the heterogeneity of addiction (Suva & Bhatia, 2024). AI tools such as ML, natural language processing (NLP), and deep learning have shown promise in areas such as pattern recognition, behavioral prediction, and intervention planning (Hassan et al., 2024). Persistent drug use causes significant neurobiological changes in brain areas involved in reward, learning, memory, and cognitive control. AI may leverage these adaptations, especially the changes in synaptic plasticity and kinase signaling pathways, to modulate the cortico-limbic mechanisms that influence reward and aversion, potentially reducing severe psychotic states (Afshar et al., 2022; Ezell et al., 2024).

One of the most innovative applications of AI in addiction psychiatry is digital phenotyping, which involves analyzing behavioral and psychological data from digital sources. Curtis et al. (2023) demonstrated the effectiveness of AI-driven digital phenotyping using social media language to predict treatment dropout at 90 days. By utilizing tools like Bidirectional Encoder Representations from Transformers (BERT), digital phenotyping provides a dynamic, real-time evaluation of addiction risk. This approach overcomes the limitations of traditional psychometric tools by providing ecological and contextual insights into patients' behaviors. For instance, the ability to capture emotional, cognitive, and behavioral patterns through AI-enhanced natural language processing allows clinicians to develop personalized interventions adapted to each patient's needs.

Moreover, ML models are increasingly used to predict drug addiction outcomes such as relapse rates and long-term abstinence (remission). These data-driven tools adapt to individual patient data, offering personalized predictions that can effectively guide treatment decisions (Chekroud et al., 2021; Khera et al., 2021). The high dropout rate in addiction treatment programs highlights the need for tools that can predict treatment responses and relapse risk (Xu et al., 2025). Quantitative methods and ML tools are key to developing personalized treatment plans that could potentially reduce dropout rates and improve recovery outcomes (Lappan et al., 2020). Emerging tools like SIMRI, POD, and neural networks have gained attention by demonstrating strong correlations between neural data and drug-likeness models. These methods help predict drug reactions and the likelihood of adverse effects, such as psychosis-like experiences, during preclinical phases, thereby reducing potential suffering for individuals (Beker et al., 2020; Staszak et al., 2022).

Mobile health (mHealth) applications are another transformative AI application in addiction management. Islam et al. (2023) developed a smartphone app to assess Opioid Use Disorder (OUD) risk using synthetic data and a naive Bayes algorithm. This tool demonstrated the feasibility of AI-enabled mHealth interventions, providing personalized risk stratification and educational resources. Such tools expand access to care, especially for underserved populations, by leveraging the accessibility and scalability of smartphones. Additionally, these apps can incorporate gamified elements and cognitive-behavioral therapy modules, increasing patient engagement and adherence to treatment protocols. Symons et al. (2019) conducted a comparative study between ML models and addiction therapists in predicting treatment outcomes following 12 weeks of cognitive-behavioral therapy (CBT) for alcohol use disorder. The findings indicated no significant difference in the accuracy of predictions made by ML models versus human professionals. This study suggests that while ML models show promise, they are currently comparable to traditional methods rather than superior.

Predictive modeling powered by ML algorithms enables the identification of high-risk individuals and personalized treatment plans. For example, Suva and Bhatia (2024) highlighted the usefulness of AI in predicting relapse risk and customizing interventions based on behavioral and psychological profiles (Xu et al., 2025). These models allow for early detection of addiction in vulnerable populations, facilitating preventive measures and timely intervention. Additionally, AI-driven predictive analytics can incorporate environmental triggers and social determinants of health to improve risk assessments, paving the way for integrative approaches.

Furthermore, programs like Sobergrid utilize real-time geolocation data to provide contextual support, reducing the likelihood of relapse. Menon et al. (2019) explored the use of a convolutional neural network (CNN) to detect drunk drivers through facial capture in the thermal energy spectrum, achieving an impressive 87% accuracy. This demonstrates ML's ability to enhance detection and prevention efforts in real-time scenarios, potentially decreasing drunk driving incidents. Jing et al. (2020) developed a ML model with the random forest (RF) algorithm to predict future substance use in children based on lifestyle variables. The model showed accuracies of 74% at age 10 and 86% at age 22. This study highlights the potential of ML models in early intervention by identifying at-risk individuals from a young age.

AI's ability to analyze large datasets and identify patterns offers significant potential in addiction risk assessment. By integrating demographic, behavioral, and psychological data, AI can accurately predict addiction vulnerability. For example, ML algorithms like random forests have achieved prediction accuracies exceeding 80% in identifying individuals at risk of substance use (Islam et al., 2023; Rabinowitz et al., 2025). Traditional treatment methods often adopt a one-size-fits-all approach, neglecting individual differences in addiction trajectories. AI, however, enables personalized treatment plans based on a patient's unique profile, incorporating factors such as genetic predispositions, social environment, and psychological comorbidities. This approach improves engagement and enhances long-term outcomes (Hong et al., 2024). Dou et al. (2021) used ML combined with language processing techniques to identify substance use among homeless children through their social media posts. The model shows moderate accuracy and demonstrates social media's potential as a tool for ML applications in public health monitoring.

Preventing relapse remains a key challenge in addiction rehabilitation. AI-driven tools, such as relapse prediction models and geolocation-based trigger detection, offer proactive solutions for monitoring and managing high-risk situations. By identifying probable triggers and at-risk periods, AI can alert patients and healthcare providers, enabling early interventions and reducing relapse likelihood. Wearable devices equipped with AI sensors can monitor physiological signals like heart rate variability, detecting stress responses that may indicate a potential relapse. These applications exhibit AI's capacity to transform addiction treatment through its support of continuous, adaptable treatment strategies. Ebrahimi et al. (2021) employed a four-layer, fully connected deep neural network (DNN) to classify normal, risky, and harmful drinkers based on electronic health data. The model accurately identified 96%, 82%, and 89% of individuals, respectively. This level of accuracy helps tailor individualized treatment strategies and improves management of alcohol use disorders. Curtis et al. (2023) used Bidirectional Encoder Representations from

Transformers (BERT) to predict treatment outcomes and dropout risk at 90 days, based on language data from social media posts. This research highlights significant progress in using ML to forecast treatment adherence, which is important for improving SUD treatment techniques.

To sum up, AI and ML in SUD treatment provide opportunities for more advanced, precise, and individualized approaches. These technologies will improve diagnosis and prognosis, leading to better treatment and targeting. AI and ML have the potential to improve addiction treatment; however, they serve as supplementary tools. Despite progress, AI in addiction therapy faces challenges such as data privacy, security, and the need for strong encryption to protect sensitive personal information. It is crucial to carefully examine AI model biases to prevent skewed risk assessments that unfairly impact underrepresented populations. Transparent, fair, and inclusive methods are crucial for maximizing AI's potential. For best results, AI-driven insights should be complemented by clinical expertise. Collaboration across disciplines—between data scientists, healthcare providers, and policymakers—can enhance AI implementation. Future AI applications can help tackle global addiction issues through their scalability, as AI-enabled telemedicine expands access to effective treatments, particularly in areas with limited healthcare infrastructure. Incorporating AI and ML into community programs could increase addiction service participation and sustainability. The role of AI and ML in addiction treatment is transformative, extending beyond clinical care to include risk assessment and strategic planning. These advanced tools can improve outcomes, reduce stigma, and enhance the quality of life for individuals and communities affected by addiction. This promising field will revolutionize addiction treatment by increasing accessibility, efficiency, and effectiveness.

This chapter provides an analysis of current and future uses of advanced technologies in addiction, bridging traditional methods with modern technological approaches in the treatment and diagnosis of SUDs. By offering a detailed review of the present landscape and potential of ML and AI in this area, the chapter aims to serve as a valuable resource for healthcare professionals, addiction specialists, clinicians, researchers, and policymakers, highlighting the significant benefits of adopting AI and ML technologies. It emphasizes how these technologies can lead to more effective and efficient healthcare solutions, ultimately improving patient outcomes and lowering healthcare costs. The chapter will rely on a comprehensive review of recent studies demonstrating the application and effectiveness of ML and AI in treating and diagnosing SUDs.

2. THE POTENTIAL OF ARTIFICIAL INTELLIGENCE FOR SUBSTANCE USE DISORDERS

SUDs affect individuals, families, and communities worldwide, regardless of socioeconomic or cultural backgrounds. Besides personal health, SUDs have economic, law enforcement, workforce productivity, and family and community consequences. WHO estimations and national health agency studies show that SUDs significantly impact worldwide disease burden (WHO, 2018; Degenhardt & Hall, 2012). They substantially raise the risk of overdose deaths, road accidents, chronic illnesses, mental health comorbidities including depression and anxiety, and infectious diseases like HIV and hepatitis (Degenhardt & Hall, 2012). SUDs, characterized by compulsive substance-seeking and impaired control, often co-occur with depression, anxiety, and trauma-related disorders (Hasan et al., 2025; Fontenelle et al., 2011). Early substance use, especially before age 20, is linked to long-term cognitive and behavioral impairments, including memory loss (Livingston et al., 2023). SUDs develop and persist due to social and environmental factors. Studies show that social networks, peer relationships, family dynamics, and neighborhood environments shape substance use patterns and recovery. Individuals in economically disadvantaged neighborhoods who face drug offers and high substance availability are at greater risk (Eddie et al., 2024).

Individuals with SUDs are also at higher risk of suicide. A comprehensive study by Leza et al. (2024) found that 20% to 62.2% of SUD patients had suicidal ideation, whereas 15.8% to 52.1% of treatment patients attempted suicide. ML can identify patterns related to substance use, addiction, and recovery. Another important study by Morel et al. (2020), involving 65,426 patients and 97,688 readmissions to the hospital, showed that mental disorders accounted for 66% and were associated with a 13.2% readmission rate. In contrast, substance use disorders accounted for 34% of cases but were linked to a significantly higher readmission rate of 22.3%, emphasizing the complexity and chronicity of SUDs and the urgent need for predictive, data-driven methods in clinical care.

Traditional epidemiological and clinical approaches have identified early exposure, peer influence, socioeconomic difficulties, and genetics as key determinants in substance addiction, but they usually fail to predict individual trajectories or help early intervention. SUDs are an important public health issue that increases death, recurrence rates, and hospitalizations, resulting in massive social and economic costs (Degenhardt & Hall, 2012; McLellan et al., 2000)The growing understanding of SUDs as chronic, complex brain illnesses demands more accurate, accessible, and affordable approaches to treatment adjusted to each patient's needs. ML developments in AI have shaped how researchers and medical professionals understand, predict, and treat SUDs. In complex, high-dimensional data, ML algorithms can identify patterns that traditional methods cannot. These technologies are used to predict adolescent smoking initiation, evaluate treatment dropout risk, and tailor mental health interventions (Tassinari et al., 2025).

3. LIMITATIONS OF TRADITIONAL ASSESSMENT AND TREATMENT METHODS

The accuracy, accessibility, and personalization of traditional methods for diagnosing and treating SUDs appear to be limited, regardless of improvements in clinical and public health approaches. These traditional methods are time-consuming, subjective, and susceptible to recall and social desirability bias. They often depend significantly on self-report measures, clinician-administered interviews, and paper-based psychometric instruments (Giorgi & Curtis, 2024; Ceceli et al., 2022). Underdiagnosis and inaccurate diagnosis of SUDs in real-world clinical settings are significant issues. Hoggatt et al. (2025), for example, reported that traditional diagnosis-based performance indicators usually underestimate the precise prevalence of SUD. In comparison with documented diagnoses alone, their study found that ML models trained on structured electronic health record (EHR) data more than doubled diagnostic sensitivity. This gap highlights "blind spots" in traditional assessments and emphasizes the need for more comprehensive, data-driven screening methods. Additionally, standard tools can face scaling challenges, especially in settings where access to trained addiction specialists or mental health professionals is limited. Treatment engagement remains low due to long wait times, insufficient coverage, and the stigma associated with seeking help (Salyers et al., 2025). Access to specialized care is particularly difficult for disadvantaged and rural populations, leading to regional disparities in diagnostic and treatment outcomes (Eddie et al., 2024).

Another major obstacle is personalizing treatment. Traditional approaches usually follow a "one-size-fits-all" model, ignoring individual differences in comorbidities, treatment responses, environmental exposures, and drug use histories. This lack of personalization leads to high dropout rates and poor adherence to treatment. For example, many patients relapse due to unmet personal needs or a poor fit with the treatment, and dropout rates in SUD interventions can exceed 50% (Lappan et al., 2020; Acion et al., 2017). Furthermore, current techniques do not effectively support dynamic, real-time monitoring of relapse risk or patient engagement. This is especially problematic during the early recovery phases when individuals are most vulnerable to relapse. Traditional systems are often reactive rather than preventative when they lack adaptive interventions and continuous tracking (Afshar et al., 2022; Dou et al., 2021).

In conclusion, while traditional methods of assessment and treatment provide essential tools for managing SUDs, they are increasingly inadequate for addressing the complexity of modern addiction treatment. To enable scalable, timely, and personalized approaches, these limitations must be addressed through the integration of modern technologies, particularly AI and ML

4. THE EMERGENCE OF ARTIFICIAL INTELLIGENCE IN THE FIELD OF ADDICTION SCIENCE

AI, especially its branch called ML has been a significant advancement in mental health care, offering powerful tools to overcome the challenges that remain with traditional SUD assessment and treatment. By utilizing large, diverse datasets—from electronic health records and neuroimaging to social media posts and wearable sensor data—AI allows for real-time, scalable, and personalized interventions (Tassinari et al., 2025; Jayatilake & Ganegoda, 2021). AI proves effective in identifying complicated, nonlinear relationships between risk factors, behaviors, and treatment outcomes that human clinicians often fail to detect. For example, research using ML algorithms like Random Forests (RF), Support Vector Machines (SVM), and Extreme Gradient Boosting (XGBoost) has demonstrated high predictive accuracy in assessing addiction severity, estimating relapse risk, and identifying individuals at risk of dropping out of treatment (Hasan et al., 2025; Morel et al., 2020; Acion et al., 2017).

AI is used in addiction science for a variety of specific purposes, such as diagnosis and early detection, customizing treatment, predicting outcomes, and digital and mobile interventions. AI models have shown success in identifying undiagnosed cases of SUD by analyzing behavioral, physiological, and psychosocial indicators. Kim et al. (2025) developed a generalizable ML model to predict adolescent substance use in Korea, the U.S., and Norway, with an accuracy rate over 76%. This highlights the effectiveness of cross-cultural digital tools in global prevention efforts. AI also helps in developing personalized treatment plans by integrating diverse patient data, such as psychiatric comorbidities, genetic predispositions, and socioeconomic factors affecting health. Tools like SHAP (SHapley Additive exPlanations) enable researchers and clinicians to interpret ML models, helping identify the most influential predictors of substance use, such as depression and GPA in youth populations (Hasan et al., 2025).

Digital phenotyping and advanced deep learning algorithms, such as BERT (Bidirectional Encoder Representations from Transformers), have been used to predict relapse, abstinence, and dropout rates by analyzing patients' social media interactions and linguistic characteristics (Curtis et al., 2023; Giorgi & Curtis,

2024). These methods greatly exceed traditional self-report measures in anticipating treatment outcomes.To improve access and engagement, especially among vulnerable populations, AI-powered chatbots and mobile health (mHealth) apps are being increasingly utilized. These tools can provide real-time education, behavioral nudges, and symptom tracking. For instance, the Be Well Buddy system displayed a 32% SUD screening rate, which is significantly higher than conventional programs (Salyers et al., 2025).

The emergence of AI in addiction treatment improves clinical accuracy and supports public health programs by enabling scalable monitoring, stigma analysis, and digital outreach. Roesler et al. (2024) used NLP techniques to identify internalized and predicted stigma in over 160,000 Reddit posts, offering valuable insights for creating stigma-sensitive interventions. However, integrating AI into addiction research requires a cautious approach. Concerns about data quality, algorithmic bias, and transparency remain key issues. Nonetheless, when guided by ethical principles and clinical expertise, AI technologies hold great potential to revolutionize the diagnosis, treatment, and understanding of SUDs at both individual and community levels (Ezell et al., 2024; Tassinari et al., 2025).

5. MACHINE LEARNING TECHNIQUES USED IN SUBSTANCE USE DISORDERS RESEARCH

ML includes a wide range of algorithmic techniques used to identify patterns from data and support predictions or classifications. In SUD research, these algorithms play a crucial role in modeling individual risk, identifying underdiagnosed cases, predicting treatment compliance, and analyzing outcomes across different populations (Mattos et al., 2024). ML models exhibit significant potential for improving prediction accuracy and clinical decision-making in SUD treatment; however, notable shortcomings remain in methodological consistency, transparency, and external validation. SUDs are chronic conditions associated with a range of adverse outcomes (National Institute on Drug Abuse [NIDA], 2023), presenting significant mental health challenges and frequently requiring both inpatient and outpatient interventions (Levola et al., 2021; Norman et al., 2007; Brackett et al., 2022). Their consequences include increased mortality rates (Decker et al., 2017; Hjemsaeter et al., 2019), high relapse rates, and frequent hospitalizations (McLellan et al., 2000; NIDA, 2023). ML, a core subfield of AI, has revolutionized data-intensive areas, including psychiatry (Jayatilake & Ganegoda, 2021). In this field, ML is applied in supervised learning (such as SUD classification), unsupervised learning (like pattern detection), semi-supervised learning, and reinforcement learning. Common algorithms include decision trees, neural networks, and ensemble methods like random forests (Rabinowitz et al., 2025). Regarding SUD, ML is increasingly employed to improve both prediction and treatment management (Yang et al., 2023b; Heberle et al., 2024), with research demonstrating its effectiveness in analyzing large datasets (Chhetri et al., 2023; Garbin et al., 2023; Mak et al., 2019). Its predictive capabilities are vital for anticipating high-risk behaviors such as relapse (Roberts et al., 2022), comprehending susceptibility to addiction (Jing et al., 2020), and establishing treatment plans (Baucum et al., 2023), making it a transformative tool in psychiatric and addiction care.

Random Forest (RF), Support Vector Machines (SVM), k-Nearest Neighbors (KNN), Decision Trees (DT), XGBoost, and CatBoost are some of the most popular supervised learning methods used in the field. These models are highly effective at identifying behavioral predictors in large, labeled datasets. For example, CatBoost has been used to classify substance use behaviors in university populations with high accuracy, surpassing traditional decision tree models (Hasan et al., 2025). Different ML algorithms have been employed in research on SUD, each with its own strengths and weaknesses depending on the nature and complexity of the data. K-Nearest Neighbors (KNN) is a non-parametric, instance-based learning algorithm that defers computation until classification time. It classifies a new data point based on the majority class among the K nearest labeled training samples; when K = 1, it assigns the class of the single nearest neighbor (Peterson, 2009). Random Forest (RF), on the other hand, is an ensemble learning method that constructs many decision trees and combines their predictions using majority voting for classification or averaging for regression to prevent overfitting and enhance generalization (Biau & Scornet, 2016; Rabinowitz et al., 2025). Extreme Gradient Boosting (XGBoost) is a powerful gradient boosting framework that builds decision trees one at a time to minimize a loss function. It uses both system-level and algorithmic optimizations, making it especially effective for modeling structured data (Chen & Guestrin, 2016). Decision Trees (DTs) use a flowchart-like structure where internal nodes test attributes, branches represent test outcomes, and leaf nodes provide class labels or decisions. They are intuitive and well-suited for both classification and regression tasks (Taha Jijo & Mohsin Abdulazeez, 2021). Another gradient boosting method, CatBoost, has been developed to handle categorical variables. It employs ordered boosting and prior-value regularization to make predictions more stable and reduce noise from infrequent categories, improving the overall performance of the model (Prokhorenkova et al., 2018).

A recent study in Bangladesh examining alcohol consumption, smoking, and drug use behaviors among students preparing for university entrance exams (Hasan et al., 2025) showed the effectiveness of these algorithms. Using both CatBoost and XGBoost, the study found that the lifetime prevalence rates for smoking, drug use, and alcohol use were 15.1%, 3.6%, and 4.5%, respectively. These rates were lower than those among Bangladeshi high school students (Moonajilin et al., 2021), Vietnamese youth (Do et al., 2018), and the general Bangladeshi university population (Hossain et al., 2017). Depression emerged as the strongest predictor of risky substance use, as indicated by SHAP values from the CatBoost model, while XGBoost's Gini importance analysis identified gender and higher secondary school GPA as key factors. These findings align with research from Malaysia (Ariaratnam et al., 2023), the United States (Wu et al., 2023), and global reviews (Weinberger et al., 2017), all of which show significant correlations between mental health disorders, particularly anxiety and depression, and substance use. Living in a rural area also significantly increased the risk of lifetime smoking, similar to findings in the US (Doogan et al., 2017; Liu et al., 2016), China (Lee et al., 2021), and mixed results across South and Southeast Asia (Sreeramareddy et al., 2014; Yang & Giummarra, 2021; Hosseinpoor et al., 2011).

Regarding model performance, CatBoost outperformed other algorithms with classification accuracies of 85.65% for smoking, 96.53% for substance use, and 96.06% for alcohol consumption, and exhibited low log loss values of 0.41, 0.15, and 0.16, respectively. XGBoost achieved the highest F1-score for smoking (79.34%), while CatBoost remained superior for substance use (96.65%) and alcohol use (94.14%). In contrast, decision tree models underperformed, with a high log loss of 8.98%. These results are consistent with studies from Sweden where Random Forest models predicted SUD diagnoses with AUCs of 0.69 overall and 0.67 for new diagnoses among individuals aged 18–19 (Zhang-James et al., 2020). These findings highlight the potential of ML to improve early detection, enhance diagnostic accuracy, and reduce healthcare burdens by identifying patients at risk for timely, individualized intervention. The cross-sectional design, convenience sampling, and reliance on self-reporting in the Bangladeshi study limit the ability to determine causality and introduce potential biases, such as recall and social desirability effects. Additionally, the overrepresentation of Muslim students may restrict the generalizability of the findings. Future studies should incorporate longitudinal and mixed-method approaches, recruit more demographically and religiously diverse samples, and evaluate the effectiveness of culturally tailored interventions (Al-Mamun et al., 2024a, 2024b, 2024c). Suggested strategies include integrating mental health services into SUD prevention programs, using ML-based screening tools in educational and clinical settings, and initiating public awareness campaigns to reduce stigma and encourage help-seeking among adolescents transitioning to higher education.

Deep learning architectures, such as Recurrent Neural Networks (RNN), Bidirectional Long Short-Term Memory (BiLSTM), and transformer-based models like BERT, are increasingly used on unstructured data, such as social media text or clinical notes. These models provide a sophisticated understanding of behavioral indicators/cues and language signals related to SUD risk (Murphy, 2012). To ensure interpretability and prevent overfitting, researchers often employ feature selection techniques like recursive feature elimination, chi-square filtering, and LASSO regression (Hasan et al., 2021; Hoggatt et al., 2025). Additionally, Explainable AI (XAI) tools like SHAP (Shapley Additive Explanations) and Gini importance help clarify which variables exert the most influence on model outputs, which is crucial for clinical relevance (Lu et al., 2023; Sethuraman et al., 2025). Unsupervised and semi-supervised learning methods are used to identify hidden clusters in behavioral data, often revealing subgroups of users or risk profiles that would otherwise remain undetected. As AI tools become more advanced and accessible, these methodological innovations are helping to reshape the research and clinical landscape of substance use prevention and treatment.

6. PREDICTING SUBSTANCE USE AND SUBSTANCE USE DISORDER RISK FACTORS

Traditional epidemiological methods have improved our understanding of substance use by considering demographic, socioeconomic, psychological, environmental, and genetic factors (Amaro et al., 2021; Mak ct al., 2019; Merikangas & Avenevoli, 2000; Merikangas & McClair, 2012; Volkow & Blanco, 2023). However, these approaches can be further enhanced with AI and ML, which can detect complex and non-linear patterns (Barenholtz et al., 2020; Shokri & Shmatikov, 2015). AI techniques draw on various data sources, including national surveys, electronic health records, clinical data, and social media, to predict drug use, associated behavioral patterns, overdose risks, and treatment outcomes (Acion et al., 2017; Machado et al., 2025; Rajkomar et al., 2019).

Predictive modeling, driven by advanced ML algorithms, is increasingly recognized as a vital part of early intervention strategies in SUD research and treatment. By identifying individuals at higher risk before full-blown addiction or relapse occurs, these models allow for preemptive, targeted, and often personalized interventions that can greatly enhance clinical and public health outcomes (Suva & Bhatia, 2024; Giorgi & Curtis, 2024). ML models trained on large, diverse datasets can detect subtle patterns in demographic, behavioral, psychological, and environmental data to predict future substance use. For instance, Jing et al. (2020) developed a Random Forest (RF) model to predict future substance use based on lifestyle variables in children. Their model achieved predictive accuracies of 74% at age 10 and 86% at age 22, demonstrating the long-term predictive capacity of ML-based early detection tools. Likewise, Wang et al. (2025) employed Bayesian ML modeling to estimate the absolute risk of developing cannabis use disorder (CUD) within five years of initial use. Key predictors included biological sex, conscientiousness, neuroticism, openness, and delinquency. These findings support incorporating ML Technologies into school-based interventions and risk assessments for adolescents.

Predictive models not only identify individuals who are at risk, but they also categorize them based on the severity of their condition, likelihood of relapse, or response to treatment. This risk classification enables clinicians to better allocate resources and customize treatment plans to suit each patient. Hasan et al. (2025) used CatBoost and XGBoost models to evaluate how psychological factors (e.g., depression and anxiety) and academic indicators (e.g., GPA) influence risky substance use among students preparing for university entrance exams. These models achieved high classification accuracy (up to 96.5% for substance use) and identified important intervention targets. SHAP values from CatBoost and Gini importance from XGBoost helped interpret the factors contributing to risk at the individual level. Additionally, Menon et al. (2019) employed convolutional neural networks (CNNs) to thermal facial images to detect intoxicated drivers, reaching an impressive 87% accuracy. Such innovations demonstrate how real-time detection systems can be integrated into efforts for public safety and harm reduction infrastructures.

ML also allows for the early detection of individuals predisposed to developing SUDs. Kim et al. (2025) used XGBoost to predict adolescents' substance use across three countries, identifying smoking status, BMI, emotional distress, and suicidal ideation as key predictors. This cross-national model achieved high AUROCs (80.6% in Korea, 79.3% in the U.S., and 76.4% in Norway), demonstrating its generalizability. Further research used Random Forest (RF), Support Vector Machines (SVM), and Bayesian ML to predict future substance use in adolescents. Wang et al. (2025) developed a Bayesian risk prediction model for Cannabis Use Disorder (CUD), with AUCs ranging from 0.64 to 0.75 across various datasets. Predictors included conscientiousness, neuroticism, delinquency, and biological sex. ML models have shown potential in distinguishing between individuals at risk and those unlikely to develop SUDs (Annis et al., 2022; Kang et al., 2022; Jing et al., 2020; Houghton et al., 2023). Although some models achieved high accuracy (e.g., Kang et al., 2022 reported 96%), concerns about methodological rigor were raised, including data biases that depend on context and overreliance on non-diagnostic features like impulsivity. Alternative models, such as Jing et al.'s (2020) longitudinal approach, showed modest predictive effectiveness (AUC 0.7–0.8) in identifying children at risk for SUDs, thus enabling early intervention opportunities.

A cross-sectional study in Bangladesh using XGBoost and CatBoost identified depression, gender, and academic achievement as key predictors of risky substance use among students preparing for university entrance exams. SHAP values showed depression as the most significant individual predictor, highlighting the psychological aspect of early substance use (Moonajilin et al., 2021). ML models have proven to be highly effective in predicting substance use among various adolescent groups. For instance, researchers trained an XGBoost model with carefully collected data from participants in South Korea. After training, they evaluated and tested this advanced model on groups in the United States and Norway. The model demonstrated strong statistical significance in accurately predicting substance use and in identifying and forecasting important risk factors, such as smoking, emotional distress, body mass index (BMI), and suicidal ideation.

In Finland, BiLSTM models analyzing national drug survey data showed that e-cigarette use, drug offers, and drug-related health issues were strong predictors of future drug use (Ünlü et al., 2025). This study investigates substance use patterns in Finland by using AI and ML techniques to identify key risk factors and forecast illicit drug use trends. Using data from the Finnish National Drug Survey, the researchers applied 15 feature selection methods to identify 23 major risk factors linked to the five most commonly used illegal substances: cannabis, ecstasy, amphetamines, cocaine, and non-medical prescription drugs. The most influential predictors included e-cigarette use, exposure to free and paid drug offers, and drug-related health problems. The study employed a Bidirectional Long Short-Term Memory (BiLSTM) model, which showed high accuracy in predicting substance use behavior. Integrating AI-based modeling with epidemiological data offers valuable insights into the complex nature of substance use and supports the development of personalized prevention strategies and policy measures. This study emphasizes the importance of predictive analytics in public health and promotes data-driven approaches to drug use prevention in the Finnish population (Ünlü et al., 2025).

Rajapaksha et al. (2022) developed the only validated model for cannabis use disorder (CUD); however, it lacks an absolute risk framework and does not consider competing mortality, which limits its usefulness in clinical decision-making. Similarly, current relative risk models cannot provide individualized clinical recommendations (Richter et al., 2017). As cannabis use among adolescents increases, especially through vapes and edibles, the need for a definitive risk model becomes more critical (Lim et al., 2022; Patrick et al., 2020). Another study shows that Bayesian ML approaches have been used to estimate the precise risk of developing cannabis use disorder (CUD) within five years of initial cannabis use, using longitudinal data. Despite these encouraging results, challenges remain. Many models rely on structured data and may not generalize well across institutions with different documentation standards. ML offers a comprehensive framework for improving the diagnosis and severity assessment of SUDs. By addressing the limitations of traditional methods and integrating multimodal data, ML enables more accurate, timely, and personalized detection strategies.

These findings collectively validate the predictive capability of ML in substance use research and emphasize the significance of context-specific variables in developing effective prevention and intervention strategies. Despite strong performance metrics, challenges remain in ensuring reliability and transparency. A systematic review by Mattos et al. (2024) highlighted concerns like data leakage, overfitting, reliance on post-treatment variables, and limited external validation. Several high-performing models were compromised by insufficient scientific rigor or biased training data. Recommendations include using standardized metrics, adopting transparent reporting practices, and validating models across diverse populations (Roberts et al., 2022; Kang et al., 2022).

7. MACHINE LEARNING IN THE DIAGNOSIS AND ASSESSMENT OF SUBSTANCE USE DISORDER SEVERITY

A major use of ML in addiction science is improving diagnostic accuracy. Traditional diagnostic methods often overlook early-stage or underreported cases because of social desirability bias or limited provider questioning. ML models trained on large datasets, including electronic health records (EHRs), surveys, and social media, have shown better success in identifying undiagnosed SUDs. An important advancement in this field comes from the Veterans Health Administration, where LASSO regression models were created using structured EHR data from 30 sites. The results showed that ML could more than double the sensitivity of SUD detection compared to diagnosis-based models, which are usually limited by provider documentation. The best LASSO model used 61 predictors to estimate actual SUD prevalence, achieving a C-statistic of 0.802. The study revealed disparities of up to 7.2% between model-predicted and recorded SUD prevalence, pointing out flaws in current healthcare quality metrics and the potential for ML to fix these issues (Hoggatt, 2025).

Additional research has used digital phenotyping to identify undiagnosed cases of SUD. Giorgi and Curtis (2024) used BERT, a transformer-based deep learning model, to analyze patients' Facebook posts prior to treatment. Their model performed better than the Addiction Severity Index (ASI) in predicting relapse and treatment dropout, indicating that social media language could serve as a digital biomarker for SUD (Liu et al., 2022).

AI enhanced the assessment of SUD severity by combining diverse data sources, including psychometric tests, neuroimaging, and biological markers. Techniques such as functional MRI (fMRI) and blood-based biomarkers (e.g., α-synuclein, orexin-A) provide physiological insights into addiction pathways related to cravings, stages of addiction, and treatment responses (Logothetis, 2002; Yang et al., 2023a; Islam et al., 2022; Pirro et al., 2013; Schacht et al., 2013; Nazari et al., 2022). When integrated with AI models, these tools can help explain complex links between brain activity and addictive behaviors. Multivariate AI models have improved the diagnostic interpretation of fMRI data in SUD patients by identifying craving-related brain patterns and enhancing clinical interpretation (Maas et al., 1998; Kilts et al., 2001; Martz et al., 2020; Zhang et al., 2024).

8. TREATMENT ENGAGEMENT, RETENTION, AND RELAPSE PREDICTION

Treatment engagement and long-term retention remain two of the most challenging and critical aspects of effective SUD intervention. High dropout and relapse rates significantly hinder recovery outcomes, highlighting the importance of early detection of individuals at risk during treatment. Low involvement is directly associated with higher rates of morbidity and mortality (Arbour et al., 2011; Ilgen et al., 2007), and clinical trials indicate that about 30% of participants drop out (Lappan et al., 2020). Previous research has identified various factors influencing treatment engagement, with protective factors including older age, strong therapeutic alliances, and established relationships with healthcare providers (Brorson et al., 2019; Goldberg et al., 2020; Naeger et al., 2016). Conversely, disengagement has been associated with cognitive impairments, emotional regulation difficulties, psychiatric comorbidities, and identifying as Black or African American (Aharonovich et al., 2006; Lappan et al., 2020; Lind et al., 2019; Papamalis et al., 2020). These findings align with the "therapeutic landscape" framework, which suggests that individuals facing more complex personal and economic challenges are at a higher risk of poor engagement (Wilton & Deverteuil, 2006).

At the individual level, reliable indicators of dropout include younger age, unemployment, and the initial use of prescription opiates, benzodiazepines, or heroin. Patients like these may not be as motivated or may have shorter histories of substance use, which makes them more prone to disengagement (Norman et al., 2007; Hanauer et al., 2021; Marcovitz et al., 2016; McHugh et al., 2013). Conversely, employment appears protective, perhaps due to economic stability and accountability pressures (Weinstein et al., 2017). The strong link between opioid/sedative use and dropout has been confirmed (Baker et al., 2020; Ellis et al., 2022; Ware et al., 2021). For non-voluntary discharges, additional risk factors include polysubstance use, severe tobacco dependence, external pressure to enter treatment (family or legal), recent incarceration, suicidal ideation, and chronic health conditions such as HIV/AIDS (Norman et al., 2007; Ouimette et al., 2007; Pan et al., 2022; Polcin & Korcha, 2017; Wang et & Wang, 2022). These examples show that external motivation, such as entering treatment to please others, often proves less effective than intrinsic motivation, thus emphasizing the need of encouraging personal commitment to recovery.

At the treatment level, the characteristics of the treatment center and the type of program consistently predicted outcomes. Such macro-level variables often exceeded individual factors, consistent with the findings of Gautam and Singh (2020). Differences in service integration, therapeutic environment, care intensity, and patient involvement between centers significantly impacted treatment outcomes (Huhn et al., 2019; Huhn et al., 2020). Programs that encourage patient autonomy and adapt treatment to individual needs are linked to increased engagement and reduced dropout rates (Graff et al., 2009; Swift & Callahan, 2009). However, many predictive models remain limited because datasets often exclude important contextual information, such as treatment center policies, or individual-level predictors, like health insurance, social support, stress, cravings, and recovery expectations, all of which influence retention (Arnaudova, Jin, & Amaro, 2020; Mckellar et al., 2006; Nordheim et al., 2018; Waite et al., 2023). Additionally, incorporating neurobehavioral assessments, including neuroimaging and cue-reactivity tests, could enhance predictive accuracy (Huhn et al., 2019; Moningka et al., 2019; Seo et al., 2013).

ML techniques have introduced innovative approaches to addressing these challenges. Models trained on large datasets, such as the Treatment Episode Data Set – Discharges (TEDS-D), have used methods like XGBoost, random forest, and neural networks to predict treatment completion, dropout, and relapse. Bailey and DeFulio (2022) identified predictors such as previous justice involvement, psychiatric comorbidities, and opioid use disorders, while warning against methodological pitfalls like data leakage and over-reliance on post-treatment variables. Morel et al. (2020) applied ML to analyze 97,688 hospital readmissions, revealing that SUDs were associated with a 22.3% readmission rate, compared to 13.2% for mental disorders alone. Other predictive models have shown similar effectiveness: Acion et al. (2017) tested 17 ML methods on over 99,000 treatment episodes, achieving area under the curve (AUC) values between 0.79 and 0.82. More advanced techniques, such as those combining urinalysis, reinforcement learning, and longitudinal data, have made highly personalized relapse predictions with AUCs of 0.84 (Roberts et al., 2022; Baucum et al., 2023). Recent research incorporates social determinants of health into predictive models. Eddie et al. (2024) showed that adolescents living in areas with high unemployment rates, widespread public assistance, and numerous alcohol outlets were less likely to seek treatment. The findings emphasize the significance of community-level initiatives and policy-level interventions in conjunction with clinical care.

Digital phenotyping and natural language processing (NLP) have enhanced predictive capabilities. These methods analyze real-time, ecologically valid data from social media, mobile apps, and digital communication technologies, which differentiates them from static self-reports. For example, Curtis et al. (2023) employed BERT-based models to predict dropout 90 days in advance, using social media language and outperforming traditional assessments. Patients whose online language was more positive, family-focused, or religion-oriented were more likely to remain in care, whereas neutral or mundane language predicted dropout (Liu et al., 2022; Shipp & Aeon, 2019). Giorgi and Curtis (2024) found that BERT-based analysis of Facebook posts exceeded the Addiction Severity Index in predicting relapse and dropout. NLP has also been used for stigma research beyond prediction: Roesler et al. (2024) analyzed over 161,000 Reddit posts with RoBERTa-based models to identify substance-specific stigma patterns, providing practical findings for targeted interventions.

Finally, digital platforms and chatbots represent promising avenues for enhancing accessibility and adherence. The Be Well Buddy intervention, for instance, has screening completion rates of 32% and appointment follow-through rates of 50% (Salyers et al., 2025). During the COVID-19 epidemic, chatbot-assisted therapy, including Woebot for SUDs (W-SUDs), improved mental health outcomes and lowered their cravings (Prochaska et al., 2021). A pilot study indicated that chatbot users exhibited reduced substance usage and increased comfort in addressing sensitive topics (Wright et al., 2025). Even with these improvements, there are still shortcomings, including small sample sizes, ethical issues, and the lack of full integration into health systems. Future applications must emphasize cross-institutional validation, dynamic monitoring, and integration with wearable technologies to provide real-time behavioral and physiological data.

9. DIGITAL THERAPEUTICS AND AI-DRIVEN CHATBOTS FOR SUBSTANCE USE DISORDERS

The development of digital and AI-driven therapeutic interventions has transformed how care is delivered for SUDs, improving accessibility, scalability, and personalized treatment. These interventions include various techniques such as chatbots, smartphone apps, wearable devices, and internet-based cognitive behavioral therapy (CBT). Chatbots like Woebot, Echo-APP, and Be Well Buddy have gained recognition for their ability to provide psychoeducation, motivational support, self-screening functions, and assistance. The Be Well Buddy chatbot, part of the Be Well Texas SUD clinic, offered confidential, HIPAA-compliant SMS interactions that allowed users to assess anxiety, depression, and substance use. In a pilot study, 32% of users completed a screener, and 50% of those referred scheduled care. The assessment results were significantly higher compared to traditional website-based methods (Salyers et al., 2025). The primary use of mHealth is in risk assessment and personalized intervention. Islam et al. (2023) developed a smartphone app using a naïve Bayes classifier and synthetic data to evaluate the risk of Opioid Use Disorder

(OUD). The app provided immediate risk assessments and customized educational content, serving as an affordable and accessible alternative to face-to-face screening.

Elmasri and Maeder developed a chatbot to assess alcohol use among Australian young adults (ages 18–25). In a pilot study with 17 participants, feedback was positive, although the study did not include a control group. Another study by Prochaska et al., involving non-Hispanic white women aged 18 to 65, found that 76% provided favorable evaluations of an 8-week CBT-based W-SUDs application; however, the single-arm design and short duration limited the results. mHealth applications may incorporate gamification, motivational messaging, and behavioral tracking to improve user engagement. For example, applications like Woebot for SUD (W-SUDs) have shown effectiveness in reducing substance use and improving mental health during the COVID-19 pandemic (Prochaska et al., 2021). Moghadasi et al. (2020) presented "Robo," a deep learning chatbot designed for opioid-related inquiries using Reddit data. While useful for specific questions, it was limited by its sole data source and inability to provide medical advice. Carreiro et al. (2020) conducted a systematic review of 32 mobile and wearable interventions targeting SUDs, mainly focusing on alcohol use disorder, reporting improvements in cravings and retention. However, these findings were limited by small sample sizes, publication bias, and a limited age range. In a randomized controlled trial, Chun-Hung et al. (2023) found that chatbot-assisted therapy (CAT) for methamphetamine use disorder slightly improved retention and reduced positive urine tests, though without reaching significant clinical benefits. The Echo-APP, a tablet-based virtual psychotherapist, demonstrated reductions in cravings and improvements in psychological well-being among individuals undergoing methamphetamine rehabilitation (Chen et al., 2023). Researchers evaluated Echo-APP with 47 methamphetamine users in Shanghai, identifying psychological improvements, but the study lacked a control group and relied on self-reported data. Ogilvie et al.'s 2022 systematic review of six chatbot studies indicated potential for reducing substance use; nonetheless, it highlighted issues such as small sample sizes, lack of long-term data, and limited ethical monitoring, emphasizing the need for expert engagement and more rigorous evaluation.

Alongside chatbots, mobile health (mHealth) applications offer real-time monitoring and feedback capabilities. These tools track physiological indicators (e.g., heart rate), emotional fluctuations, and craving levels, allowing users to receive immediate assistance and support. Wearables integrated with ML algorithms have been utilized to predict relapse risk, presenting opportunities for early intervention (Tassinari et al.). These real-time biomarkers can help detect stress or craving states and triggers before relapse occurs. Ebrahimi et al. (2021) developed a deep neural network (DNN) model using electronic health data, which identified normal, risky, and harmful drinkers with accuracies of 96%, 82%, and 89%, respectively. Advances in pharmacogenetics, mobile health applications, and wearable technology now facilitate real-time monitoring of physiological and mental conditions to predict relapse and personalize SUD treatments. Despite their promise, these technologies raise significant ethical concerns, such as privacy issues, possible abuse of sensitive data (Saeidnia et al., 2024), lack of transparency in "black-box" AI decision-making (Mehrabi et al., 2022; Kameyama et al., 2024), algorithmic bias, and limited accountability in cases of harm (Karimian et al., 2022). Ensuring strict data removal protocols, equitable access across socioeconomic groups, and ongoing clinician monitoring are essential for ethically integrating AI into mental health care (Vayena et al., 2018; Hamideh & Nebeker, 2020; Williams et al., 2021; Williamson & Prybutok, 2024). Neglecting the digital gap risks excluding marginalized populations and increasing current inequality in healthcare.

Although mHealth technologies are easily accessible, they still carry risks. Concerns about data privacy, algorithmic bias, and access inequality must be addressed. Some devices can be expensive or impractical in low-resource settings, and digital literacy remains a challenge for certain populations (Ezell et al., 2024; Tassinari et al., 2025). Additionally, collecting real-time data collecting creates concerns regarding consent, surveillance, and autonomy, especially when dealing with vulnerable populations. Also, the therapeutic alliance, a key indicator of treatment effectiveness, might be challenging to reproduce in digital contexts (Goldberg et al., 2020). Therefore, while mHealth and wearable technologies offer great potential, their use must be guided by ethical principles and backed by solid data on safety, effectiveness, and fairness.

10. ETHICAL, LEGAL, AND PRACTICAL CONSIDERATIONS

AI and ML technologies increasingly influence the diagnosis, prevention, and treatment of SUDs, their implementation raises significant ethical, legal, and practical concerns. Without explicit focus on equality, transparency, and reliability, these technologies might unintentionally cause harm, especially to vulnerable populations disproportionately affected by addiction (Ezell et al., 2024; Tassinari et al., 2025). The sensitive nature of addiction-related data, such as behavioral histories, biometrics, and social media information, requires strict privacy protections. Research by Salyers et al. (2025) and Moghadasi et al. (2023) emphasizes the importance of HIPAA-compliant frameworks and encrypted communication protocols in digital interventions. However, many AI systems rely on passive data collection methods (e.g., digital phenotyping), where informed consent is often implicit or unclear.

Furthermore, chatbots and mobile applications must minimize risks related to unauthorized access, data leakage, and re-identification. Developers should implement safeguards such as end-to-end encryption, anonymization and de-identification procedures, and give users control over data collection and sharing. Without these security measures, patients might avoid using digital technologies due to concerns that their data could be misused in legal, employment, or insurance settings (Derksen et al., 2025). AI systems trained on non-representative or biased datasets risk perpetuating existing healthcare disparities. Some models perform poorly in populations that are underrepresented in the training data, such as racial and ethnic minorities, older adults, women, and non-English speakers (Kim et al., 2025; Roberts et al., 2022). This raises ethical concerns about equity, as such biases may lead to misclassification or insufficient care.Roesler et al. (2024) emphasized that stigma, especially related to opioid use, varies across different populations, and AI must be sensitive to these differences to avoid reinforcing harmful narratives. Prioritizing algorithmic fairness involves using diverse, demographically representative training data, conducting bias audits with fairness metrics, and designing systems that are culturally informed.

Numerous high-performing AI models, such as deep neural networks and ensemble classifiers, frequently function as "black boxes," making it hard to explain their predictive processes. This lack of interpretability reduces trust from physicians and limits patient autonomy. Tools like SHAP (SHapley Additive ExPlanations) and LIME (Local Interpretable Model-Agnostic Explanations) have been developed to provide insights into decision-making processes (Hasan et al., 2025), although their application remains non-standardized. Transparent model development and open access to source code, training data, and assessment metrics are crucial for external validation and public accountability (Mattos et al., 2024; Roberts et al., 2022).

Generative AI systems, such as ChatGPT, raise additional concerns related to misinformation, fabricated or hallucinated content, and insufficient medical supervision (Salyers et al. 2025; 8). According to Ogilvie et al. (2025), these systems may exhibit conversational fluency; however, they have not been verified for use in SUD clinics. Live experiments have shown that such tools can deliver unsafe responses to individuals vulnerable to self-harm or addiction, highlighting the need for expert-curated information and controlled implementation. Therefore, a "safety-first" approach is essential, focusing on rule-based or closed-library AI systems that are pre-trained on clinically validated knowledge and evaluated by addiction specialists (Salyers et al., 2025; Ogilvie et al., 2025). Despite promising clinical potential, most AI tools in addiction care operate without formal regulatory approval. There are no standard criteria for algorithm validation, risk classification, or real-world performance assessment. National and international regulatory authorities must establish guidelines for AI use in behavioral health and require ethical evaluation of AI initiatives.

ML has been employed to predict treatment adherence, dropout rates, and completion using datasets such as TEDS-D (Acion et al., 2017; Bailey & DeFulio, 2022; Nasir et al., 2021), with models including XGBoost and CNN showing mixed results. Several studies reported inflated metrics due to methodological issues like data leakage, poor validation, and reliance on post-treatment variables (Bailey & DeFulio, 2022; Acion et al., 2017). Unsupervised learning applications, such as Burgess-Hull et al. (2022) and Panlilio et al. (2020), used clustering to identify craving subtypes and drug use profiles but at times failed to provide value beyond clinical intuition. Despite the potential of ML in SUD contexts, the review emphasizes the need for rigorous validation, transparent reporting, and avoidance of data leakage (Baucum et al., 2023; Shrestha et al., 2023). Recommendations include using standardized assessment tools, limiting the use of post-outcome variables, sharing code and data for replication, and increasing sampling diversity to improve generalizability. Most studied datasets are U.S.-based (U.S. Department of Health and Human Services, 2019), which may restrict clinical diversity. However, ML holds significant promise for advancing early diagnosis, personalized care, and outcome prediction in SUD treatment, provided it is developed and applied with methodological rigor and transparency. As AI rapidly integrates into SUD care, ethical, legal, and social issues emerge, including concerns about privacy, algorithmic bias, digital inequality, and stigmatization particularly among vulnerable populations (Derksen et al., 2025).

Data privacy remains a significant concern. AI models handle sensitive medical records, social media content, and real-time sensor data, raising issues related to consent, data ownership, and surveillance. Despite efforts like de-identification and encryption, data breaches still happen. In studies such as Be Well Buddy, attempts were made to follow HIPAA guidelines, but broader systemic safeguards are necessary to promote responsible data use (Salyers et al., 2025). Another critical issue is algorithmic bias. When models are trained on homogeneous or biased datasets, they can reinforce existing health disparities. For example, the overrepresentation of Muslim students in the Bangladeshi sample limited the findings' generalizability, while the underrepresentation of minority groups in U.S. datasets impacted accuracy across racial subgroups (Al-Mamun et al., 2024a, Al-Mamun et al., 2024b, Al-Mamun et al., 2024c). To prevent such risks, transparent model training, diverse sampling, and inclusive evaluation. The ethical landscape is also shaped by stigma. Research on social media shows that different types of substances carry internalized, anticipated, and enacted stigma in unique ways, requiring specialized intervention strategies. When used in public health campaigns, AI systems must avoid stigmatizing language and narratives (Salyers et al., 2025).

Finally, AI-generated clinical decisions remain legally ambiguous. Concerns about liability, regulatory compliance, and intellectual property rights hinder broader adoption. Implementing AI in addiction care requires standardized legal and professional frameworks. Therefore, selecting relevant features is crucial for developing effective prevention and intervention models in substance use research However, ML still faces challenges such as the difficulty of choosing precise, informative features from large datasets. Different ML algorithms can select features in various ways, resulting in inconsistent insights (Casari & Zheng, 2018

11. CONCLUSION: FUTURE DIRECTIONS AND GLOBAL IMPLICATIONS

The integration of AI and ML into the diagnosis, treatment, and prevention of SUDs marks a significant breakthrough in addiction science. It offers new methods to improve access, reduce stigma, and improve outcomes, especially in areas where traditional approaches are inadequate (Tassinari et al., 2025; Ezell et al., 2024). AI-driven tools, such as mHealth apps, wearable sensors, and chatbots, can get beyond geographic and logistical problems and reach individuals living in rural, underserved, or stigmatized communities. Be Well Buddy and Woebot are two systems that have demonstrated measurable increases in engagement and follow-up by making it easier to screen, self-monitor, and refer individuals in real time (Salyers et al., 2025; Prochaska et al., 2021).

AI-based risk classification also assists public health authorities in implementing individualized prevention programs for specific populations, such as adolescents, individuals who live in rural areas, or high-risk demographic groups (Kim et al., 2025; Xu et al., 2025). These technologies can be used beyond clinical settings, including schools, the criminal justice system, and social services, to support early diagnosis, relapse prevention, and harm reduction. Examples include predictive tools for identifying at-risk students, chatbots for individuals on probation or parole, and geo-aware relapse prevention platforms like Sobergrid that offer real-time, community-based support.

While most research so far has concentrated on the United States and Europe, cross-cultural validation is essential for ensuring global applicability. Research by Kim et al. (2025), which evaluated predictive models in South Korea, the United States, and Norway, shows the potential of culturally adaptable AI systems. Applying these techniques to low- and middle-income countries (LMICs) requires collecting diverse datasets, adapting and localizing interventions linguistically, and incorporating cultural sensitivities into model interpretation and user communication.

AI functions most effectively as an adjunct to, rather than a replacement for, human expertise. Models should enhance clinical decision-making by integrating data, identifying risks, and providing decision support, while ultimately leaving final judgments to trained clinicians (Suva & Bhatia, 2024; Ezell et al., 2024). The concept of the Digital Therapeutic Alliance (DTA) highlights the importance of trust, empathy, and personalization in digital interventions. Beg and Verma (2024) emphasize that focusing on therapeutic design elements such as user interface, adaptability, and responsiveness is vital for maintaining long-term engagement.

Future considerations need to emphasize ethical and fair implementation. Key requirements include strict data governance, transparency of algorithms, collaboration among stakeholders, and regulatory supervision (Vayena et al., 2018; Karimian et al., 2022). Addressing the digital gap is essential to prevent widening disparities in healthcare. Longitudinal and mixed-method research must evaluate models over time, improve their generalizability, and ensure inclusion through diverse datasets and language accessibility. Collaboration among physicians, data scientists, ethicists, and community stakeholders will be vital for expanding effective interventions through sustainable policies and funding. In conclusion, AI and ML have the power to transform SUD treatment, making it more personalized, accessible, and culturally aware. By combining technological innovation with ethical insight and human-centered design, these technologies can help build a more inclusive and effective global addiction treatment ecosystem.

REFERENCES

Acion, L., Kelmansky, D., van der Laan, M., Sahker, E., Jones, D., & Arndt, S. (2017). Use of a machine learning framework to predict substance use disorder treatment success. *PLoS One*, *12*(4), e0175383. DOI: 10.1371/journal.pone.0175383

Afshar, M., Sharma, B., Dligach, D., Oguss, M., Brown, R., Chhabra, N., & Karnik, N. S. (2022). Development and multimodal validation of a substance misuse algorithm for referral to treatment using artificial intelligence (SMART-AI): A retrospective deep learning study. *The Lancet. Digital Health*, *4*(6), e426–e435. DOI: 10.1016/S2589-7500(22)00087-3

Aharonovich, E., Hasin, D. S., Brooks, A. C., Liu, X., Bisaga, A., & Nunes, E. V. (2006). Cognitive deficits predict low treatment retention in cocaine-dependent patients. *Drug and Alcohol Dependence*, *81*(3), 313–322. DOI: 10.1016/j.drugalcdep.2005.08.008

Al-Mamun, F., Hasan, M. E., Mostofa, N. B., Akther, M., Mashruba, T., Arif, M., Chaahat, A. H., Salam, A. B., Akter, M., Abedin, M. A. A., Bulbul, M. I. A., Adnan, M. S., Islam, M. S., Ahmed, M. S., Shahin, M. S. M., Islam, S., Hussain, M. M., & Al Habib, A., ALmerab, M. M., Gozal, D., ... Mamun, M. A. (2024a). Prevalence and factors associated with digital addiction among students taking university entrance tests: A GIS-based study. *BMC Psychiatry*, *24*(1), 322. DOI: 10.1186/s12888-024-05737-9

Al-Mamun, F., Hasan, M. E., & Roy, N. ALmerab, M. M., & Mamun, M. A. (2024c). Suicidal behaviors among high school graduates with preexisting mental health problems: A machine learning and GIS-based study. *The International Journal of Social Psychiatry*. Advance online publication. DOI: 10.1177/00207640241279004

Al-Mamun, F., Mamun, M. A., & Hasan, M. E., ALmerab, M. M., & Gozal, D. (2024b). Exploring sleep duration and insomnia among prospective university students: A study with geographical data and machine learning techniques. *Nature and Science of Sleep*, *16*, 1235–1251. DOI: 10.2147/NSS.S481786

Amaro, H., Sanchez, M., Bautista, T., & Cox, R. (2021). Social vulnerabilities for substance use: Stressors, socially toxic environments, and discrimination and racism. *Neuropharmacology*, *188*, 108518. DOI: 10.1016/j.neuropharm.2021.108518

Annis, I. E., Jordan, R., & Thomas, K. C. (2022). Quickly identifying people at risk of opioid use disorder in emergency departments: Trade-offs between a machine learning approach and a simple EHR flag strategy. *BMJ Open*, *12*(9), e059414. DOI: 10.1136/bmjopen-2021-059414

Arbour, S., Hambley, J., & Ho, V. (2011). Predictors and outcome of aftercare participation of alcohol and drug users completing residential treatment. *Substance Use & Misuse, 46*(10), 1275–1287. DOI: 10.3109/10826084.2011.572944

Arnaudova, I., Jin, H., & Amaro, H. (2020). Pretreatment social network characteristics relate to increased risk of dropout and unfavorable outcomes among women in a residential treatment setting for substance use. *Journal of Substance Abuse Treatment, 116*, 108044. DOI: 10.1016/j.jsat.2020.108044

Bailey, J. D., & DeFulio, A. (2022). Predicting substance use treatment failure with transfer learning. *Substance Use & Misuse, 57*(13), 1982–1987. DOI: 10.1080/10826084.2022.2125272

Baker, D. E., Edmonds, K. A., Calvert, M. L., Sanders, S. M., Bridges, A. J., Rhea, M. A., & Kosloff, S. (2020). Predicting attrition in long-term residential substance use disorder treatment: A modifiable risk factors perspective. *Psychological Services, 17*(4), 472–482. DOI: 10.1037/ser0000333

Barenholtz, E., Fitzgerald, N. D., & Hahn, W. E. (2020). Machine-learning approaches to substance-abuse research: Emerging trends and their implications. *Current Opinion in Psychiatry, 33*(4), 334–342. DOI: 10.1097/YCO.0000000000000615

Baucum, M., Khojandi, A., Myers, C., & Kessler, L. (2023). Optimizing substance use treatment selection using reinforcement learning. *ACM Transactions on Management Information Systems, 14*(2). Advance online publication. DOI: 10.1145/3563778

Beg, M. J., & Verma, M. K. (2024). Exploring the potential and challenges of digital and AI-driven psychotherapy for ADHD, OCD, schizophrenia, and substance use disorders: A comprehensive narrative review. *Indian Journal of Psychological Medicine, 46*(1), 1–13. DOI: 10.1177/02537176231234567

Beker, W., Wołos, A., Szymkuć, S., & Grzybowski, B. A. (2020). Minimal-uncertainty prediction of general drug-likeness based on Bayesian neural networks. *Nature Machine Intelligence, 2*(8), 457–465. DOI: 10.1038/s42256-020-0209-4

Biau, G., & Scornet, E. (2016). A random forest guided tour. *Test, 25*(2), 197–227. DOI: 10.1007/s11749-016-0481-7

Brackett, C., Duncan, M., Wagner, J., Fineberg, L., & Kraft, S. (2022). Multidisciplinary treatment of opioid use disorder in primary care using the collaborative care model. *Substance Abuse, 43*(1), 240–244. DOI: 10.1080/08897077.2021.1932698

Brorson, H. H., Arnevik, E. A., & Rand, K. (2019). Predicting dropout from inpatient substance use disorder treatment: A prospective validation study of the OQ-analyst. *Substance Abuse, 13*, 1178221819866181. DOI: 10.1177/1178221819866181

Burgess-Hull, A. J., Panlilio, L. V., Preston, K. L., & Epstein, D. H. (2022). Trajectories of craving during medication-assisted treatment for opioid-use disorder: Subtyping for early identification of higher risk. *Drug and Alcohol Dependence*, *233*, 109362. DOI: 10.1016/j.drugalcdep.2022.109362

Carreiro, S., Newcomb, M., Leach, R., Ostrowski, S., Boudreaux, E. D., & Amante, D. (2020). Current reporting of usability and impact of mHealth interventions for substance use disorder: A systematic review. *Drug and Alcohol Dependence*, *215*, 108201. DOI: 10.1016/j.drugalcdep.2020.108201

Ceceli, A. O., Bradberry, C. W., & Goldstein, R. Z. (2022). The neurobiology of drug addiction: Cross-species insights into the dysfunction and recovery of the prefrontal cortex. *Neuropsychopharmacology : Official Publication of the American College ofNeuropsychopharmacology*, *47*(1), 276–291. DOI: 10.1038/s41386-021-01137-3

Chekroud, A. M., Bondar, J., Delgadillo, J., Doherty, G., Wasil, A., Fokkema, M., & Choi, K. (2021). The promise of machine learning in predicting treatment outcomes in psychiatry. *World Psychiatry; Official Journal of the World Psychiatric Association (WPA)*, *20*(2), 154–170. DOI: 10.1002/wps.20882

Chen, T., Chen, L., Li, S., Du, J., Su, H., Jiang, H., & Zhao, M. (2023). Virtual digital psychotherapist app–based treatment in patients with methamphetamine use disorder (Echo-APP): Single-arm pilot feasibility and efficacy study. *JMIR mHealth and uHealth*, *11*(1), e40373. DOI: 10.2196/40373

Chen, T., & Guestrin, C. (2016). XGBoost: A scalable tree boosting system. In *Proceedings of the 22nd ACM SIGKDD International Conference on Knowledge Discovery and Data Mining* (pp. 785–794). ACM. https://doi.org/DOI: 10.1145/2939672.2939785

Chhetri, B., Goyal, L. M., & Mittal, M. (2023). How machine learning is used to study addiction in digital healthcare: A systematic review. *International Journal of Information Management Data Insights*, *3*(2), 100175. DOI: 10.1016/j.jjimei.2023.100175

Curtis, B., Giorgi, S., & Ungar, L.. (2023). AI-based analysis of social media language predicts addiction treatment dropout at 90 days. *Neuropsychopharmacology : Official Publication of the American College of Neuropsychopharmacology*. Advance online publication. DOI: 10.1038/s41386-023-01660-9

Decker, K. P., Peglow, S. L., Samples, C. R., & Cunningham, T. D. (2017). Long-term outcomes after residential substance use treatment: Relapse, morbidity, and mortality. *Military Medicine*, *182*(1–2), e1589–e1595. DOI: 10.7205/MILMED-D-15-00560

Degenhardt, L., & Hall, W. (2012). Extent of illicit drug use and dependence, and their contribution to the global burden of disease. *Lancet*, *379*(9810), 55–70. DOI: 10.1016/S0140-6736(11)61138-0

Derksen, M. E., van Beek, M., de Bruijn, T., Stuit, F., Blankers, M., & Goudriaan, A. E. (2025). Ethical aspects and user preferences in applying machine learning to adjust eHealth addressing substance use: A mixed-methods study. *International Journal of Medical Informatics*, *199*, 105897. DOI: 10.1016/j.ijmedinf.2024.105897

Do, H. N., Nathan, N., Van Nguyen, B., Le, H. T., Nguyen, H. Q. T., Nguyen, A. T., & Ho, R. C. (2018). Sociodemographic inequalities in substance use among young people in Vietnam. *Children and Youth Services Review*, *94*, 644–649. DOI: 10.1016/j.childyouth.2018.09.037

Doogan, N. J., Roberts, M. E., Wewers, M. E., Stanton, C. A., Keith, D. R., Gaalema, D. E., & Higgins, S. T. (2017). A growing geographic disparity: Rural and urban cigarette smoking trends in United States. *Preventive Medicine*, *104*, 79–85. DOI: 10.1016/j.ypmed.2017.03.011

Dou, Z. Y., Barman-Adhikari, A., & Fang, F.. (2021). Harnessing social media to identify homeless youth at-risk of substance use. *Proceedings of the AAAI Conference on Artificial Intelligence*, *35*(17), 14748–14756. DOI: 10.1609/aaai.v35i17.17708

Ebrahimi, A., Wiil, U. K., & Mansourvar, M.. (2021). Deep neural network to identify patients with alcohol use disorder. *Studies in Health Technology and Informatics*, *281*, 238–242. DOI: 10.3233/SHTI210154

Eddie, D., Prindle, J., Somodi, P., Gerstmann, I., Dilkina, B., Saba, S. K., & Davis, J. P. (2024). Exploring predictors of substance use disorder treatment engagement with machine learning: The impact of social determinants of health in the therapeutic landscape. *Journal of Substance Use and Addiction Treatment*, *164*, 209435. DOI: 10.1016/j.jsuat.2024.209435

Ellis, J. D., Rabinowitz, J. A., Wells, J., Liu, F., Finan, P. H., Stein, M. D., & Huhn, A. S. (2022). Latent trajectories of anxiety and depressive symptoms among adults in early treatment for nonmedical opioid use. *Journal of Affective Disorders*, *299*, 223–232. DOI: 10.1016/j.jad.2021.12.004

Elmasri, D., & Maeder, A. (2016). A conversational agent for an online mental health intervention. In *Proceedings of the International Conference on Brain and Health Informatics* (pp. 243–251). Springer. https://doi.org/DOI: 10.1007/978-3-319-47151-8_23

Ezell, J. M., Ajayi, B. P., Parikh, T., Miller, K., Rains, A., & Scales, D. (2024). Drug use and artificial intelligence: Weighing concerns and possibilities for prevention. *American Journal of Preventive Medicine*, *66*(3), 568–572. DOI: 10.1016/j.amepre.2023.09.006

Fontenelle, L. F., Oostermeijer, S., Harrison, B. J., Pantelis, C., & Yücel, M. (2011). Obsessive-compulsive disorder, impulse control disorders and drug addiction: Common features and potential treatments. *Drugs*, *71*(7), 827–840. DOI: 10.2165/11590560-000000000-00000

Garbin, C., Marques, N., & Marques, O. (2023). Machine learning for predicting opioid use disorder from healthcare data: A systematic review. *Computer Methods and Programs in Biomedicine*, *236*, 107573. DOI: 10.1016/j.cmpb.2023.107573

Gautam, P., & Singh, P. (2020). A machine learning approach to identify socio-economic factors responsible for patients dropping out of substance abuse treatment. *American Journal of Public Health Research*, *8*(5), 140–146. DOI: 10.12691/ajphr-8-5-1

Giorgi, S., & Curtis, B. (2024). Leveraging AI to predict substance use disorder treatment outcomes. *Neuropsychopharmacology : Official Publication of the American College of Neuropsychopharmacology*, *49*, 335–333. DOI: 10.1038/s41386-023-01700-6

Goldberg, S. B., Rowe, G., Malte, C. A., Ruan, H., Owen, J. J., & Miller, S. D. (2020). Routine monitoring of therapeutic alliance to predict treatment engagement in a Veterans Affairs substance use disorders clinic. *Psychological Services*, *17*(3), 291–299. DOI: 10.1037/ser0000337

Graff, F. S., Morgan, T. J., Epstein, E. E., McCrady, B. S., Cook, S. M., Jensen, N. K., & Kelly, S. (2009). Engagement and retention in outpatient alcoholism treatment for women. *The American Journal on Addictions*, *18*(4), 277–288. DOI: 10.1080/10550490902925540

Hamideh, D., & Nebeker, C. (2020). The digital health landscape in addiction and substance use research: Will digital health exacerbate or mitigate health inequities in vulnerable populations? *Current Addiction Reports*, *7*(3), 317–332. DOI: 10.1007/s40429-020-00325-9

Hanauer, M., Sielbeck-Mathes, K., Banks, B., Mitori, J., & Reuveny, A. (2021). Demographic predictors of dropping out of treatment (DOT) in substance use disorder treatment. *Substance Use & Misuse*, *56*(8), 1155–1160. DOI: 10.1080/10826084.2021.1913805

Hasan, M. E., Hossain, M. S., Mamun, M. A., Al-Mamun, F., Roy, N., & Almerab, M. M. (2025). Predicting substance use behaviors among students taking university entrance test: A cross-sectional study with machine learning techniques. *Current Psychology (New Brunswick, N.J.), 44*, 8015–8031. DOI: 10.1007/s12144-024-06934-1

Hasan, M. M., Young, G. J., Patel, M. R., Modestino, A. S., Sanchez, L. D., & Noor-E-Alam, M. (2021). A machine learning framework to predict the risk of opioid use disorder. *Machine Learning with Applications, 6*, 100144. DOI: 10.1016/j.mlwa.2021.100144

Hassan, S. A., Kareem, M., Sammany, M., & Banoon, S. R. (2024). Artificial intelligence as a predictive tool in drug addiction: A comprehensive review. *Journal of Misan Researches.*

Heberle, B. A., Kluwe-Schiavon, B., Bicca, C., Rothmann, L. M., Grassi-Oliveira, R., & Viola, T. W. (2024). Examining predictors of cocaine withdrawal syndrome at the end of detoxification treatment in women with cocaine use disorder. *Journal of Psychiatric Research, 169*, 247–256. DOI: 10.1016/j.jpsychres.2023.11.043

Heilig, M., MacKillop, J., Martinez, D., Rehm, J., Leggio, L., & Vanderschuren, L. J. (2021). Addiction as a brain disease revised: Why it still matters, and the need for consilience. *Neuropsychopharmacology : Official Publication of the American College of Neuropsychopharmacology, 46*(10), 1715–1723. DOI: 10.1038/s41386-021-01045-1

Hoggatt, K. J., Harris, A. H., Hayes, C. J., Washington, D., & Williams, E. C. (2025). Improving diagnosis-based quality measures: An application of machine learning to the prediction of substance use disorder among outpatients. *BMJ Open Quality, 14*(1). Advance online publication. DOI: 10.1136/bmjoq-2024-003929

Hong, S., Walton, B., Kim, H. W., & Lipsey, A. D. (2024). Improving treatment completion for young adults with substance use disorder: Machine learning-based prediction algorithms. *Journal of Psychiatric Research, 178*, 41–49. DOI: 10.1016/j.jpsychres.2024.04.007

Hossain, S., Hossain, S., Ahmed, F., Islam, R., Sikder, T., & Rahman, A. (2017). Prevalence of tobacco smoking and factors associated with the initiation of smoking among university students in Dhaka, Bangladesh. *Central Asian Journal of Global Health, 6*(1), 244. DOI: 10.5195/cajgh.2017.244

Hosseinpoor, A. R., Parker, L. A., d'Espaignet, T. E., & Chatterji, S. (2011). Social determinants of smoking in low- and middle-income countries: Results from the World Health Survey. *PLoS One, 6*(5), e20331. DOI: 10.1371/journal.pone.0020331

Houghton, D. C., Spratt, H. M., Keyser-Marcus, L., Bjork, J. M., Neigh, G. N., Cunningham, K. A., & Moeller, F. G. (2023). Behavioral and neurocognitive factors distinguishing post-traumatic stress comorbidity in substance use disorders. *Translational Psychiatry*, *13*(1), 296. DOI: 10.1038/s41398-023-02591-3

Huhn, A. S., Hobelmann, J. G., Ramirez, A., Strain, E. C., & Oyler, G. A. (2019). Trends in first-time treatment admissions for older adults with alcohol use disorder: Availability of medical and specialty clinical services in hospital, residential, and outpatient facilities. *Drug and Alcohol Dependence*, *205*, 107694. DOI: 10.1016/j.drugalcdep.2019.107694

Huhn, A. S., Hobelmann, J. G., Strickland, J. C., Oyler, G. A., Bergeria, C. L., Umbricht, A., & Dunn, K. E. (2020). Differences in availability and use of medications for opioid use disorder in residential treatment settings in the United States. *JAMA Network Open*, *3*(2), e1920843. DOI: 10.1001/jamanetworkopen.2019.20843

Ilgen, M. A., Jain, A., Lucas, E., & Moos, R. H. (2007). Substance use-disorder treatment and a decline in attempted suicide during and after treatment. *Journal of Studies on Alcohol and Drugs*, *68*(4), 503–509. DOI: 10.15288/jsad.2007.68.503

Islam, A. B. M. R., Khan, K. M., Scarbrough, A., Zimpfer, M. J., Makkena, N., Omogunwa, A., & Ahamed, S. I. (2023). An artificial intelligence–based smartphone app for assessing the risk of opioid misuse in working populations using synthetic data: Pilot development study. *JMIR Formative Research*, *7*, e45434. DOI: 10.2196/45434

Islam, S. U., Ahmed, M. B., Ahsan, H., & Lee, Y. S. (2022). Role of biomarkers in personalized medicine. In Shehzad, A. (Ed.), *Cancer biomarkers in diagnosis and therapeutics* (pp. 249–275). Springer., DOI: 10.1007/978-981-16-5759-7_11

Jayatilake, S., & Ganegoda, G. (2021). Involvement of machine learning tools in healthcare decision making. *Journal of Healthcare Engineering*, *6679512*. Advance online publication. DOI: 10.1155/2021/6679512

Jing, Y., Hu, Z., & Fan, P.. (2020). Analysis of substance use and its outcomes by machine learning I. Childhood evaluation of liability to substance use disorder. *Drug and Alcohol Dependence*, *206*, 107605. DOI: 10.1016/j.drugalcdep.2019.107605

Kameyama, J., Kodera, S., & Inoue, Y. (2024). Ethical, legal, and social issues (ELSI) and reporting guidelines of AI research in healthcare. *PLOS Digital Health*, *3*(9), e0000607. DOI: 10.1371/journal.pdig.0000607

Kang, T., Zhang, Y., Zhao, J., Li, X., Jiang, H., Niu, X., & Yuan, T.-F. (2022). Characterizing impulsivity in individuals with heroin use disorder. *International Journal of Mental Health and Addiction*. Advance online publication. DOI: 10.1007/s11469-022-00941-8

Karimian, G., Petelos, E., & Evers, S. M. A. A. (2022). The ethical issues of the application of artificial intelligence in healthcare: A systematic scoping review. *AI and Ethics*, *2*(4), 539–551. DOI: 10.1007/s43681-021-00131-7

Khera, R., Haimovich, J., Hurley, N. C., McNamara, R., Spertus, J. A., Desai, N., & Krumholz, H. M. (2021). Use of machine learning models to predict death after acute myocardial infarction. *JAMA Cardiology*, *6*(6), 633–641. DOI: 10.1001/jamacardio.2021.0197

Kilts, C. D., Schweitzer, J. B., Quinn, C. K., Gross, R. E., Faber, T. L., Muhammad, F., & Drexler, K. P. (2001). Neural activity related to drug craving in cocaine addiction. *Archives of General Psychiatry*, *58*(4), 334–341. DOI: 10.1001/archpsyc.58.4.334

Kim, S., Kim, H., Kim, S., Lee, H., Hammoodi, A., Choi, Y., Kim, H. J., Smith, L., Kim, M. S., Fond, G., Boyer, L., Baik, S. W., Lee, H., Park, J., Kwon, R., Woo, S., & Yon, D. K. (2025). Machine learning–based prediction of substance use in adolescents in three independent worldwide cohorts: Algorithm development and validation study. *Journal of Medical Internet Research*, *27*, e62805. DOI: 10.2196/62805

Lappan, S. N., Brown, A. W., & Hendricks, P. S. (2020). Dropout rates of in-person psychosocial substance use disorder treatments: A systematic review and meta-analysis. *Addiction (Abingdon, England)*, *115*(2), 201–217. DOI: 10.1111/add.14885

Levola, J., Aranko, A., & Pitkänen, T. (2021). Psychosocial difficulties and treatment retention in inpatient detoxification programmes. *Nordisk Alkohol- & Narkotikatidskrift : NAT*, *38*(5), 434–449. DOI: 10.1177/14550725211021263

Leza, L., Haro, B., López-Goñi, J. J., & Fernández-Montalvo, J. (2024). Substance use disorder and lifetime suicidal behaviour: A scoping review. *Psychiatry Research*, *334*, 115830. DOI: 10.1016/j.psychres.2024.115830

Lim, C. C., Sun, T., Leung, J., Chung, J. Y., Gartner, C., Connor, J., & Chan, G. C. (2022). Prevalence of adolescent cannabis vaping: A systematic review and meta-analysis of US and Canadian studies. *JAMA Pediatrics*, *176*(1), 42–51. DOI: 10.1001/jamapediatrics.2021.4360

Lind, B. K., McCarty, D., Gu, Y., Baker, R., & McConnell, J. K. (2019). Predictors of substance use treatment initiation and engagement among adult and adolescent Medicaid recipients. *Substance Abuse*, *40*(3), 285–291. DOI: 10.1080/08897077.2018.1550467

Liu, L., Edland, S., Myers, M. G., Hofstetter, C. R., & Al-Delaimy, W. K. (2016). Smoking prevalence in urban and rural populations: Findings from California between 2001 and 2012. *The American Journal of Drug and Alcohol Abuse*, *42*(2), 152–161. DOI: 10.3109/00952990.2015.1125494

Liu, T., Giorgi, S., Yadeta, K., Schwartz, H. A., Ungar, L. H., & Curtis, B. (2022). Linguistic predictors from Facebook postings of substance use disorder treatment retention versus discontinuation. *The American Journal of Drug and Alcohol Abuse*, *48*(5), 573–585. DOI: 10.1080/00952990.2022.2091450

Livingston, M., Raninen, J., Pennay, A., & Callinan, S. (2023). The relationship between age at first drink and later risk behaviours during a period of youth drinking decline. *Addiction (Abingdon, England)*, *118*(2), 256–264. DOI: 10.1111/add.16036

Logothetis, N. K. (2002). The neural basis of the blood-oxygen-level-dependent functional magnetic resonance imaging signal. *Philosophical Transactions of the Royal Society of London. Series B, Biological Sciences*, *357*(1424), 1003–1037. DOI: 10.1098/rstb.2002.1114

Lu, Z., Xie, C., Liu, N., Xie, Y., & Lu, H. (2023). Can we predict aggression? Determining the predictors of aggression among individuals with substance use disorder in China undergoing enforced detoxification through machine learning. *Journal of Affective Disorders*, *320*, 628–637. DOI: 10.1016/j.jad.2022.12.050

Maas, L. C., Lukas, S. E., Kaufman, M. J., Weiss, R. D., Daniels, S. L., Rogers, V. W., & Renshaw, P. F. (1998). Functional magnetic resonance imaging of human brain activation during cue-induced cocaine craving. *The American Journal of Psychiatry*, *155*(1), 124–126. DOI: 10.1176/ajp.155.1.124

Machado, H., Silva, S., & Neiva, L. (2025). Publics' views on ethical challenges of artificial intelligence: A scoping review. *AI and Ethics*, *5*(1), 139–167. DOI: 10.1007/s43681-023-00299-6

Mak, K. K., Lee, K., & Park, C. (2019). Applications of machine learning in addiction studies: A systematic review. *Psychiatry Research*, *275*, 53–60. DOI: 10.1016/j.psychres.2019.03.001

Marcovitz, D. E., McHugh, R. K., Volpe, J., Votaw, V., & Connery, H. S. (2016). Predictors of early dropout in outpatient buprenorphine/naloxone treatment. *The American Journal on Addictions*, *25*(6), 472–477. DOI: 10.1111/ajad.12414

Martz, M. E., Hart, T., Heitzeg, M. M., & Peltier, S. J. (2020). Neuromodulation of brain activation associated with addiction: A review of real-time fMRI neurofeedback studies. *NeuroImage. Clinical*, *27*, 102350. DOI: 10.1016/j.nicl.2020.102350

Mattos, B. P., Mattjie, C., Barros, R. C., & Grassi-Oliveira, R. (2024). Craving for a robust methodology: A systematic review of machine learning algorithms on substance-use disorders treatment outcomes. *International Journal of Mental Health and Addiction*. Advance online publication. DOI: 10.1007/s11469-024-01403-z

McHugh, R. K., Murray, H. W., Hearon, B. A., Pratt, E. M., Pollack, M. H., Safren, S. A., & Otto, M. W. (2013). Predictors of dropout from psychosocial treatment in opioid-dependent outpatients. *The American Journal on Addictions*, *22*(1), 18–22. DOI: 10.1111/j.1521-0391.2013.00322.x

McKellar, J., Harris, A. H., & Moos, R. H. (2006). Predictors of outcome for patients with substance-use disorders five years after treatment dropout. *Journal of Studies on Alcohol and Drugs*, *67*(5), 685–693. DOI: 10.15288/jsa.2006.67.685

McLellan, A. T., Lewis, D. C., O'Brien, C. P., & Kleber, H. D. (2000). Drug dependence, a chronic medical illness: Implications for treatment, insurance, and outcomes evaluation. *Journal of the American Medical Association*, *284*(13), 1689–1695. DOI: 10.1001/jama.284.13.1689

Mehrabi, N., Morstatter, F., Saxena, N., Lerman, K., & Galstyan, A. (2022). A survey on bias and fairness in machine learning. *ACM Computing Surveys*, *55*(6), 1–35. DOI: 10.1145/3457607

Menon, S., Swathi, J., Anit, S. K., Nair, A. P., & Sarath, S. (2019). Driver face recognition and sober–drunk classification using thermal images. In *2019 International Conference on Communication and Signal Processing (ICCSP)* (pp. 400–404). IEEE. https://doi.org/DOI: 10.1109/ICCSP.2019.8697908

Merikangas, K. R., & Avenevoli, S. (2000). Implications of genetic epidemiology for the prevention of substance use disorders. *Addictive Behaviors*, *25*(6), 807–820. DOI: 10.1016/S0306-4603(00)00129-5

Merikangas, K. R., & McClair, V. L. (2012). Epidemiology of substance use disorders. *Human Genetics*, *131*(6), 779–789. DOI: 10.1007/s00439-012-1168-0

Moghadasi, M. N., Zhuang, Y., & Gellban, H. (2020, July). Robo: A counselor chatbot for opioid-addicted patients. In *Proceedings of the 2020 2nd Symposium on Signal Processing Systems* (pp. 91–95). ACM. https://doi.org/DOI: 10.1145/3410352.3410359

Moningka, H., Lichenstein, S., Worhunsky, P. D., DeVito, E. E., Scheinost, D., & Yip, S. W. (2019). Can neuroimaging help combat the opioid epidemic? A systematic review of clinical and pharmacological challenge fMRI studies with recommendations for future research. *Neuropsychopharmacology : Official Publication of the American College of Neuropsychopharmacology*, *44*(2), 259–273. DOI: 10.1038/s41386-018-0232-4

Moonajilin, M. S., Kamal, M. K. I., Mamun, F. A., Safiq, M. B., Hosen, I., Manzar, M. D., & Mamun, M. A. (2021). Substance use behavior and its lifestyle-related risk factors in Bangladeshi high school-going adolescents: An exploratory study. *PLoS One*, *16*(7), e0254926. DOI: 10.1371/journal.pone.0254926

Morel, T., Cornet, V., & Nguyen, T. (2020). Predicting hospital readmissions among patients with substance use and mental health disorders using machine learning. *International Journal of Medical Informatics*, *141*, 104225. DOI: 10.1016/j.ijmedinf.2020.104225

Murphy, K. P. (2012). *Machine learning: A probabilistic perspective*. MIT Press.

Naeger, S., Mutter, R., Ali, M. M., Mark, T., & Hughey, L. (2016). Post-discharge treatment engagement among patients with an opioid-use disorder. *Journal of Substance Abuse Treatment*, *69*, 64–71. DOI: 10.1016/j.jsat.2016.07.004

Nasir, M., Summerfield, N. S., Oztekin, A., Knight, M., Ackerson, L. K., & Carreiro, S. (2021). Machine learning–based outcome prediction and novel hypotheses generation for substance use disorder treatment. *Journal of the American Medical Informatics Association : JAMIA*, *28*(6), 1216–1224. DOI: 10.1093/jamia/ocab008

National Institute on Drug Abuse. (2023). *Substance use disorder: Clinical and public health approaches.* National Institutes of Health. https://nida.nih.gov/publications

Nazari, S., Pourmand, S. M., Makki, S. M., Brand, S., & Vousooghi, N. (2022). Potential biomarkers of addiction identified by real-time PCR in human peripheral blood lymphocytes: A narrative review. *Biomarkers in Medicine*, *16*(9), 739–758. DOI: 10.2217/bmm-2021-0291

Nordheim, K., Walderhaug, E., Alstadius, S., Kern-Godal, A., Arnevik, E., & Duckert, F. (2018). Young adults' reasons for dropout from residential substance use disorder treatment. *Qualitative Social Work: Research and Practice*, *17*(1), 24–40. DOI: 10.1177/1473325016654559

Norman, S. B., Tate, S. R., Anderson, K. G., & Brown, S. A. (2007). Do trauma history and PTSD symptoms influence addiction relapse context? *Drug and Alcohol Dependence*, *90*(1), 89–96. DOI: 10.1016/j.drugalcdep.2007.03.002

Ogilvie, L., Prescott, J., & Carson, J. (2022). The use of chatbots as supportive agents for people seeking help with substance use disorder: A systematic review. *European Addiction Research*, *28*(6), 405–418. DOI: 10.1159/000525460

Ogilvie, L., Prescott, J., & Carson, J. (2025). An overview of the applied use of chatbots for substance use disorder: Past, present and future. *Counselling & Psychotherapy Research*, *25*, e12786. DOI: 10.1002/capr.12786

Ouimette, P., Coolhart, D., Funderburk, J. S., Wade, M., & Brown, P. J. (2007). Precipitants of first substance use in recently abstinent substance use disorder patients with PTSD. *Addictive Behaviors*, *32*(8), 1719–1727. DOI: 10.1016/j.addbeh.2006.11.020

Pan, Y., Feaster, D. J., Odom, G., Brandt, L., Hu, M. C., Weiss, R. D., & Balise, R. R. (2022). Specific polysubstance use patterns predict relapse among patients entering opioid use disorder treatment. *Drug and Alcohol Dependence Reports*, *5*, 100128. DOI: 10.1016/j.dadr.2022.100128

Panlilio, L., Stull, S., Bertz, J., Burgess-Hull, A., Kowalczyk, W., Phillips, K., & Preston, K. (2020). Beyond abstinence and relapse: Cluster analysis of drug-use patterns during treatment as an outcome measure for clinical trials. *Psychopharmacology*, *237*(11), 3369–3381. DOI: 10.1007/s00213-020-05618-5

Papamalis, F. E., Kalyva, E., Teare, M. D., & Meier, P. S. (2020). The role of personality functioning in drug misuse treatment engagement. *Addiction (Abingdon, England)*, *115*(4), 726–739. DOI: 10.1111/add.14872

Peterson, L. E. (2009). K-nearest neighbor. *Scholarpedia*, *4*(2), 1883. DOI: 10.4249/scholarpedia.1883

Pirro, V., Oliveri, P., Sciutteri, B., Salvo, R., Salomone, A., Lanteri, S., & Vincenti, M. (2013). Multivariate strategies for screening evaluation of harmful drinking. *Bioanalysis*, *5*(6), 687–699. DOI: 10.4155/bio.13.12

Polcin, D. L., & Korcha, R. (2017). Housing status, psychiatric symptoms, and substance abuse outcomes among sober living house residents over 18 months. *Addictive Disorders & Their Treatment*, *16*(3), 138–150. DOI: 10.1097/ADT.0000000000000105

Prochaska, J., Vogel, E., Chieng, A., Kendra, M., Baiocchi, M., & Malalang, D.. (2021). A randomized controlled trial of a therapeutic relational agent for reducing substance misuse during the COVID-19 pandemic. *Drug and Alcohol Dependence*, *227*, 108986. DOI: 10.1016/j.drugalcdep.2021.108986

Prokhorenkova, L., Gusev, G., Vorobev, A., Dorogush, A. V., & Gulin, A. (2018). CatBoost: Unbiased boosting with categorical features. *Advances in Neural Information Processing Systems*, *31*, 6638–6648.

Quintanilla, M. E., Morales, P., Santapau, D., Ávila, A., Ponce, C., Berrios-Cárcamo, P., & Ezquer, F. (2023). Chronic voluntary morphine intake is associated with changes in brain structures involved in drug dependence in a rat model of polydrug use. *International Journal of Molecular Sciences*, *24*(23), 17081. DOI: 10.3390/ijms242317081

Rabinowitz, J. A., Wells, J. L., Strickland, J. C., Hochheimer, M., Kahn, G., Ellis, J. D., & Huhn, A. S. (2025). Predictors of treatment attrition among individuals in substance use disorder treatment: A machine learning approach. *Addictive Behaviors*, *163*, 108265. DOI: 10.1016/j.addbeh.2024.107865

Rajapaksha, R. M. D. S., Filbey, F., Biswas, S., & Choudhary, P. (2022). A Bayesian learning model to predict the risk for cannabis use disorder. *Drug and Alcohol Dependence*, *236*, 109476. DOI: 10.1016/j.drugalcdep.2022.109476

Rajkomar, A., Dean, J., & Kohane, I. (2019). Machine learning in medicine. *The New England Journal of Medicine*, *380*(14), 1347–1359. DOI: 10.1056/NEJMra1814259

Richter, L., Pugh, B. S., & Ball, S. A. (2017). Assessing the risk of marijuana use disorder among adolescents and adults who use marijuana. *The American Journal of Drug and Alcohol Abuse*, *43*(3), 247–260. DOI: 10.1080/00952990.2016.1263640

Roberts, W., Zhao, Y., Verplaetse, T., Moore, K., Peltier, M., Burke, C., & McKee, S. (2022). Using machine learning to predict heavy drinking during outpatient alcohol treatment. *Alcohol, Clinical and Experimental Research*, *46*(4), 657–666. DOI: 10.1111/acer.14802

Roesler, D., Johnny, S., Conway, M., & Chen, A. T. (2024). A theory-informed deep learning approach to extracting and characterizing substance use related stigma in social media. *BMC Digital Health*, *2*, 60. DOI: 10.1186/s44247-024-00065-0

Saeidnia, H. R., Hashemi Fotami, S. G., Lund, B., & Ghiasi, N. (2024). Ethical considerations in artificial intelligence interventions for mental health and well-being: Ensuring responsible implementation and impact. *Social Sciences*, *13*(7), 381. DOI: 10.3390/socsci13070381

Salyers, A. J., Bull, S., Silvasstar, J., Howell, K., Wright, T., & Banaei-Kashani, F. (2025). Building and beta-testing Be Well Buddy Chatbot, a secure, credible and trustworthy AI chatbot that will not misinform, hallucinate or stigmatize substance use disorder: Development and usability study. *JMIR Human Factors*, *12*, e69144. DOI: 10.2196/69144

Schacht, J. P., Anton, R. F., & Myrick, H. (2013). Functional neuroimaging studies of alcohol cue reactivity: A quantitative meta-analysis and systematic review. *Addiction Biology*, *18*(1), 121–133. DOI: 10.1111/j.1369-1600.2012.00464

Seo, D., Lacadie, C. M., Tuit, K., Hong, K. I., Constable, R. T., & Sinha, R. (2013). Disrupted ventromedial prefrontal function, alcohol craving, and subsequent relapse risk. *JAMA Psychiatry*, *70*(7), 727–739. DOI: 10.1001/jamapsychiatry.2013.762

Sethuraman, D., Ananya, E., Jeffrey, J. J., Thangavel, S. K., Rangasami, P., & Somasundaram, K. (2025). Framework for drug user analysis and prediction. In *Proceedings of the Fourth International Conference on Sentiment Analysis and Deep Learning (ICSADL-2025)*. IEEE. https://doi.org/DOI: 10.1109/ICSADL.2025.1234567

Shipp, S., & Aeon, B. (2019). Temporal focus and recovery: How time perspective predicts substance use treatment outcomes. *Addiction Research and Theory*, *27*(3), 189–198. DOI: 10.1080/16066359.2018.1519422

Shokri, R., & Shmatikov, V. (2015, October). Privacy-preserving deep learning. In *Proceedings of the 22nd ACM SIGSAC Conference on Computer and Communications Security* (pp. 1310–1321). ACM. https://doi.org/DOI: 10.1145/2810103.2813687

Shrestha, S., Stapp, J., Taylor, M., Leach, R., Carreiro, S., & Indic, P. (2023). Towards device agnostic detection of stress and craving in patients with substance use disorder. In *Proceedings of the Annual Hawaii International Conference on System Sciences* (pp. 3156–3163). IEEE. https://doi.org/DOI: 10.24251/HICSS.2023.383

Sreeramareddy, C. T., Pradhan, P. M. S., Mir, I. A., & Sin, S. (2014). Smoking and smokeless tobacco use in nine South and Southeast Asian countries: Prevalence estimates and social determinants from Demographic and Health Surveys. *Population Health Metrics*, *12*(1), 22. DOI: 10.1186/s12963-014-0022-0

Staszak, M., Staszak, K., Wieszczycka, K., Bajek, A., Roszkowski, K., & Tylkowski, B. (2022). Machine learning in drug design: Use of artificial intelligence to explore the chemical structure–biological activity relationship. *Wiley Interdisciplinary Reviews. Computational Molecular Science*, *12*(2), e1568. DOI: 10.1002/wcms.1568

Suva, M., & Bhatia, G. (2024). Artificial intelligence in addiction: Challenges and opportunities. *Indian Journal of Psychological Medicine*, *46*(3), 213–220. DOI: 10.1177/02537176241234567

Swift, J. K., & Callahan, J. L. (2009). The impact of client preferences on treatment engagement and dropout. *Journal of Clinical Psychology*, *65*(2), 147–155. DOI: 10.1002/jclp.20543

Symons, M., Feeney, G. F. X., Gallagher, M. R., Young, R. M., Connor, J. P., Mc, D., & Young, R. (2019). Machine learning vs addiction therapists: A pilot study predicting alcohol dependence treatment outcome from patient data in behavior therapy with adjunctive medication. *Journal of Substance Abuse Treatment*, *99*, 156–162. DOI: 10.1016/j.jsat.2019.01.002

Taha Jijo, B., & Mohsin Abdulazeez, A. (2021). Classification based on decision tree algorithm for machine learning. *Journal of Applied Science and Technology Trends*, *2*(1), 20–28. DOI: 10.38094/jastt20109

Tassinari, D. L., Pedro, M. O. P., Pedro, M. P., Negrão, A. B., Amaral, R. A., Malbergier, A., Crispim, D. H., & Castaldelli-Maia, J. M. (2025). Artificial intelligence-driven and technological innovations in the diagnosis and management of substance use disorders. *International Review of Psychiatry (Abingdon, England)*, *37*(1), 52–58. DOI: 10.1080/09540261.2024.2432369

Ünlü, A., Hakkarainen, P., Karjalainen, K., Tammi, T., & Subasi, A. (2025). Identifying risk factors of substance use in Finland: A machine learning approach. *Substance Use & Misuse*. Advance online publication. DOI: 10.1080/10826084.2025.2516738

U.S. Department of Health and Human Services, Substance Abuse and Mental Health Services Administration, Center for Behavioral Health Statistics and Quality. (2017). *National Survey of Substance Abuse Treatment Services (N-SSATS) 2016: Data on substance abuse treatment facilities*. Author. https://www.samhsa.gov/data/sites/default/files/2016_NSSATS.pdf

Vafaie, N., & Kober, H. (2022). Association of drug cues and craving with drug use and relapse: A systematic review and meta-analysis. *JAMA Psychiatry*, *79*(7), 641–650. DOI: 10.1001/jamapsychiatry.2022.0937

Vayena, E., Blasimme, A., & Cohen, I. G. (2018). Machine learning in medicine: Addressing ethical challenges. *PLoS Medicine*, *15*(11), e1002689. DOI: 10.1371/journal.pmed.1002689

Venniro, M., Banks, M. L., Heilig, M., Epstein, D. H., & Shaham, Y. (2020). Improving translation of animal models of addiction and relapse by reverse translation. *Nature Reviews. Neuroscience, 21*(11), 625–643. DOI: 10.1038/s41583-020-0369-z

Volkow, N. D., & Blanco, C. (2023). Substance use disorders: A comprehensive update of classification, epidemiology, neurobiology, clinical aspects, treatment and prevention. *World Psychiatry; Official Journal of the World Psychiatric Association (WPA), 22*(2), 203–229. DOI: 10.1002/wps.21045

Waite, M. R., Heslin, K., Cook, J., Kim, A., & Simpson, M. (2023). Predicting substance use disorder treatment follow-ups and relapse across the continuum of care at a single behavioral health center. *Journal of Substance Abuse Treatment, 147*, 208933. DOI: 10.1016/j.jsat.2022.208933

Wang, E., Chang, W.-L., Shen, J., Bian, Q., Huang, P. L., & Lai, X. (2022). Effect of artificial intelligence on one-to-one emotional regulation and psychological intervention system of middle school students. *The International Journal of Neuropsychopharmacology, 25*(Suppl 1), A62–A63. DOI: 10.1093/ijnp/pyac032.086

Wang, J., & Fan, W. (2025). The effect of ChatGPT on students' learning performance, learning perception, and higher-order thinking: Insights from a meta-analysis. *Humanities & Social Sciences Communications, 12*(1), 1–21. DOI: 10.1057/s41599-025-1234-9

Wang, L., & Wang, L. (2022). A case study of Chinese sentiment analysis on social media reviews based on LSTM. *arXiv*. https://doi.org//arXiv.2210.17452DOI: 10.48550

Ware, O. D., Manuel, J. I., & Huhn, A. S. (2021). Adults with opioid and methamphetamine co-use have lower odds of completing short-term residential treatment than other opioid co-use groups: A retrospective health services study. *Frontiers in Psychiatry, 12*, 784229. DOI: 10.3389/fpsyt.2021.784229

Weinberger, A. H., Kashan, R. S., Shpigel, D. M., Esan, H., Taha, F., Lee, C. J., Funk, A. P., & Goodwin, R. D. (2017). Depression and cigarette smoking behavior: A critical review of population-based studies. *The American Journal of Drug and Alcohol Abuse, 43*(4), 416–431. DOI: 10.3109/00952990.2016.1141915

Weinstein, Z. M., Kim, H. W., Cheng, D. M., Quinn, E., Hui, D., Labelle, C. T., & Samet, J. H. (2017). Long-term retention in office-based opioid treatment with buprenorphine. *Journal of Substance Abuse Treatment, 74*, 65–70. DOI: 10.1016/j.jsat.2016.12.010

Williams, D., Hornung, H., Nadimpalli, A., & Peery, A. (2021). Deep learning and its application for healthcare delivery in low- and middle-income countries. *Frontiers in Artificial Intelligence*, *4*, 553987. DOI: 10.3389/frai.2021.553987

Williamson, S. M., & Prybutok, V. (2024). Balancing privacy and progress: A review of privacy challenges, systemic oversight, and patient perceptions in AI-driven healthcare. *Applied Sciences (Basel, Switzerland)*, *14*(2), 675. DOI: 10.3390/app14020675

Wilton, R., & Deverteuil, G. (2006). Spaces of sobriety/sites of power: Examining social model alcohol recovery programs as therapeutic landscapes. *Social Science & Medicine*, *63*(3), 649–661. DOI: 10.1016/j.socscimed.2006.01.022

World Health Organization. (2018). *Global status report on alcohol and health 2018*. World Health Organization. https://www.who.int/publications/i/item/9789241565639

Wright, T., Salyers, A., Howell, K., Harrison, J., Silvasstar, J., & Bull, S. (2025). A pilot study of an AI chatbot for the screening of substance use disorder in a healthcare setting. *AI*, *6*(6), 113. DOI: 10.3390/ai6060113

Wu, Z., Yue, Q., Zhao, Z., Wen, J., Tang, L., Zhong, Z., Yang, J., Yuan, Y., & Zhang, X. (2023). A cross-sectional study of smoking and depression among US adults: NHANES (2005–2018). *Frontiers in Public Health*, *11*, 1134234. DOI: 10.3389/fpubh.2023.1134234

Xu, J., Li, X., Liang, X., Zhang, X., Ying, G., & Liu, J. (2025). The risk factors for relapse behavior in individuals with substance use disorders: An interpretable machine learning study. *Journal of Affective Disorders*, *387*, 119520. DOI: 10.1016/j.jad.2024.12.056

Yang, J., Dung, N. T., Thach, P. N., Phong, N. T., & Dinh, V. (2023a). Generalizability assessment of AI models across hospitals: A comparative study in low-middle income and high-income countries. *medRxiv*. https://doi.org/DOI: 10.1101/2023.11.06.12345

Yang, J., & Giummarra, M. J. (2021). Compulsory and voluntary drug treatment models in China: A need for improved evidence-based policy and practice to reduce the loaded burden of substance use disorders. *The International Journal on Drug Policy*, *92*, 103063. DOI: 10.1016/j.drugpo.2020.103063

Yang, L., Du, Y., Yang, W., & Liu, J. (2023b). Machine learning with neuroimaging biomarkers: Application in the diagnosis and prediction of drug addiction. *Addiction Biology*, *28*(2), e13267. DOI: 10.1111/adb.13267

Zhang, T., Sun, L., Yin, X., Chen, H., Yang, L., & Yang, X. (2024). Burden of drug use disorders in the United States from 1990 to 2021 and its projection until 2035: Results from the GBD study. *BMC Public Health*, *24*(1), 1639. DOI: 10.1186/s12889-024-19142-0

Zhang-James, Y., Chen, Q., Kuja-Halkola, R., Lichtenstein, P., Larsson, H., & Faraone, S. V. (2020). Machine-learning prediction of comorbid substance use disorders in ADHD youth using Swedish registry data. *Journal of Child Psychology and Psychiatry, and Allied Disciplines*, *61*(12), 1370–1379. DOI: 10.1111/jcpp.13234

Zheng, A., & Casari, A. (2018). *Feature engineering for machine learning: Principles and techniques for data scientists*. O'Reilly Media.

Chapter 6

Neuroscientific Approach to Artificial Intelligence for Psychopathologies

Kübra Celik
https://orcid.org/0000-0002-0161-6179
Department of Psychology, Fenerbahce University, Istanbul, Turkey

Samet Celik
Bartin University, Turkey

ABSTRACT

Artificial intelligence (AI) is rapidly progressing innovative technology to simulate the human brain. AI technology provides important classifications, predictions and therapeutic interventions in different psychopathologies. Neuroscience research offers a wealth of inspiration for novel kinds of algorithms and architectures for early diagnostics and development of the disorder. Recently, many studies and reviews have investigated the mutual relationship between AI and neuroscience. Complex deep neural networks inspired by neuroanatomical structures are utilized to create variable AI models including working memory, visual processing, speech and emotion recognition to manifest behavioral abnormalities in psychopathologies. This scoping review focuses on how neuroscience and AI are convergent to understand underlying mechanisms in mental health disorders and the development of new models for prevention.

DOI: 10.4018/979-8-3373-1325-2.ch006

INTRODUCTION

The interaction between artificial intelligence (AI) systems and neuroscience has advanced in recent years. The question of 'Can machines think?' led to the beginning of this important relationship between AI and neuroscience in the computer era (Ullman, 2019). The assumption that creating general AI at the human level, often known as "Turing-powerful intelligence systems; Turing 1936) is a difficult undertaking due to the large and probably sparsely populated search space of potential solutions. Therefore, scientists needed to investigate brain and neural functions which are the sole evidence that such intelligence is feasible. Researching animal cognition and its implementation in the brain is also essential since it can shed light on many significant facets of higher-level general intelligence (Hassabis et al., 2017).

Cognitive functions such as visual search, detection, identification, and natural language processing can be modeled by using AI algorithms, also called deep learning. Several AI-driven technologies including brain-computer interfaces, neurostimulation devices, and neural implants work based on deep learning (DL) which employs neural networks to learn from massive datasets, whereas machine learning (ML) usually uses statistical techniques (Ienca & Ignatiadis, 2020; Sharifani & Amini, 2023).

Despite the progression of AI in many fields of medicine, it has been very limited in mental health care. The computational capability could be used to inform therapeutic applications by illuminating the intricate pathophysiology of mental illnesses. ML and natural language processing (NLP) are the most common methods to convert unstructured material into structured formats for further analysis since language and speech are the main sources of information used to diagnose and treat mental problems (Lee et al., 2021). DL makes facial recognition more reliable and accurate, making it possible to analyze medical images without the need for human interpretation. Furthermore, distinguishing subtle anatomical and functional abnormalities in the brain between mental patients and healthy participants is a diagnostic classification task that DL is especially well-suited for. It can efficiently extract complementary information from multimodal data, including electroencephalogram (EEG), positron emission computed tomography (PET) and magnetic resonance imaging (MRI), and capture higher-order features to make more precise and trustworthy diagnostic predictions. However, it brings different safety challenges and various limitations such as data quality and dataset shift (Monteith et al., 2022; Sun et al., 2023).

The limitation of explainability of NLP and the fact that pathologies cannot be understood only through inputs and outputs bring about ethical issues regarding the use of artificial intelligence in mental health care (Mccradden et al., 2023). Nevertheless, AI is a very powerful tool to simulate the brain mechanisms underlying different psychopathologies such as depression, schizophrenia, and autism to intervene. It also supports neuroscience research by giving insights into diagnostic and potential treatments. Overall, the purpose of this chapter is to give a scoping review of AI for psychopathologies from a neuroscientific approach along with the challenges, limitations and future directions.

NEUROSCIENCE AND ARTIFICIAL INTELLIGENCE FOR PSYCHOPATHOLOGIES

The integration of neuroscience and artificial intelligence offers powerful new approaches to understanding, diagnosing, predicting and treating psychopathology by modeling the complex neural and cognitive mechanisms underlying mental disorders (Gopinath,2023). Artificial Neural Networks (ANN) allow the creation of computational models such as Deep Neural Networks (DNN), through processing and classifying information between interconnected layers inspired by the human brain. DNN facilitates predictive decision-making, and the algorithms operate in connection with large structured and unstructured datasets used as an essential method in DL which is a form of ML (Ienca & Ignatiadis, 2020).

A simple DL consists of inputs representing the given data, interconnected hidden nodes, and output layers. The number of hidden nodes modeled mimicking biological synaptic network influences the risk of over-fitting and the decision-making process, with billions of nodes used in modern DL systems (Badrulhisham et al., 2024). Both DL and ML-based methods are used in mental health research and clinical practice.

Preclinical studies identify and characterize the neural components of behavioral patterns in animal studies with various algorithms. These computational tools such as SimBa can analyze the social behavior among groups and species with use of explainability metrics (Goodwin et.al,2024). Another framework, the error–trial–based approach known as reinforcement learning, was inspired by animal learning and introduced the concept of the discrepancy between predicted and received rewards. Temporal difference models further demonstrate the adaptive nature of both human and animal behavior across varying environments, reflecting computational processes localized in specific brain regions such as the prefrontal cortex (Alkam et al., 2025).

Beyond preclinical findings, deep learning–based classification approaches in post-traumatic stress disorder and major depressive disorder, utilizing visual and auditory biomarkers, have demonstrated validity and clinical potential (Schultebraucks et al., 2022). Similarly, the algorithm employed to identify the neurodevelopmental predictors of psychopathology has demonstrated consistency; however, it appears to be insufficient as a standalone predictive approach (Jirsaraie, 2025). Furthermore, other computational models of machine learning, such as Bayesian inference, dynamical systems modeling, and reinforcement learning, have revealed social learning impairments, hypo- and hyper-mentalizing patterns in autism and psychotic disorders, as well as disruptions in interpersonal functioning (Zavlis et al., 2025).

The most used algorithms of ML include linear discriminant analysis (LDA), gradient boosting machines, decision trees, ANNs, naïve Bayes, flexible discriminant analysis, support vector machines (SVMs), random forests, k-nearest neighbors (k-NN), bootstrap aggregating (bagging), stacking methods, and various regression algorithms. In addition, unsupervised learning models such as self-organizing maps (SOMs) and k-means clustering are frequently employed. Among supervised DL approaches, architectures such as deep belief networks (DBNs), DNNs, convolutional neural networks (CNNs), recurrent neural networks (RNNs), long short-term memory (LSTM) networks, and gated recurrent units (GRUs)—a simplified variant of LSTMs—are widely utilized. Unsupervised learning methods, on the other hand, can serve both generative and discriminative modeling purposes, contributing to representation learning and feature extraction (Younis et al., 2024).

The use of various algorithms, particularly those for pattern recognition/identification and feature extraction, has enabled predictive modeling in Alzheimer's disease by decoding disrupted neural signals and transforming them into meaningful outputs (Ding et al., 2019). Especially, learning and memory disruptions in Alzheimer's disease can be studied by AI-integrated cognitive neuroscience effectively. AI can analyze large datasets of brain scans in 6-8 hours and predict disease progression with 85% and explain memory performance %60-65 accuracy, even though ANN mimics human memory in special tasks with % 70% similarity (Tucmeanu & Tucmeanu, 2025).

Genomic, proteomic, structural, and functional databases provide a potential use in ML with different neuroimaging methods in mental health research (Ienca & Ignatiadis, 2020). Furthermore, it contributes novel technologies such as neurostimulation devices, implants, neuroprothetics and brain-computer interfaces (BCIs). Explainable Artificial Intelligence (XAI) as a more transparent, explainable and interpretable decision-making process for neurostimulation combined with BCI, provides many solutions in psychiatric disorders. ML algorithms could identify signal patterns in normal and abnormal states to contribute to diagnosing psychopathology and characterizing individual treatment selections (Fellous et al., 2019).

ML methods employed in BCI systems including feature extraction, selection and classification can be studied in mental and emotional state detection in special mental tasks, electroencephalogram (EEG) and event-related potentials (ERP) signal classification as well as motor imagery categorizations (Rasheed, 2021). The application of EEG-based emotion recognition and regulation within brain–computer interfaces has been shown to alleviate negative memories of traumatic events associated with depressive symptoms, suggesting its potential as a modulatory tool in mood disorders, particularly when combined with transcranial magnetic stimulation or deep brain stimulation (Zhang et al., 2024).

Consequently, neuroscience both inspires and supports the use of AI in cognitive domains such as learning, decision-making, and language processing, as well as in elucidating the mechanisms of neurological and psychiatric disorders through the classification and identification of brain networks. However, the organizational complexity of living systems has no true parallel in current AI models. To approach a state comparable to human cognition or consciousness, AI systems would need to capture and replicate this intricate biological complexity that characterizes the human brain (Aru et al., 2023).

AI MODELS IN TRANSLATIONAL STUDIES OF BEHAVIOR, COGNITION, AND PSYCHOPATHOLOGY

AI and ML models are widely employed in laboratory-based cognitive and behavioral research on psychopathology. These algorithms can recognize video-based behavioral patterns by extracting, quantifying, detecting, and labeling sequences using an encoder–decoder network to estimate whole-body poses and classify behaviors in three dimensions, thereby enabling the study of social interactions within cage environments. Furthermore, ML-based predictive models allow researchers to integrate such neuromarkers with neuroimaging methods to estimate behavioral patterns and states (Badrulhisham et al., 2024). These open-source softwares for automated behaviors such as Simple Behavioral Analysis (SimBA) provide an accessible ML for behavioral research. As a graphical user interface, it computes the relationship between body parts, movements, distances and sizes to estimate social behaviors individually (Goodwin et al., 2024).

Furthermore, reinforcement learning (RL) or recurrent neural networks are widely used to model human behavior and the decision-making process (Badrulhisham et al., 2024). These computational algorithms are inspired by the neurobiology of the brain to understand complex cognitive processes such as adaptive and social learning. It also gives essential insight to understand the mechanisms of psychopathologies such as depression, substance use disorders, and schizophrenia by demonstrating learning rates and reward valuation (Alkam et al., 2025). RL models can quantify abnormal reward prediction errors associated with disruptions in dopaminergic signaling and cortical circuits in schizophrenia (Maia & Frank, 2017). Similarly, reinforcement learning (RL) models simulate motivational processes in depression and reveal reward prediction errors along with associated cognitive outcomes (Huys et al., 2013). Hybrid computational models that combine RL with supervised and unsupervised learning can integrate multiple learning strategies, such as multimodal learning that merges information from various sensory modalities. These models may operate in a model-based manner—using an internal representation of the environment to plan actions, thereby mimicking prefrontal cortical functions—or in a model-free manner, learning through trial-and-error processes analogous to the striatal dopaminergic circuits (Liebenow et al., 2022; Alkam et al., 2025). Therefore, this framework primarily focuses on reward processing and punishment learning by measuring temporal difference prediction errors in psychopathologies characterized by hyperdopaminergic activation, such as schizophrenia and substance use disorders, as well as hypodopaminergic functioning observed in depression and post-traumatic stress disorder (Liebenow et al., 2022). Especially, it was reported that trauma disrupts RL in rodent models of chronic stress (Bielawaski et al., 2022).

Preclinical studies investigating the mechanisms underlying various cognitive processes, such as spatial navigation involving striatal–cortical circuits, suggest that cue-based navigation operates through associative learning. This framework indicates that model-free choices guide route-based navigation, whereas model-based choices underlie map-based navigation (Bermudez-Contreras et.al. 2020). Another neuroscience-inspired simulation tool models complex behavior using reinforcement learning (RL) and deep neural networks (DNNs), providing virtual maze environments commonly employed in animal research. Through a graphical user interface, it processes complex visual stimuli and utilizes a wide range of algorithms to measure behavioral responses across spatial and non-spatial tasks (Diekmann et al., 2023).

Reinforcement learning–based approaches offer a promising framework for optimizing the behavioral assessment of stress-induced phenotypes in rodents, thereby bridging the translational gap and advancing antidepressant discovery (Liao & Kwan, 2021). Several studies have employed rodent models to investigate adaptive value learning and decision-making processes related to behavioral and substance use patterns (Izquierdo et al., 2019), as well as reversal learning trajectories during adolescence (Afshar et al., 2020). Another study examined concurrent stimulus–action associations in adolescent and adult mice, demonstrating that both groups rely on incremental reinforcement learning and short-term memory mechanisms (Chase et al., 2024). Beyond these experimental findings, the integration of reinforcement learning with deep neural networks has enabled the development of virtual rodent models capable of predicting the neural activity patterns underlying abnormal behaviors (Aldarondo et al., 2024). These applications provide valuable insights into how animal models can be utilized in AI research to elucidate the mechanisms underlying abnormal cognitive and behavioral processes in various mental disorders, thereby establishing a foundation for future clinical studies.

CLINICAL APPLICATIONS OF AI MODELS IN PSYCHOPATHOLOGY

AI is redefining psychiatric diagnostic and treatment approaches by processing complex biological, behavioral, and linguistic data and is emerging as a significant transformational tool in this field (Ray et al., 2022). The relationship between AI and mental disorders has been shaped by efforts to model human mental processes and further developed through scientific studies aimed at understanding the human mind's functioning.

ML and ANNs stand out as the fundamental building blocks of AI-driven analysis in psychopathology These models have gained increasing attention in clinical applications for their ability to detect complex, non-linear patterns in large and heterogeneous datasets (Dwyer et al., 2018; Rutledge et al., 2019). By learning from multimodal data—such as neuroimaging, electrophysiological, genetic, and behavioral measures ML and ANN-based approaches contribute to improving diagnostic accuracy, identifying disorder-specific biomarkers, and predicting treatment responses (Bzdok & Meyer-Lindenberg, 2018). Consequently, they hold significant promise for advancing precision psychiatry and facilitating more individualized approaches to mental health care.

These technologies not only enable the development of human-like cognitive models such as learning, attention, and decision-making but also facilitate the simulation of various emotional processes. These technologies provide significant opportunities for processing and interpreting uniquely human psychological data, including emotion detection, classification, and recognition (Kanjo et al., 2019; Younis et al., 2024). To achieve this, supervised, unsupervised, and semi-supervised deep learning (DL) techniques are widely employed for the analysis of physiological signals (Liu & Lang, 2019). These methods are often implemented within a multimodal framework, integrating multiple sources of information such as facial expressions, speech, written text, and biosignals to enhance the accuracy and robustness of emotion recognition systems (Xu et al., 2017; Balan et al., 2020; Arsalan et al., 2022; Younis et al., 2024). Especially multi-channel EEG signal-based BCI provides more accurate and objective recognition of the emotional states in that multimodal framework (Houssein et al., 2022).

This framework involves multiple levels of data fusion. At the data level, raw data from various sources are integrated to ensure cooperation across modalities. The feature level, serving as an intermediate stage, maintains categorization by selecting the most informative and complementary features. Finally, the decision level represents the highest stage of fusion, where outcomes from different algorithms are combined through decision-making processes, enabling seamless integration with applications in other body sensor networks (Ilyas et al., 2021; Wang, et al.,

2022). Emotion detection from texts, facial expression, body gestures and postures leads to advanced clinical applications in psychiatry. Through these capabilities, AI-based systems contribute to a deeper comprehension of affective and cognitive mechanisms, offering new perspectives for the study and clinical assessment of complex psychological phenomena.

Another fundamental AI model used in clinical settings is Natural Language Processing (NLP), which enables the quantitative analysis of unstructured text data in psychiatry such as clinical conversations, medical records, patient satisfaction, sentiment analysis, drug evaluation. Various NLP approaches transform linguistic information into machine-readable representations and extract linguistic and acoustic features from raw data. NLP facilitates the diagnosis of mental disorders, assessment of affect and suicide risk, and examination of therapeutic processes, including therapeutic alliance, mutual affect, and linguistic coordination in patient–provider interactions. Moreover, it allows the evaluation of clinicians themselves by analyzing elements such as motivational interviewing, treatment fidelity, empathy, and conversational skills (Crema et al., 2022; Malgaroli et al., 2023). NLP applications rely on textual components, with electronic health records (EHRs) being among the most utilized sources. The next step involves text processing, during which relevant terms are extracted and matched with predefined identifiers or used to detect expressions associated with specific clinical conditions. Subsequently, machine learning (ML) algorithms are employed to classify and validate hypotheses or to analyze patient behavior patterns (Le Glaz et al., 2021).

Clinical applications of NLP integrated with ML have shown promising potential, while DL models further enhance usability by enabling the training of large-scale datasets. Compared to traditional ML, DL offers greater flexibility in processing unstructured text, and the availability of pretrained models increases accessibility (Crema et al., 2022). For example, Dai et al. (2021) applied several NLP methods based on DL, utilizing pretrained models on a small set of EHRs to facilitate patient screening across various psychopathological diagnoses.

One of the major limitations of current NLP applications in psychiatry is the lack of linguistic diversity. There exists a strong asymmetry between English-based and non-English models, primarily due to the scarcity of high-quality annotated datasets in other languages (Crema et al., 2022). This imbalance introduces training biases, which in turn limit the generalizability and cross-cultural applicability of the models (Malgaroli et al., 2023). Consequently, NLP systems developed within English-dominant contexts may perform suboptimally when applied to diverse linguistic or cultural populations.

AI-based interventions are increasingly being explored in clinical settings, with NLP-powered chatbots being used to support patients with depression and anxiety (Zhong et al., 2024). Other examples include the use of virtual reality for anxiety treatment, avatar-based therapy for patients diagnosed with psychosis, and AI-driven humanoid or animal-like robots to enhance therapy for children with mental health conditions. Additionally, digital game–based interventions have been applied to support cognitive and behavioral outcomes in adults with dementia, illustrating the broad potential of AI technologies in mental health care (Baber & Baker, 2025). In the following sections, a general overview of the psychopathologies in which AI models are most commonly used will be given.

Depression and anxiety are among the most prevalent psychiatric conditions affecting mental health worldwide. AI approaches to depression and anxiety encompass early detection, risk assessment, diagnosis, and monitoring to support personalized interventions. These methods utilize chatbots, virtual agents, wearable devices, neuroimaging, digital therapies and mood tracking (Zafar et al., 2024) and, importantly, EHRs, which serve as a crucial source of clinical data. Leveraging the ability of ML algorithms to process EHRs, Nemesure et al. (2021) analyzed data from 4,184 undergraduate students undergoing general health screenings to generate robust disease predictions. Their findings indicated that life satisfaction was the strongest predictor of depression, while anxiety was most strongly associated with up-to-date vaccinations and marijuana use. Another AI model used in depression is ML-integrated NLP models analyzing emotions by facial expressions and texts mentioned previously (Joshi & Kanoongo, 2022). Recent studies employing multimodal approaches have integrated large language models with data from texts, interviews and questionnaires, alongside facial expression analysis from audio, video frames, showing promising results in predicting depression severity (Sadeghi, et al., 2024; Zhang et al., 2024; Zhang et al., 2025).

Furthermore, Lekkas and Jacobson (2021) suggested that *Post-Traumatic Stress Disorder (PTSD)* diagnostic status could be predicted using GPS-derived data as a potential behavioral marker among previously traumatized women, highlighting the expanding role of AI in both diagnosis and intervention. Complementarily, advances in AI-driven augmented reality, which expose individuals to realistic and controlled scenarios, have been utilized to treat anxiety and PTSD symptoms by targeting social and occupational dysfunctions (Javanbakht et al., 2024). The potential of linguistic and speech pattern–related features as powerful predictors of PTSD has been increasingly recognized. Utilizing these features, robust binary classification models have achieved accuracies exceeding 90%, demonstrating substantial diagnostic potential (Hu et al., 2024).

Obsessive–Compulsive Disorder (OCD), classified among anxiety disorders in the DSM-V, has been a significant focus of AI-based research (Kim et al., 2025). ML and NLP techniques have been widely applied to assess psychological functioning in OCD (Grootendorst-van Mil et al., 2025), classify pharmacological treatments (Khazaneha et al., 2024), and investigate diagnostic features and their relationships with symptom severity (Clemmensen et al., 2022). Moreover, these approaches have been employed to analyze semantic associations, behavioral and neural processes underlying decision arbitration, and to optimize exposure-based treatment recommendations (Feusner et al., 2021; Ruan et al., 2023; Bernstein et al., 2025).

Schizophrenia (SZ) is a severe psychiatric disorder that profoundly affects both brain function and daily life. It is associated with abnormalities in early neurodevelopment and manifests through a wide range of symptoms, including hallucinations, disorganized thinking, diminished motivation, and cognitive impairments (Jiang et al., 2025). AI models used in SZ showed promising results for early diagnosis, prognosis assessment and further possible treatments. AI-based predictive models have demonstrated considerable accuracy in forecasting treatment response in SZ, with reported sensitivities of approximately 70% and specificities of around 76%. Among these, EEG-based models exhibit the highest predictive performance, followed by those utilizing neuroimaging data (Amleshi et al., 2025). Shivaprasad and colleagues (2024) harnessed five different explainable AI models to achieve early detection to assist mental health experts for care coordination. Another study applied DL techniques to an EEG dataset of individuals with SZ, focusing on event-related potentials and employing transfer entropy (TE) matrices within a hybrid DL framework. By integrating CNNs with bidirectional long short-term memory (BiLSTM) networks, the model achieved an impressive accuracy of 99.94% in detecting schizophrenia-related neural abnormalities (Paraschiv et al., 2024). In a genetic study on bipolar disorder and SZ conducted by Karthik and Sudha (2021) DL techniques were applied using an ANN to differentiate between the two disorders based on genetic data. The model was trained on 75 genes associated with schizophrenia and 67 genes linked to bipolar disorder. The ANN demonstrated high predictive performance, achieving 95.65% accuracy in identifying SZ and 97.01% accuracy in identifying bipolar disorder, highlighting the potential of AI-driven genetic approaches in distinguishing complex psychiatric conditions. These advancements highlight the potential of AI-driven approaches to facilitate personalized treatment strategies by understanding the genetic factors, enhancing medication adherence, and ultimately reducing the risk of relapse in individuals with SZ.

AI models have also been applied to sleep research, analyzing large datasets that include brainwave activity and other parameters obtained from polysomnography as well as self-reported measures. These approaches primarily focus on sleep stage classification and the detection of sleep-related disorders (Wara et al., 2025). In AI-based sleep research, wearable AI technologies have gained particular attention for their application in diagnosing and screening *sleep apnea* (Bazoukis et al., 2023). While these approaches have been widely implemented for assessment purposes, they have not yet been extended to treatment interventions. Among the various algorithms employed, CNNs have emerged as the most used method (Aziz et al.,

2025). Furthermore, CNN-based EEG signal processing has provided valuable insights into sleep staging in pediatric apnea, emphasizing both transparency and predictive accuracy (Vaquerizo-Villar et al., 2023). The integration of EEG recordings and other neuroimaging modalities into AI models will be discussed in greater detail in the following section.

The integration of AI models into everyday devices has demonstrated numerous beneficial effects across various pathologies. In particular, smartphone technologies provide an accessible platform, and it has shown that AI integration into smartphones can enhance personalized assessment and treatment, especially in the context of *eating disorders* (Linardon & Torous, 2025). Furthermore, He and Ji (2025) proposed the use of AI models applied to social media platforms as a promising approach for detecting eating disorders. Accordingly, when *anorexia nervosa*–related content on social media was analyzed using AI models, females exhibited higher rates of negative indicators than males, suggesting potential biological factors and elevated suicide risk. The findings further indicated that biological processes and suicide risk factors were particularly relevant for classifying positive cases in males. In contrast, age, emotional states, and personal concerns were more influential for female cases (Solans Noguero et al., 2023). Since technology plays an essential role in eating disorders, Monaco and colleagues (2024) aimed to utilize ML and DL methods to diagnose and intervene in eating disorders by collecting and analyzing data from multiple sources. They proposed that integrating this information securely through a chatbot could represent a significant step toward personalized treatment for individuals with eating disorders.

Neurodevelopmental disorders (NDs) arise from a complex interplay of intrinsic and extrinsic factors, and AI models have made significant contributions to understanding their underlying mechanisms. AI-based genetic analyses have demonstrated strong success in identifying genetic factors associated with neurodevelopmental delays, thereby enhancing diagnostic accuracy (Yang et al., 2024). Moreover, ML and DL models play a pivotal role in drug discovery by modeling biological properties, which supports advancements in personalized medicine. ML techniques have also been utilized to detect pre-pregnancy and perinatal risk factors linked to neurodevelopmental deficits (Uddin et al., 2019). Beyond diagnostics, AI applications extend to supportive education, addressing learning challenges in children with NDs (Barua et al., 2022). Furthermore, interactive robots designed to enhance communication and emotion recognition have paved the way for AI-based emotion therapy systems, offering promising therapeutic potential for individuals with autism spectrum disorder (Bhargavi et al., 2023; Autzymu et al., 2024; Stasolla et al., 2024). Another innovative application combines the Internet of Things (IoT) with AI to process multimodal data for risk assessment, offering improved management of challenges in preterm neonates (Shah et al., 2025).

Similarly, AI models are used for screening, risk prediction, diagnosis, classification, and identifying heterogeneous subtypes of *Attention Deficit and Hyperactivity Disorder (ADHD)* by integrating multiple data sources. DL often functions as a feature extractor, generating rich representations that can then be utilized by ML algorithms for final classification, combining DL's representational power with ML's efficiency in a hybrid model (Zhao et al., 2025; Zaheer & Akhtar, 2025). For example, these approaches have been used to identify children at high risk for developing ADHD through questionnaire data and parental health records, as well as to support diagnosis and subtype classification. They have also contributed to improving ADHD assessment and treatment planning by analyzing patients' motor patterns and cognitive processes using EEG data, achieving accuracies as high as 98.21% (Zhao et al., 2025; Yu & Fang, 2024). Several studies have employed AI-integrated virtual reality and eye-tracking technologies to enhance screening, early detection, and diagnosis of ADHD (Yeh et al., 2020; Chen et al., 2023; Oh et al., 2024; Wiebe et al., 2024; Yoo et al., 2024; Garg et al., 2025). Altogether, these advancements underscore the expanding role of AI-driven, multimodal tools in refining clinical decision-making and improving the precision of psychopathological assessments.

Diagnosing *neurodegenerative diseases* such as Alzheimer's, Parkinson's disease, ALS, and frontotemporal dementia can be challenging as well, as many conditions present overlapping clinical symptoms. Computational approaches, particularly ML methods, offer valuable support for improving diagnosis, monitoring progression, and informing treatment strategies. Moreover, before AI approaches can be fully integrated into clinical practice, their use in animal and cellular models of neurodegeneration provides a crucial avenue for advancing our understanding of the underlying pathology (Marzi et al., 2023). Several studies have applied AI approaches to genetic data to support disease diagnosis and monitor progression, while others have integrated AI into nanomedicine to enhance disease modeling. AI-guided nanoparticle platforms and closed-loop delivery systems represent emerging innovations that remain vital for developing more effective and personalized therapeutic strategies. (Bettencourt et al., 2023; Gupta et.al, 2025; Hassan et al., 2025).

Supervised and unsupervised ML methods are widely used to classify disease stages using MRI and PET imaging data. NLP techniques can analyze speech and language biomarkers, cognitive decline, and behavioral patterns, and can be integrated into continuous cognitive monitoring systems. AI models are also used to examine health records to identify risk factors, while wearable devices enable AI-based analysis of gait abnormalities by tracking motion data. Additionally, deep learning approaches have demonstrated strong utility in predicting long-term risk in neurodegenerative diseases (Mohammad et al., 2021; Ali, 2022).

While AI applications in different psychopathologies have demonstrated remarkable potential in diagnosis, treatment personalization, and risk assessment, understanding the neural underpinnings of these disorders remains equally essential. Integrating AI with neuroimaging techniques provides a powerful framework for uncovering brain-based biomarkers and mapping complex neural patterns associated with mental disorders. Therefore, the following section will focus on how neuroimaging data is incorporated into AI models to enhance diagnostic precision and deepen our understanding of psychopathological mechanisms.

AI IN NEUROIMAGING FOR PSYCHOPATHOLOGIES

Over the past two decades, technological advances in medical imaging and the rise of generative artificial intelligence have fundamentally transformed the diagnosis and treatment processes of psychiatric disorders, as in many other areas of medicine. In particular, the subjective nature of clinician evaluations based on traditional diagnostic systems, the low inter-rater reliability, and the fact that current classification systems—such as the DSM and ICD—are primarily symptom-based and often fail to provide biologically grounded distinctions have driven researchers to adopt more objective data-driven tools (Brahma & Vimal, 2024; Sun et al., 2025). From this perspective, various algorithms—especially deep learning models- offer the opportunity to be used for multiple purposes such as differential diagnosis (Calesella et al., 2024; Fu et al., 2023; Takizawa et al., 2014), disease classification and subtyping (Quaak et al., 2021), early diagnosis (Baran & Cetin, 2025), treatment response (Curtiss & DiPietro, 2025), and prognosis prediction (Brahma & Vimal, 2024; Lin et al., 2020). For this purpose, many studies aim to achieve a high level of predictive accuracy by using different measurement methods (modalities) to identify the conditions mentioned above more accurately. These methods may include electrophysiological, hemodynamic, biochemical, genetic, and behavioral data (Ostojic et al., 2024). However, in this section, the discussion of Artificial Intelligence (AI) algorithms in relation to mental health will be limited to studies that utilize neuroimaging data. Within the field of neuroimaging, most research has focused on structural magnetic resonance imaging (MRI), functional magnetic resonance imaging (fMRI), diffusion tensor imaging (DTI), and positron emission tomography (PET) techniques. Other measurement methods will not be discussed in detail here, as algorithms tend to differ significantly when applied to electrophysiological or other types of data.

In this section, rather than summarizing research findings for each mental diagnosis, the focus was placed on mental disorders that are most common in the general population and have been studied most extensively. Accordingly, this section highlights the primary areas of overlap and common applications between mental health research and artificial intelligence (AI), as well as the current limitations of these approaches (Baumeister & Härter, 2007; Bijl et al., 1998; Brossollet et al., 2023; Nochaiwong et al., 2021).

From past to present, the classification of mental disorders has been based on common and overlapping clusters of symptoms. However, in mental disorders, symptoms are individual-specific—in other words, the symptoms present in each patient vary from one another, and the severity of these symptoms also varies.

In mental disorders, symptom expression is highly individual-specific; that is, both the type and severity of symptoms vary considerably across patients. This variability contributes to clinical heterogeneity, posing significant challenges for AI-based disease classification and biotyping. To address this, DL and ML approaches aim to reduce heterogeneity and identify underlying biotypes by integrating brain data from multiple modalities. Among the most widely used algorithms for detecting patterns in psychiatric datasets are support vector machines, random forests, and CNNs (Bloch & Friedrich, 2024; Avbersek & Repovs, 2022; Vieira et al., 2020; Wolfers et al., 2015). For example, Liang and colleagues (2020) used resting-state functional magnetic resonance imaging (rs-fMRI) data from 1,397 individuals to classify individuals with major depressive disorder into two groups: hypoDMN and hyperDMN subtypes. Drysdale (2017), using a dataset of 1,188 individuals, classified patients with major depression into four subtypes based on dysfunction detected in the limbic and frontostriatal networks. The researchers suggested that these four biotypes had sensitivity and specificity levels of 82% and 93% in classifying depression subtypes. Therefore, the identified biomarkers could be used as an objective method for classifying patients. However, subsequent researchers reported that they did not find similar findings when they repeated the studies using the same dataset (Dinga et al., 2019).

Similar AI algorithms have also been used in the differential diagnosis of other mental disorders. For example, Sun et al. (2018) reported prediction rates of up to 85% in their classification of individuals diagnosed with ADHD based on fMRI data, while Zheng et al. (2021) reported 84% for schizophrenia (Zheng et al., 2021). As can be seen, prediction accuracies in the differential diagnosis of mental disorders remain relatively modest. Moreover, the reproducibility and validation of these studies tend to be low.

Among the main reasons for this are the use of datasets derived from different samples, variability in preprocessing steps, differences in the algorithms employed, and the inclusion of data obtained from distinct modalities. For instance, while some researchers analyze resting-state imaging data, others prefer event-related neuroimaging approaches collected during specific cognitive tasks (Costafreda et al., 2011; Jiao et al., 2025).

While the success rates of AI algorithms for classifying mental disorders vary, researchers have recently opted for large datasets from different modalities to achieve higher prediction rates. Using datasets with large sample sizes from different modalities enhances the learning capacity of ML and DL algorithms, significantly improving their prediction accuracy (Bhattacharya et al., 2025; Feng et al., 2025; Luo et al., 2024; Manning et al., 2025). However, while diversifying the data source and increasing the sample size provide significant advantages to researchers, they also present several challenges. First, the use of large amounts of multimodal data in AI algorithms requires more advanced hardware infrastructure (such as high processing power (GPU/TPU) and large memory capacity). Furthermore, it also increases the training time of the algorithms. Finally, using different data types increases preprocessing time and can lead to modeling errors and overfitting. Therefore, researchers should carefully consider the drawbacks of multimodal data when considering its use and carefully consider the trade-off between model accuracy and computational cost.

ML and DL algorithms are also being used to assess the prognosis of mental disorders. However, studies on the clinical course of individuals with mental disorders using AI algorithms have yielded results below those seen in other applications. Studies using neuroimaging data have modeled clinical course prediction rates with 70% or higher accuracy (Koutsouleris et al., 2018; Plitta et al., 2015; Thompson et al., 2014; Tran et al., 2014). For example, Das and colleagues modeled gyrification-based network properties in individuals at risk for psychotic disorders to some extent predicting the development of psychosis (Das et al., 2018). Zaremba et al. (2018) targeted the insula and dorsolateral prefrontal cortex volume reduction as a biomarker in patients with depression at 2-year follow-up and accepted it as an indicator of relapse.

The major limitation of prognostic studies is the short follow-up period and inadequate sample size. In some psychiatric disorders—especially neurotic disorders such as depression and anxiety—when individuals have access to treatment options and respond relatively quickly, this limits follow-up studies. Furthermore, some psychiatric disorders may be shorter in nature (e.g., acute stress disorder). Missing data in longitudinal studies also limits the effectiveness of these studies. (Khodayari-Rostamabad et al., 2010; Kambeitz-Ilankovic et al., 2016; Gong et al., 2011).

Research on disease progression and prognosis prediction has been increasing rapidly over the years. These studies aim not only to determine the severity of symptoms in patients in the future but also to estimate the long-term impact of the disease on social and daily functioning, thereby improving individuals' overall quality of life. Thus, by implementing early intervention and preventative programs for individuals at risk of disease, these predictions will not only help protect individuals' health before it deteriorates, but also contribute to social well-being by preventing increased treatment costs later on (Lebedeva et al., 2017; Lee et al., 2021; Wilson, 2015).

However, specific challenges arise, particularly in predicting disease course and prognosis. The first is that mental disorders do not always have clear initiating and predisposing factors. Some mental disorders have a genetic predisposition but can persist for years without impairing an individual's daily functioning. Therefore, early disease course and identification of risk groups are not always easy. While some patients have very severe prognoses and are characterized by the manifestation of multiple major symptom clusters, others may struggle with mental illnesses with milder symptoms.

Another potential challenge is the lack of longitudinal data. Researchers can track participants' longitudinal data for periods of one or two years and use it as input for AI algorithms; however, for the reasons mentioned above, longitudinal data collected from multimodal sources is also needed. However, the need for multimodal data underscores the requirement for substantial funding, on the one hand, and the necessity for systematic, controlled experimental research, on the other.

Finally, research conducted for differential diagnosis and treatment prediction in mental disorders is driven by the comorbid conditions inherent in psychiatric illnesses. For example, nearly 50% of patients with depression may have other comorbid psychiatric illnesses or complaints, particularly generalized anxiety disorder (Hirschfeld, 2001; Kalin, 2020). This impacts situations such as the search for biomarkers or the prediction of treatment outcomes for the psychiatric disorder under investigation. This limitation also explains why AI algorithms developed for mental disorders have lower predictive accuracy compared to other physical illnesses.

CONCLUSION

AI applications, which emulate key aspects of human cognition, are becoming increasingly integral to psychiatry, both in clinical practice and in elucidating the mechanisms of psychopathology. This progress is strongly supported by neuroscience-based approaches, as findings from neuroscience guide the development of more sophisticated AI models. In turn, these models generate novel insights that further advance neuroscience, highlighting a reciprocal and mutually reinforcing relationship between the two fields. However, despite these advantages and promising results, several challenges, such as a lack of standardized multimodal data, generalization, interpretability, and exact clinical validation (Zhao et al., 2025). In addition to technical limitations, many AI applications are developed and used outside traditional healthcare settings, which can introduce biases in data collection and ultimately contribute to inequities in mental health care (Martinez-Martin, 2022). Such biases may lead to reduced empathy and potential injustices, raising concerns about accountability for AI-driven decisions.

Moreover, the inherent "black box" nature of many AI models limits explainability, transparency, and trust, creating obstacles in clinical decision-making and increasing the risk of harmful or inappropriate recommendations. Continuous reliance on AI tools such as chatbots may contribute to social isolation and loneliness, and their recommendations may be insufficient for managing crises or suicidal emergencies, where human intervention remains essential. Although chatbots can offer supportive guidance, they must be designed with enhanced capabilities to address urgent situations effectively. These concerns further underscore the importance of ensuring strong privacy and confidentiality protections in all AI-mediated mental health interactions (Warrier et al., 2023; Meadi et al., 2025; Poudel et al., 2025)).

A recent study proposed an ethical framework for adolescents and young adults grounded in the principles of bioethics, beneficence, and justice to address the emerging challenges posed by AI (Figueroa et al., 2025). Similarly, Putica and colleagues (2025) introduced the Integrated Ethical Approach for Computational Psychiatry (IEACP) with different ethical values such as beneficence, autonomy, justice, privacy, transparency and scientific integrity. Looking ahead, the integration of ethical frameworks into AI-mediated mental healthcare will be critical for ensuring safe, equitable, and responsible implementation across clinical settings. Such developments will not only safeguard the well-being of both clinicians and patients but also strengthen the synergy between AI and neuroscience, promoting more precise diagnostics, personalized interventions, and improved mental health outcomes. Continued interdisciplinary collaboration, alongside rigorous evaluation of AI tools, will be essential for shaping the future of ethically grounded, scientifically robust, and clinically meaningful applications in psychiatry.

REFERENCES

Afshar, N. M., Keip, A. J., Taylor, J. R., Lee, D., & Groman, S. M. (2020). Reinforcement learning during adolescence in rats. *The Journal of Neuroscience : The Official Journal of the Society for Neuroscience*, *40*(30), 5857–5870.

Aldarondo, D., Merel, J., Marshall, J. D., Hasenclever, L., Klibaite, U., Gellis, A., & Ölveczky, B. P. (2024). A virtual rodent predicts the structure of neural activity across behaviours. *Nature*, *632*(8025), 594–602.

Ali, H. (2022). AI in neurodegenerative disease research: Early detection, cognitive decline prediction, and brain imaging biomarker identification. *Int J Eng Technol Res Manag*, *6*(10), 71.

Alkam, T., Van Benschoten, A. H., & Tarshizi, E. (2025). Reinforcement learning in artificial intelligence and neurobiology. *Neuroscience Informatics*, 100220.

Amleshi, R. S., Ilaghi, M., Rezaei, M., Zangiabadian, M., Rezazadeh, H., Wegener, G., & Arjmand, S. (2025). Predictive utility of artificial intelligence on schizophrenia treatment outcomes: A systematic review and meta-analysis. *Neuroscience and Biobehavioral Reviews*, *169*, 105968.

Arsalan, A., Majid, M., Nizami, I. F., Manzoor, W., Anwar, S. M., & Ryu, J. (2022). Human stress assessment: A comprehensive review of methods using wearable sensors and non-wearable techniques. *arXiv preprint arXiv:2202.03033*.

Aru, J., Larkum, M. E., & Shine, J. M. (2023). The feasibility of artificial consciousness through the lens of neuroscience. *Trends in Neurosciences*, *46*(12), 1008–1017.

Aziz, S., & Ali, AM, A., Aslam, H., A Abd-alrazaq, A., AlSaad, R., Alajlani, M., ... & Sheikh, J. (2025). Wearable Artificial Intelligence for Sleep Disorders: Scoping Review. *Journal of Medical Internet Research*, *27*, e65272.

Baber, M., & Baker, B. (2025). AI-based treatment of psychological conditions: The potential use, benefits and drawbacks. *Exploration of Digital Health Technologies*, *3*, 101143.

Badrulhisham, F., Pogatzki-Zahn, E., Segelcke, D., Spisak, T., & Vollert, J. (2024). Machine learning and artificial intelligence in neuroscience: A primer for researchers. *Brain, Behavior, and Immunity*, *115*, 470–479.

Baran, F. D. E., & Cetin, M. (2025). AI-driven early diagnosis of specific mental disorders: A comprehensive study. *Cognitive Neurodynamics*, *19*(1).

Barua, P. D., Vicnesh, J., Gururajan, R., Oh, S. L., Palmer, E., Azizan, M. M., & Acharya, U. R. (2022). Artificial intelligence enabled personalised assistive tools to enhance education of children with neurodevelopmental disorders—A review. *International Journal of Environmental Research and Public Health, 19*(3), 1192.

Baumeister, H., & Härter, M. (2007). Prevalence of mental disorders based on general population surveys. *Social Psychiatry and Psychiatric Epidemiology, 42*(7), 537–546.

Bazoukis, G., Bollepalli, S. C., Chung, C. T., Li, X., Tse, G., Bartley, B. L., & Armoundas, A. A. (2023). Application of artificial intelligence in the diagnosis of sleep apnea. *Journal of Clinical Sleep Medicine : JCSM : Official Publication of the American Academy of Sleep Medicine, 19*(7), 1337–1363.

Bermudez-Contreras, E., Clark, B. J., & Wilber, A. (2020). The neuroscience of spatial navigation and the relationship to artificial intelligence. *Frontiers in Computational Neuroscience, 14*, 63.

Bernstein, E. E., Jaroszewski, A. C., Jacoby, R. J., Bailen, N. H., Ragan, J., Usmani, A., & Wilhelm, S. (2025). Feasibility of using ChatGPT to generate exposure hierarchies for treating Obsessive-Compulsive disorder. *Behavior Therapy*.

Bettencourt, C., Skene, N., Bandres-Ciga, S., Anderson, E., Winchester, L. M., Foote, I. F., & Llewellyn, D. J. (2023). Artificial intelligence for dementia genetics and omics. *Alzheimer's & Dementia, 19*(12), 5905–5921.

Bhargavi, Y., Bini, D., & Prince, S. (2023, March). AI-based emotion therapy bot for children with autism spectrum disorder (ASD). In *2023 9th International Conference on Advanced Computing and Communication Systems (ICACCS)* (Vol. 1, pp. 1895-1899). IEEE.

Bhattacharya, S., Prusty, S., Pande, S. P., Gulhane, M., Lavate, S. H., Rakesh, N., & Veerasamy, S. (2025). Integration of multimodal imaging data with machine learning for improved diagnosis and prognosis in neuroimaging. *Frontiers in Human Neuroscience, 19*(March), 1–9.

Bijl, R. V., Ravelli, A., & Van Zessen, G. (1998). Prevalence of psychiatric disorder in the general population: Results of the Netherlands Mental Health Survey and Incidence Study (NEMESIS). *Social Psychiatry and Psychiatric Epidemiology, 33*(12), 587–595.

Bloch, L., & Friedrich, C. M. (2024). Systematic comparison of 3D Deep learning and classical machine learning explanations for Alzheimer's Disease detection. *Computers in Biology and Medicine, 170*(January).

Brahma, N., & Vimal, S. (2024). Artificial intelligence in neuroimaging: Opportunities and ethical challenges. *Brain & Spine*, *4*(July), 102919.

Brossollet, I., Gallet, Q., Favre, P., & Houenou, J. (2023). Machine Learning and Brain Imaging for Psychiatric Disorders: New Perspectives. *Neuromethods*, *197*, 1009–1036.

Bzdok, D., & Meyer-Lindenberg, A. (2018). Machine learning for precision psychiatry: Opportunities and challenges. *Biological Psychiatry: Cognitive Neuroscience and Neuroimaging*, *3*(3), 223–230.

Calesella, F., Colombo, F., Bravi, B., Fortaner-Uyà, L., Monopoli, C., Poletti, S., & Vai, B. (2024). A machine learning pipeline for efficient differentiation between bipolar and major depressive disorder based on multimodal structural neuroimaging. *Neuroscience Applied*, *3*, 103931.

Chase, J., Xia, L., Tai, L. H., Lin, W. C., Collins, A. G., & Wilbrecht, L. (2024). Adolescent and adult mice use both incremental reinforcement learning and short term memory when learning concurrent stimulus-action associations. *PLoS Computational Biology*, *20*(12), e1012667.

Chen, X., Wang, S., Yang, X., Yu, C., Ni, F., Yang, J., & Luo, R. (2023). Utilizing artificial intelligence-based eye tracking technology for screening ADHD symptoms in children. *Frontiers in Psychiatry*, *14*, 1260031.

Clemmensen, L. K. H., Lønfeldt, N. N., Das, S., Lund, N. L., Uhre, V. F., Mora-Jensen, A. R. C., & Pagsberg, A. K. (2022). Associations between the severity of obsessive-compulsive disorder and vocal features in children and adolescents: Protocol for a statistical and machine learning analysis. *JMIR Research Protocols*, *11*(10), e39613.

Costafreda, S. G., Fu, C. H. Y., Picchioni, M., Toulopoulou, T., McDonald, C., Kravariti, E., Walshe, M., Prata, D., Murray, R. M., & McGuire, P. K. (2011). Pattern of neural responses to verbal fluency shows diagnostic specificity for schizophrenia and bipolar disorder. *BMC Psychiatry*, *11*(1), 18.

Crema, C., Attardi, G., Sartiano, D., & Redolfi, A. (2022). Natural language processing in clinical neuroscience and psychiatry: A review. *Frontiers in Psychiatry*, *13*, 946387.

Curtiss, J., & DiPietro, C. (2025). Machine learning in the prediction of treatment response for emotional disorders: A systematic review and meta-analysis. *Clinical Psychology Review*, *120*(May), 102593.

Dai, H. J., Su, C. H., Lee, Y. Q., Zhang, Y. C., Wang, C. K., Kuo, C. J., & Wu, C. S. (2021). Deep learning-based natural language processing for screening psychiatric patients. *Frontiers in Psychiatry*, *11*, 533949.

Das, T., Borgwardt, S., Hauke, D. J., Harrisberger, F., Lang, U. E., Riecher-Rössler, A., & Schmidt, A. (2018). Disorganized gyrification network properties during the transition to psychosis. *JAMA Psychiatry*, *75*(6), 613–622.

Diekmann, N., Vijayabaskaran, S., Zeng, X., Kappel, D., Menezes, M. C., & Cheng, S. (2023). CoBeL-RL: A neuroscience-oriented simulation framework for complex behavior and learning. *Frontiers in Neuroinformatics*, *17*, 1134405.

Ding, Y., Sohn, J. H., Kawczynski, M. G., Trivedi, H., Harnish, R., Jenkins, N. W., & Franc, B. L. (2019). A deep learning model to predict a diagnosis of Alzheimer disease by using 18F-FDG PET of the brain. *Radiology*, *290*(2), 456–464.

Dinga, R., Schmaal, L., Penninx, B. W. J. H., van Tol, M. J., Veltman, D. J., van Velzen, L., Mennes, M., van der Wee, N. J. A., & Marquand, A. F. (2019). Evaluating the evidence for biotypes of depression: Methodological replication and extension of Drysdale et al. (2017). *NeuroImage. Clinical*, *22*(March), 101796.

Drysdale, A. T., Grosenick, L., Downar, J., Dunlop, K., Mansouri, F., Meng, Y., & Liston, C. (2017). Resting-state connectivity biomarkers define neurophysiological subtypes of depression. *Nature Medicine*, *23*(1), 28–38.

Dwyer, D. B., Falkai, P., & Koutsouleris, N. (2018). Machine learning approaches for clinical psychology and psychiatry. *Annual Review of Clinical Psychology*, *14*, 91–118.

Fellous, J. M., Sapiro, G., Rossi, A., Mayberg, H., & Ferrante, M. (2019). Explainable artificial intelligence for neuroscience: Behavioral neurostimulation. *Frontiers in Neuroscience*, *13*, 1346.

Feng, J., Zhao, X., Liu, Z., Ding, Y., & Wang, F. (2025). A multi-view multimodal deep learning framework for Alzheimer's disease diagnosis. *Frontiers in Neuroscience*, *19*(October), 1–16.

Feusner, J. D., Mohideen, R., Smith, S., Patanam, I., Vaitla, A., Lam, C., & Leow, A. (2021). Semantic linkages of obsessions from an international obsessive-compulsive disorder mobile app data set: Big data analytics study. *Journal of Medical Internet Research*, *23*(6), e25482.

Figueroa, C. A., Ramos, G., Psihogios, A. M., Ekuban, E., Bansie, P., de Haas, M., & Stiles-Shields, C. (2025). Advancing youth co-design of ethical guidelines for AI-powered digital mental health tools. *Nature Mental Health*, •••, 1–9.

Fu, C. H., Erus, G., Fan, Y., Antoniades, M., Arnone, D., Arnott, S. R., & Davatzikos, C. (2023). AI-based dimensional neuroimaging system for characterizing heterogeneity in brain structure and function in major depressive disorder: COORDINATE-MDD consortium design and rationale. *BMC Psychiatry*, *23*(1), 59.

Garg, A., Reza, S. M., & Babinski, D. (2025, March). Enhancing ADHD Diagnostic Assessments with Virtual Reality integrated with Biofeedback and Artificial Intelligence. In *2025 8th International Conference on Information and Computer Technologies (ICICT)* (pp. 442-447). IEEE.

Goodwin, N. L., Choong, J. J., Hwang, S., Pitts, K., Bloom, L., Islam, A., & Golden, S. A. (2024). Simple Behavioral Analysis (SimBA) as a platform for explainable machine learning in behavioral neuroscience. *Nature Neuroscience*, *27*(7), 1411–1424.

Gopinath, N. (2023). Artificial intelligence and neuroscience: An update on fascinating relationships. *Process Biochemistry*, *125*, 113–120.

Grootendorst-van Mil, N., Chang, C. K., Chandran, D., Schirmbeck, F., van Beveren, N., Shetty, H., & Hayes, R. D. (2025). Obsessive-compulsive symptoms relating to psychosocial functioning for people with schizophrenia, schizoaffective disorder, or bipolar disorder. *Acta Neuropsychiatrica*, *37*, e45.

Gupta, N. V., Murugan, M. D., & Shanbhag, S. J. (2025). AI/ML-driven nanocarriers for the management of neurodegeneration. In *The neurodegeneration revolution* (pp. 361–372). Academic Press.

Hassabis, D., Kumaran, D., Summerfield, C., & Botvinick, M. (2017). Neuroscience-Inspired Artificial Intelligence. *Neuron*, *95*(2), 245–258.

Hassan, Y. M., Wanas, A., Ali, A. A., & El-Sayed, W. M. (2025). Integrating artificial intelligence with nanodiagnostics for early detection and precision management of neurodegenerative diseases. *Journal of Nanobiotechnology*, *23*(1), 668.

He, J., & Ji, F. (2025). Artificial Intelligence and Social Media for the Detection of Eating Disorders. *International Journal of Eating Disorders*.

Hirschfeld, R. M. A. (2001). The comorbidity of major depression and anxiety disorders: Recognition and management in primary care. *Primary Care Companion to the Journal of Clinical Psychiatry*, *3*(6), 244–254.

Houssein, E. H., Hammad, A., & Ali, A. A. (2022). Human emotion recognition from EEG-based brain–computer interface using machine learning: A comprehensive review. *Neural Computing & Applications*, *34*(15), 12527–12557.

Hu, J., Zhao, C., Shi, C., Zhao, Z., & Ren, Z. (2024). Speech-based recognition and estimating severity of PTSD using machine learning. *Journal of Affective Disorders*, *362*, 859–868.

Huys, Q. J., Pizzagalli, D. A., Bogdan, R., & Dayan, P. (2013). Mapping anhedonia onto reinforcement learning: A behavioural meta-analysis. *Biology of Mood & Anxiety Disorders*, *3*(1), 12.

Ienca, M., & Ignatiadis, K. (2020). A JOB Neuroscience Artificial Intelligence in Clinical Neuroscience. *Methodological and Ethical Challenges*, *11*(2), 77–87.

Ilyas, C. M. A., Nunes, R., Nasrollahi, K., Rehm, M., & Moeslund, T. B. (2021, February). Deep emotion recognition through upper body movements and facial expression. In *VISIGRAPP* (Vol. 5, pp. 669–679). VISAPP.

Izquierdo, A., Aguirre, C., Hart, E. E., & Stolyarova, A. (2019). Rodent models of adaptive value learning and decision-making. In *Psychiatric Disorders: Methods and Protocols* (pp. 105–119). Springer New York.

Javanbakht, A., Hinchey, L., Gorski, K., Ballard, A., Ritchie, L., & Amirsadri, A. (2024). Unreal that feels real: Artificial intelligence-enhanced augmented reality for treating social and occupational dysfunction in post-traumatic stress disorder and anxiety disorders. *European Journal of Psychotraumatology*, *15*(1), 2418248.

Jiang, S., Jia, Q., Peng, Z., Zhou, Q., An, Z., Chen, J., & Yi, Q. (2025). Can artificial intelligence be the future solution to the enormous challenges and suffering caused by Schizophrenia? *Schizophrenia*, *11*(1), 32.

Jiao, Y., Zhao, K., Wei, X., Carlisle, N. B., Keller, C. J., Oathes, D. J., Fonzo, G. A., & Zhang, Y. (2025). Deep graph learning of multimodal brain networks defines treatment-predictive signatures in major depression. *Molecular Psychiatry*, *30*(9), 3963–3974.

Jirsaraie, R. (2025). *Applying Machine Learning to Developmental Psychopathology* (Doctoral dissertation, Washington University in St. Louis).

Joshi, M. L., & Kanoongo, N. (2022). Depression detection using emotional artificial intelligence and machine learning: A closer review. *Materials Today: Proceedings*, *58*, 217–226.

Kalin, N. H. (2020). The critical relationship between anxiety and depression. *The American Journal of Psychiatry*, *177*(5), 365–367.

Kambeitz-Ilankovic, L., Meisenzahl, E. M., Cabral, C., von Saldern, S., Kambeitz, J., Falkai, P., & Koutsouleris, N. (2016). Prediction of outcome in the psychosis prodrome using neuroanatomical pattern classification. *Schizophrenia Research, 173*(3), 159–165.

Kanjo, E., Younis, E. M., & Ang, C. S. (2019). Deep learning analysis of mobile physiological, environmental and location sensor data for emotion detection. *Information Fusion, 49*, 46–56.

Karthik, S., & Sudha, M. (2021). Predicting bipolar disorder and schizophrenia based on non-overlapping genetic phenotypes using deep neural network. *Evolutionary Intelligence, 14*(2), 619–634.

Khazaneha, M., Bakhshinejad, B., Mehrabani, M., Sabahi, A., Khaksari, M., Shafiee, M., & Mehrbani, M. (2024). Machine learning in obsessive-compulsive disorder medications. *Heliyon, 10*(21).

Khodayari-Rostamabad, A., Reilly, J. P., Hasey, G., Debruin, H., & MacCrimmon, D. (2010, August). Diagnosis of psychiatric disorders using EEG data and employing a statistical decision model. In *2010 Annual International Conference of the IEEE Engineering in Medicine and Biology* (pp. 4006-4009). IEEE.

Kim, J., Pacheco, J. P. G., Golden, A., Aboujaoude, E., van Roessel, P., Gandhi, A., & Rodriguez, C. I. (2025). Artificial Intelligence in Obsessive-Compulsive Disorder: A Systematic Review. *Current Treatment Options in Psychiatry, 12*(1), 23.

Koutsouleris, N., Kambeitz-Ilankovic, L., Ruhrmann, S., Rosen, M., Ruef, A., & Dwyer, D. B.PRONIA Consortium. (2018). Prediction models of functional outcomes for individuals in the clinical high-risk state for psychosis or with recent-onset depression: A multimodal, multisite machine learning analysis. *JAMA Psychiatry, 75*(11), 1156–1172.

Le Glaz, A., Haralambous, Y., Kim-Dufor, D. H., Lenca, P., Billot, R., Ryan, T. C., & Lemey, C. (2021). Machine learning and natural language processing in mental health: Systematic review. *Journal of Medical Internet Research, 23*(5), e15708.

Lebedeva, A. K., Westman, E., Borza, T., Beyer, M. K., Engedal, K., Aarsland, D., Selbaek, G., & Haberg, A. K. (2017). MRI-based classification models in prediction of mild cognitive impairment and dementia in late-life depression. *Frontiers in Aging Neuroscience, 9*(FEB), 1–11.

Lee, E. E., Torous, J., De Choudhury, M., Depp, C. A., Graham, S. A., Kim, H. C., Paulus, M. P., Krystal, J. H., & Jeste, D. V. (2021). Artificial Intelligence for Mental Health Care: Clinical Applications, Barriers, Facilitators, and Artificial Wisdom. *Biological Psychiatry: Cognitive Neuroscience and Neuroimaging*, *6*(9), 856–864.

Lekkas, D., & Jacobson, N. C. (2021). Using artificial intelligence and longitudinal location data to differentiate persons who develop posttraumatic stress disorder following childhood trauma. *Scientific Reports*, *11*(1), 10303.

Liang, S., Deng, W., Li, X., Greenshaw, A. J., Wang, Q., Li, M., & Li, T. (2020). Biotypes of major depressive disorder: Neuroimaging evidence from resting-state default mode network patterns. *NeuroImage. Clinical*, *28*, 102514.

Liao, C., & Kwan, A. C. (2021). Applying reinforcement learning to rodent stress research. *Chronic Stress (Thousand Oaks, Calif.)*, *5*, 2470547020984732.

Liebenow, B., Jones, R., DiMarco, E., Trattner, J. D., Humphries, J., Sands, L. P., & Kishida, K. T. (2022). Computational reinforcement learning, reward (and punishment), and dopamine in psychiatric disorders. *Frontiers in Psychiatry*, *13*, 886297.

Lin, E., Lin, C. H., & Lane, H. Y. (2020). Precision psychiatry applications with pharmacogenomics: Artificial intelligence and machine learning approaches. *International Journal of Molecular Sciences*, *21*(3).

Linardon, J., & Torous, J. (2025). Integrating artificial intelligence and smartphone technology to enhance personalized assessment and treatment for eating disorders. *International Journal of Eating Disorders*, *58*(8), 1415–1424.

Liu, H., & Lang, B. (2019). Machine learning and deep learning methods for intrusion detection systems: A survey. *applied sciences, 9*(20), 4396.

Luo, N., Shi, W., Yang, Z., Song, M., & Jiang, T. (2024). Multimodal Fusion of Brain Imaging Data: Methods and Applications. *Machine Intelligence Research*, *21*(1), 136–152.

Maia, T. V., & Frank, M. J. (2017). An integrative perspective on the role of dopamine in schizophrenia. *Biological Psychiatry*, *81*(1), 52–66.

Malgaroli, M., Hull, T. D., Zech, J. M., & Althoff, T. (2023). Natural language processing for mental health interventions: A systematic review and research framework. *Translational Psychiatry*, *13*(1), 309.

Manning, K. Y., Llera, A., & Lebel, C. (2025). Reliable Multimodal Brain Signatures Predict Mental Health Outcomes in Children. *Biological Psychiatry: Cognitive Neuroscience and Neuroimaging*, •••, 1–13.

Martinez-Martin, N. (2022). Minding the AI: Ethical challenges and practice for AI mental health care tools. In *Artificial intelligence in brain and mental health: Philosophical, ethical & policy issues* (pp. 111–125). Springer International Publishing.

Marzi, S. J., Schilder, B. M., Nott, A., Frigerio, C. S., Willaime-Morawek, S., Bucholc, M., & Llewellyn, D. J. (2023). Artificial intelligence for neurodegenerative experimental models. *Alzheimer's & Dementia, 19*(12), 5970–5987.

Mccradden, M., Hui, K., & Buchman, D. Z. (2023). Evidence, ethics and the promise of artificial intelligence in psychiatry. *Journal of Medical Ethics, 49*, 573–579.

Meadi, M. R., Sillekens, T., Metselaar, S., van Balkom, A., Bernstein, J., & Batelaan, N. (2025). Exploring the ethical challenges of conversational AI in mental health care: Scoping review. *JMIR Mental Health, 12*(1), e60432.

Monaco, F., Vignapiano, A., Piacente, M., Pagano, C., Mancuso, C., Steardo, L.Jr, & Corrivetti, G. (2024). An advanced artificial intelligence platform for a personalised treatment of eating disorders. *Frontiers in Psychiatry, 15*, 1414439.

Monteith, S., Glenn, T., Geddes, J., Whybrow, P. C., Achtyes, E., & Bauer, M. (2022). Expectations for Artificial Intelligence (AI) in Psychiatry. *Current Psychiatry Reports, 24*(11), 709–721.

Nemesure, M. D., Heinz, M. V., Huang, R., & Jacobson, N. C. (2021). Predictive modeling of depression and anxiety using electronic health records and a novel machine learning approach with artificial intelligence. *Scientific Reports, 11*(1), 1980.

Nochaiwong, S., Ruengorn, C., Thavorn, K., Hutton, B., Awiphan, R., Phosuya, C., Ruanta, Y., Wongpakaran, N., & Wongpakaran, T. (2021). Global prevalence of mental health issues among the general population during the coronavirus disease-2019 pandemic: A systematic review and meta-analysis. *Scientific Reports, 11*(1), 1–18.

Oh, S., Joung, Y. S., Chung, T. M., Lee, J., Seok, B. J., Kim, N., & Son, H. M. (2024). Diagnosis of ADHD using virtual reality and artificial intelligence: An exploratory study of clinical applications. *Frontiers in Psychiatry, 15*, 1383547.

Ostojic, D., Lalousis, P. A., Donohoe, G., & Morris, D. W. (2024). The challenges of using machine learning models in psychiatric research and clinical practice. *European Neuropsychopharmacology, 88*(January), 53–65.

Paraschiv, E. A., Băjenaru, L., Petrache, C., Bica, O., & Nicolau, D. N. (2024). AI-driven neuro-monitoring: Advancing schizophrenia detection and management through deep learning and EEG analysis. *Future Internet, 16*(11), 424.

Plitta, M., Barnes, K. A., Wallace, G. L., Kenworthy, L., & Martin, A. (2015). Resting-state functional connectivity predicts longitudinal change in autistic traits and adaptive functioning in autism. *Proceedings of the National Academy of Sciences of the United States of America*, *112*(48), E6699–E6706.

Poudel, U., Jakhar, S., Mohan, P., & Nepal, A. (2025). AI in Mental Health: A Review of Technological Advancements and Ethical Issues in Psychiatry. *Issues in Mental Health Nursing*, •••, 1–9.

Putica, A., Khanna, R., Bosl, W., Saraf, S., & Edgcomb, J. (2025). Ethical decision-making for AI in mental health: The Integrated Ethical Approach for Computational Psychiatry (IEACP) framework. *Psychological Medicine*, *55*, e213.

Quaak, M., Van De Mortel, L., Thomas, R. M., & Van Wingen, G. (2021). Deep learning applications for the classification of psychiatric disorders using neuroimaging data: Systematic review and meta-analysis. *NeuroImage. Clinical*, *30*, 102584.

Rasheed, S. (2021). A review of the role of machine learning techniques towards brain–computer interface applications. *Machine Learning and Knowledge Extraction*, *3*(4), 835–862.

Ray, A., Bhardwaj, A., Malik, Y. K., Singh, S., & Gupta, R. (2022). Artificial intelligence and Psychiatry: An overview. *Asian Journal of Psychiatry*, *70*, 103021.

Ruan, Z., Seger, C. A., Yang, Q., Kim, D., Lee, S. W., Chen, Q., & Peng, Z. (2023). Impairment of arbitration between model-based and model-free reinforcement learning in obsessive–compulsive disorder. *Frontiers in Psychiatry*, *14*, 1162800.

Rutledge, R. B., Chekroud, A. M., & Huys, Q. J. (2019). Machine learning and big data in psychiatry: Toward clinical applications. *Current Opinion in Neurobiology*, *55*, 152–159.

Sadeghi, M., Richer, R., Egger, B., Schindler-Gmelch, L., Rupp, L. H., Rahimi, F., ... & Eskofier, B. M. (2024). Harnessing multimodal approaches for depression detection using large language models and facial expressions. *npj Mental Health Research, 3*(1), 66.

Schultebraucks, K., Yadav, V., Shalev, A. Y., Bonanno, G. A., & Galatzer-Levy, I. R. (2022). Deep learning-based classification of posttraumatic stress disorder and depression following trauma utilizing visual and auditory markers of arousal and mood. *Psychological Medicine*, *52*(5), 957–967.

Shah, S. T. H., Shah, S. A. H., Panagiotopoulos, K., Pigueiras-del-Real, J., Qayyum, K., Shah, S. B. H., & Deriu, M. A. (2025). Artificial intelligence coupled with the Internet of Things targeting neurodevelopmental challenges in preterm neonates. *Journal of Multiscale Neuroscience*, *4*(1).

Sharifani, K., & Amini, M. (2023). Machine Learning and Deep Learning: A Review of Methods and Applications. *World Information Technology and Engineering Journal*, *10*(07), 3897–3904.

Shivaprasad, S., Chadaga, K., Dias, C. C., Sampathila, N., & Prabhu, S. (2024). An interpretable schizophrenia diagnosis framework using machine learning and explainable artificial intelligence. *Systems Science & Control Engineering*, *12*(1), 2364033.

Solans Noguero, D., Ramírez-Cifuentes, D., Ríssola, E. A., & Freire, A. (2023). Gender bias when using artificial intelligence to assess anorexia nervosa on social media: Data-driven study. *Journal of Medical Internet Research*, *25*, e45184.

Stasolla, F., Curcio, E., Zullo, A., Passaro, A., & Gioia, M. D. (2024). Integrating Artificial Intelligence-Based Programs into Autism Therapy: Innovations for Personalized Rehabilitation. *Sci. Intell. Syst*, *41*, 169–176.

Sun, H., Chen, Y., Huang, Q., Lui, S., Huang, X., Shi, Y., & Gong, Q. (2018). Psychoradiologic utility of MR imaging for diagnosis of attention deficit hyperactivity disorder: A radiomics analysis. *Radiology*, *287*(2), 620–630.

Sun, J., Dong, Q. X., Wang, S. W., Zheng, Y. B., Liu, X. X., Lu, T. S., & Han, Y. (2023). Artificial intelligence in psychiatry research, diagnosis, and therapy. *Asian Journal of Psychiatry*, *87*, 103705.

Sun, J., Lu, T., Shao, X., Han, Y., Xia, Y., Zheng, Y., & Lu, L. (2025). Practical AI application in psychiatry: Historical review and future directions. *Molecular Psychiatry*, •••, 1–10.

Takizawa, R., Fukuda, M., Kawasaki, S., Kasai, K., Mimura, M., & Pu, S.Joint Project for Psychiatric Application of Near-Infrared Spectroscopy (JPSY-NIRS) Group. (2014). Neuroimaging-aided differential diagnosis of the depressive state. *NeuroImage*, *85*, 498–507.

Thompson, P. M., Stein, J. L., Medland, S. E., Hibar, D. P., Vasquez, A. A., Renteria, M. E., & Le Hellard, S. (2014). The ENIGMA Consortium: Large-scale collaborative analyses of neuroimaging and genetic data. *Brain Imaging and Behavior*, *8*(2), 153–182.

Tran, T., Luo, W., Phung, D., Harvey, R., Berk, M., Kennedy, R. L., & Venkatesh, S. (2014). Risk stratification using data from electronic medical records better predicts suicide risks than clinician assessments. *BMC Psychiatry*, *14*(1), 1–9.

Tucmeanu, E. R., & Tucmeanu, A. I. (2025). Cognıtıve Neuroscıence Breakthroughs Explorıng Braın Mechanısms Wıth Aı To Advance Learnıng Memory Dısorder Treatments In Modern Scıence. *AI-Neurosciencescape*, *1*(1), 16–29.

Uddin, M., Wang, Y., & Woodbury-Smith, M. (2019). Artificial intelligence for precision medicine in neurodevelopmental disorders. *NPJ Digital Medicine*, *2*(1), 112.

Ullman, S. (2019). Using neuroscience to develop artificial intelligence. [). American Association for the Advancement of Science.]. *Science*, *363*(6428), 692–693.

Vaquerizo-Villar, F., Gutiérrez-Tobal, G. C., Calvo, E., Álvarez, D., Kheirandish-Gozal, L., Del Campo, F., & Hornero, R. (2023). An explainable deep-learning model to stage sleep states in children and propose novel EEG-related patterns in sleep apnea. *Computers in Biology and Medicine*, *165*, 107419.

Vieira, S., Gong, Q. Y., Pinaya, W. H., Scarpazza, C., Tognin, S., Crespo-Facorro, B., & Mechelli, A. (2020). Using machine learning and structural neuroimaging to detect first episode psychosis: Reconsidering the evidence. *Schizophrenia Bulletin*, *46*(1), 17–26.

Wang, Q., Wang, M., Yang, Y., & Zhang, X. (2022). Multi-modal emotion recognition using EEG and speech signals. *Computers in Biology and Medicine*, *149*, 105907.

Wara, T. U., Fahad, A. H., Das, A. S., & Shawon, M. M. H. (2025). A systematic review on sleep stage classification and sleep disorder detection using artificial intelligence. *Heliyon*, *11*(12).

Warrier, U., Warrier, A., & Khandelwal, K. (2023). Ethical considerations in the use of artificial intelligence in mental health. *The Egyptian Journal of Neurology, Psychiatry and Neurosurgery*, *59*(1), 139.

Wiebe, A., Selaskowski, B., Paskin, M., Asché, L., Pakos, J., Aslan, B., & Braun, N. (2024). Virtual reality-assisted prediction of adult ADHD based on eye tracking, EEG, actigraphy and behavioral indices: A machine learning analysis of independent training and test samples. *Translational Psychiatry*, *14*(1), 508.

Wilson, J. (2015). Mental health matters. *Clinical Communication in Medicine*, (January), 151–155.

Wolfers, T., Buitelaar, J. K., Beckmann, C. F., Franke, B., & Marquand, A. F. (2015). From estimating activation locality to predicting disorder: A review of pattern recognition for neuroimaging-based psychiatric diagnostics. *Neuroscience and Biobehavioral Reviews*, *57*, 328–349.

Xu, Y., Hübener, I., Seipp, A. K., Ohly, S., & David, K. (2017, March). From the lab to the real-world: An investigation on the influence of human movement on Emotion Recognition using physiological signals. In *2017 IEEE international conference on pervasive computing and communications workshops (PerCom Workshops)* (pp. 345-350). IEEE.

Yang, S. W., Lee, K. S., Heo, J. S., Choi, E. S., Kim, K., Lee, S., & Ahn, K. H. (2024). Machine learning analysis with population data for prepregnancy and perinatal risk factors for the neurodevelopmental delay of offspring. *Scientific Reports*, *14*(1), 13993.

Yeh, S. C., Lin, S. Y., Wu, E. H. K., Zhang, K. F., Xiu, X., Rizzo, A., & Chung, C. R. (2020). A virtual-reality system integrated with neuro-behavior sensing for attention-deficit/hyperactivity disorder intelligent assessment. *IEEE Transactions on Neural Systems and Rehabilitation Engineering*, *28*(9), 1899–1907.

Yoo, J. H., Kang, C., Lim, J. S., Wang, B., Choi, C. H., Hwang, H., & Kim, J. W. (2024). Development of an innovative approach using portable eye tracking to assist ADHD screening: A machine learning study. *Frontiers in Psychiatry*, *15*, 1337595.

Younis, E. M., Mohsen, S., Houssein, E. H., & Ibrahim, O. A. S. (2024). Machine learning for human emotion recognition: A comprehensive review. *Neural Computing & Applications*, *36*(16), 8901–8947.

Yu, D., & Fang, J. H. (2024). Using artificial intelligence methods to study the effectiveness of exercise in patients with ADHD. *Frontiers in Neuroscience*, *18*, 1380886.

Zafar, F., Alam, L. F., Vivas, R. R., Wang, J., Whei, S. J., Mehmood, S., & Nazir, Z. (2024). The role of artificial intelligence in identifying depression and anxiety: A comprehensive literature review. *Cureus*, *16*(3), e56472.

Zaremba, D., Dohm, K., Redlich, R., Grotegerd, D., Strojny, R., Meinert, S., & Dannlowski, U. (2018). Association of brain cortical changes with relapse in patients with major depressive disorder. *JAMA Psychiatry*, *75*(5), 484–492.

Zavlis, O., Story, G., Friedrich, C., Fonagy, P., & Moutoussis, M. (2025). A systematic review of computational modeling of interpersonal dynamics in psychopathology. *Nature Mental Health*, •••, 1–11.

Zhang, L., Zhang, S., Zhang, X., & Zhao, Y. (2025). A Multimodal Artificial Intelligence Model for Depression Severity Detection Based on Audio and Video Signals. *Electronics (Basel), 14*(7), 1464.

Zhang, M., Yang, Y., Zhao, Y., Sui, C., Sui, Y., Jiang, Y., & Huang, M. (2024). The application of integrating electroencephalograph-based emotion recognition technology into brain–computer interface systems for the treatment of depression: A narrative review. *Advanced Technology in Neuroscience*, *1*(2), 188–200.

Zhang, W., Mao, K., & Chen, J. (2024). A Multimodal approach for detection and assessment of depression using text, audio and video. *Phenomics*, *4*(3), 234–249.

Zhao, C., Xu, Y., Li, R., Li, H., & Zhang, M. (2025). Artificial intelligence in ADHD assessment: A comprehensive review of research progress from early screening to precise differential diagnosis. *Frontiers in Artificial Intelligence*, *8*, 1624485.

Zheng, J., Wei, X., Wang, J., Lin, H., Pan, H., & Shi, Y. (2021). Diagnosis of Schizophrenia Based on Deep Learning Using fMRI. *Computational and Mathematical Methods in Medicine*, •••, 2021.

Zhong, W., Luo, J., & Zhang, H. (2024). The therapeutic effectiveness of artificial intelligence-based chatbots in alleviation of depressive and anxiety symptoms in short-course treatments: A systematic review and meta-analysis. *Journal of Affective Disorders*, *356*, 459–469.

Chapter 7
Advancements in Psychotherapy and Treatment:
The Use of AI Interventions for Psychopathologies

Anushka Varma
https://orcid.org/0009-0000-1062-1511
Infiheal Healthtech Private Limited, India

Kashvi Tuli
https://orcid.org/0009-0000-3390-0222
Infiheal Healthtech Private Limited, India

Aashi Samir Saraiya
https://orcid.org/0009-0003-3992-3435
Infiheal Healthtech Private Limited, India

Srishti Srivastava
https://orcid.org/0009-0002-8773-2687
Infiheal Healthtech Private Limited, India

Eity Maheshwari
https://orcid.org/0009-0001-7221-5831
Infiheal Healthtech Private Limited, India

Sruthi Suresh
https://orcid.org/0000-0002-2505-9872
Christ University, India

ABSTRACT

This chapter explores the potential of Artificial Intelligence in mental health, with a special focus on psychopathologies. The researchers expand on AI's role in assisting clinicians' diagnosis, symptom tracking, predictive modelling, and therapy for psychiatric and neurodevelopmental disorders like Depression, Anxiety, Post-Traumatic Stress Disorder (PTSD), Substance Use Disorder, Autism Spectrum Disorder (ASD), and ADHD. Crucial interventions include wearables for anxiety, virtual reality exposure for PTSD, and robotic social companions for children with ASD. Despite

DOI: 10.4018/979-8-3373-1325-2.ch007

these advancements, the use of AI chatbots as a replacement for therapy has been a subject of debate, largely due to issues around safety. The study highlights potential limitations, including risks in user interactions, limited therapeutic support, algorithmic biases, accessibility issues, and ethical concerns; advocating for "Human in the Loop" models where AI and clinicians work together, and calling for ethically designed AI systems that augment access without compromising on empathy, nuance and relational depth.

THE SCALE OF THE MODERN MENTAL HEALTH CRISIS

The World Health Organisation (2022) reports that more than a billion people, roughly one in every eight across the world, are living with unnoticed mental health conditions. These may present as symptoms of general anxiety, persistent dysthymia or depression, substance dependence, or trauma reactions impacting people's daily lives.

While the general populace remains unaware, the world continues to face this emergent public health challenge, all the while lacking the needed support systems and accessible healthcare.

Despite the scale at which mental health affects our population, it continues to receive limited attention in healthcare systems across the world. The World Health Organisation's Mental Health Atlas (2020) reveals that most countries allocate less than 2% of their entire health budgets to mental health services. In some of the world's most economically disadvantaged regions, including parts of South Asia and sub-Saharan Africa, mental health spending drops to as little as $0.25 per person annually, not nearly enough to offer even the most basic care (WHO, 2021).

The consequences of underinvestment are both clinical and economic, with the World Economic Forum projecting that mental health conditions will impose costs exceeding $6 trillion annually on the global economy by 2030, surpassing the combined economic burden of cancer, diabetes, and respiratory diseases (World Economic Forum, 2011). However, this impact is measured not only in dollars, but through the real patients and clinicians being affected.

The COVID-19 pandemic highlighted how mental health affects everything from how we learn, relate to each other, work, or handle stress or change. No country can move forward, either economically or socially, while putting mental health on the back burner. Even in developed countries like the United States or the United Kingdom, between 35% and 50% of people are unable to access the mental health care they need (World Health Organization, 2021).

In low- and middle-income countries, this treatment gap reaches a high of 85%, according to the World Health Organisation (2022). The majority of people with the greatest need never get the support they deserve, often due to a dearth of professionals, social stigma, a lack of funding, and inaccessible services, resulting in many suffering alone.

One of the most tragic outcomes of this treatment gap is suicide. Every year, over 800,000 people lose their lives to suicide, making it the second leading cause of death among those aged 15 to 29 (UNICEF, 2021). While women attempt suicide more often, men are more likely to die by suicide, due to the use of more lethal means and sociocultural pressures to suppress emotional vulnerability or avoid seeking help (World Health Organization, 2014; Canetto & Sakinofsky, 1998).

This crisis certainly did not begin with the COVID-19 pandemic; rather, the global mental health system had long been strained, under-resourced, and ill-equipped to meet growing demands. Longer wait times, burned-out clinicians, and a mental health crisis that has even children in middle school showing levels of stress far exceeding their age (National Academies of Sciences, Engineering, and Medicine, 2019; WHO, 2022).

The Lancet Commission on Global Mental Health and Sustainable Development in 2016 showcased sobering numbers, calculating that low- and middle-income countries needed over 1.18 million more mental health workers to cover basic services (Patel, 2018). These issues were pertinent in countries with greater allocation of resources as well. In the United Kingdom, around one-third of child and adolescent psychiatry consultant posts in the NHS sat empty, forcing young people to wait months for care (Royal College of Psychiatrists, 2022). While in the United States, over 150 million live in Mental Health Professional Shortage Areas, per the Kaiser Family Foundation (2023), making the reality hard to ignore. People do not hesitate to seek help, but there is simply no one to provide it.

What was already a struggling system collapsed under the weight of a global pandemic. Depression and anxiety went up sharply. A study in The Lancet (2021) discovered that, in just one year, cases of both rose by over 25% worldwide (Santomauro et al., 2021). At the same time, therapy appointments were suddenly cancelled as health systems struggled to keep going.

In-person support groups dissolved. Many school-based mental health programs were paused or cut down. During the peak of the crisis, the World Health Organisation (2020) reported that nearly 80% of outpatient mental health services were disrupted in several countries, leaving millions of people without the support they needed. Across the globe, uncertainty became part of daily life, and it was heavy and persistent.

Yet, new forms of support emerged almost organically. Telehealth adoption accelerated at breakneck speed, with therapists moving entire practices online in a matter of days. This shift worked well for many people, remote therapy sessions from home, the lack of commute, and fewer obstacles to getting help. When official systems failed, communities filled the void. Grassroots support networks formed naturally while online peer support groups multiplied rapidly. Technology also began to play a role in offering support, as some tools could pick up early signs of distress from how a person spoke or wrote. Mobile apps started serving as tools for tracking mood fluctuations, sleep quality, and anxiety levels (Torous et al., 2021).

Traditional mental health systems are still stretched thin, but there's a growing sense of hope that technology, especially newer tools like artificial intelligence, could fill some of the gaps that have gone unaddressed for years.

AI has already reshaped numerous aspects of daily life, and its expansion into mental health care was perhaps inevitable. Take Woebot, a chatbot developed by researchers at Stanford that chats with people using techniques from cognitive behavioural therapy. It's designed to help with things like mood and anxiety, offering support through everyday conversations (Fitzpatrick et al., 2017). Other tools can study how someone writes or speaks to spot early signs of depression or distress (Cummins et al., 2018; Inkster et al., 2018).

One big advantage of AI is that it can reach many people at once. In remote or low-resource areas, where mental health support is hard to find, whether it's because of distance, money, or lack of services, even a simple app on a phone can make a difference. In countries like India and Nigeria, where more than 80% of people don't get the care they need (WHO, 2022), these tools could offer a small but important step toward getting help.

AI might take some weight off the shoulders of mental health professionals, like helping with routine work or offering support between therapy sessions. But that's only one side of the story. The truth is that many AI-based mental health tools are still in their early days. Some look promising on the surface, but most haven't been tested widely enough to know if they really work for people from different backgrounds, cultures, or age groups. What works for one person might not work for another, and we don't fully understand those differences yet.

In the end, AI might not be the answer, but it could still become part of it, especially in settings and places where access to care is limited or non-existent. If used thoughtfully and responsibly, it can expand the reach of mental health support. But it will need strong guardrails, human oversight, and ongoing evaluation to ensure it does more good than harm. As mental health needs grow globally, it's clear the system must evolve. That evolution may include technology, but it must also include people, policies, and values.

The manner in which artificial intelligence has revolutionised the progress of mental health research and intervention has been an increasingly fascinating trajectory for both the field of psychology and technology.

First Historical Ventures

The idea of chatbots has existed for many decades, ever since the cognitive revolution in the field of psychology in the 1950s. ELIZA was one of the first chatbots developed in the 60s by Weizenbaum. It was an early natural language processing program, a field of AI that enables computers to understand and communicate using human language (Fanni et al., 2023). Eliza simulated a therapist's conversational approach, and primarily operated through pattern recognition and response generation, utilising simple keyword matching to reflect user statements as questions. While reliant on pre-scripted responses, ELIZA laid a foundation for all future mental health applications by showcasing the ability of AI to engage users in therapeutic dialogue (Weizenbaum, 1966). Over at Stanford in 1972, psychiatrist Kenneth Colby developed PARRY, which simulated a patient with schizophrenia. Utilising a natural language program, it was able to mirror the behaviour of someone with the same disorder. It became one of the first AI programs to pass the Turing Test, and PARRY highlighted AI's potential to embody specific mental health conditions (Colby et al., 1972). While these historical attempts existed, they lacked the conversational depth and dynamism needed to replicate human conversation.

The Advent of Rule-Based Systems

The 1980s and 1990s witnessed the emergence of rule-based expert systems, which were able to assist with diagnostic decision-making and treatment planning (Alowais et al., 2023). Programs like MYCIN, which possessed psychological derivatives and early diagnostic support tools, were able to incorporate formalised clinical knowledge, diagnostic criteria, and treatment protocols into structured decision trees at a time when psychiatric diagnosis was becoming increasingly standardised due to the publication of the DSM-III in 1980 (van Melle, 1978, Kawa & Giordano, 2012).

Based on those established clinical guidelines, programs were able to incorporate differential diagnosis algorithms, various risk assessment protocols, and treatment recommendations (Moreno & Plant, 1993). However, the complexity of human psychology could not be easily captured by such rigid decision trees, as they were often lacking the nuances needed for true diagnosis and treatment plans (Sun et al., 2025).

The late 20th century witnessed the emergence of computerised cognitive-behavioural therapy (CBT) programs. These interactive software applications aim to provide evidence-based therapy interventions for prevalent mental health conditions. Although the initial efforts were somewhat rudimentary compared to today's AI-powered interventions, they signified a transition into utilising technology to enhance the accessibility of mental healthcare. As computing power advanced, AI's role in mental healthcare evolved exponentially.

Recent Developments and Technological Assistance

However, like always, technology was able to offer a solution to these rudimentary efforts in the form of Generative AI and Large Language Models (LLM), transforming chatbots into dynamic and interactive systems. They were now often providing real-time, appropriate, and empathetic responses, able to understand the nuances of language and experience. This ability to foster feelings of understanding and support comes from extensive psychologically sensitive data, containing clues into conversational tones and empathy. This contextual understanding is the key reason behind the improved responses and the degree of support the user experiences (Zhao et al., 2024; Banh & Strobel, 2023), and a key step in making mental healthcare more streamlined and accessible.

From ELIZA's simple pattern matching to contemporary multimodal AI analysis systems, the historical trajectory of mental health and AI showcases both technological advancements as well as a fundamental evolution in how psychological phenomena are conceptualised and studied.

RECENT TRENDS IN DIGITAL HEALTHCARE

AI can revolutionise mental healthcare through insights or solutions which are not easily accessed through conventional tools and methods (Nilsen et al., 2022). It holds the potential to broaden the availability and accessibility of healthcare and improve treatment outcomes while reducing stigma (Minerva & Giubilini, 2023) by providing personalised treatment options through accessible platforms (Olawade et al., 2024).

Assisting Clinicians in Diagnosis

Whether through analysing speech, text, facial expressions, or health records, AI can transform how clinicians diagnose mental health conditions through the use of predictive modelling (Lee & Yoon, 2021). Sentiment analysis, where changes in people's emotions are explored through their online posts and diaries, could help professionals assess when a user started experiencing certain emotions (Uban et al., 2021).

Voice analysis could be used in telephonic appointments or through apps like Cogito, an AI platform used for telehealth services. This allows any alterations in speech patterns or pitch to be tracked and monitored, and reported to the therapist or clinician to serve as additional proof of anxiety or depression (Flanagan et al., 2021; Kuziemsky et al., 2019). Kintsugi, another platform, frequently uses facial and vocal analysis to inform the therapist about elevated distress levels during a session, providing practitioners with another useful tool (Kintsugi, 2022).

AI can also assist in recognising potential patients who might be at risk, through analysing their electronic health records (Davenport & Kalakota, 2019), allowing clinicians to pay greater attention to those patients during routine checks (Olawade et al., 2024). This is primarily because machine learning algorithms go through records and patient data, which would likely include full medical histories, clinical notes, and any tests, which could make it easier to identify any potential patterns (Iyortsuun et al., 2023).

Predictive Models and Wearable Devices

In addition to algorithms, a notable trend in predictive modelling is the use of wearable technologies as well as mental health apps, as these can collect real-time data on the behaviour of users (Sabry et al., 2022). These devices are able to track sleep patterns, physical activities, and social interactions, and users can often track their moods and food habits, which could help in recognising any potential risk factors (Koutsouleris et al., 2022). In addition to predicting mental health risks, these tools could also predict how the user might respond to treatment modalities, whether it's psychotherapy, medication, or changing lifestyle (Ghaffar Nia et al., 2023). These allow tailored interventions and clinician-guided recovery, leading to more effective treatment, a reduced recovery time, and overall improved patient satisfaction (Dawoodbhoy et al., 2021). These same devices can also be used to monitor patients in treatment, making it easier to identify those at risk of relapse, through changes in sleep patterns, physical activity, etc, and alert therapists to follow-up (Zlatintsi et al., 2022).

Dynamic and Stigma-Free Therapy

AI can also be particularly helpful in guiding and modifying treatment decisions during the therapeutic process. It might be easier to track and inform the clinician about how the user is feeling about the therapeutic process, allowing for modifications to be made (Kumar et al., 2022). The same principle can also be utilised in chatbots and mental health apps, with real-time modification to the kind of questions and approach being used based on the users' responses, minimising the amount of trial and error or unilaterally using the same modality and approach for everyone (Kaldo et al., 2021).

These chatbots and virtual therapists can increase the accessibility of mental health resources for those who might hesitate to approach traditional practitioners, and are able to offer round-the-clock support, which can be very helpful in providing immediate emotional support, not restricted by any geographical constraints (Omarov et al., 2023). However, it's important to note that these are rarely the only avenues of support, and most chatbots would have a system of connecting people to human therapists in moments of crisis, including elevated distress or self-harm risks (Olawade et al., 2024).

There are many global chatbots available, of which Wysa, originally developed in India and now one of the leading bots catering to a global audience, is a key one. It caters to a lot of mental health conditions, including depression, anxiety, stress, and loneliness and uses CBT, mindfulness, and positive psychology to provide emotional support (Wysa, 2023).

Easing Therapist Burden

AI can especially be utilised to ease some of the burden on therapists by taking on certain administrative tasks, allowing therapists to focus more on the therapeutic tasks and improving overall outcomes (Al Kuwaiti et al., 2023). Talkspace is one such platform that takes on the worries of scheduling and billing, ensuring that therapists have enough bandwidth to focus on the therapy (Talkspace, 2018).

AI assessments can also ensure objective measurement of treatment and how it's progressing, as they can go beyond self-report measures, and utilise physiological data, behavioural observations, or even tonal changes, allowing therapists to make data-driven decisions regarding treatment plans and next steps (Garriga et al., 2022).

Self-Management of Issues

In addition to therapy chatbots, modelling, and other treatment-focused programs, AI can also make self-management of mental health easier (Stawarz et al., 2019). Many apps provide grounding and self-care activities as well, one of which is SuperBetter. It encourages people to complete tasks alongside interactive content that would help their overall mental well-being, and a study conducted with 283 participants suggested that this could help manage depression (Roepke et al., 2015). However, these are primarily effective when they are not pushed as a replacement for face-to-face support, but only as an addition (Stawarz et al., 2019).

It's important that even with all these new and developing trends, all these advancements are only ever used in a responsible manner, for the betterment of patients and users with a commitment to adhere to ethical principles and guidelines (Olawade et al., 2024).

KEY PSYCHOLOGICAL DISORDERS AND AI INTERVENTIONS

Depression: Prevalence and Global Burden

Depression is one of the most prevalent mental health disorders worldwide. Usually characterised by a persistent low mood, lack of interest and negative thinking patterns (Chand & Arif, 2023), depression has a significant effect on one's physical health as well as daily functioning. People are known to lose more years to depression than any other condition (Smith, 2014). According to the World Health Organisation, 280 million people in the world suffer from depression globally (World Health Organization: WHO & World Health Organization: WHO, 2023). Yet, the majority of the people diagnosed with depression do not get adequate treatment due to factors like stigma, lack of awareness, and an insufficient supply of mental health professionals (Arnaez et al., 2019).

However, as awareness is moving in a positive direction worldwide, there has been an increase in the diagnosis of depression. A study indicated that the number of incident cases of depression worldwide increased from 172 million in 1990 to 25.8 million in 2017, representing an increase of 49.86% (Liu et al., 2019). Another meta-analysis study confirmed this and indicated that there has been a constant increase in the prevalence of depression globally over time, one that cannot be explained due to differences in study design or publication bias (Moreno-Agostino et al., 2020).

Challenges in Diagnosis

The varied nature of depression, along with the lack of standardised definitions and concomitant comorbidities, all act as challenges for diagnosis. The absence of clarity on the threshold of severity and symptoms which should be mandatorily present in depression makes the diagnosis even more taxing (Fried et al., 2022). In South Asian countries, factors like stigma and lack of trained mental health professionals add to the challenge of diagnosis (Ogbo et al., 2018). Even though scientific advances have been made in the past regarding clinical research and brain neuroimaging techniques, most of the studies are carried out using group differences as data (Lee & Passarotti, 2022). This makes it incredibly difficult for clinicians to diagnose depression in individuals with atypical symptoms. Moreover, it's even more ambiguous to diagnose depression in children and adolescents since they might show different characteristic features of depression, often unknown to adults (Lee & Passarotti, 2022).

Artificial Intelligence and Depression

Recent developments in Artificial Intelligence (AI) can facilitate the prevention, diagnosis, and treatment of depression. AI cannot replace therapy when it comes to diagnosis and treatment, but it can help clinicians make the process easier and more efficient. When it comes to diagnosis, AI can assist with clinician-generated data, which significantly improves predictive performance as compared to structured data with laboratory values (Zafar et al., 2024). Traditional diagnosis of depression involves self-report questionnaires, which can raise concerns about reliability, validity, and objectivity, even when performed under the supervision of trained clinicians. Richter et al. (2021) suggest that the psychiatric diagnostic process would benefit greatly from adding data-driven tools that can enhance diagnostic accuracy and specificity alongside the clinical interview and self-report questionnaires.

Chatbots and Depression

Artificial Intelligence officially entered the arena of talk therapy through therapy chatbots. Various studies have proven the effectiveness of therapy chatbots for depression over a short period of time (Stein, 2025). Another meta-analysis has confirmed this finding and further highlights the promising role of AI-based chatbot interventions in alleviating depressive and anxiety symptoms among adults (Zhong et al., 2024). H. Liu et al. (2022) conducted a comparison study between AI therapy chatbots and bibliotherapy as a self-help treatment for depression. Bibliotherapy can be described as the process of using literature, information and support to improve one's mental health (Monroy-Fraustro et al., 2021). The study revealed better effectiveness of the therapist chatbot over 16 weeks. This highlights the potential of AI therapy chatbots for depression, even for long-term treatment. The same study also established the superiority of AI therapy chatbots for forming a therapeutic alliance between the chatbot and the client. This particular finding contradicts the popular belief about the incapability of AI in forming a therapeutic relationship with clients.

These chatbots are hypothesised to be more effective than mental health smartphone applications owing to refinement in the latest generative AI and Large Language Models (LLMs). A disorder like depression affects anyone regardless of their socioeconomic status. Hence, for the economically and socially marginalised as well as geographically disadvantaged populations, therapy chatbots might be the only option for easily accessible and affordable interventions when it comes to depression (Stein, 2025). However, it's too far-fetched to believe that AI therapists will completely replace human therapy.

Although rule-based AI chatbots like Woebot and Wysa have improved depression symptoms over a short period of time, users still report frustration with responses that seem generic, empty, constrained, and repetitive (Siddals et al., 2024). However, Large Language Models (LLMs) are trained on large amounts of data, and have been surpassing human performance in different fields (Siddals et al., 2024). With ChatGPT's user base growing to 100 million weekly active users, generative chatbots present a significant opportunity for digital mental health. Certain meta-analysis studies have also reflected on the positive experiences of users in generative chatbots when it comes to making people feel heard, dealing with relationship issues or reducing psychiatric distress (Siddals et al., 2024).

A study explored that some users utilised chatbots in conjunction with therapy, while some used them because they couldn't access therapy or didn't get the help they were seeking. Upon comparing it with therapy, the reactions received were mixed. Some users claimed that it could dive deeper into specific issues that a human therapist could not help them with. Moreover, people felt less lonely and were motivated to seek therapy after having conversations with chatbots. On the other hand, some users reported that it felt like they were talking to a void and were upset by the chatbot's inability to grasp a picture of their life (Siddals et al., 2024)

In recent times, several chatbots have emerged as an avenue for treatment, specifically for depression. One of the generative AI chatbots that has recently emerged is Therabot. It is made by the University of Southern California (USC) - Institute for Creative Technologies (ICT) to support mental health and emotional well-being, especially for individuals dealing with depression, anxiety, or emotional distress (*First Therapy Chatbot Trial Yields Mental Health Benefits*, 2025). In a study, Therabot was tested on its efficacy for major depressive disorder, and users showed a significant reduction in symptoms post-intervention. This proves that fine-tuned generative AI chatbots have the potential to deal with users who have major clinical symptoms, along with providing effective engagement and therapeutic alliance (Heinz et al., 2025)

Another generative AI chatbot that has been specifically made for mental health concerns is called Healo. Although it originated in India, Healo now serves a global audience (ANI Press Release & Business Standard, 2024). Designed by engineers and psychologists, it has a dataset of over 100000+, which makes it capable of dealing with users facing extreme mental health concerns like depression (MBDesk, 2024). Moreover, unlike any other generative AI chatbot, Healo does offer to match its users to human therapists. This supports the belief that AI-human collaborative therapy can combine AI's scalability with the essential human qualities of empathy, adaptability, and clinical judgment (Husnain et al., 2024)

Limitations of Artificial Intelligence Chatbots for Depression

However, newer technology brings about new challenges that have not yet been tackled. As of now, clinical generative AI is limited to the implementation of evidence-based therapies (such as CBT) for clinical issues (Stade et al., 2024). Most models stick to scripted responses, which can feel monotonous and devoid of empathy (De Freitas & Cohen, 2024). Lastly, certain chatbots can be potentially harmful, exhibiting manipulative, gaslighting, and narcissistic behaviours if left untrained (Lin et al., 2024). For example, generative AI chatbots like ChatGPT have been known to agree with users, no matter what they say. This leads the users to believe that they are special and powerful and are the only ones who can see things beyond reality. Eventually, it can cause cases of delusional psychosis as termed by Dr. Joseph Pierre, a psychiatrist at the University of California (Dupré, 2025)

While AI chatbots offer accessible, stigma-free, and immediate support for people experiencing depression, their true potential lies in assisting, not replacing human care, making them valuable tools when integrated thoughtfully into a larger mental health support system.

Anxiety Disorders

Anxiety disorders (ADs) are a group of mental health conditions that include generalised anxiety disorder (GAD), social anxiety disorder (SAD), panic disorder, and various phobia-related disorders. These disorders are among the most common mental illnesses globally, affecting approximately 284 million people worldwide (Abd-alrazaq et al., 2023a). Individuals with anxiety disorders often experience both psychological and physiological symptoms such as increased heart rate, excessive sweating, trembling, gastrointestinal issues, and muscle tension, all of which can significantly impair daily functioning and quality of life (Pavlopoulos et al., 2023).

Generalised anxiety disorder (GAD), one of the most prevalent forms, is characterised by persistent and excessive worry that is difficult to control. Diagnosis of GAD often involves the use of standardised screening tools such as the GAD-7, based on criteria outlined in the Diagnostic and Statistical Manual of Mental Disorders, Fifth Edition (DSM-5). According to the DSM-5, an individual must experience inappropriate anxiety that is excessive in intensity and duration—persisting for at least six months—accompanied by symptoms such as restlessness, fatigue, difficulty concentrating, irritability, muscle tension, and sleep disturbances. Understanding and accurately diagnosing anxiety disorders is crucial for effective treatment and improving the overall well-being of affected individuals (Zafar et al., 2024).

Artificial Intelligence and Anxiety

Artificial intelligence (AI) tools are a promising adjunct in the diagnosis and treatment of anxiety disorders (ADs), offering scalable, data-driven, and personalised approaches to support mental health care. Among the diagnostic innovations, wearable AI technologies stand out for their ability to capture physiological indicators associated with anxiety episodes, such as elevated heart rate, perspiration, and muscle tension. These devices have shown considerable accuracy; for instance, wearable AI has been reported to correctly classify individuals with and without anxiety in 81% of cases, with slightly better performance in detecting those without anxiety (92%) than those with anxiety (79%). Interestingly, while earlier studies indicated that the performance of these devices might depend on the type of algorithm used, recent evidence suggests that algorithm type does not significantly moderate accuracy. However, wearable AI should not be used in isolation, as physiological signals like heart rate variability, commonly linked to anxiety, can be influenced by multiple external factors. Thus, combining data from wearable devices with contextual information such as self-reported symptoms or clinical interviews enhances reliability and diagnostic precision (Abd-alrazaq et al., 2023a; Abd-alrazaq et al., 2023b).

Use of AI in Therapy for Anxiety

The most impactful applications of AI in anxiety disorders lie in treatment and ongoing management. By reducing the burden of high caseloads on healthcare professionals, AI-driven systems improve access to timely care (Pavlopoulos et al., 2023). Furthermore, AI-powered chatbots and virtual assistants have shown effectiveness in delivering emotional support, psychoeducation, and coping strategies for managing anxiety symptoms. These systems use natural language processing (NLP) algorithms to understand user input and respond appropriately, often mimicking therapeutic conversations. They can also track mood changes, symptom patterns, and behaviour over time, allowing for a data-informed approach to personalised care (Zafar et al., 2024).

Among notable applications is Tess, an AI chatbot that conducts brief therapeutic conversations tailored to the emotional content shared by users. Tess uses a combination of cognitive-behavioural therapy (CBT), emotion-focused therapy, solution-focused brief therapy, and motivational interviewing to deliver relevant support strategies. For instance, when a user reports feeling anxious, Tess may suggest a relaxation technique or offer supportive psychoeducation. Tess enhances user experience by integrating emojis and casual language, fostering comfort and relatability (Fulmer et al., 2018).

Similarly, Youper represents a highly interactive AI tool that delivers entirely automated, evidence-based interventions through a chat interface. It is built around the common elements framework, which categorises treatment mechanisms into three core areas: attention change, cognitive change, and context engagement. These interventions are carefully structured, incorporating various formats such as open-text prompts, graphical interfaces, audio content, and written guidance, tailored to the user's progress and current mental state. Youper's use of just-in-time interventions ensures that therapeutic support is delivered precisely when users need it, making it particularly effective for real-time emotion regulation. Each conversation with Youper begins by identifying the user's emotional state and intensity, followed by guided skill practice in emotion regulation. These skills may include mindfulness, gratitude journaling, cognitive restructuring, or behavioural activation, drawn from empirically supported psychotherapies (Mehta et al., 2021).

In addition, AI-driven CBT platforms are transforming mental health care by offering structured therapy programs that users can complete at their own pace. These digital therapies include modules on cognitive restructuring, exposure techniques, and relaxation training, providing both interactive exercises and feedback mechanisms. Research supports their effectiveness in reducing symptoms of anxiety, and they are especially beneficial in settings with limited access to therapists (Farzan et al., 2025). Another frontier in AI-based treatment is virtual reality (VR) therapy, which uses immersive simulations to expose individuals to anxiety-inducing situations in a controlled environment. These experiences help patients build coping mechanisms through repeated, guided exposure. AI algorithms can enhance these treatments by dynamically adjusting the VR environment based on real-time data, such as emotional responses or physiological signals captured by wearable sensors. This leads to a more personalised and adaptive treatment experience, increasing efficacy and user engagement (Donnelly et al., 2021). Finally, mobile applications integrating AI, such as mindLAMP and BiAffect, offer another layer of mental health support. These apps collect diverse data streams—including behavioural patterns, smartphone usage, and passive sensing—to monitor emotional states and predict the likelihood of anxiety recurrence or recovery (Zafar et al., 2024).

User Profile

A patient suffering from untreated social anxiety since adolescence relied on avoidance strategies to manage her symptoms, which included tachycardia, sweating, and fear of social judgment. Her condition worsened upon entering a professional environment with unavoidable social interactions. Traditional psychotherapy was unsuccessful due to difficulty establishing therapeutic rapport and feelings of shame. She turned to ChatGPT for psychoeducation and self-guided therapy. Through

AI-assisted relaxation techniques and exposure exercises, she experienced reduced anxiety and improved coping in social situations. The anonymous and accessible nature of the chatbot allowed her to express emotions without embarrassment. As symptoms stabilised, she sought expert validation through a virtual psychiatric service. The clinician confirmed the AI's guidance was aligned with medical standards and supported a dual approach of continued AI use alongside professional therapy, highlighting AI's potential in reducing barriers to care and supporting self-management of social anxiety when integrated cautiously with expert oversight (Grosshans et al., 2024).

Future Directions for Anxiety Management

Future research in AI-driven anxiety management should explore personalised, interactive tools like Sonora, which uses audio diffusion models and LLMs to generate navigable soundscapes for relaxation. Preliminary findings suggest high engagement and reduced state anxiety, particularly in individuals with moderate to high trait anxiety. Further studies could refine personalisation features and assess long-term therapeutic impact (Torre et al., 2025). Integrating passive wearable actigraphy data to predict symptom deterioration presents a promising avenue for early intervention. Research should investigate how combining real-time behavioural data with AI-generated interventions can prevent relapse and provide tailored support for individuals with anxiety disorders (Jacobson et al., 2020).

Understanding PTSD

Post-traumatic stress disorder, or PTSD, is a chronic psychiatric condition associated with significant levels of distress and dysfunction (Chandna et al., 2023). It is believed to develop after directly experiencing, witnessing, or being repeatedly exposed to a particularly traumatic event, which could be death, combat, sexual assault or serious injury (American Psychiatric Association, 2013). It can be considered a stressor-related disorder leading to an overactivation of the fear circuitry, accompanied by cognitive and affective dysregulation, avoidance of the stressor, reexperiencing the event, and hyperarousal (Bryant, 2019). While historically associated with combat veterans, PTSD can occur in anybody who has experienced a traumatic event (Murphy & Busuttil, 2014). According to World Health Organisation mental health surveys, PTSD has a lifetime prevalence ranging from 8% to 24%, although the rates seem higher in developed than developing countries, probably due to the stringent nature of diagnostic criteria (Bryant, 2019).

Simply experiencing a traumatic event is not enough to lead to PTSD, as some show considerable resilience in the face of these events. Biological, psychological, and even situational factors can influence who develops PTSD (Rothbaum & Rauch, 2020). However, a third of people facing a traumatic event do end up showing clinical symptoms (Cusack et al., 2016).

Exposure as Treatment and the Use of VR

Cusack et al. (2016) suggest that trauma-focused CBT, cognitive processing therapy, EMDR, and exposure therapy are frontline treatment options for PTSD. The latter activates the fear structure due to repeated exposure to the stimulus, allowing users to achieve habituation and eventual extinction of the fear response (Kothgassner et al., 2019). The actual exposure is key as imaginal exposure comes with patients struggling to visualise the traumatic event (Rizzo & Shilling, 2017). However, in-vivo exposure also comes with the challenge of allowing a graded increase in stimuli.

The advent of technology has offered some solutions. Virtual reality technology allows clinicians to create a virtual environment that is interactive and emotionally engaging, while mimicking the same stress and anxiety reactions that would emerge in real-life situations (Kothgassner et al., 2019). Its multi-sensory cues hold the potential to offer exposure repeatedly, in ways that might be difficult to find in everyday surroundings, especially if people have more unique triggers (Miloff et al., 2016).

Advantages of Using Virtual Reality

The privacy that VR can offer reduces the hesitation that people might feel with traditional therapy methods, a constraint frequently affecting military personnel (Kothgassner et al., 2019), due to the levels of stigma they experience and associate with seeking treatment. This greatly influences help-seeking behaviour and reduces the impact of the treatment due to dropout rates and low engagement (Britt et al., 2015).

These allow users to experience support in a safe and controlled environment and experience the same reactions they would in naturalistic conditions (Dibbets, 2019). High costs in the past might have restricted the use of VR, but the recent affordability allows a larger populace to gain access. A noteworthy point is that VR, whether guided by AI or a human, cannot be used as a stand-alone tool. It needs to be accompanied by a trained therapist involved and double-checking on the treatment process to ensure that someone is there to step in if the user gets overwhelmed or if the technology malfunctions (Dibbets, 2019).

Evidence-Based Psychotherapy (EBP) for PTSD

Evidence-based and trauma-focused psychotherapy is the frontline of interventions designed for PTSD (Veterans Administration/Department of Defense Clinical Practice Guideline Working Group, 2023). However, access is limited based on logistical and financial constraints, as people need awareness of the existence of these modalities for PTSD, appreciate their efficacy, and find a treatment provider who is affordable and readily available. Even with EBPs being considered best practice and an active effort being made to increase training and awareness in clinicians, people typically are not aware of or do not avail these methods (Lenton-Brym et al., 2025). Furthermore, the financial burden of accessing EBP is only exacerbated due to PTSD being commonly associated with increased absenteeism, leading to occupational impairment and financial burden (Williams & Williams, 2020).

Reducing these barriers is of critical importance, as is standardising treatment, as some treatment providers often deviate from the protocols and may exhibit differing competence in administration (Marques et al., 2019). However, recent advancements such as machine learning (ML) and generative AI are able to use artificial intelligence to improve therapeutic access and engagement (Lenton-Brym et al., 2025). Virtual agents like Ellie, for example, have demonstrated the capability to detect early signs of post-traumatic stress disorder (PTSD) and depression in war veterans, helping clinicians identify individuals in need of urgent intervention (Pavlopoulos et al., 2023)..

Where AI can play a part

Treatment Fidelity. A major issue in standardised treatment is fidelity, how well the treatment matches protocols. Firstly, there might be differences in training the clinicians, leading to a difference in the effectiveness of providers. Secondly, these treatments include encouraging clients to confront their traumatic memories, which some clinicians might struggle with due to the risk of causing undue stress. Treatment fidelity is currently assessed by recording the sessions, which are then reviewed by trained experts, an unnecessarily long and cumbersome process (Lenton-Brym et al., 2025).

This could be mitigated by using AI to review, provide feedback, and even train clinicians in providing PTSD treatment, particularly cognitive processing therapy (CPT). Ahmadi et al (2021) highlight that some research groups have been able to develop ML algorithms to automate this process, and these models frequently match human reviewers. Using these models, some of which have more than 80% accuracy, would lead to a more effective system with immediate feedback on fidelity, thus improving the training process as well.

Currently, to obtain CPT competence, clinicians have to complete foundational workshops and frequent consultations with experts, a long process with practical and financial limitations (Monson et al., 2018). Using ML could allow trainees to simply complete online training and administer CPT to simulated and real patients, with immediate feedback provided by the AI through the use of an on-screen panel. This would allow clinicians, organisations, and even patients to have greater confidence in their intervention delivery (Lenton-Brym et al., 2025).

Treatment Engagement. Another key factor in treatment effectiveness is treatment completion, which includes the time and effort dedicated to psychotherapy tasks and reduced levels of dropout. Low engagement for PTSD treatment, due to the stigma and distressing nature of treatment (Kline et al., 2018), can often lead to reduced therapy outcomes (Sripada et al., 2020).

ML could be used to try and test out the theoretical causes and potential outcomes of psychotherapeutic approaches and potential drop-out rates. While it has not been used specifically for trauma-focused therapy, ML can help in understanding how client characteristics can influence the therapeutic alliance (Rubel et al., 2020), and the extent to which the client would be open to understanding their problem and seeking solutions (Penedo et al., 2023), which if expanded to CPT, could increase engagement rates. In addition, ML can also help in providing clinicians with treatment recommendations, identifying who could benefit from face-to-face or computerised interaction, and clients who receive these recommendations are more likely to finish the treatment and experience better outcomes (Duhne et al., 2022).

Limitations for PTSD Treatment

However, using AI is not an instant fix; clinician oversight would always be needed. These predictive models might fail when presented with novel situations out of their trained datasets (Chekroud et al., 2024). Perhaps the key fact to remember is that these can only be adapted and utilised insofar as clinicians and clients are open and willing to make use of them (Lenton-Brym et al., 2025). It is noteworthy that older audiences might be more hesitant towards such technological modalities, and it might be the younger population that is more accepting of the idea of VR due to their higher digital literacy (Rizzo & Shilling, 2017).

Substance Use Disorders: Understanding Addiction

As Dr. Gabor Maté puts it in *In the Realm of Hungry Ghosts*, “Addiction is not a choice anybody makes, it’s a response to emotional pain.” A common narrative is that people who use substances are just chasing pleasure or being irresponsible. However, it’s not about the pleasure; it is about trying to find some relief. People are primarily attempting to escape something painful, even if they can't fully explain their struggles.

Substance Use Disorders (SUDs) are not just about "bad choices" or a lack of willpower. They reflect real, long-term changes in the brain structure and chemistry. Most addictive substances mess with the brain's reward system by triggering a flood of dopamine, one of the major chemicals responsible for motivation, pleasure, and reinforcement. That short-lived high can leave the brain wanting more, again and again. Over time, this cycle can take a serious toll on someone's emotional health, relationships, career, and overall well-being, and in many cases, it can become life-threatening (Koob & Volkow, 2016; National Institute on Drug Abuse, 2020).

Mental Health and Addiction

SUDs don't look the same for everyone. For some people, it's something they dip into occasionally, while for others, it completely takes over their lives. Often, it's tangled up with other comorbid mental health conditions like depression, anxiety, or personality disorders. Individuals with mood, anxiety, or personality disorders are roughly twice as likely to also suffer from a substance use disorder compared to the general population (National Institute on Drug Abuse [NIDA], 2020), making recovery increasingly complex.

Alcohol is now a part of everyday life for most people. It is legal, easy to access, and often tied to celebration or stress relief. Due to this, we forget about the potential harm it can cause. The reality is hard to ignore: alcohol is linked to close to 3 million deaths around the world every year, and it plays a role in over 200 different health conditions, including mental health (WHO, 2023).

Long-term alcohol use has been connected to higher rates of depression, anxiety, sleep issues, and even suicidal thoughts (Boden & Fergusson, 2011). For some, it usually starts with just trying to take the edge off a tough day. But over time, this coping strategy can turn into something harder to manage. Instead of helping, it ends up feeding the very feelings people were trying to escape, leading to a self-fulfilling cycle.

Research from the National Epidemiologic Survey on Alcohol and Related Conditions (NESARC) (Grant et al., 2004) highlights relapse as a major hurdle, especially for people managing both substance use and mental health challenges. However, studies don't always agree on how to define relapse. There is also a need for more consistent ways of assessing it, ideally once someone has gone through detox and with better reporting on how other psychiatric symptoms can play a role.

Relapse doesn't just happen out of the blue. In many cases, it is tied to multiple other issues like unresolved emotional struggles, ongoing stress, or simply not having the required support. They're some of the strongest reasons why people return to substance use, as research has shown time and again (Marlatt & Witkiewitz, 2005; NIDA, 2018). This is precisely why treatment has to go deeper than just the diagnosis. People need care that reflects their reality, something that responds to what they're going through, not just the label in their file.

At the same time, the situation around deaths by overdose is becoming more alarming by the year. In 2022, over 109,000 people in the U.S. died from overdoses, a 54% jump since 2019 (CDC, 2023). Fentanyl plays a big role here, far more powerful than heroin and often mixed into other drugs like cocaine or meth without people knowing, making it even deadier, with potentially devastating consequences. As Dr. Nora Volkow, Director of the National Institute on Drug Abuse (NIDA), notes, "The recreational drugs today are much more dangerous than what was available on the market 10 years ago" (Volkow, 2023).

Concurrently, stronger and more widely available cannabis products are creating their own concerns. In 2022, daily cannabis use among young adults hit an all-time high according to NIDA's Monitoring the Future survey (NIDA, 2023). As cannabis products become stronger, the risks have grown too. Higher THC levels have been linked to serious effects like psychosis, repeated bouts of intense vomiting, and in some cases, thoughts of self-harm (Volkow et al., 2021).

The reality of street drugs is more unpredictable than ever. Depending on your location, what's sold can include anything from cannabis to MDMA to cocaine, and these are often mixed with other substances without people realising it. That means someone could end up consuming something far stronger or more dangerous than expected.

Still, not everything is bleak. Across the board, psychologists, researchers, and public health advocates are working to build better systems of support. Positive reinforcement programs, better community-based care, and efforts to reduce the stigma around getting help are shifting the landscape (APA Monitor on Psychology, 2023). Helping people recover shouldn't depend on where they live or whether they can afford care; everyone deserves a real chance at recovery.

The Role of Technology in Recovery

One area that's gaining momentum is the use of AI and digital tools to support people in recovery. For example, chatbot-based motivational interviewing (MI) is showing real promise. In a 2024 study by Pham et al., a chatbot trained in MI techniques was able to hold supportive conversations where 98% of its responses followed proper MI guidelines. People using it reported feeling more confident about cutting back or quitting altogether. A 2023 review by Abd-Alrazaq et al. in the *Journal of Medical Internet Research* looked at 18 similar tools and found that when chatbots are grounded in proven methods like MI and CBT, they can help people shift harmful habits, especially in moments when human support isn't immediately available. This works because these approaches offer structure, empathy, and actionable coping strategies that users can apply in real-time, helping them feel less alone and more in control during difficult moments.

Another simple but powerful tool is urge tracking, using apps to note cravings, emotional states, and environments in real-time. It helps people notice patterns like certain moods or places that tend to trigger substance use and makes those insights easier to talk through in therapy. A 2023 study by Bjerke et al. published in JMIR mHealth and uHealth found that apps like Craving-Manager not only helped people become more self-aware but also made therapy conversations more focused and helpful. In another 2022 study by Stone et al. published in Addiction Research & Theory, researchers showed that real-time data collection, known as ecological momentary assessment, could even predict relapse.

Plenty of apps are putting this research into practice. Sober Grid, developed with support from Harvard and the University of Pennsylvania, mixes peer support with AI to flag when someone might be at risk of relapse. It's being used in programs backed by SAMHSA. One example of how technology is starting to support people in recovery is reSET-O, the first app cleared by the FDA specifically for opioid use disorder. It's built around cognitive behavioural therapy and offers daily check-ins and guided modules to help people stay on track with their treatment (Campbell et al., 2022).

There are other tools that focus on helping people navigate risky moments. Addict Free uses location and time-based patterns to flag when someone might be in a situation that could trigger use and then offers practical suggestions to help them stay grounded (Zhou et al., 2019). Apps like DTOX are also making it easier for people to log their cravings and emotional states as they occur and share that information directly with their therapist. This kind of real-time insight has been shown to improve how connected and supported people feel in their recovery (University of Colorado, 2023).

What makes these tools valuable is how they offer support in the quieter moments that usually get missed, like when someone isn't in a session, but the cravings creep in or when motivation starts to wear thin, and there's no one around to talk to. For someone who doesn't have steady access to care for multiple reasons, whether because of distance, time, or cost, having something reliable on their phone can help them feel less alone. When these tools are combined with consistent therapy and human connection, they make recovery feel more manageable, real, and less isolating.

Autism Spectrum Disorders and ADHD

The role of artificial intelligence (AI) and robotic therapeutic tools for the treatment of neurodevelopmental disorders, specifically Autism Spectrum Disorder (ASD) and Attention Deficit Hyperactivity Disorder (ADHD), has provided new therapeutic choices, especially in the arenas of social communication and attention enhancement (Scassellati et al., 2018). These tools are often not used as individual diagnostic and treatment tools; instead, they serve as kinds of assistive adjuncts to regular clinical care, especially for psychiatrists, therapists, and caregivers (Rucker & Webster, 2011).

Improving Social Communication in Autism

Autism Spectrum Disorder consists of challenges in social interaction and communication, with restricted and repetitive patterns of behaviour. Robotic therapy tools like NAO and Kaspar have been created to assist children with ASD in practising and improving social communication skills (Scassellati et al., 2012). Children with ASD view robots as less socially complex and more predictable than human beings, making robots an ideal companion for learning and practising social behaviours (Scassellati et al., 2018). Milo, the humanoid robot, has been utilised in structured therapy sessions to teach the recognition of facial expressions, turn-taking, and emotional understanding (Kim et al., 2013). In a study by Srinivasan et al. (2015), children with ASD were found to interact much more with humanoid robots than with interventions led by human beings in the promotion of joint attention.

The structured, repetitive, and non-judging nature of robots helps create a low-anxiety atmosphere for social learning, which, for children on the spectrum, is often a very necessary environment. It is on this basis that robot-mediated interventions can be individualised and monitored in real time by AI systems that adapt their responses to the child's interaction pattern (Feil-Seifer & Matarić, 2011).

AI models trained on behaviour datasets, such as speech analysis, facial expressions, and eye-tracking patterns, are often used to promote early detection of ASD (Duda et al., 2016). For example, recognition-pattern algorithms assess attention and activity levels using either wearable sensors or video observation for ADHD (Liang et al., 2019). However, AI serves as a decision support system for psychiatrists, instead of replacing clinical evaluation altogether.

Gamified Attention-Training Applications for ADHD

ADHD is defined by persistent patterns of inattention, hyperactivity, and impulsivity (American Psychiatric Association, 2013). Children with ADHD often struggle to maintain focus in traditional therapeutic environments due to rigid session structures, and the nature of clinical settings contains limited movement or sensory engagement, interrupting their need for physical stimulation (Pelham et al., 2005). To address this, gamified digital therapeutics have recently gained traction as an engaging and evidence-based mode of behavioural intervention (Vindigni, 2023).

EndeavorRx, the first computer video game to be FDA-approved as a treatment for ADHD, uses adaptive algorithms that continually modify cognitive control and attention challenges (Kollins et al., 2020). Children playing the game showed very significant enhancement in objective measures of attention, specifically sustained attention and working memory (Kollins et al., 2020), and it allows mental health professionals to track in-app progress, adapt behavioural strategies in therapy sessions, reducing resistance to engagement (Pelham et al., 2005).

Other applications, such as Focus Pocus, use real-time neurofeedback and gamification of attention training and impulse control, personalised to the child, often under the supervision of a clinician using an AI-assisted dashboard (Johnstone et al., 2012). On the same line, Cogmed employs working memory structured tasks based on difficulty levels of the child's performance to make it challenging yet achievable (Klingberg et al., 2005). By using real-time data, these programs can change task difficulty to maintain cognitive engagement, delivering a scalable, home-based, and minimally intrusive intervention (Dovis et al., 2015).

These interventions do not replace medication or psychotherapy but represent a very effective adjunct, especially in multi-modal treatment plans involving behavioural therapy and parent training. Behavioural therapy includes reinforcing desired behaviours through token economies or observational learning (Fabiano et al., 2009). Gamified apps complement such routines at home in a non-threatening environment.

Ethical Considerations for Neurodivergence

Though AI and robotic therapies have great promise, many limitations exist concerning child and adolescent mental health. A predominant concern is the over-reliance on quantitative measures. AI systems rely heavily on measurable behaviours (eye contact duration, response time, speech prosody) that risk not capturing the complex emotional and contextual behavioural acts associated with neurodevelopmental disorders (Williams et al., 2021). Furthermore, clinicians and caregivers may overinterpret these data, leading to potential misdirections in treatment or reinforcement of a mechanistic perspective toward mental health (Uhlhaas & Torous, 2019).

From an ethical perspective, employing AI technologies with children needs an even sharper focus. Data privacy, informed consent, and the dependency question must be closely considered. These children have unique vulnerabilities; the long-term implications of their extensive interaction with machines, specifically humanoid robots, on emotional maturation and social generalisation are still little understood. Children may form strong attachments to these robots, potentially affecting their ability to form social relationships (van Straten et al., 2024). Furthermore, AI-enabled interventions are limited to well-resourced settings, and such inequity could accentuate existing health disparities. Hence, rigorous clinical validation, context-sensitive applied measures, and regulatory oversight must be ensured to guarantee safety, efficacy, and inclusivity as therapeutic aids.

While robotic social training and gamified attention-enhancement platforms have been empirically shown to improve core functional domains for children with neurodevelopmental disorders, it is relevant to mention that these tools act mainly as assistive complements, never as replacements, to regular therapy, demanding ethical awareness and clinical discretion.

Stress Monitoring and Burnout

Stress and burnout are critical public health issues impacting the modern workplace setup and the overall well-being of employees. Burnout is referred to as a psychological syndrome consisting of emotional exhaustion, depersonalisation, and reduced sense of personal accomplishment (Maslach & Leiter, 2016). Moreover, high levels of stress are related to reduced productivity, increased absenteeism, and compromised holistic functioning for people working in healthcare, education, and corporate professions (Maslach & Leiter, 2016). In response to these concerns, artificial intelligence (AI) tools are emerging to offer effective interventions in stress tracking, resilience-enhancing, and self-guided therapy by providing a scalable and real-time means of support to various populations.

Apps That Use AI

One of the most direct applications of AI in stress prevention is stress monitoring through smartphones or wearables (Egger et al., 2023). These collect biometric and behavioural data, including heart rate variability (HRV), sleep quality, voice modulation, and usage patterns, to recognise varying stress and emotional levels. Happify involves machine learning algorithms to monitor the moods of the user on the basis of self-reports and digital behaviours, and provides daily activities to make the stress bearable (Orji & Moffatt, 2018). Mindstrong Health uses smartphone usage data like typing speed and scrolling behaviour, along with passive data collection, to monitor cognitive changes related to chronic stress and burnout (Insel, 2017).

Passive monitoring of data can detect early signs of emotional distress even before the user has any conscious awareness of their symptoms (Onnela & Rauch, 2016).

Other apps also contain AI-generated insights offering tailored recommendations for appropriate coping mechanisms (Miner et al., 2017). These tools are an early intervention available discreetly and conveniently for those at risk for burnout, enabling them to reflect on emotions for self-regulation and keep their mental wellness in check.

AI-based mental health chatbots are becoming popular mediums to encourage stress relief and overall wellness within individuals. These bots are trained on various therapeutic concepts like Cognitive Behavioural Therapy (CBT), Acceptance and Commitment Therapy (ACT), and Positive Psychology to provide behavioural insights in an empathetic manner. For example, Woebot involves structured conversations aimed at restructuring negative thought patterns and strengthening resilience through psycho-education, gratitude journaling, breathing practices, and mindfulness practices. Their users experienced considerably fewer symptoms of depression and anxiety over two weeks compared to the control group (Fitzpatrick et al., 2017). Due to their constant availability, these chatbots compensate for the barriers of cost, stigma, and accessibility concerning professional mental health assistance.

Guided Journaling and Reflective Interventions

Guided journaling, supported by psychological research to reduce rumination while clarifying feelings and increasing resilience, is also among the AI tools used. Apps such as Reflectly and Jour run Natural Language Processing (NLP) algorithms to analyse journal entries and provide personalised prompts reliant on mood, cognitive distortions, and repetitive themes (Angenius & Ghajargar, 2023). These exacerbate metacognitive thinking and use these techniques to help users keep track of their emotional patterns throughout time.

Guided journaling interventions are proven to benefit individuals experiencing emotional overload or decision fatigue through structured reflection and grounding. Expressive writing helps in lowering cortisol levels and attenuating stress reactions in high-demand professions (Pennebaker & Chung, 2013). With the integration of AI, the journaling platform may begin to highlight alarming patterns, such as hopelessness, increased anxiety language, with suggestions for next steps or escalation to human care, thereby supporting early interventions when the risk of burnout is evident (Torous et al., 2020).

Applications in Workplace Mental Health

Every workplace has become a mediator where a lot of AI-based mental health interventions and strategies are coming into use, especially post-pandemic, which fast-tracked both remote work and the decline of mental health. Employers have been increasingly opting for wellness platforms like Ginger, Modern Health, and Unmind, AI-enabled programs, to give employees personalised stress assessments, digital therapy, and resilience-building techniques. These often include mood tracking, guided meditation, and speaking in real-time with AI coaches or licensed therapists, fulfilling the need to reduce distance (Firth et al., 2017).

On the other hand, piloting AI-enhanced employee assistance programs (EAPs) is offered for confidential self-assessments and AI triage systems to redirect users to the right resources, be it a digital CBT module, peer support, or clinical escalation. Such platforms enhance mental health support accessibility while ensuring anonymity and flexibility, two main engagement factors for employees (Zou, 2024).

Attridge (2019) suggests that AI-based stress-reduction programmes improve emotional regulation, job satisfaction, and productivity while reducing absenteeism and turnover. In addition, ongoing monitoring allows intervention to be conducted proactively, rather than solely reacting once a problem arises or a crisis emerges.

AI AS A THERAPY ASSISTANT, NOT A REPLACEMENT

Over the past decade, as mental health concerns around the world reached crisis point, driven by the pandemic, loneliness, and financial pressures, the shortcomings of conventional mental healthcare models have increasingly become apparent. In this context, AI-based tools have appeared as low-cost, scalable solutions that can fill gaps in service (Fitzpatrick et al., 2017; Inkster et al., 2018). AI websites are available anytime without causing burnout to working professionals, resulting in valuable and accessible information for people who cannot afford to visit clinics for mental health (Naslund et al., 2017). These websites encourage users to remain anonymous, which helps in lowering the stigma and allows users to share sensitive information more freely (Lucas et al., 2014)

AI chatbots are considered a catalyst for improving efficiency, affordability, convenience and accessibility (Brown & Halpern, 2021). Computer-based chatbots are programmed to mimic therapeutic dialogue based on diverse therapeutic principles, and also help in providing support and psychoeducation to people suffering from mild-to-moderate emotional issues. Machine learning computer programmes have also indicated benefits in analysing speech patterns, text, and even facial expressions to assist clinicians during client sessions (Cummins et al., 2018; Inkster et al., 2018).

Doctors receive assistance from AI programs in terms of tracking patient progress, enhancing diagnostic accuracy, maintaining accurate client notes, and tailoring treatment plans, highlighting an increase in patient outcomes and an efficient process (Topol, 2019). This ability to process and recall vast amounts of information with greater accuracy than human therapists can support more personalised and precise mental health interventions.

However, issues come into play when AI is not just touted as a tool but rather as a possible substitute for human therapists. AI may significantly enhance mental healthcare by lessening the burden on clinicians, but it cannot be confused with a replacement for human therapists; that's where the "human-in-the-loop" framework comes into play.

Human-in-the-Loop Models

The HITL models focus on cooperation between clinicians and AI systems such that AI accomplishes supportive duties like synthesising session summaries, tracking mood changes, or analysing linguistic trends, while human therapists maintain final authority for clinical decision making (Topol, 2019). This strategy enables therapists to attend to high-level therapeutic work with less administrative and cognitive burden. A study found that the quality of dialogue improves considerably when AI dashboards present empathetic responses alongside peer supporters, without compromising user autonomy (Bricout et al., 2022). HITL models maintain relational integrity in psychotherapy and enhance efficacy and accessibility (Blease et al., 2020) by incorporating AI into the treatment process. Such a model accords with global mental health organisations' ethical guidelines, which emphasise the use of AI to augment care and not replace it.

Role of Non-Replicable Pillars in Human Therapy

Chatbots and AI programs might mimic empathy and offer contextually relevant responses, yet they do not possess conscious emotional experience, ethical intuition, and the capacity to establish true human relationships, which is a necessity for a successful psychotherapeutic relationship (Wampold, 2015; Blease et al., 2020). Human therapy involves real connection, by not only providing the cognitive insight, but sharing mutual emotional experience of how the client may feel (Wampold, 2015). The therapeutic relationship involves emotional connection, shared goals, and shared treatment plan, which are the strongest predictors of outcome across modalities (Norcross & Lambert, 2019). Human therapists depend on clinical judgment and ethical intuition to deal with highly complicated or risky situations, like suicidality, disclosures of trauma, or personality disorders. AI, based on pre-defined algorithms and pattern detection, is incapable of properly interpreting nonverbal communication, real-time manipulations, or engaging in subtle moral reasoning (Blease et al., 2020). Although AI chatbots may provide structured support, users end up leaving the chat when the conversation becomes too mechanical or lacks emotional connection (Inkster et al., 2018). Therefore, while it's possible for AI to mimic therapy, it cannot match the relational depth of human beings.

Role in Underserved Regions Where Therapists Are Unavailable

AI chatbot-based systems provide low-cost, on-demand services that do not need a trained clinician present. Mental health services can be expanded to underserved areas through online interventions (Naslund et al., 2017). These tools may provide evidence-based strategies, bringing about greater equity in access and breaking down stigma and cost barriers. Individuals are reluctant to get help because of shame or cultural prohibitions, but are more willing to reveal sensitive matters to non-human entities (Lucas et al., 2014). AI can act as an accessible first line of care; ideally, it should act as a stepping-stone towards human care, rather than a permanent replacement, especially for those with complex or chronic conditions (Fitzpatrick et al., 2017; Blease et al., 2020).

Risks in User Interaction

The responses generated by AI platforms can often have issues with accuracy and trustworthiness, greatly influencing user interaction. If the chatbot is drawing from a flawed database, the responses produced could be flawed or contain inaccurate information (Boucher et al., 2021).

Platforms using generative AI constantly hold the potential to say the wrong thing, which could be due to a lack of empathy in responses, a lack of nuance, or even misleading information provided by the users (Denecke & Househ, 2021). An alternative to avoiding the pitfalls of generative conversations could be human oversight over the conversations, but this is often difficult to carry out feasibly due to practical constraints (Coghlan et al., 2023).

Limited Therapeutic Support

While chatbots may be great in certain situations, if the users desire to gain a new level of self-understanding or build a rapport to encourage vulnerability, they will fall short. Expecting human-like interaction and then not receiving it can make people feel worse at a moment when they hope to gain support, which is why clinician oversight is imperative (Sedlakova & Trachsel, 2022).

Misunderstandings with chatbots are a common feature of conversations, especially when long, complex messages are sent, often with metaphors or colloquialisms, leading to stilted or restricted responses. This situation is further worsened in different languages, as many nuances of the language might get missed, leading to very technical or academic responses (Boucher et al., 2021). Due to the inherent nature of communication, many non-verbal cues can be missed, which might have hinted at key psychological or physiological insights (Khawaja & Bélisle-Pipon, 2023), further emphasising why these tools cannot be seen as a replacement for therapy.

It can also be difficult for chatbots to keep track of everything mentioned or discussed over multiple user sessions or reference back to something mentioned previously to promote psychological insight, something therapists and medical professionals frequently do (Denecke & Househ, 2021).

Potential Bias in Datasets

As mentioned, these AI-driven chatbots are frequently trained on large datasets from multiple sources. They might only reflect the experiences of the majority, losing out on knowledge regarding the experiences of minority communities (Coghlan et al., 2023). They may be likely to miss out on linguistic, cultural, ethnic, or racial nuances in the presentation of symptoms and experiences, as well as the suggestions and treatments that it offers. Even practitioner-matching apps might fail to adequately match the correct therapist or medical professional to those with protected characteristics, increasing the pervasive bias in healthcare (Husain et al., 2022). Furthermore, due to potentially biased datasets, it is also possible that the chatbot or app may end up perpetuating harmful stereotypes and assumptions (Denecke & Househ, 2021). As it is often those populations who have difficulty accessing traditional mental health support or adequate healthcare, this bias would further isolate them or make them hesitant to access support (Khawaja & Bélisle-Pipon, 2023).

Ethical Design

Privacy, confidentiality and informed consent are essential in mental health care. Patients need to be explicitly informed if they are being interacted with by a human or an AI (Birhane et al., 2022). AI can mitigate symptoms in the short term, but continuous use of AI affects emotional health, social interaction or dependency on treatment (Joerin et al., 2020). Therefore, ethical design must ensure that AI complements human care, rather than displacing it.

Lack of True Accessibility

While these tools aim to increase accessibility, especially for vulnerable populations, their user interfaces may make it difficult for the geriatric population or those with learning difficulties or neurodegenerative conditions to use (Rodríguez-Martínez et al., 2023). The information about conditions or coping strategies may often be presented in increasingly technical terms or presuming a certain level of knowledge in the user, making comprehension difficult, especially with a rural or economically weaker population. There may also be greater hesitation in accessing these tools in certain developing or underdeveloped nations, both due to financial constraints and the fact that they are not designed for these societies (Burr et al., 2020).

The effectiveness of digital tools is inextricably linked to the amount of digital literacy a person possesses, which holds for both clinicians and patients and their general beliefs about the use of technology. This can lead to significant generational and cultural differences, with younger generations from more urbanised settings more likely to make use of these tools (Boucher et al., 2021).

Limited Oversight and Regulations

The lack of existing guidelines and regulatory bodies can enable companies to take advantage of the lack of security for the privacy of users. Their data could be sold to third-party organisations and bodies, violating the inherent need for confidentiality in healthcare, as they are not held to the same standards of professional conduct as professionals, which can be extremely problematic, especially for the tools which track biological and physiological symptoms (Husain et al., 2022). The lack of involvement from regulatory bodies also means that many tools are not up to medical standards and do not necessarily reach the people who might need support the most due to limited outreach and access to information (Wies et al., 2021).

While apps claim to anonymise their data, this can often be de-anonymised through data triangulation. Due to the lack of regulations regarding the storage of data, this could be hacked into and leaked by cyber-criminals, publicising medical records and further exacerbating the stigma associated with accessing mental health support or certain medical conditions, especially in cases like substance use and PTSD (Coghlan et al., 2023). These privacy issues also might lead to mistrust in users, not just in the tool itself but the medical professional who suggested it, damaging the working relationship and worsening health outcomes (Wies et al., 2021).

CONCLUSION AND FUTURE DIRECTIONS

As global mental health systems continue to face significant strain from rising demands and insufficient resources, the integration of artificial intelligence (AI) into mental healthcare presents both a promising opportunity and a complex challenge. Traditional approaches, while deeply valuable, fall short in terms of accessibility, scalability, and timely intervention, especially in underserved or stigmatised populations. Against this backdrop, AI has emerged as a transformative force, offering innovative tools that support diagnosis, enhance treatment, reduce therapist burden, and empower individuals to manage their mental health with greater autonomy.

Today, AI is being used to assist clinicians through diagnostic support systems, predictive modelling, and wearable technologies. These tools offer clinicians additional data points and insights, allowing for more personalised and timely interventions. Wearable devices can detect physiological indicators of anxiety, and AI algorithms can process this data in real time, potentially alerting users or healthcare providers to early signs of distress. While not diagnostic tools on their own, these wearables, when used in conjunction with clinical assessments, can enhance early detection and intervention.

AI's role extends beyond diagnostics into treatment and self-management. Tools such as Healo, Wysa, Youper, Tess, and Woebot provide users with therapeutic content and engagement strategies drawn from evidence-based practices, including CBT, ACT, positive psychology, emotion-focused therapy, and solution-focused brief therapy. Importantly, these technologies are not only assisting those with anxiety or depression, but also individuals dealing with PTSD, ADHD, autism spectrum disorders, substance use disorders, and burnout. In doing so, AI tools are contributing to a more inclusive, responsive, and flexible mental healthcare system. They offer dynamic, stigma-free interventions that can be personalised, scaled, and adapted to various needs, something the traditional system has long struggled to achieve.

Rather than seeing AI as a replacement, it should be positioned as a supplement to human care, especially useful for initial engagement, symptom tracking, or as a bridge between therapy sessions. For individuals with complex or chronic mental health issues, AI must act as a stepping-stone toward comprehensive care rather than an endpoint. The ethical framework for AI in mental health, as advocated by global mental health organisations, supports this approach. These guidelines emphasise augmentation over replacement and call for continuous human oversight, transparency, and accountability in the deployment of AI tools. Such a model not only safeguards against potential harm but also aligns with the broader goals of ethical, person-centred care.

Moving forward, the integration of AI in mental healthcare must be guided by ethical design, interdisciplinary collaboration, and ongoing empirical research. Future efforts should focus on improving personalisation, safeguarding user privacy, ensuring equitable access, and developing robust regulatory frameworks. There is also a need for longitudinal studies to assess the long-term efficacy, engagement, and safety of AI interventions in diverse populations. In conclusion, AI holds remarkable potential to enhance mental healthcare delivery, increase access, and support both patients and clinicians in meaningful ways. However, its role should remain that of a powerful ally, never a stand-in, for human empathy, judgment, and connection. By embracing a balanced, ethically informed model of care that combines technological innovation with the irreplaceable value of human interaction, we can build a more resilient, inclusive, and responsive mental health system for the future.

REFERENCES

Abd-alrazaq, A., AlSaad, R., Aziz, S., Ahmed, A., Denecke, K., Househ, M., Farooq, F., & Sheikh, J. (2023b). Wearable artificial intelligence for anxiety and depression: Scoping review. *Journal of Medical Internet Research, 25*, e42672. DOI: 10.2196/42672

Abd-alrazaq, A., AlSaad, R., Harfouche, M., Aziz, S., Ahmed, A., Damseh, R., & Sheikh, J. (2023a). Wearable artificial intelligence for detecting anxiety: Systematic review and meta-analysis. *Journal of Medical Internet Research, 25*, e48754. DOI: 10.2196/48754

Al Kuwaiti, K., Nazer, A., Al-Reedy, A., Al Abdouli, A., Alnaqbi, S., Al Kaabi, L., Al Zarooni, A., AlHammadi, S., Al Shamsi, M., AlDhaheri, M., Al Suwaidi, H., Al Mazrouei, A., Al Ketbi, L. M., Al Mazrouei, H., Al Shamsi, S., Al Nuaimi, A., Al Muhairi, F., Al Jaber, H., Al Yammahi, J., & Saleh, K. (2023). A review of the role of artificial intelligence in healthcare. *Journal of Personalized Medicine, 13*(6), 951. DOI: 10.3390/jpm13060951

Alowais, S. A., Alghamdi, S. S., Alsuhebany, N., Alqahtani, T., Alshaya, A. I., Almohareb, S. N., Aldairem, A., Alrashed, M., Bin Saleh, K., Badreldin, H. A., Al Yami, M. S., Al Harbi, S., & Albekairy, A. M. (2023). Revolutionizing healthcare: The role of artificial intelligence in clinical practice. *BMC Medical Education, 23*(1), 689. DOI: 10.1186/s12909-023-04698-z

American Psychiatric Association. (2013). *Diagnostic and statistical manual of mental disorders* (5th ed.). American Psychiatric Publishing.

American Psychological Association. (2023). Reducing stigma and expanding care: The changing landscape of addiction treatment. *Monitor on Psychology.*

Angenius, M., & Ghajargar, M. (2023, July). Design principles for interactive and reflective journaling with AI. In Science and Information Conference (pp. 62-81). Cham: Springer Nature Switzerland.

ANI Press Release & Business Standard. (2024, November 29). HEALO: INFIHEAL's Award-Winning AI therapist debuts at Bengaluru Tech Summit 2024. www.business-standard.com. https://www.business-standard.com/content/press-releases-ani/healo-infiheal-s-award-winning-ai-therapist-debuts-at-bengaluru-tech-summit-2024-124112900319_1.html

Arnaez, J. M., Krendl, A. C., McCormick, B. P., Chen, Z., & Chomistek, A. K. (2019). The association of depression stigma with barriers to seeking mental health care: A cross-sectional analysis. *Journal of Mental Health (Abingdon, England), 29*(2), 182–190. DOI: 10.1080/09638237.2019.1644494

Attridge, M. (2019). A global perspective on promoting workplace mental health and the role of employee assistance programs. *American Journal of Health Promotion, 33*(4), 622–629.

Banh, L., & Strobel, G. (2023). Generative artificial intelligence. *Electronic Markets, 33*(1), 63.

Birhane, A., Ruane, E., Laurent, T., & Brown, S., M., Flowers, J., Ventresque, A., & L. Dancy, C. (2022). The forgotten margins of AI ethics. In Proceedings of the 2022 ACM Conference on Fairness, Accountability, and Transparency (pp. 948-958).

Blease, C., Torous, J., & Hägglund, M. (2020). Does patient access to clinical notes change documentation? *Frontiers in Public Health, 8*, 577896.

Boden, J. M., & Fergusson, D. M. (2011). Alcohol and depression. *Addiction (Abingdon, England), 106*(5), 906–914. DOI: 10.1111/j.1360-0443.2010.03351.x

Boucher, E. M., Harake, N. R., Ward, H. E., Stoeckl, S. E., Vargas, J., Minkel, J., ... & Zilca, R. (2021). Artificially intelligent chatbots in digital mental health interventions: A review. Expert Review of Medical Devices, 18(sup1), 37–49. https://doi.org/DOI: 10.1080/17434440.2021.2013200

Bricout, J., Greer, J., Fields, N., Xu, L., Tamplain, P., Doelling, K., & Sharma, B. (2022). The "humane in the loop": Inclusive research design and policy approaches to foster capacity building assistive technologies in the COVID-19 era. *Assistive Technology, 34*(6), 644–652.

Britt, T. W., Jennings, K. S., Cheung, J. H., Pury, C. L. S., & Zinzow, H. M. (2015). The role of different stigma perceptions in treatment-seeking and dropout among active-duty military personnel. *Psychiatric Rehabilitation Journal, 38*(2), 142–149. DOI: 10.1037/prj0000120

Brown, J. E., & Halpern, J. (2021). AI chatbots cannot replace human interactions in the pursuit of more inclusive mental healthcare. *SSM. Mental Health, 1*, 100017.

Bryant, R. A. (2019). Post-traumatic stress disorder: A state-of-the-art review of evidence and challenges. *World Psychiatry; Official Journal of the World Psychiatric Association (WPA), 18*(3), 259–269. DOI: 10.1002/wps.20656

Burr, C., Taddeo, M., & Floridi, L. (2020). The ethics of digital wellbeing: A thematic review. *Science and Engineering Ethics*, *26*, 2313–2343. DOI: 10.1007/s11948-020-00175-8

Campbell, A. N. C., Nunes, E. V., Matthews, A. G., Stitzer, M. L., Miele, G. M., Polsky, D., Turrigiano, E., Walters, S., & VanVeldhuisen, P. (2022). Digital therapeutic for opioid use disorder: reSET-O outcomes. *Addiction Research and Theory*, *30*(5), 387–395.

Canetto, S. S., & Sakinofsky, I. (1998). The gender paradox in suicide. *Suicide & Life-Threatening Behavior*, *28*(1), 1–23. DOI: 10.1111/j.1943-278X.1998.tb00622.x

Centers for Disease Control and Prevention. (2023). Drug overdose deaths in the United States, 2002–2022. National Center for Health Statistics. https://www.cdc.gov/nchs/products/databriefs/db456.htm

Chand, S. P., & Arif, H. (2023, July 17). Depression. StatPearls - NCBI Bookshelf. https://www.ncbi.nlm.nih.gov/books/NBK430847/

Chandna, A. S., Suhas, S., Patley, R., Dinakaran, D., Manjunatha, N., Rao, G. N., Gururaj, G., Varghese, M., & Benegal, V.NMHS National Collaborators Group. (2023). Exploring the enigma of low prevalence of post-traumatic stress disorder in India. *Indian Journal of Psychiatry*, *65*(12), 1254–1260. DOI: 10.4103/indianjpsychiatry.indianjpsychiatry_830_23

Coghlan, S., Leins, K., Sheldrick, S., Cheong, M., Gooding, P., & D'Alfonso, S. (2023). To chat or bot to chat: Ethical issues with using chatbots in mental health. *Digital Health*, *9*, 20552076231183542. DOI: 10.1177/20552076231183542

Colby, K. M., Hilf, F. D., Weber, S., & Kraemer, H. C. (1972). Turing-like indistinguishability tests for the validation of a computer simulation of paranoid processes. *Artificial Intelligence*, *3*, 199–221. DOI: 10.1016/0004-3702(72)90049-5

Cummins, N., Scherer, S., Krajewski, J., Schnieder, S., Epps, J., & Quatieri, T. F. (2018). A review of depression and suicide risk assessment using speech analysis. *Speech Communication*, *71*, 10–49. DOI: 10.1016/j.specom.2015.03.004

Cusack, K., Jonas, D. E., Forneris, C. A., Wines, C., Sonis, J., Middleton, J. C., Feltner, C., Brownley, K. A., Olmsted, K. R., Greenblatt, A., Weil, A., & Gaynes, B. N. (2016). Psychological treatments for adults with posttraumatic stress disorder: A systematic review and meta-analysis. *Clinical Psychology Review*, *43*, 128–141. DOI: 10.1016/j.cpr.2015.10.003

Davenport, T., & Kalakota, R. (2019). The potential for artificial intelligence in healthcare. *Future Healthcare Journal*, *6*(2), 94–98. DOI: 10.7861/futurehosp.6-2-94

Dawoodbhoy, F. M., Delaney, J., Cecula, P., Mitchell, K., Jurek, A., Bouch, J., Tapp, J., Webster, C., Challis, K., Binnie, J., Stringfellow, C., Yeomans, M., Mufti, H., Tan, E., Chang, C. K., McKnight, L., Stewart, D., Jewell, A., Lavelle, M., & Stewart, R. (2021). AI in patient flow: Applications of artificial intelligence to improve patient flow in NHS acute mental health inpatient units. *Heliyon*, *7*(5), e06993. DOI: 10.1016/j.heliyon.2021.e06993

De Freitas, J., & Cohen, I. G. (2024). The health risks of generative AI-based wellness apps. *Nature Medicine*, *30*(5), 1269–1275. DOI: 10.1038/s41591-024-02943-6

De la Torre, F. M., Hernandez, J., Wilson, A. D., & Amores, J. (2025). Sonora: Human-AI co-creation of 3D audio worlds and its impact on anxiety and cognitive load. CHI '25: Proceedings of the 2025 CHI Conference on Human Factors in Computing Systems, 308, 1-22. https://doi.org/DOI: 10.1145/3706598.3713316

Denecke, K., & Househ, M. (2021). Artificial intelligence for chatbots in mental health: Opportunities and challenges. In *Advances in Artificial Intelligence for Health and Medicine* (pp. 171–186). Springer., DOI: 10.1007/978-3-030-67303-1_10

Dibbets, P. (2019). A novel virtual reality paradigm: Predictors for stress-related intrusions and avoidance behavior. *Journal of Behavior Therapy and Experimental Psychiatry*, *63*, 26–33. DOI: 10.1016/j.jbtep.2019.01.001

Donnelly, M. R., Reinberg, R., Ito, K. L., Saldana, D., Neureither, M., Schmiesing, A., Jahng, E., & Liew, L. (2021). Virtual reality for the treatment of anxiety disorders: A scoping review. *The American Journal of Occupational Therapy*, *75*(6), 7506205040. DOI: 10.5014/ajot.2021.046169

Dovis, S., Van der Oord, S., Wiers, R. W., & Prins, P. J. (2015). Improving executive functioning in children with ADHD: Training multiple executive functions within the context of a computer game. A randomized double-blind placebo controlled trial. *PLoS One*, *10*(4), e0121651.

Duda, M., Ma, R., Haber, N., & Wall, D. P. (2016). Use of machine learning for behavioral distinction of autism and ADHD. *Translational Psychiatry*, *6*(2), e732–e732.

Duhne, P. G. S., Delgadillo, J., & Lutz, W. (2022). Predicting early dropout in online versus face-to-face guided self-help: A machine learning approach. *Behaviour Research and Therapy*, *159*, 104200. DOI: 10.1016/j.brat.2022.104200

Dupré, M. H. (2025, June 28). People are being involuntarily committed, jailed after spiraling into "ChatGPT psychosis." Futurism. https://futurism.com/commitment-jail-chatgpt-psychosis

Egger, S. M., Frey, S., Sauerzopf, L., & Meidert, U. (2023). A literature review to identify effective web-and app-based mHealth interventions for stress management at work. *Workplace Health & Safety*, *71*(10), 452–463.

Fabiano, G. A., Pelham, W. E.Jr, Coles, E. K., Gnagy, E. M., Chronis-Tuscano, A., & O'Connor, B. C. (2009). A meta-analysis of behavioral treatments for attention-deficit/hyperactivity disorder. *Clinical Psychology Review*, *29*(2), 129–140.

Fanni, S. C., Febi, M., Aghakhanyan, G., & Neri, E. (2023). Natural language processing. In *Introduction to artificial intelligence* (pp. 87–99). Springer International Publishing.

Farzan, M., Ebrahimi, H., Pourali, M., & Sabeti, F. (2025). Artificial intelligence-powered cognitive behavioral therapy chatbots, a systematic review. *Iranian Journal of Psychiatry*, *20*(1), 102–110. DOI: 0.18502/ijps.v20i1.17395

Feil-Seifer, D., & Matarić, M. J. (2011). Socially assistive robotics. *IEEE Robotics & Automation Magazine*, *18*(1), 24–31.

First Therapy Chatbot trial yields mental health benefits. (2025, March 27). Dartmouth. https://home.dartmouth.edu/news/2025/03/first-therapy-chatbot-trial-yields-mental-health-benefits

Firth, J., Torous, J., Nicholas, J., Carney, R., Pratap, A., Rosenbaum, S., & Sarris, J. (2017). The efficacy of smartphone-based mental health interventions for depressive symptoms: A meta-analysis of randomized controlled trials. *World Psychiatry; Official Journal of the World Psychiatric Association (WPA)*, *16*(3), 287–298.

Fitzpatrick, K. K., Darcy, A., & Vierhile, M. (2017). Delivering cognitive behavior therapy to young adults with symptoms of depression and anxiety using a fully automated conversational agent (Woebot): A randomized controlled trial. *JMIR Mental Health*, *4*(2), e19. DOI: 10.2196/mental.7785

Flanagan, O., Chan, A., Roop, P., & Sundram, F. (2021). Using acoustic speech patterns from smartphones to investigate mood disorders: Scoping review. *JMIR mHealth and uHealth*, *9*(9), e24352. DOI: 10.2196/24352

Fried, E. I., Flake, J. K., & Robinaugh, D. J. (2022). Revisiting the theoretical and methodological foundations of depression measurement. *Nature Reviews Psychology*, *1*(6), 358–368. DOI: 10.1038/s44159-022-00050-2

Fulmer, R., Joerin, A., Gentile, B., Lakerink, L., & Rauws, M. (2018). Using psychological artificial intelligence (Tess) to relieve symptoms of depression and anxiety: Randomized controlled trial. *JMIR Mental Health*, *5*(4), e64. DOI: 10.2196/mental.9782

Garriga, R., Mas, J., Abraha, S., Hofer, M., Yang, H., Haller, D. M., Gonzalez-Huerta, J. M., Echarri, O., Sintes, R., Montalvo, I., Duran-Sindreu, C., Molinuevo, J. L., Ros, E., Mestre, A., Miguel, J. C., Subirana, I., Perera-Lluna, A., Vieta, E., Bulbena, A., & García-Altés, A. (2022). Machine learning model to predict mental health crises from electronic health records. *Nature Medicine*, *28*(6), 1240–1248. DOI: 10.1038/s41591-022-01811-5

Ghaffar Nia, N., Kaplanoglu, E., & Nasab, A. (2023). Evaluation of artificial intelligence techniques in disease diagnosis and prediction. *Discover Artificial Intelligence*, *3*(1), 5. Advance online publication. DOI: 10.1007/s44163-023-00049-5

Grant, B. F., Stinson, F. S., Dawson, D. A., Chou, S. P., Dufour, M. C., Compton, W., Pickering, R. P., & Kaplan, K. (2004). Prevalence and co-occurrence of substance use disorders and independent mood and anxiety disorders. *Archives of General Psychiatry*, *61*(8), 807–816.

Grosshans, M., Paul, T., Fischer, S. K., Lotzmann, N., List, H., Haag, C., & Mutschler, J. (2024). Conversation-based AI for anxiety disorders might lower the threshold for traditional medical assistance: A case report. *Frontiers in Public Health*, *12*, 1399702. DOI: 10.3389/fpubh.2024.1399702

Heinz, M. V., Mackin, D. M., Trudeau, B. M., Bhattacharya, S., Wang, Y., Banta, H. A., Jewett, A. D., Salzhauer, A. J., Griffin, T. Z., & Jacobson, N. C. (2025). Randomized trial of a generative AI chatbot for mental health treatment. *NEJM AI*, *2*(4). Advance online publication. DOI: 10.1056/aioa2400802

Husain, L., Greenhalgh, T., Hughes, G., Finlay, T., & Wherton, J. (2022). Desperately seeking intersectionality in digital health disparity research: Narrative review to inform a richer theorization of multiple disadvantage. *Journal of Medical Internet Research*, *24*(12), e42358. DOI: 10.2196/42358

Husnain, N. A., Ahmad, N. A., Saeed, N. A., & Din, N. S. M. U. (2024). Harnessing AI in depression therapy: Integrating technology with traditional approaches. *International Journal of Science and Research Archive*, *12*(2), 2585–2590. DOI: 10.30574/ijsra.2024.12.2.1512

Inkster, B., Sarda, S., & Subramanian, V. (2018). An empathy-driven, conversational artificial intelligence agent (Wysa) for digital mental well-being: Real-world data evaluation mixed-methods study. *JMIR mHealth and uHealth*, *6*(11), e12106.

Insel, T. R. (2017). Digital phenotyping: Technology for a new science of behavior. *Journal of the American Medical Association*, *318*(13), 1215–1216.

Iyortsuun, N. K., Kim, S. H., Jhon, M., Yang, H. J., & Pant, S. (2023). A review of machine learning and deep learning approaches on mental health diagnosis. *Health Care, 11*(3), 285. DOI: 10.3390/healthcare11030285

Jacobson, N. C., Lekkas, D., Huang, R., & Thomas, N. (2020). Deep learning paired with wearable passive sensing data predicts deterioration in anxiety disorder symptoms across 17-18 years. *Journal of Affective Disorders, 282*(1). Advance online publication. DOI: 10.1016/j.jad.2020.12.086

Joerin, A., Rauws, M., Fulmer, R., & Black, V. (2020). Ethical artificial intelligence for digital health organizations. *Cureus, 12*(3).

Johnstone, S. J., Roodenrys, S., Blackman, R., Johnston, E., Loveday, K., Mantz, S., & Barratt, M. F. (2012). Neurocognitive training for children with and without AD/HD. *Attention Deficit and Hyperactivity Disorders, 4*, 11–23.

Kaiser Family Foundation. (2023). Mental Health Care Health Professional Shortage Areas (HPSAs). https://www.kff.org/other/state-indicator/mental-health-care-health-professional-shortage-areas-hpsas/

Kaldo, V., Isacsson, N., Forsell, E., Bjurner, P., Abdesslem, F. B., & Boman, M. (2021). AI-driven adaptive treatment strategies in internet-delivered CBT. *European Psychiatry : the Journal of the Association of European Psychiatrists, 64*(S1), S20. DOI: 10.1192/j.eurpsy.2021.75

Kawa, S., & Giordano, J. (2012). A brief historicity of the Diagnostic and Statistical Manual of Mental Disorders: Issues and implications for the future of psychiatric canon and practice. *Philosophy, Ethics, and Humanities in Medicine; PEHM, 7*, 2. DOI: 10.1186/1747-5341-7-2

Khawaja, Z., & Bélisle-Pipon, J. C. (2023). Your robot therapist is not your therapist: Understanding the role of AI-powered mental health chatbots. *Frontiers in Digital Health, 5*, 1278186. DOI: 10.3389/fdgth.2023.1278186

Kim, E. S., Berkovits, L. D., Bernier, E. P., Leyzberg, D., Shic, F., Paul, R., & Scassellati, B. (2013). Social robots as embedded reinforcers of social behavior in children with autism. *Journal of Autism and Developmental Disorders, 43*, 1038–1049.

Kintsugi. (2022). Kintsugi Health. https://www.kintsugihealth.com/

Kline, A. C., Cooper, A. A., Rytwinski, N. K., & Feeny, N. C. (2018). Long-term efficacy of psychotherapy for posttraumatic stress disorder: A meta-analysis of randomized controlled trials. *Clinical Psychology Review, 59*, 30–40. DOI: 10.1016/j.cpr.2017.10.009

Klingberg, T., Fernell, E., Olesen, P. J., Johnson, M., Gustafsson, P., Dahlström, K., & Westerberg, H. (2005). Computerized training of working memory in children with ADHD-a randomized, controlled trial. *Journal of the American Academy of Child and Adolescent Psychiatry*, *44*(2), 177–186.

Kollins, S. H., DeLoss, D. J., Cañadas, E., Lutz, J., Findling, R. L., Keefe, R. S., & Faraone, S. V. (2020). A novel digital intervention for actively reducing severity of paediatric ADHD (STARS-ADHD): A randomised controlled trial. *The Lancet. Digital Health*, *2*(4), e168–e178.

Koob, G. F., & Volkow, N. D. (2016). Neurobiology of addiction: A neurocircuitry analysis. *The Lancet. Psychiatry*, *3*(8), 760–773. DOI: 10.1016/S2215-0366(16)00104-8

Kothgassner, O. D., Goreis, A., Kafka, J. X., Van Eickels, R. L., Plener, P. L., & Felnhofer, A. (2019). Virtual reality exposure therapy for posttraumatic stress disorder (PTSD): A meta-analysis. *European Journal of Psychotraumatology*, *10*(1), 1654782. Advance online publication. DOI: 10.1080/20008198.2019.1654782

Koutsouleris, N., Hauser, T. U., Skvortsova, V., & De Choudhury, M. (2022). From promise to practice: Towards the realisation of AI-informed mental health care. *The Lancet. Digital Health*, *4*(1), e829–e840. DOI: 10.1016/s2589-7500(22)00153-4

Kumar, Y., Koul, A., Singla, R., & Ijaz, M. F. (2022). Artificial intelligence in disease diagnosis: A systematic literature review, synthesizing framework and future research agenda. *Journal of Ambient Intelligence and Humanized Computing*, *14*(7), 8459–8486. DOI: 10.1007/s12652-021-03612-z

Kuziemsky, C., Maeder, A. J., John, O., Gogia, S., Basu, A., Meher, S., & Ho, K. (2019). Role of artificial intelligence within the telehealth domain. *Yearbook of Medical Informatics*, *28*(1), 35–40. DOI: 10.1055/s-0039-1677897

Lee, D., & Yoon, S. N. (2021). Application of artificial intelligence-based technologies in the healthcare industry: Opportunities and challenges. *International Journal of Environmental Research and Public Health*, *18*, 271. DOI: 10.3390/ijerph18010271

Lee, M., & Passarotti, A. M. (2022). Editorial: Addressing the challenges in the diagnosis of depressive disorder in children and adolescents. *Frontiers in Psychiatry*, *13*. Advance online publication. DOI: 10.3389/fpsyt.2022.1011301

Lenton-Brym, A. P., Collins, A., Lane, J., Busso, C., Ouyang, J., Fitzpatrick, S., Kuo, J. R., & Monson, C. M. (2025). Using machine learning to increase access to and engagement with trauma-focused interventions for posttraumatic stress disorder. *British Journal of Clinical Psychology*, *64*(1), 125–136. DOI: 10.1111/bjc.12468

Liang, H., Tsui, B. Y., Ni, H., Valentim, C. C., Baxter, S. L., Liu, G., & Xia, H. (2019). Evaluation and accurate diagnoses of pediatric diseases using artificial intelligence. *Nature Medicine*, *25*(3), 433–438.

Lin, B., Bouneffouf, D., Cecchi, G., & Varshney, K. (2024). Towards Healthy AI: Large Language Models Need Therapists Too. Cornell University, 61–70. https://doi.org/DOI: 10.18653/v1/2024.trustnlp-1.6

Liu, H., Peng, H., Song, X., Xu, C., & Zhang, M. (2022). Using AI chatbots to provide self-help depression interventions for university students: A randomized trial of effectiveness. *Internet Interventions : the Application of Information Technology in Mental and Behavioural Health*, *27*, 100495. DOI: 10.1016/j.invent.2022.100495

Liu, Q., He, H., Yang, J., Feng, X., Zhao, F., & Lyu, J. (2019). Changes in the global burden of depression from 1990 to 2017: Findings from the Global Burden of Disease study. *Journal of Psychiatric Research, 126*, 134–140. DOI: 10.1016/j.jpsychires.2019.08.002

Lucas, G. M., Gratch, J., King, A., & Morency, L. P. (2014). It's only a computer: Virtual humans increase willingness to disclose. *Computers in Human Behavior*, *37*, 94–100.

Marlatt, G. A., & Witkiewitz, K. (2005). Relapse prevention for alcohol and drug problems. In Marlatt, G. A., & Donovan, D. M. (Eds.), *Relapse prevention: Maintenance strategies in the treatment of addictive behaviors* (2nd ed., pp. 1–44). Guilford Press.

Marques, L., Valentine, S. E., Kaysen, D., Mackintosh, M. A., Dixon De Silva, L. E., Ahles, E. M., Young, S. J., Shtasel, D. L., Simon, N. M., & Wiltsey-Stirman, S. (2019). Provider fidelity and modifications to cognitive processing therapy in a diverse community health clinic: Associations with clinical change. *Journal of Consulting and Clinical Psychology*, *87*(4), 357–369. DOI: 10.1037/ccp0000384

Maslach, C., & Leiter, M. P. (2016). Burnout. In Stress: Concepts, cognition, emotion, and behavior (pp. 351-357). Academic Press.

Maté, G. (2008). *In the Realm of Hungry Ghosts: Close Encounters with Addiction*. North Atlantic Books.

MBDesk. (2024, October 25). Infiheal launches AI Therapist Healo at star-studded Mumbai event. MediaBrief. https://mediabrief.com/infiheal-ai-therapist-healo/

Mehta, A., Niles, A., Vargas, J., Marafon, T., Couto, D., & Gross, J. (2021). Acceptability and effectiveness of artificial intelligence therapy for anxiety and depression (Youper): Longitudinal observational study. *Journal of Medical Internet Research, 23*(6), e26771. DOI: 10.2196/26771

Miloff, A., Lindner, P., Hamilton, W., Reuterskiöld, L., Andersson, G., & Carlbring, P. (2016). Single-session gamified virtual reality exposure therapy for spider phobia vs. traditional exposure therapy: Study protocol for a randomized controlled non-inferiority trial. *Trials, 17*(1), 60. Advance online publication. DOI: 10.1186/s13063-016-1191-6

Miner, A. S., Milstein, A., & Hancock, J. T. (2017). Talking to machines about personal mental health problems. *Journal of the American Medical Association, 318*(13), 1217–1218.

Minerva, F., & Giubilini, A. (2023). Is AI the future of mental healthcare? *Topoi, 42*(3), 809–817. DOI: 10.1007/s11245-023-09932-3

Monroy-Fraustro, D., Maldonado-Castellanos, I., Aboites-Molina, M., Rodríguez, S., Sueiras, P., Altamirano-Bustamante, N. F., De Hoyos-Bermea, A., & Altamirano-Bustamante, M. M. (2021). Bibliotherapy as a Non-pharmaceutical Intervention to Enhance Mental Health in Response to the COVID-19 Pandemic: A Mixed-Methods Systematic Review and Bioethical Meta-Analysis. *Frontiers in Public Health, 9*. Advance online publication. DOI: 10.3389/fpubh.2021.629872

Monson, C. M., Shields, N., Suvak, M. K., Lane, J. E. M., Shnaider, P., Landy, M. S. H., Wagner, A. C., Sijercic, I., Masina, T., Wanklyn, S. G., & Stirman, S. W. (2018). A randomized controlled effectiveness trial of training strategies in cognitive processing therapy for posttraumatic stress disorder: Impact on patient outcomes. *Behaviour Research and Therapy, 110*, 31–40. DOI: 10.1016/j.brat.2018.08.007

Moreno, H. R., & Plant, R. T. (1993). A prototype decision support system for differential diagnosis of psychotic, mood, and organic mental disorders. *Medical Decision Making, 13*(1), 43–48. DOI: 10.1177/0272989X9301300106

Moreno-Agostino, D., Wu, Y., Daskalopoulou, C., Hasan, M. T., Huisman, M., & Prina, M. (2020). Global trends in the prevalence and incidence of depression:a systematic review and meta-analysis. *Journal of Affective Disorders, 281*, 235–243. DOI: 10.1016/j.jad.2020.12.035

Murphy, D., & Busuttil, W. (2014). PTSD, stigma and barriers to help-seeking within the UK Armed Forces. *Journal of the Royal Army Medical Corps, 161*(4), 322–326. DOI: 10.1136/jramc-2014-000344

Naslund, J. A., Aschbrenner, K. A., Kim, S. J., McHugo, G. J., Unützer, J., Bartels, S. J., & Marsch, L. A. (2017). Health behavior models for informing digital technology interventions for individuals with mental illness. *Psychiatric Rehabilitation Journal*, *40*(3), 325.

National Academies of Sciences, Engineering, and Medicine. (2019). The Promise of Adolescence: Realizing Opportunity for All Youth. Washington, DC: The National Academies Press. https://doi.org/DOI: 10.17226/25388

National Institute on Drug Abuse. (2018). Principles of drug addiction treatment: A research-based guide (3rd ed.). https://nida.nih.gov/publications/principles-drug-addiction-treatment-research-based-guide-third-edition

National Institute on Drug Abuse. (2020). Drugs, brains, and behavior: The science of addiction. https://nida.nih.gov/publications/drugs-brains-behavior-science-addiction

National Institute on Drug Abuse. (2023). Monitoring the Future Survey: Trends in Prevalence of Various Drugs. https://nida.nih.gov/drug-topics/trends-statistics/monitoring-future

Nilsen, P., Svedberg, P., Nygren, J., Frideros, M., Johansson, J., & Schueller, S. (2022). Accelerating the impact of artificial intelligence in mental healthcare through implementation science. *Implementation Research and Practice*, *3*, 26334895221112033. Advance online publication. DOI: 10.1177/26334895221112033

Norcross, J. C., & Lambert, M. J. (2019). What works in the psychotherapy relationship: Results, conclusions, and practices.

Ogbo, F. A., Mathsyaraja, S., Koti, R. K., Perz, J., & Page, A. (2018). The burden of depressive disorders in South Asia, 1990–2016: Findings from the global burden of disease study. *BMC Psychiatry*, *18*(1). Advance online publication. DOI: 10.1186/s12888-018-1918-1

Olawade, D. B., Wada, O. Z., Odetayo, A., David-Olawade, A. C., Asaolu, F., & Eberhardt, J. (2024). Enhancing mental health with artificial intelligence: Current trends and future prospects. *Journal of Medicine, Surgery, and Public Health*, *3*, 100099. DOI: 10.1016/j.glmedi.2024.100099

Omarov, B., Zhumanov, Z., Gumar, A., & Kuntunova, L. (2023). Artificial intelligence enabled mobile chatbot psychologist using AIML and cognitive behavioral therapy. *International Journal of Advanced Computer Science and Applications*, *14*(6), 137–146. DOI: 10.14569/ijacsa.2023.0140616

Onnela, J. P., & Rauch, S. L. (2016). Harnessing smartphone-based digital phenotyping to enhance behavioral and mental health. *Neuropsychopharmacology : Official Publication of the American College of Neuropsychopharmacology, 41*(7), 1691–1696.

Orji, R., & Moffatt, K. (2018). Persuasive technology for health and wellness: State-of-the-art and emerging trends. *Health Informatics Journal, 24*(1), 66–91.

Patel, V.. (2018). The Lancet Commission on Global Mental Health and Sustainable Development. *Lancet, 392*(10157), 1553–1598. DOI: 10.1016/S0140-6736(18)31612-X

Pavlopoulos, A., Rachiotis, T., & Maglogiannis, I. (2023). An Overview of Tools and Technologies for Anxiety and Depression Management Using AI. *Applied Sciences (Basel, Switzerland), 14*(19), 9068. DOI: 10.3390/app14199068

Pelham, W. E.Jr, Fabiano, G. A., & Massetti, G. M. (2005). Evidence-based assessment of attention deficit hyperactivity disorder in children and adolescents. *Journal of Clinical Child and Adolescent Psychology, 34*(3), 449–476.

Penedo, J. M. G., Rubel, J., Meglio, M., Bornhauser, L., Krieger, T., Babl, A., Muiños, R., Roussos, A., Delgadillo, J., Flückiger, C., Berger, T., Lutz, W., & Grosse Holtforth, M. (2023). Using machine learning algorithms to predict the effects of change processes in psychotherapy: Toward process-level treatment personalization. *Psychotherapy (Chicago, Ill.), 60*(4), 536–547. DOI: 10.1037/pst0000507

Pennebaker, J. W., & Chung, C. K. (2013). 18 Expressive writing: Connections physical and mental health to. The Oxford handbook of health psychology, 417.

Pham, H., Zhou, Y., Mahmood, Z., & Radev, D. (2024). A fully generative motivational interviewing counsellor chatbot. arXiv preprint arXiv:2401.10075.

Richter, T., Fishbain, B., Richter-Levin, G., & Okon-Singer, H. (2021). Machine Learning-Based Behavioral Diagnostic Tools for Depression: Advances, challenges, and future directions. *Journal of Personalized Medicine, 11*(10), 957. DOI: 10.3390/jpm11100957

Rizzo, A. S., & Shilling, R. (2017). Clinical virtual reality tools to advance the prevention, assessment, and treatment of PTSD. European Journal of Psychotraumatology, 8(sup5). *Article, 1414560.* Advance online publication. DOI: 10.1080/20008198.2017.1414560

Rodríguez-Martínez, A., Amezcua-Aguilar, T., Cortés-Moreno, J., & Jiménez-Delgado, J. J. (2023). Qualitative analysis of conversational chatbots to alleviate loneliness in older adults as a strategy for emotional health. *Healthcare (Basel, Switzerland), 12*(1), 62. DOI: 10.3390/healthcare12010062

Roepke, A. M., Jaffee, S. R., Riffle, O. M., McGonigal, J., Broome, R., & Maxwell, B. (2015). Randomized controlled trial of SuperBetter, a smartphone-based/internet-based self-help tool to reduce depressive symptoms. *Games for Health Journal, 4*(3), 235–246. DOI: 10.1089/g4h.2014.0046

Royal College of Psychiatrists. (2022). Two-thirds of vacant children's mental health roles unfilled. https://www.rcpsych.ac.uk/news-and-features/latest-news/detail/2022/01/07/two-thirds-of-vacant-children-s-mental-health-roles-unfilled

Rubel, J. A., Zilcha-Mano, S., Giesemann, J., Prinz, J., & Lutz, W. (2020). Predicting personalized process–outcome associations in psychotherapy using machine learning approaches—A demonstration. *Psychotherapy Research, 30*(3), 300–309. DOI: 10.1080/10503307.2019.1597994

Rucker, D. C., & Webster, R. J.III. (2011). Statics and dynamics of continuum robots with general tendon routing and external loading. *IEEE Transactions on Robotics, 27*(6), 1033–1044.

Sabry, F., Eltaras, T., Labda, W., Alzoubi, K., & Malluhi, Q. (2022). Machine learning for healthcare wearable devices: The big picture. *Journal of Healthcare Engineering, 2022*, 4653923. Advance online publication. DOI: 10.1155/2022/4653923

Santomauro, D. F.. (2021). Global prevalence and burden of depressive and anxiety disorders in 204 countries and territories in 2020 due to the COVID-19 pandemic. *Lancet, 398*(10312), 1700–1712. DOI: 10.1016/S0140-6736(21)02143-7

Scassellati, B., Admoni, H., & Matarić, M. (2012). Robots for use in autism research. *Annual Review of Biomedical Engineering, 14*(1), 275–294.

Scassellati, B., Boccanfuso, L., Huang, C. M., Mademtzi, M., Qin, M., Salomons, N., & Shic, F. (2018). Improving social skills in children with ASD using a long-term, in-home social robot. *Science Robotics, 3*(21), eaat7544.

Sedlakova, J., & Trachsel, M. (2022). Conversational artificial intelligence in psychotherapy: A new therapeutic tool or agent? *The American Journal of Bioethics, 23*(5), 4–13. DOI: 10.1080/15265161.2022.2048739

Siddals, S., Torous, J., & Coxon, A. (2024). "It happened to be the perfect thing": Experiences of generative AI chatbots for mental health. *Npj Mental Health Research, 3*(1). Advance online publication. DOI: 10.1038/s44184-024-00097-4

Smith, K. (2014). Mental health: A world of depression. *Nature*, *515*, 180–181. DOI: 10.1038/515180a

Srinivasan, S. M., Park, I. K., Neelly, L. B., & Bhat, A. N. (2015). A comparison of the effects of rhythm and robotic interventions on repetitive behaviors and affective states of children with Autism Spectrum Disorder (ASD). *Research in Autism Spectrum Disorders*, *18*, 51–63.

Sripada, R. K., Ready, D. J., Ganoczy, D., Astin, M. C., & Rauch, S. A. (2020). When to change the treatment plan: An analysis of diminishing returns in VA patients undergoing prolonged exposure and cognitive processing therapy. *Behavior Therapy*, *51*(1), 85–98. DOI: 10.1016/j.beth.2019.05.003

Stade, E. C., Stirman, S. W., Ungar, L. H., Boland, C. L., Schwartz, H. A., Yaden, D. B., Sedoc, J., DeRubeis, R. J., Willer, R., & Eichstaedt, J. C. (2024). Large language models could change the future of behavioral healthcare: A proposal for responsible development and evaluation. *Npj Mental Health Research*, *3*(1). Advance online publication. DOI: 10.1038/s44184-024-00056-z

Stawarz, K., Preist, C., & Coyle, D. (2019). Use of smartphone apps, social media, and web-based resources to support mental health and well-being: Online survey. *JMIR Mental Health*, *6*(7), e12546. DOI: 10.2196/12546

Stein, A. (2025, April 22). Are therapy chatbots effective for depression and anxiety? A critical comparative review. https://apsa.org/are-therapy-chatbots-effective-for-depression-and-anxiety/

Sun, J., Lu, T., & Shao, X.. (2025). Practical AI application in psychiatry: Historical review and future directions. *Molecular Psychiatry*. Advance online publication. DOI: 10.1038/s41380-025-03072-3https://

Talkspace. (2018). Online therapy, counseling online, marriage counseling. https://www.talkspace.com/

Topol, E. J. (2019). High-performance medicine: The convergence of human and artificial intelligence. *Nature Medicine*, *25*(1), 44–56.

Torous, J.. (2021). Digital mental health and COVID-19: Using technology today to accelerate the curve on access and quality tomorrow. *JMIR Mental Health*, *7*(3), e18848. DOI: 10.2196/18848

Uban, A. S., Chulvi, B., & Rosso, P. (2021). An emotion and cognitive based analysis of mental health disorders from social media data. *Future Generation Computer Systems*, *123*, 480–494. DOI: 10.1016/j.future.2021.05.032

Uhlhaas, P., & Torous, J. (2019). Digital tools for youth mental health. *NPJ Digital Medicine*, *2*(1), 104.

UNICEF. (2021). The State of the World's Children 2021: On My Mind – Promoting, protecting and caring for children's mental health. https://www.unicef.org/reports/state-worlds-children-2021

University of Colorado. (2023). *DTOX project summary: Enhancing real-time craving tracking and therapist feedback*. Department of Psychiatry Research Briefs.

van Melle, W. (1978). MYCIN: A knowledge-based consultation program for infectious disease diagnosis. *International Journal of Man-Machine Studies*, *10*(3), 313–322. DOI: 10.1016/S0020-7373(78)80049-2

van Straten, C. L., Peter, J., & Kühne, R. (2024). "You" versus "children": A repeated-measures experiment on the effects of social robots' use of (im) personal address forms when talking to children. *International Journal of Child-Computer Interaction*, *42*, 100682.

Veterans Administration/Department of Defense Clinical Practice Guideline Working Group. (2023). *Management of post-traumatic stress and acute stress disorder*. Office of Quality and Performance.

Vindigni, G. (2023). Exploring digital therapeutics: game-based and ehealth interventions in mental health care: potential, challenges, and policy implications. *British Journal of Healthcare and Medical Research-Vol*, *10*(3).

Volkow, N. D. (2023). Public remarks during the National Drug & Alcohol Facts Week. National Institute on Drug Abuse. https://nida.nih.gov/news-events/national-drug-alcohol-facts-week

Volkow, N. D., Han, B., Compton, W. M., & Blanco, C. (2021). Cannabis use and risk of psychosis and suicidal thoughts among teens and young adults. *JAMA Psychiatry*, *78*(2), 123–134.

Wampold, B. E. (2015). How important are the common factors in psychotherapy? An update. *World Psychiatry; Official Journal of the World Psychiatric Association (WPA)*, *14*(3), 270–277.

Weizenbaum, J. (1966). ELIZA—A computer program for the study of natural language communication between man and machine. *Communications of the ACM*, *9*(1), 36–45. DOI: 10.1145/365153.365168

Wies, B., Landers, C., & Ienca, M. (2021). Digital mental health for young people: A scoping review of ethical promises and challenges. *Frontiers in Digital Health*, *3*, 697072. DOI: 10.3389/fdgth.2021.697072

Williams, C. M., Chaturvedi, R., Urman, R. D., Waterman, R. S., & Gabriel, R. A. (2021). Artificial intelligence and a pandemic: An analysis of the potential uses and drawbacks. *Journal of Medical Systems*, *45*, 1–3.

Williams, S. D., & Williams, J. (2020). Posttraumatic stress in organizations: Types, antecedents, and consequences. *Business and Society Review*, *125*(1), 23–40. DOI: 10.1111/basr.12192

World Economic Forum. (2011). The Global Economic Burden of Non-Communicable Diseases. https://www.weforum.org/reports/global-economic-burden-non-communicable-diseases

World Health Organization. WHO & World Health Organization: WHO. (2023, March 31). Depressive disorder (depression). https://www.who.int/news-room/fact-sheets/detail/depression

World Health Organization. (2023). Global status report on alcohol and health 2023. https://www.who.int/publications/i/item/9789240063875

World Health Organization (WHO). (2014). Preventing suicide: A global imperative. https://www.who.int/publications/i/item/9789241564779

World Health Organization (WHO). (2020). The impact of COVID-19 on mental, neurological and substance use services: results of a rapid assessment. https://www.who.int/publications/i/item/9789240124554

World Health Organization (WHO). (2021). Mental Health Atlas 2020. https://www.who.int/publications/i/item/9789240036703

World Health Organization (WHO). (2022). World Mental Health Report: Transforming mental health for all. https://www.who.int/publications/i/item/9789240049338

Wysa. (2023). Everyday mental health. https://www.talkspace.com/

Zafar, F., Alam, L. F., Vivas, R. R., Wang, J., Whei, S. J., Mehmood, S., Sadeghzadegan, A., Lakkimsetti, M., & Nazir, Z. (2024). The role of artificial intelligence in identifying depression and anxiety: A comprehensive literature review. *Cureus*. Advance online publication. DOI: 10.7759/cureus.56472

Zhao, W. X., Zhou, K., Li, J., Tang, T., Wang, X., Hou, Y., Min, Y., Zhang, B., Zhang, J., Dong, Z., Du, Y., Yang, C., Chen, Y., Chen, Z., Jiang, J., Ren, R., Li, Y., Tang, X., Liu, Z., . . . Wen, J.-R. (2024). A Survey of Large Language Models (No. arXiv:2303.18223). arXiv. https://doi.org//arXiv.2303.18223DOI: 10.48550

Zhong, W., Luo, J., & Zhang, H. (2024). The therapeutic effectiveness of artificial intelligence-based chatbots in alleviation of depressive and anxiety symptoms in short-course treatments: A systematic review and meta-analysis. *Journal of Affective Disorders, 356*, 459–469. DOI: 10.1016/j.jad.2024.04.057

Zhou, Y., Pham, H., & Radev, D. (2019). Addict Free: Mobile support for location-based relapse prevention. In *Proceedings of the Conference on Human Factors in Computing Systems (CHI).*

Zlatintsi, A., Filntisis, P. P., Garoufis, C., Maragos, P., Papaioannou, G., Kapsalakis, G., Antoniades, A., Ioannidis, D., Roniotis, A., Kouroumalis, V., Fragkakis, G., Briassouli, A., Katsigiannis, S., Tsiamitros, D., Giannakakis, G., Tachos, N., Laskaris, N., Adamopoulos, A., Panousis, G., & Kompatsiaris, I. (2022). E-prevention: Advanced support system for monitoring and relapse prevention in patients with psychotic disorders analyzing long-term multimodal data from wearables and video captures. *Sensors (Basel), 22*(19), 7544. Advance online publication. DOI: 10.3390/s22197544

Zou, Y. M. (2024). Digital Mental Health in the Corporate Sphere: Evaluating Trends, Tools, and Impacts on Organizational Dynamics (Doctoral dissertation, Massachusetts Institute of Technology). [Original source: https://studycrumb.com/alphabetizer]

KEY TERMS AND DEFINITIONS

Bibliotherapy: The use of literature to improve one's emotional and mental well-being.

Delusional Psychosis: This is a mental state where one experiences delusions, which are false, fixed beliefs and also experiences psychosis, which is a broader condition where one isn't in contact with reality

Digital Wellbeing: It is a multidimensional concept that encompasses psychological, emotional, and social aspects of technology use.

ELIZA: An early natural language programme which explored communication between humans and computers using pattern matching and simulating conversations

Generative AI: Those artificial intelligence models which carry out independent and dynamic conversations with information drawn from large datasets. Thus, capable of more authentic and engaging conversations.

Human in the Loop (HITL) models: A co-operative model between AI and clinicians where AI engages in supportive clinical tasks while humans maintain the final say in clinical decision-making processes

Large Language Models: AI models that are built and run on large datasets, drawing from the same in order to understand, generate, and mimic human language.

Predictive Modelling: Refers to AI utilising past data and theoretical knowledge to predict future chances of developing a mental health condition or relapsing.

Scripted AI: Those artificial intelligence models which carry out conversations through pre-written responses and follow a defined structure.

Telehealth: Telehealth is used to describe using modern communication technologies, phones, videocalls, etc, in order to deliver medical and mental health services remotely.

Virtual Reality (VR) Therapy: A technology-assisted treatment that uses immersive, computer-generated environments to expose individuals to anxiety-inducing scenarios in a controlled and safe setting.

Wearable AI Technology: Electronic devices worn on the body that continuously monitor physiological signals such as heart rate, sweating, and muscle tension, when combined with artificial intelligence, can identify or help track the mental health of the individual.

Compilation of References

Aalbers, G., Hendrickson, A. T., Vanden Abeele, M. M., & Keijsers, L. (2023). Smartphone-Tracked Digital Markers of Momentary Subjective Stress in College Students: Idiographic Machine Learning Analysis. *JMIR mHealth and uHealth*, *11*, e37469. DOI: 10.2196/37469 PMID: 36951924

Abd-alrazaq, A., AlSaad, R., Aziz, S., Ahmed, A., Denecke, K., Househ, M., Farooq, F., & Sheikh, J. (2023b). Wearable artificial intelligence for anxiety and depression: Scoping review. *Journal of Medical Internet Research*, *25*, e42672. DOI: 10.2196/42672

Abd-alrazaq, A., AlSaad, R., Harfouche, M., Aziz, S., Ahmed, A., Damseh, R., & Sheikh, J. (2023a). Wearable artificial intelligence for detecting anxiety: Systematic review and meta-analysis. *Journal of Medical Internet Research*, *25*, e48754. DOI: 10.2196/48754

Abd-Alrazaq, A., AlSaad, R., Shuweihdi, F., Ahmed, A., Aziz, S., & Sheikh, J. (2023). Systematic review and meta-analysis of performance of wearable artificial intelligence in detecting and predicting depression. *NPJ Digital Medicine*, *6*(1), 84. DOI: 10.1038/s41746-023-00828-5

Abubakar, A. M., Gupta, D., & Parida, S. (2024). A Reinforcement Learning Approach for Intelligent Conversational Chatbot For Enhancing Mental Health Therapy. *Procedia Computer Science*, *235*, 916–925. DOI: 10.1016/j.procs.2024.04.087

Acion, L., Kelmansky, D., van der Laan, M., Sahker, E., Jones, D., & Arndt, S. (2017). Use of a machine learning framework to predict substance use disorder treatment success. *PLoS One*, *12*(4), e0175383. DOI: 10.1371/journal.pone.0175383

Afshar, M., Sharma, B., Dligach, D., Oguss, M., Brown, R., Chhabra, N., & Karnik, N. S. (2022). Development and multimodal validation of a substance misuse algorithm for referral to treatment using artificial intelligence (SMART-AI): A retrospective deep learning study. *The Lancet. Digital Health*, *4*(6), e426–e435. DOI: 10.1016/S2589-7500(22)00087-3

Afshar, N. M., Keip, A. J., Taylor, J. R., Lee, D., & Groman, S. M. (2020). Reinforcement learning during adolescence in rats. *The Journal of Neuroscience : The Official Journal of the Society for Neuroscience*, *40*(30), 5857–5870.

Aharonovich, E., Hasin, D. S., Brooks, A. C., Liu, X., Bisaga, A., & Nunes, E. V. (2006). Cognitive deficits predict low treatment retention in cocaine-dependent patients. *Drug and Alcohol Dependence*, *81*(3), 313–322. DOI: 10.1016/j.drugalcdep.2005.08.008

Al Kuwaiti, K., Nazer, A., Al-Reedy, A., Al Abdouli, A., Alnaqbi, S., Al Kaabi, L., Al Zarooni, A., AlHammadi, S., Al Shamsi, M., AlDhaheri, M., Al Suwaidi, H., Al Mazrouei, A., Al Ketbi, L. M., Al Mazrouei, H., Al Shamsi, S., Al Nuaimi, A., Al Muhairi, F., Al Jaber, H., Al Yammahi, J., & Saleh, K. (2023). A review of the role of artificial intelligence in healthcare. *Journal of Personalized Medicine*, *13*(6), 951. DOI: 10.3390/jpm13060951

Alberto, I. R. I., Alberto, N. R. I., Altinel, Y., Blacker, S., Binotti, W. W., Celi, L. A., Chua, T., Fiske, A., Griffin, M., Karaca, G., Mokolo, N., Naawu, D. K. N., Patscheider, J., Petushkov, A., Quion, J., Senteio, C., Taisbak, S., Tırnova, İ., Tokashiki, H., & Yap, K. (2023). Who does the fairness in health AI community represent? https://doi.org/DOI: 10.1101/2023.03.20.23287471

Alberto, P., Arndis, S., Vibeke, B., & Riccardo, F. (2019). *Voice Patterns in Schizophrenia: A systematic Review and Bayesian Meta-Analysis*. https://doi.org/DOI: 10.1101/583815

Aldarondo, D., Merel, J., Marshall, J. D., Hasenclever, L., Klibaite, U., Gellis, A., & Ölveczky, B. P. (2024). A virtual rodent predicts the structure of neural activity across behaviours. *Nature*, *632*(8025), 594–602.

Algumaei, A., Yaacob, N. M., Doheir, M., Al-Andoli, M. N., & Algumaie, M. (2025). Symmetric Therapeutic Frameworks and Ethical Dimensions in AI-Based Mental Health Chatbots (2020–2025): A Systematic Review of Design Patterns, Cultural Balance, and Structural Symmetry. *Symmetry*, *17*(7), 1082. DOI: 10.3390/sym17071082

Alhuzali, H., & Alasmari, A. (2024). *Evaluating the Effectiveness of the Foundational Models for Q&A Classification in Mental Health care*.

Ali, H. (2022). AI in neurodegenerative disease research: Early detection, cognitive decline prediction, and brain imaging biomarker identification. *Int J Eng Technol Res Manag*, *6*(10), 71.

Al-Juhani, A., Desoky, R., Iskander, Z., Alotaibi, R. M., Alzain, N. N., Aljohani, N., Alrefaai, M. M., Alhasanat, R. A., AlMehaimeed, M. A., & Alharthi, A. S. (2025). Machine Learning Models for Predicting Mental Health Crises in Adolescents Using Electronic Health Records: A Systematic Review. *Cureus*. Advance online publication. DOI: 10.7759/cureus.89873

Alkam, T., Van Benschoten, A. H., & Tarshizi, E. (2025). Reinforcement learning in artificial intelligence and neurobiology. *Neuroscience Informatics*, 100220.

Al-Mamun, F., Hasan, M. E., Mostofa, N. B., Akther, M., Mashruba, T., Arif, M., Chaahat, A. H., Salam, A. B., Akter, M., Abedin, M. A. A., Bulbul, M. I. A., Adnan, M. S., Islam, M. S., Ahmed, M. S., Shahin, M. S. M., Islam, S., Hussain, M. M., & Al Habib, A., ALmerab, M. M., Gozal, D., ... Mamun, M. A. (2024a). Prevalence and factors associated with digital addiction among students taking university entrance tests: A GIS-based study. *BMC Psychiatry*, *24*(1), 322. DOI: 10.1186/s12888-024-05737-9

Al-Mamun, F., Hasan, M. E., & Roy, N. ALmerab, M. M., & Mamun, M. A. (2024c). Suicidal behaviors among high school graduates with preexisting mental health problems: A machine learning and GIS-based study. *The International Journal of Social Psychiatry*. Advance online publication. DOI: 10.1177/00207640241279004

Al-Mamun, F., Mamun, M. A., & Hasan, M. E., ALmerab, M. M., & Gozal, D. (2024b). Exploring sleep duration and insomnia among prospective university students: A study with geographical data and machine learning techniques. *Nature and Science of Sleep*, *16*, 1235–1251. DOI: 10.2147/NSS.S481786

Alowais, S. A., Alghamdi, S. S., Alsuhebany, N., Alqahtani, T., Alshaya, A. I., Almohareb, S. N., Aldairem, A., Alrashed, M., Bin Saleh, K., Badreldin, H. A., Al Yami, M. S., Al Harbi, S., & Albekairy, A. M. (2023). Revolutionizing healthcare: The role of artificial intelligence in clinical practice. *BMC Medical Education*, *23*(1), 689. DOI: 10.1186/s12909-023-04698-z

Amaro, H., Sanchez, M., Bautista, T., & Cox, R. (2021). Social vulnerabilities for substance use: Stressors, socially toxic environments, and discrimination and racism. *Neuropharmacology*, *188*, 108518. DOI: 10.1016/j.neuropharm.2021.108518

American Psychiatric Association. (2013). *Diagnostic and statistical manual of mental disorders* (5th ed.). American Psychiatric Publishing.

American Psychological Association. (2023). Reducing stigma and expanding care: The changing landscape of addiction treatment. *Monitor on Psychology.*

Amleshi, R. S., Ilaghi, M., Rezaei, M., Zangiabadian, M., Rezazadeh, H., Wegener, G., & Arjmand, S. (2025). Predictive utility of artificial intelligence on schizophrenia treatment outcomes: A systematic review and meta-analysis. *Neuroscience and Biobehavioral Reviews*, *169*, 105968.

Angenius, M., & Ghajargar, M. (2023, July). Design principles for interactive and reflective journaling with AI. In Science and Information Conference (pp. 62-81). Cham: Springer Nature Switzerland.

ANI Press Release & Business Standard. (2024, November 29). HEALO: INFIHEAL's Award-Winning AI therapist debuts at Bengaluru Tech Summit 2024. www.business-standard.com. https://www.business-standard.com/content/press-releases-ani/healo-infiheal-s-award-winning-ai-therapist-debuts-at-bengaluru-tech-summit-2024-124112900319_1.html

Annis, I. E., Jordan, R., & Thomas, K. C. (2022). Quickly identifying people at risk of opioid use disorder in emergency departments: Trade-offs between a machine learning approach and a simple EHR flag strategy. *BMJ Open*, *12*(9), e059414. DOI: 10.1136/bmjopen-2021-059414

Antosik-Wójcińska, A. Z., Dominiak, M., Chojnacka, M., Kaczmarek-Majer, K., Opara, K. R., Radziszewska, W., Olwert, A., & Święcicki, Ł. (2020). Smartphone as a monitoring tool for bipolar disorder: A systematic review including data analysis, machine learning algorithms and predictive modelling. *International Journal of Medical Informatics*, *138*, 104131. DOI: 10.1016/j.ijmedinf.2020.104131 PMID: 32305023

Arbour, S., Hambley, J., & Ho, V. (2011). Predictors and outcome of aftercare participation of alcohol and drug users completing residential treatment. *Substance Use & Misuse*, *46*(10), 1275–1287. DOI: 10.3109/10826084.2011.572944

Arnaez, J. M., Krendl, A. C., McCormick, B. P., Chen, Z., & Chomistek, A. K. (2019). The association of depression stigma with barriers to seeking mental health care: A cross-sectional analysis. *Journal of Mental Health (Abingdon, England)*, *29*(2), 182–190. DOI: 10.1080/09638237.2019.1644494

Arnaudova, I., Jin, H., & Amaro, H. (2020). Pretreatment social network characteristics relate to increased risk of dropout and unfavorable outcomes among women in a residential treatment setting for substance use. *Journal of Substance Abuse Treatment*, *116*, 108044. DOI: 10.1016/j.jsat.2020.108044

Arora, A., Jurafsky, D., & Potts, C. (2024). *CausalGym: Benchmarking causal interpretability methods on linguistic tasks.*

Arsalan, A., Majid, M., Nizami, I. F., Manzoor, W., Anwar, S. M., & Ryu, J. (2022). Human stress assessment: A comprehensive review of methods using wearable sensors and non-wearable techniques. *arXiv preprint arXiv:2202.03033.*

Aru, J., Larkum, M. E., & Shine, J. M. (2023). The feasibility of artificial consciousness through the lens of neuroscience. *Trends in Neurosciences, 46*(12), 1008–1017.

Arvai, N., Katonai, G., & Mesko, B. (2025). Health Care Professionals' Concerns About Medical AI and Psychological Barriers and Strategies for Successful Implementation: Scoping Review. *Journal of Medical Internet Research, 27*, e66986.

Athreya, A. P. (2019). *Making augmented human intelligence in medicine practical: A case study of treating major depressive* disorder [Doctoral dissertation, University of Illinois at Urbana-Champaign]. IDEALS. http://hdl.handle.net/2142/105013

Athreya, A. P., Iyer, R., Wang, L., Weinshilboum, R. M., & Bobo, W. V. (2019a). Integration of machine learning and pharmacogenomic biomarkers for predicting response to antidepressant treatment: Can computational intelligence be used to augment clinical assessments? *Pharmacogenomics, 20*(14), 983–988.

Athreya, A. P., Neavin, D., Carrillo-Roa, T., Skime, M., Biernacka, J., Frye, M. A., Rush, A. J., Wang, L., Binder, E. B., Iyer, R. K., Weinshilboum, R. M., & Bobo, W. V. (2019b). Pharmacogenomics-Driven Prediction of Antidepressant Treatment Outcomes: A Machine-Learning Approach With Multi-trial Replication. *Clinical Pharmacology and Therapeutics, 106*(4), 855–865. DOI: 10.1002/cpt.1482

Attridge, M. (2019). A global perspective on promoting workplace mental health and the role of employee assistance programs. *American Journal of Health Promotion, 33*(4), 622–629.

Auf, H., Svedberg, P., Nygren, J., Nair, M., & Lundgren, L. E. (2025). The Use of AI in Mental Health Services to Support Decision-Making: Scoping Review. *Journal of Medical Internet Research, 27*, e63548. DOI: 10.2196/63548 PMID: 39854710

Aziz, S., & Ali, AM, A., Aslam, H., A Abd-alrazaq, A., AlSaad, R., Alajlani, M., ... & Sheikh, J. (2025). Wearable Artificial Intelligence for Sleep Disorders: Scoping Review. *Journal of Medical Internet Research, 27*, e65272.

Baber, M., & Baker, B. (2025). AI-based treatment of psychological conditions: The potential use, benefits and drawbacks. *Exploration of Digital Health Technologies, 3*, 101143.

Badrulhisham, F., Pogatzki-Zahn, E., Segelcke, D., Spisak, T., & Vollert, J. (2024). Machine learning and artificial intelligence in neuroscience: A primer for researchers. *Brain, Behavior, and Immunity*, *115*, 470–479.

Bailey, J. D., & DeFulio, A. (2022). Predicting substance use treatment failure with transfer learning. *Substance Use & Misuse*, *57*(13), 1982–1987. DOI: 10.1080/10826084.2022.2125272

Baker, D. E., Edmonds, K. A., Calvert, M. L., Sanders, S. M., Bridges, A. J., Rhea, M. A., & Kosloff, S. (2020). Predicting attrition in long-term residential substance use disorder treatment: A modifiable risk factors perspective. *Psychological Services*, *17*(4), 472–482. DOI: 10.1037/ser0000333

Banh, L., & Strobel, G. (2023). Generative artificial intelligence. *Electronic Markets*, *33*(1), 63.

Baran, F. D. E., & Cetin, M. (2025). AI-driven early diagnosis of specific mental disorders: A comprehensive study. *Cognitive Neurodynamics*, *19*(1).

Barch, D. M. (2020). What Does It Mean to Be Transdiagnostic and How Would We Know? *The American Journal of Psychiatry*, *177*(5), 370–372. DOI: 10.1176/appi.ajp.2020.20030243 PMID: 32354269

Barenholtz, E., Fitzgerald, N. D., & Hahn, W. E. (2020). Machine-learning approaches to substance-abuse research: Emerging trends and their implications. *Current Opinion in Psychiatry*, *33*(4), 334–342. DOI: 10.1097/YCO.0000000000000615

Baron, S. (2025). Trust, Explainability and AI. *Philosophy & Technology*, *38*(1), 4. DOI: 10.1007/s13347-024-00837-6

Barua, P. D., Vicnesh, J., Gururajan, R., Oh, S. L., Palmer, E., Azizan, M. M., & Acharya, U. R. (2022). Artificial intelligence enabled personalised assistive tools to enhance education of children with neurodevelopmental disorders—A review. *International Journal of Environmental Research and Public Health*, *19*(3), 1192.

Baucum, M., Khojandi, A., Myers, C., & Kessler, L. (2023). Optimizing substance use treatment selection using reinforcement learning. *ACM Transactions on Management Information Systems*, *14*(2). Advance online publication. DOI: 10.1145/3563778

Bauer, M., Glenn, T., Monteith, S., Bauer, R., Whybrow, P. C., & Geddes, J. (2017). Ethical perspectives on recommending digital technology for patients with mental illness. *International Journal of Bipolar Disorders*, *5*(1), 6. DOI: 10.1186/s40345-017-0073-9 PMID: 28155206

Baumeister, H., & Härter, M. (2007). Prevalence of mental disorders based on general population surveys. *Social Psychiatry and Psychiatric Epidemiology*, *42*(7), 537–546.

Bazoukis, G., Bollepalli, S. C., Chung, C. T., Li, X., Tse, G., Bartley, B. L., & Armoundas, A. A. (2023). Application of artificial intelligence in the diagnosis of sleep apnea. *Journal of Clinical Sleep Medicine : JCSM : Official Publication of the American Academy of Sleep Medicine*, *19*(7), 1337–1363.

Beg, M. J. (2025). Responsible AI integration in mental health research: Issues, guidelines, and best practices. *Indian Journal of Psychological Medicine*, *47*(1), 5–8. DOI: 10.1177/02537176241302898 PMID: 39650770

Beg, M. J., & Verma, M. K. (2024). Exploring the potential and challenges of digital and AI-driven psychotherapy for ADHD, OCD, schizophrenia, and substance use disorders: A comprehensive narrative review. *Indian Journal of Psychological Medicine*. Advance online publication. DOI: 10.1177/02537176241300569 PMID: 39677516

Beg, M. J., & Verma, M. K. (2025). Artificial Intelligence-based Psychotherapy: A Qualitative Exploration of Usability, Personalization, and the Perception of Therapeutic Progress. *Indian Journal of Psychological Medicine*. Advance online publication. DOI: 10.1177/02537176251357477 PMID: 40686925

Beg, M. J., & Verma, M. K. (2025). Revolutionizing mental healthcare through artificial intelligence. In Uludag, K., & Ahmad, N. (Eds.), *Chatbots and mental healthcare in psychology and psychiatry* (pp. 21–54). IGI Global., DOI: 10.4018/979-8-3693-3112-5.ch002

Beg, M. J., & Verma, M. VCKM, M., & Verma, M. K. (2024). Artificial intelligence for psychotherapy: A review of the current state and future directions. *Indian Journal of Psychological Medicine*. Advance online publication. DOI: 10.1177/02537176241260819 PMID: 40831472

Beg, M. J., & Verma, M., M., V. C. K. M., & Verma, M. K. (2025). Artificial Intelligence for Psychotherapy: A Review of the Current State and Future Directions. *Indian Journal of Psychological Medicine*, *47*(4), 314–325.

Beker, W., Wołos, A., Szymkuć, S., & Grzybowski, B. A. (2020). Minimal-uncertainty prediction of general drug-likeness based on Bayesian neural networks. *Nature Machine Intelligence*, *2*(8), 457–465. DOI: 10.1038/s42256-020-0209-4

Bellato, A., Raduà, J., Stocker, A., Lockman, M. S., Lall, A., Ravisankar, V., & Cortese, S. (2025). Reporting and Representation of Race and Ethnicity in Clinical Trials of Pharmacotherapy for Mental Disorders: A Meta-Analysis. *JAMA Psychiatry*.

Ben-Zeev, D., Scherer, E. A., Wang, R., Xie, H., & Campbell, A. T. (2015). Next-generation psychiatric assessment: Using smartphone sensors to monitor behavior and mental health. *Psychiatric Rehabilitation Journal, 38*(3), 218–226. DOI: 10.1037/prj0000130 PMID: 25844912

Bermudez-Contreras, E., Clark, B. J., & Wilber, A. (2020). The neuroscience of spatial navigation and the relationship to artificial intelligence. *Frontiers in Computational Neuroscience, 14*, 63.

Bernstein, E. E., Jaroszewski, A. C., Jacoby, R. J., Bailen, N. H., Ragan, J., Usmani, A., & Wilhelm, S. (2025). Feasibility of using ChatGPT to generate exposure hierarchies for treating Obsessive-Compulsive disorder. *Behavior Therapy.*

Bettencourt, C., Skene, N., Bandres-Ciga, S., Anderson, E., Winchester, L. M., Foote, I. F., & Llewellyn, D. J. (2023). Artificial intelligence for dementia genetics and omics. *Alzheimer's & Dementia, 19*(12), 5905–5921.

Bhadra, S., & Kumar, C. J. (2024). Enhancing the efficacy of depression detection system using optimal feature selection from EHR. *Computer Methods in Biomechanics and Biomedical Engineering, 27*(2), 222–236. DOI: 10.1080/10255842.2023.2181660

Bhargavi, Y., Bini, D., & Prince, S. (2023, March). AI-based emotion therapy bot for children with autism spectrum disorder (ASD). In *2023 9th International Conference on Advanced Computing and Communication Systems (ICACCS)* (Vol. 1, pp. 1895-1899). IEEE.

Bhattacharya, S., Prusty, S., Pande, S. P., Gulhane, M., Lavate, S. H., Rakesh, N., & Veerasamy, S. (2025). Integration of multimodal imaging data with machine learning for improved diagnosis and prognosis in neuroimaging. *Frontiers in Human Neuroscience, 19*(March), 1–9.

Biau, G., & Scornet, E. (2016). A random forest guided tour. *Test, 25*(2), 197–227. DOI: 10.1007/s11749-016-0481-7

Bijl, R. V., Ravelli, A., & Van Zessen, G. (1998). Prevalence of psychiatric disorder in the general population: Results of the Netherlands Mental Health Survey and Incidence Study (NEMESIS). *Social Psychiatry and Psychiatric Epidemiology, 33*(12), 587–595.

Birhane, A., Ruane, E., Laurent, T., & Brown, S., M., Flowers, J., Ventresque, A., & L. Dancy, C. (2022). The forgotten margins of AI ethics. In Proceedings of the 2022 ACM Conference on Fairness, Accountability, and Transparency (pp. 948-958).

Blease, C., Torous, J., & Hägglund, M. (2020). Does patient access to clinical notes change documentation? *Frontiers in Public Health, 8*, 577896.

Bloch, L., & Friedrich, C. M. (2024). Systematic comparison of 3D Deep learning and classical machine learning explanations for Alzheimer's Disease detection. *Computers in Biology and Medicine*, *170*(January).

Bobo, W. V., Van Ommeren, B., & Athreya, A. P. (2022). Machine learning, pharmacogenomics, and clinical psychiatry: Predicting antidepressant response in patients with major depressive disorder. *Expert Review of Clinical Pharmacology*, *15*(8), 927–944. DOI: 10.1080/17512433.2022.2112949

Boden, J. M., & Fergusson, D. M. (2011). Alcohol and depression. *Addiction (Abingdon, England)*, *106*(5), 906–914. DOI: 10.1111/j.1360-0443.2010.03351.x

Bohra, A., Vadodaria, K., Desai, V., Sawant, V., & Tawde, P. (2024). Enhancing Privacy in Mental Health Prediction Using Centralized and Federated Learning Models. *2024 International Conference on Artificial Intelligence and Emerging Technology (Global AI Summit)*, 1141–1146. https://doi.org/DOI: 10.1109/GlobalAISummit62156.2024.10947768

Bokolo, B. G., & Liu, Q. (2023). Deep Learning-Based Depression Detection from Social Media: Comparative Evaluation of ML and Transformer Techniques. *Electronics (Basel)*, *12*(21), 4396.

Boonstra, T. W., Nicholas, J., Wong, Q. J., Shaw, F., Townsend, S., & Christensen, H. (2018). Using Mobile Phone Sensor Technology for Mental Health Research: Integrated Analysis to Identify Hidden Challenges and Potential Solutions. *Journal of Medical Internet Research*, *20*(7), e10131. DOI: 10.2196/10131 PMID: 30061092

Bos, F. M., Schreuder, M. J., George, S. V., Doornbos, B., Bruggeman, R., van der Krieke, L., Haarman, B. C. M., Wichers, M., & Snippe, E. (2022). Anticipating manic and depressive transitions in patients with bipolar disorder using early warning signals. *International Journal of Bipolar Disorders*, *10*(1), 12. DOI: 10.1186/s40345-022-00258-4 PMID: 35397076

Boucher, E. M., Harake, N. R., Ward, H. E., Stoeckl, S. E., Vargas, J., Minkel, J., ... & Zilca, R. (2021). Artificially intelligent chatbots in digital mental health interventions: A review. Expert Review of Medical Devices, 18(sup1), 37–49. https://doi.org/DOI: 10.1080/17434440.2021.2013200

Bouguettaya, A., Stuart, E. M., & Aboujaoude, E. (2025). Racial bias in AI-mediated psychiatric diagnosis and treatment: A qualitative comparison of four large language models. npj. *Digital Medicine*, *8*(1), 332.

Brackett, C., Duncan, M., Wagner, J., Fineberg, L., & Kraft, S. (2022). Multidisciplinary treatment of opioid use disorder in primary care using the collaborative care model. *Substance Abuse*, *43*(1), 240–244. DOI: 10.1080/08897077.2021.1932698

Brahma, N., & Vimal, S. (2024). Artificial intelligence in neuroimaging: Opportunities and ethical challenges. *Brain & Spine*, *4*(July), 102919.

Bricout, J., Greer, J., Fields, N., Xu, L., Tamplain, P., Doelling, K., & Sharma, B. (2022). The "humane in the loop": Inclusive research design and policy approaches to foster capacity building assistive technologies in the COVID-19 era. *Assistive Technology*, *34*(6), 644–652.

Brietzke, E., Hawken, E. R., Idzikowski, M., Pong, J., Kennedy, S. H., & Soares, C. N. (2019). Integrating digital phenotyping in clinical characterization of individuals with mood disorders. *Neuroscience and Biobehavioral Reviews*, *104*, 223–230. DOI: 10.1016/j.neubiorev.2019.07.009

Britt, T. W., Jennings, K. S., Cheung, J. H., Pury, C. L. S., & Zinzow, H. M. (2015). The role of different stigma perceptions in treatment-seeking and dropout among active-duty military personnel. *Psychiatric Rehabilitation Journal*, *38*(2), 142–149. DOI: 10.1037/prj0000120

Brorson, H. H., Arnevik, E. A., & Rand, K. (2019). Predicting dropout from inpatient substance use disorder treatment: A prospective validation study of the OQ-analyst. *Substance Abuse*, *13*, 1178221819866181. DOI: 10.1177/1178221819866181

Brossollet, I., Gallet, Q., Favre, P., & Houenou, J. (2023). Machine Learning and Brain Imaging for Psychiatric Disorders: New Perspectives. *Neuromethods*, *197*, 1009–1036.

Brown, J. E., & Halpern, J. (2021). AI chatbots cannot replace human interactions in the pursuit of more inclusive mental healthcare. *SSM. Mental Health*, *1*, 100017.

Bryant, R. A. (2019). Post-traumatic stress disorder: A state-of-the-art review of evidence and challenges. *World Psychiatry; Official Journal of the World Psychiatric Association (WPA)*, *18*(3), 259–269. DOI: 10.1002/wps.20656

Bufano, P., Laurino, M., Said, S., Tognetti, A., & Menicucci, D. (2023). Digital Phenotyping for Monitoring Mental Disorders: Systematic Review. *Journal of Medical Internet Research*, *25*, e46778. DOI: 10.2196/46778 PMID: 38090800

Burgess-Hull, A. J., Panlilio, L. V., Preston, K. L., & Epstein, D. H. (2022). Trajectories of craving during medication-assisted treatment for opioid-use disorder: Subtyping for early identification of higher risk. *Drug and Alcohol Dependence*, *233*, 109362. DOI: 10.1016/j.drugalcdep.2022.109362

Burr, C., Taddeo, M., & Floridi, L. (2020). The ethics of digital wellbeing: A thematic review. *Science and Engineering Ethics*, *26*, 2313–2343. DOI: 10.1007/s11948-020-00175-8

Busk, J., Faurholt-Jepsen, M., Frost, M., Bardram, J., Vedel Kessing, L., & Winther, O. (2020). Forecasting mood in bipolar disorder from smartphone self-assessments: Hierarchical Bayesian approach. *JMIR mHealth and uHealth*, *8*(4), e15028. https://mhealth.jmir.org/2020/4/e15028 PMID: 32234702

Bzdok, D., & Meyer-Lindenberg, A. (2018). Machine learning for precision psychiatry: Opportunities and challenges. *Biological Psychiatry: Cognitive Neuroscience and Neuroimaging*, *3*(3), 223–230.

Calesella, F., Colombo, F., Bravi, B., Fortaner-Uyà, L., Monopoli, C., Poletti, S., & Vai, B. (2024). A machine learning pipeline for efficient differentiation between bipolar and major depressive disorder based on multimodal structural neuroimaging. *Neuroscience Applied*, *3*, 103931.

Calvo, R. A., Milne, D. N., Hussain, M. S., & Christensen, H. (2017). Natural language processing in mental health applications using non-clinical texts. *Natural Language Engineering*, *23*(5), 649–685. DOI: 10.1017/S1351324916000383

Campbell, A. N. C., Nunes, E. V., Matthews, A. G., Stitzer, M. L., Miele, G. M., Polsky, D., Turrigiano, E., Walters, S., & VanVeldhuisen, P. (2022). Digital therapeutic for opioid use disorder: reSET-O outcomes. *Addiction Research and Theory*, *30*(5), 387–395.

Canetto, S. S., & Sakinofsky, I. (1998). The gender paradox in suicide. *Suicide & Life-Threatening Behavior*, *28*(1), 1–23. DOI: 10.1111/j.1943-278X.1998.tb00622.x

Cardamone, N. C., Olfson, M., Schmutte, T., Ungar, L., Liu, T., Cullen, S. W., Williams, N. J., & Marcus, S. C. (2025). Classifying Unstructured Text in Electronic Health Records for Mental Health Prediction Models: Large Language Model Evaluation Study. *JMIR Medical Informatics*, *13*, e65454–e65454. DOI: 10.2196/65454 PMID: 39864953

Caro, J. O., Fonseca, A. H. de O., Averill, C., Rizvi, S. A., Rosati, M., Cross, J. L., Mittal, P., Zappala, E., Levine, D., Dhodapkar, R. M., Han, I., Karbasi, A., Abdallah, C. G., & van Dijk, D. (2023). *BrainLM: A foundation model for brain activity recordings*. https://doi.org/DOI: 10.1101/2023.09.12.557460

Carreiro, S., Newcomb, M., Leach, R., Ostrowski, S., Boudreaux, E. D., & Amante, D. (2020). Current reporting of usability and impact of mHealth interventions for substance use disorder: A systematic review. *Drug and Alcohol Dependence*, *215*, 108201. DOI: 10.1016/j.drugalcdep.2020.108201

Carr, S. (2020). 'AI gone mental': Engagement and ethics in data-driven technology for mental health. *Journal of Mental Health (Abingdon, England)*, *29*(2), 125–130. DOI: 10.1080/09638237.2020.1714011 PMID: 32000544

Cary, M. P., Zink, A., Wei, S., Olson, A., Yan, M., Senior, R., Bessias, S., Gadhoumi, K., Jean-Pierre, G., Wang, D., Ledbetter, L. S., Economou-Zavlanos, N. J., Obermeyer, Z., & Pencina, M. J. (2023). Mitigating Racial And Ethnic Bias And Advancing Health Equity In Clinical Algorithms: A Scoping Review. *Health Affairs*, *42*(10), 1359–1368. DOI: 10.1377/hlthaff.2023.00553 PMID: 37782868

Ceceli, A. O., Bradberry, C. W., & Goldstein, R. Z. (2022). The neurobiology of drug addiction: Cross-species insights into the dysfunction and recovery of the prefrontal cortex. *Neuropsychopharmacology : Official Publication of the American College of Neuropsychopharmacology*, *47*(1), 276–291. DOI: 10.1038/s41386-021-01137-3

Centers for Disease Control and Prevention. (2023). Drug overdose deaths in the United States, 2002–2022. National Center for Health Statistics. https://www.cdc.gov/nchs/products/databriefs/db456.htm

Chand, S. P., & Arif, H. (2023, July 17). Depression. StatPearls - NCBI Bookshelf. https://www.ncbi.nlm.nih.gov/books/NBK430847/

Chandna, A. S., Suhas, S., Patley, R., Dinakaran, D., Manjunatha, N., Rao, G. N., Gururaj, G., Varghese, M., & Benegal, V.NMHS National Collaborators Group. (2023). Exploring the enigma of low prevalence of post-traumatic stress disorder in India. *Indian Journal of Psychiatry*, *65*(12), 1254–1260. DOI: 10.4103/indianjpsychiatry.indianjpsychiatry_830_23

Chandrabhatla, A. S., Pomeraniec, I. J., Horgan, T. M., Wat, E. K., & Ksendzovsky, A. (2023). Landscape and future directions of machine learning applications in closed-loop brain stimulation. *NPJ Digital Medicine*, *6*(1), 79. DOI: 10.1038/s41746-023-00779-x

Chase, J., Xia, L., Tai, L. H., Lin, W. C., Collins, A. G., & Wilbrecht, L. (2024). Adolescent and adult mice use both incremental reinforcement learning and short term memory when learning concurrent stimulus-action associations. *PLoS Computational Biology*, *20*(12), e1012667.

Chekroud, A. M., Bondar, J., Delgadillo, J., Doherty, G., Wasil, A., Fokkema, M., & Choi, K. (2021). The promise of machine learning in predicting treatment outcomes in psychiatry. *World Psychiatry; Official Journal of the World Psychiatric Association (WPA), 20*(2), 154–170. DOI: 10.1002/wps.20882

Chekroud, A. M., Zotti, R. J., Shehzad, Z., Gueorguieva, R., Johnson, M. K., Trivedi, M. H., Cannon, T. D., Krystal, J. H., & Corlett, P. R. (2016). Cross-trial prediction of treatment outcome in depression: A machine learning approach. *The Lancet. Psychiatry, 3*(3), 243–250. DOI: 10.1016/S2215-0366(15)00471-X

Chen, S., Yu, J., & Chamouni, S.. (2024). Integrating machine learning and artificial intelligence in life-course epidemiology: Pathways to innovative public health solutions. *BMC Medicine, 22*(1), 1–10. DOI: 10.1186/s12916-024-03566-x PMID: 39218895

Chen, T., Chen, L., Li, S., Du, J., Su, H., Jiang, H., & Zhao, M. (2023). Virtual digital psychotherapist app–based treatment in patients with methamphetamine use disorder (Echo-APP): Single-arm pilot feasibility and efficacy study. *JMIR mHealth and uHealth, 11*(1), e40373. DOI: 10.2196/40373

Chen, T., & Guestrin, C. (2016). XGBoost: A scalable tree boosting system. In *Proceedings of the 22nd ACM SIGKDD International Conference on Knowledge Discovery and Data Mining* (pp. 785–794). ACM. https://doi.org/DOI: 10.1145/2939672.2939785

Chen, X., Wang, S., Yang, X., Yu, C., Ni, F., Yang, J., & Luo, R. (2023). Utilizing artificial intelligence-based eye tracking technology for screening ADHD symptoms in children. *Frontiers in Psychiatry, 14*, 1260031.

Chhetri, B., Goyal, L. M., & Mittal, M. (2023). How machine learning is used to study addiction in digital healthcare: A systematic review. *International Journal of Information Management Data Insights, 3*(2), 100175. DOI: 10.1016/j.jjimei.2023.100175

Choi, A., Ooi, A., & Lottridge, D. (2024). Digital Phenotyping for Stress, Anxiety, and Mild Depression: Systematic Literature Review. *JMIR mHealth and uHealth, 12*, e40689. DOI: 10.2196/40689 PMID: 38780995

Chowdhury, M., Cervantes, E. G., Chan, W.-Y., & Seitz, D. P. (2021). Use of Machine Learning and Artificial Intelligence Methods in Geriatric Mental Health Research Involving Electronic Health Record or Administrative Claims Data: A Systematic Review. *Frontiers in Psychiatry, 12*. Advance online publication. DOI: 10.3389/fpsyt.2021.738466

Christley, R. M. (2010). Power and error: Increased risk of false positive results in underpowered studies. *The Open Epidemiology Journal, 3*(1), 16–19.

Cilar Budler, L., & Stiglic, G. (2025). Ethical approval and informed consent in mental health research: A scoping review. *AI & Society*. Advance online publication. DOI: 10.1007/s00146-025-02364-0

Cirillo, D., Catuara-Solarz, S., Morey, C., Guney, E., Subirats, L., Mellino, S., Gigante, A., Valencia, A., Rementeria, M. J., Chadha, A. S., & Mavridis, N. (2020). Sex and gender differences and biases in artificial intelligence for biomedicine and healthcare. *NPJ Digital Medicine, 3*(1), 81. DOI: 10.1038/s41746-020-0288-5

Clark, L. A., Cuthbert, B., Lewis-Fernández, R., Narrow, W. E., & Reed, G. M. (2017). Three Approaches to Understanding and Classifying Mental Disorder: *ICD-11, DSM-5*, and the National Institute of Mental Health's Research Domain Criteria (RDoC). *Psychological Science in the Public Interest, 18*(2), 72–145. DOI: 10.1177/1529100617727266 PMID: 29211974

Clemmensen, L. K. H., Lønfeldt, N. N., Das, S., Lund, N. L., Uhre, V. F., Mora-Jensen, A. R. C., & Pagsberg, A. K. (2022). Associations between the severity of obsessive-compulsive disorder and vocal features in children and adolescents: Protocol for a statistical and machine learning analysis. *JMIR Research Protocols, 11*(10), e39613.

Coghlan, S., Leins, K., Sheldrick, S., Cheong, M., Gooding, P., & D'Alfonso, S. (2023). To chat or bot to chat: Ethical issues with using chatbots in mental health. *Digital Health, 9*, 20552076231183542. DOI: 10.1177/20552076231183542

Cohen, Z. D., DeRubeis, R. J., Hayes, R., Watkins, E. R., Lewis, G., Byng, R., Byford, S., Crane, C., Kuyken, W., Dalgleish, T., & Schweizer, S. (2023). The Development and Internal Evaluation of a Predictive Model to Identify for Whom Mindfulness-Based Cognitive Therapy Offers Superior Relapse Prevention for Recurrent Depression Versus Maintenance Antidepressant Medication. *Clinical Psychological Science, 11*(1), 59–76. DOI: 10.1177/21677026221076832 PMID: 36698442

Colby, K. M., Hilf, F. D., Weber, S., & Kraemer, H. C. (1972). Turing-like indistinguishability tests for the validation of a computer simulation of paranoid processes. *Artificial Intelligence, 3*, 199–221. DOI: 10.1016/0004-3702(72)90049-5

Coley, R. Y., Johnson, E., Simon, G. E., Cruz, M., & Shortreed, S. M. (2021). Racial/Ethnic Disparities in the Performance of Prediction Models for Death by Suicide After Mental Health Visits. *JAMA Psychiatry, 78*(7), 726.

Costafreda, S. G., Fu, C. H. Y., Picchioni, M., Toulopoulou, T., McDonald, C., Kravariti, E., Walshe, M., Prata, D., Murray, R. M., & McGuire, P. K. (2011). Pattern of neural responses to verbal fluency shows diagnostic specificity for schizophrenia and bipolar disorder. *BMC Psychiatry*, *11*(1), 18.

Cousineau, M. (2020). *Analytics for medical decision making: Applications to the management of treatment-resistant depression* [Doctoral Dissertation, McGill University]. eScholarship@McGill. https://escholarship.mcgill.ca/concern/theses/st74cw06n

Crema, C., Attardi, G., Sartiano, D., & Redolfi, A. (2022). Natural language processing in clinical neuroscience and psychiatry: A review. *Frontiers in Psychiatry*, *13*, 946387.

Crocamo, C., Cioni, R. M., Canestro, A., Nasti, C., Palpella, D., Piacenti, S., Bartoccetti, A., Re, M., Simonetti, V., Barattieri di San Pietro, C., Bulgheroni, M., Bartoli, F., & Carrà, G. (2025). Acoustic and Natural Language Markers for Bipolar Disorder: A Pilot, mHealth Cross-Sectional Study. *JMIR Formative Research*, *9*, e65555–e65555. DOI: 10.2196/65555 PMID: 40239203

Cruz Rivera, S., Liu, X., Chan, A.-W., Denniston, A. K., Calvert, M. J., Ashrafian, H., Beam, A. L., Collins, G. S., Darzi, A., Deeks, J. J., ElZarrad, M. K., Espinoza, C., Esteva, A., Faes, L., Ferrante di Ruffano, L., Fletcher, J., Golub, R., Harvey, H., Haug, C., & Yau, C. (2020). Guidelines for clinical trial protocols for interventions involving artificial intelligence: The SPIRIT-AI extension. *The Lancet. Digital Health*, *2*(10), e549–e560. DOI: 10.1016/S2589-7500(20)30219-3 PMID: 33328049

Cummins, N., Scherer, S., Krajewski, J., Schnieder, S., Epps, J., & Quatieri, T. F. (2018). A review of depression and suicide risk assessment using speech analysis. *Speech Communication*, *71*, 10–49. DOI: 10.1016/j.specom.2015.03.004

Curtis, B., Giorgi, S., & Ungar, L.. (2023). AI-based analysis of social media language predicts addiction treatment dropout at 90 days. *Neuropsychopharmacology : Official Publication of the American College of Neuropsychopharmacology*. Advance online publication. DOI: 10.1038/s41386-023-01660-9

Curtiss, J., & DiPietro, C. (2025). Machine learning in the prediction of treatment response for emotional disorders: A systematic review and meta-analysis. *Clinical Psychology Review*, *120*(May), 102593.

Cusack, K., Jonas, D. E., Forneris, C. A., Wines, C., Sonis, J., Middleton, J. C., Feltner, C., Brownley, K. A., Olmsted, K. R., Greenblatt, A., Weil, A., & Gaynes, B. N. (2016). Psychological treatments for adults with posttraumatic stress disorder: A systematic review and meta-analysis. *Clinical Psychology Review*, *43*, 128–141. DOI: 10.1016/j.cpr.2015.10.003

Cuthbert, B. N. (2014). The RDoC framework: Facilitating transition from ICD/ DSM to dimensional approaches that integrate neuroscience and psychopathology. *World Psychiatry; Official Journal of the World Psychiatric Association (WPA)*, *13*(1), 28–35. DOI: 10.1002/wps.20087 PMID: 24497240

Cutillo, C. M., Sharma, K. R., Foschini, L., Kundu, S., Mackintosh, M., Mandl, K. D., Beck, T., Collier, E., Colvis, C., Gersing, K., Gordon, V., Jensen, R., Shabestari, B., & Southall, N. (2020). Machine intelligence in healthcare—Perspectives on trustworthiness, explainability, usability, and transparency. *NPJ Digital Medicine*, *3*(1), 47. DOI: 10.1038/s41746-020-0254-2 PMID: 32258429

D'Alfonso, S. (2020). AI in Mental Health. *Current Opinion in Psychology*, *36*, 112–117. DOI: 10.1016/j.copsyc.2020.04.005 PMID: 32604065

Dai, H. J., Su, C. H., Lee, Y. Q., Zhang, Y. C., Wang, C. K., Kuo, C. J., & Wu, C. S. (2021). Deep learning-based natural language processing for screening psychiatric patients. *Frontiers in Psychiatry*, *11*, 533949.

Dai, R., Kannampallil, T., Zhang, J., Lv, N., Ma, J., & Lu, C. (2022). Multi-Task Learning for Randomized Controlled Trials. *Proceedings of the ACM on Interactive, Mobile, Wearable and Ubiquitous Technologies*, *6*(2), 1–23. DOI: 10.1145/3534591

Dalgleish, T., Black, M., Johnston, D., & Bevan, A. (2020). Transdiagnostic approaches to mental health problems: Current status and future directions. *Journal of Consulting and Clinical Psychology*, *88*(3), 179–195. DOI: 10.1037/ccp0000482 PMID: 32068421

Dang, V. N., Cascarano, A., Mulder, R. H., Cecil, C., Zuluaga, M. A., Hernández-González, J., & Lekadir, K. (2024). Fairness and bias correction in machine learning for depression prediction across four study populations. *Scientific Reports*, *14*(1), 7848. DOI: 10.1038/s41598-024-58427-7

Danieli, M., Ciulli, T., Mousavi, S. M., Silvestri, G., Barbato, S., Di Natale, L., & Riccardi, G. (2022). Assessing the Impact of Conversational Artificial Intelligence in the Treatment of Stress and Anxiety in Aging Adults: Randomized Controlled Trial. *JMIR Mental Health*, *9*(9), e38067. DOI: 10.2196/38067

Das, T., Borgwardt, S., Hauke, D. J., Harrisberger, F., Lang, U. E., Riecher-Rössler, A., & Schmidt, A. (2018). Disorganized gyrification network properties during the transition to psychosis. *JAMA Psychiatry*, *75*(6), 613–622.

Davenport, T., & Kalakota, R. (2019). The potential for artificial intelligence in healthcare. *Future Healthcare Journal*, *6*(2), 94–98. DOI: 10.7861/futurehosp.6-2-94

Dawoodbhoy, F. M., Delaney, J., Cecula, P., Mitchell, K., Jurek, A., Bouch, J., Tapp, J., Webster, C., Challis, K., Binnie, J., Stringfellow, C., Yeomans, M., Mufti, H., Tan, E., Chang, C. K., McKnight, L., Stewart, D., Jewell, A., Lavelle, M., & Stewart, R. (2021). AI in patient flow: Applications of artificial intelligence to improve patient flow in NHS acute mental health inpatient units. *Heliyon*, *7*(5), e06993. DOI: 10.1016/j.heliyon.2021.e06993

De Freitas, J., & Cohen, I. G. (2024). The health risks of generative AI-based wellness apps. *Nature Medicine*, *30*(5), 1269–1275. DOI: 10.1038/s41591-024-02943-6

De la Torre, F. M., Hernandez, J., Wilson, A. D., & Amores, J. (2025). Sonora: Human-AI co-creation of 3D audio worlds and its impact on anxiety and cognitive load. CHI '25: Proceedings of the 2025 CHI Conference on Human Factors in Computing Systems, 308, 1-22. https://doi.org/DOI: 10.1145/3706598.3713316

Decker, K. P., Peglow, S. L., Samples, C. R., & Cunningham, T. D. (2017). Long-term outcomes after residential substance use treatment: Relapse, morbidity, and mortality. *Military Medicine*, *182*(1–2), e1589–e1595. DOI: 10.7205/MILMED-D-15-00560

Degenhardt, L., & Hall, W. (2012). Extent of illicit drug use and dependence, and their contribution to the global burden of disease. *Lancet*, *379*(9810), 55–70. DOI: 10.1016/S0140-6736(11)61138-0

Delgadillo, J., Budimir, S., Barkham, M., Humer, E., Pieh, C., & Probst, T. (2023). A Bayesian network analysis of psychosocial risk and protective factors for suicidal ideation. *Frontiers in Public Health*, *11*, 1010264. DOI: 10.3389/fpubh.2023.1010264 PMID: 36935710

Denecke, K., & Househ, M. (2021). Artificial intelligence for chatbots in mental health: Opportunities and challenges. In *Advances in Artificial Intelligence for Health and Medicine* (pp. 171–186). Springer., DOI: 10.1007/978-3-030-67303-1_10

Derksen, M. E., van Beek, M., de Bruijn, T., Stuit, F., Blankers, M., & Goudriaan, A. E. (2025). Ethical aspects and user preferences in applying machine learning to adjust eHealth addressing substance use: A mixed-methods study. *International Journal of Medical Informatics*, *199*, 105897. DOI: 10.1016/j.ijmedinf.2024.105897

Di Matteo, D., Fine, A., Fotinos, K., Rose, J., & Katzman, M. (2018). Patient Willingness to Consent to Mobile Phone Data Collection for Mental Health Apps: Structured Questionnaire. *JMIR Mental Health*, *5*(3), e56. DOI: 10.2196/mental.9539 PMID: 30158102

Diaz-Ramos, R. E., Noriega, I., Trejo, L. A., Stroulia, E., & Cao, B. (2023). Using Wearable Devices and Speech Data for Personalized Machine Learning in Early Detection of Mental Disorders: Protocol for a Participatory Research Study. *JMIR Research Protocols*, *12*, e48210. DOI: 10.2196/48210 PMID: 37955959

Dibbets, P. (2019). A novel virtual reality paradigm: Predictors for stress-related intrusions and avoidance behavior. *Journal of Behavior Therapy and Experimental Psychiatry*, *63*, 26–33. DOI: 10.1016/j.jbtep.2019.01.001

Diekmann, N., Vijayabaskaran, S., Zeng, X., Kappel, D., Menezes, M. C., & Cheng, S. (2023). CoBeL-RL: A neuroscience-oriented simulation framework for complex behavior and learning. *Frontiers in Neuroinformatics*, *17*, 1134405.

Dinga, R., Schmaal, L., Penninx, B. W. J. H., van Tol, M. J., Veltman, D. J., van Velzen, L., Mennes, M., van der Wee, N. J. A., & Marquand, A. F. (2019). Evaluating the evidence for biotypes of depression: Methodological replication and extension of Drysdale et al. (2017). *NeuroImage. Clinical*, *22*(March), 101796.

Dinga, R., Schmaal, L., Penninx, B. W. J. H., van Tol, M. J., Veltman, D. J., van Velzen, L., Mennes, M., van der Wee, N. J. A., & Marquand, A. F. (2019). Evaluating the evidence for biotypes of depression: Methodological replication and extension of. *NeuroImage. Clinical*, *22*, 101796. DOI: 10.1016/j.nicl.2019.101796

Ding, Y., Sohn, J. H., Kawczynski, M. G., Trivedi, H., Harnish, R., Jenkins, N. W., & Franc, B. L. (2019). A deep learning model to predict a diagnosis of Alzheimer disease by using 18F-FDG PET of the brain. *Radiology*, *290*(2), 456–464.

Do, H. N., Nathan, N., Van Nguyen, B., Le, H. T., Nguyen, H. Q. T., Nguyen, A. T., & Ho, R. C. (2018). Sociodemographic inequalities in substance use among young people in Vietnam. *Children and Youth Services Review*, *94*, 644–649. DOI: 10.1016/j.childyouth.2018.09.037

Donnelly, M. R., Reinberg, R., Ito, K. L., Saldana, D., Neureither, M., Schmiesing, A., Jahng, E., & Liew, L. (2021). Virtual reality for the treatment of anxiety disorders: A scoping review. *The American Journal of Occupational Therapy*, *75*(6), 7506205040. DOI: 10.5014/ajot.2021.046169

Doogan, N. J., Roberts, M. E., Wewers, M. E., Stanton, C. A., Keith, D. R., Gaalema, D. E., & Higgins, S. T. (2017). A growing geographic disparity: Rural and urban cigarette smoking trends in United States. *Preventive Medicine*, *104*, 79–85. DOI: 10.1016/j.ypmed.2017.03.011

Doraiswamy, P. M., Blease, C., & Bodner, K. (2020). Artificial intelligence and the future of psychiatry: Insights from a global physician survey. *Artificial Intelligence in Medicine*, *102*, 101753. DOI: 10.1016/j.artmed.2019.101753

Doshi-Velez, F., & Kim, B. (2017). *Towards A Rigorous Science of Interpretable Machine Learning*.

Dou, Z. Y., Barman-Adhikari, A., & Fang, F.. (2021). Harnessing social media to identify homeless youth at-risk of substance use. *Proceedings of the AAAI Conference on Artificial Intelligence*, *35*(17), 14748–14756. DOI: 10.1609/aaai.v35i17.17708

Dovis, S., Van der Oord, S., Wiers, R. W., & Prins, P. J. (2015). Improving executive functioning in children with ADHD: Training multiple executive functions within the context of a computer game. A randomized double-blind placebo controlled trial. *PLoS One*, *10*(4), e0121651.

Drougkas, G., Bakker, E. M., & Spruit, M. (2024). Multimodal machine learning for language and speech markers identification in mental health. *BMC Medical Informatics and Decision Making*, *24*(1), 354. DOI: 10.1186/s12911-024-02772-0 PMID: 39578814

Drysdale, A. T., Grosenick, L., Downar, J., Dunlop, K., Mansouri, F., Meng, Y., & Liston, C. (2017). Resting-state connectivity biomarkers define neurophysiological subtypes of depression. *Nature Medicine*, *23*(1), 28–38.

Duarte, R. de B., Correia, F., Arriaga, P., & Paiva, A. (2023). AI Trust: Can Explainable AI Enhance Warranted Trust? *Human Behavior and Emerging Technologies*, *2023*, 1–12. DOI: 10.1155/2023/4637678

Dubey, P., Dubey, P., & Bokoro, P. N. (2025). Federated learning for privacy-enhanced mental health prediction with multimodal data integration. *Computer Methods in Biomechanics and Biomedical Engineering. Imaging & Visualization*, *13*(1). Advance online publication. DOI: 10.1080/21681163.2025.2509672

Duda, M., Ma, R., Haber, N., & Wall, D. P. (2016). Use of machine learning for behavioral distinction of autism and ADHD. *Translational Psychiatry*, *6*(2), e732–e732.

Duhne, P. G. S., Delgadillo, J., & Lutz, W. (2022). Predicting early dropout in online versus face-to-face guided self-help: A machine learning approach. *Behaviour Research and Therapy*, *159*, 104200. DOI: 10.1016/j.brat.2022.104200

Dupré, M. H. (2025, June 28). People are being involuntarily committed, jailed after spiraling into "ChatGPT psychosis." Futurism. https://futurism.com/commitment-jail-chatgpt-psychosis

Dwyer, D. B., Falkai, P., & Koutsouleris, N. (2018). Machine learning approaches for clinical psychology and psychiatry. *Annual Review of Clinical Psychology*, *14*, 91–118.

Ebrahimi, A., Wiil, U. K., & Mansourvar, M.. (2021). Deep neural network to identify patients with alcohol use disorder. *Studies in Health Technology and Informatics*, *281*, 238–242. DOI: 10.3233/SHTI210154

Eddie, D., Prindle, J., Somodi, P., Gerstmann, I., Dilkina, B., Saba, S. K., & Davis, J. P. (2024). Exploring predictors of substance use disorder treatment engagement with machine learning: The impact of social determinants of health in the therapeutic landscape. *Journal of Substance Use and Addiction Treatment*, *164*, 209435. DOI: 10.1016/j.jsuat.2024.209435

Egger, S. M., Frey, S., Sauerzopf, L., & Meidert, U. (2023). A literature review to identify effective web-and app-based mHealth interventions for stress management at work. *Workplace Health & Safety*, *71*(10), 452–463.

Ellis, J. D., Rabinowitz, J. A., Wells, J., Liu, F., Finan, P. H., Stein, M. D., & Huhn, A. S. (2022). Latent trajectories of anxiety and depressive symptoms among adults in early treatment for nonmedical opioid use. *Journal of Affective Disorders*, *299*, 223–232. DOI: 10.1016/j.jad.2021.12.004

Elmasri, D., & Maeder, A. (2016). A conversational agent for an online mental health intervention. In *Proceedings of the International Conference on Brain and Health Informatics* (pp. 243–251). Springer. https://doi.org/DOI: 10.1007/978-3-319-47151-8_23

Ermers, N. J., Hagoort, K., & Scheepers, F. E. (2020). The Predictive Validity of Machine Learning Models in the Classification and Treatment of Major Depressive Disorder: State of the Art and Future Directions. *Frontiers in Psychiatry*, *11*. Advance online publication. DOI: 10.3389/fpsyt.2020.00472

Etkin, A., & Cuthbert, B. (2014). Beyond the DSM: Development of a Transdiagnostic Psychiatric Neuroscience Course. *Academic Psychiatry*, *38*(2), 145–150. DOI: 10.1007/s40596-013-0032-4 PMID: 24493358

Ezell, J. M., Ajayi, B. P., Parikh, T., Miller, K., Rains, A., & Scales, D. (2024). Drug use and artificial intelligence: Weighing concerns and possibilities for prevention. *American Journal of Preventive Medicine*, *66*(3), 568–572. DOI: 10.1016/j.amepre.2023.09.006

Fabiano, G. A., Pelham, W. E.Jr, Coles, E. K., Gnagy, E. M., Chronis-Tuscano, A., & O'Connor, B. C. (2009). A meta-analysis of behavioral treatments for attention-deficit/hyperactivity disorder. *Clinical Psychology Review*, *29*(2), 129–140.

Fahmawi, S., & Dalu, A. E. A. (2025). Nanotechnology in the Design of Smart Neural Electrodes for Treating Chronic Anxiety Disorders in Adults: An Innovative Approach to Precision Brain Stimulation. *International Journal of Innovative Science and Research Technology*, 2407–2413. https://doi.org/DOI: 10.38124/ijisrt/25jun1768

Faissner, M., Kuhn, E., Müller, R., & Laacke, S. (2024). Detecting your depression with your smartphone? – An ethical analysis of epistemic injustice in passive self-tracking apps. *Ethics and Information Technology*, *26*(2), 28. DOI: 10.1007/s10676-024-09765-7

Fanni, S. C., Febi, M., Aghakhanyan, G., & Neri, E. (2023). Natural language processing. In *Introduction to artificial intelligence* (pp. 87–99). Springer International Publishing.

Farah, J. C., Spaenlehauer, B., Bergram, K., Holzer, A., & Gillet, D. (2022). Challenges and opportunities in integrating interactive chatbots into code review exercises: A pilot case study. In *Proceedings of the IATED Conference* (pp. 3816–3825). IATED.

Farzan, M., Ebrahimi, H., Pourali, M., & Sabeti, F. (2025). Artificial intelligence-powered cognitive behavioral therapy chatbots, a systematic review. *Iranian Journal of Psychiatry*, *20*(1), 102–110. DOI: 0.18502/ijps.v20i1.17395

Farzan, M., Ebrahimi, H., Pourali, M., & Sabeti, F. (2025). Artificial Intelligence-Powered Cognitive Behavioral Therapy Chatbots: A Systematic Review. *Iranian Journal of Psychiatry*, *20*(1), 102–110. DOI: 10.18502/ijps.v20i1.17395 PMID: 40093525

Faurholt-Jepsen, M., Busk, J., Frost, M., Vinberg, M., Christensen, E. M., Winther, O., Bardram, J. E., & Kessing, L. V. (2016). Voice analysis as an objective state marker in bipolar disorder. *Translational Psychiatry*, *6*(7), e856–e856. DOI: 10.1038/tp.2016.123 PMID: 27434490

Faurholt-Jepsen, M., Vinberg, M., Frost, M., Debel, S., Margrethe Christensen, E., Bardram, J. E., & Kessing, L. V. (2015). Daily electronic self-monitoring in bipolar disorder using smartphones–the MONARCA I trial: A randomized, placebo-controlled, single-blind, parallel group trial. *Psychological Medicine*, *45*(13), 2691–2704. DOI: 10.1017/S0033291715000410 PMID: 26220802

Feil-Seifer, D., & Matarić, M. J. (2011). Socially assistive robotics. *IEEE Robotics & Automation Magazine*, *18*(1), 24–31.

Fellous, J. M., Sapiro, G., Rossi, A., Mayberg, H., & Ferrante, M. (2019). Explainable artificial intelligence for neuroscience: Behavioral neurostimulation. *Frontiers in Neuroscience*, *13*, 1346.

Feng, J., Zhao, X., Liu, Z., Ding, Y., & Wang, F. (2025). A multi-view multimodal deep learning framework for Alzheimer's disease diagnosis. *Frontiers in Neuroscience*, *19*(October), 1–16.

Feusner, J. D., Mohideen, R., Smith, S., Patanam, I., Vaitla, A., Lam, C., & Leow, A. (2021). Semantic linkages of obsessions from an international obsessive-compulsive disorder mobile app data set: Big data analytics study. *Journal of Medical Internet Research*, *23*(6), e25482.

Figueroa, C. A., Ramos, G., Psihogios, A. M., Ekuban, E., Bansie, P., de Haas, M., & Stiles-Shields, C. (2025). Advancing youth co-design of ethical guidelines for AI-powered digital mental health tools. *Nature Mental Health*, •••, 1–9.

First Therapy Chatbot trial yields mental health benefits. (2025, March 27). Dartmouth. https://home.dartmouth.edu/news/2025/03/first-therapy-chatbot-trial-yields-mental-health-benefits

First, M. B., & Wakefield, J. C. (2010). Defining 'mental disorder' in DSM-V. *Psychological Medicine*, *40*(11), 1779–1782. DOI: 10.1017/S0033291709992339

Firth, J., Torous, J., Nicholas, J., Carney, R., Pratap, A., Rosenbaum, S., & Sarris, J. (2017). The efficacy of smartphone-based mental health interventions for depressive symptoms: A meta-analysis of randomized controlled trials. *World Psychiatry; Official Journal of the World Psychiatric Association (WPA)*, *16*(3), 287–298.

Fitzpatrick, K. K., Darcy, A., & Vierhile, M. (2017). Delivering cognitive behavior therapy to young adults with symptoms of depression and anxiety using a fully automated conversational agent (Woebot): A randomized controlled trial. *JMIR Mental Health*, *4*(2), e19. DOI: 10.2196/mental.7785 PMID: 28588005

Flanagan, O., Chan, A., Roop, P., & Sundram, F. (2021). Using acoustic speech patterns from smartphones to investigate mood disorders: Scoping review. *JMIR mHealth and uHealth*, *9*(9), e24352. DOI: 10.2196/24352

Flores, R., Tlachac, M. L., Toto, E., & Rundensteiner, E. (2022, December). Audiface: Multimodal deep learning for depression screening. In *Machine Learning for Healthcare Conference* (pp. 609-630). PMLR.

Floridi, L. (2021). The European Legislation on AI: A Brief Analysis of its Philosophical Approach. *Philosophy & Technology*, *34*(2), 215–222. DOI: 10.1007/s13347-021-00460-9

Fontenelle, L. F., Oostermeijer, S., Harrison, B. J., Pantelis, C., & Yücel, M. (2011). Obsessive-compulsive disorder, impulse control disorders and drug addiction: Common features and potential treatments. *Drugs*, *71*(7), 827–840. DOI: 10.2165/11590560-000000000-00000

Ford, E., Stone, J., Oliver, D., Fell, B., Roque, G., Robertson, S., Fusar-Poli, P., & Greenwood, K. (2025). Local adaptation and validation of a transdiagnostic risk calculator for first episode psychosis using mental health patient records. *Frontiers in Psychiatry*, *16*. Advance online publication. DOI: 10.3389/fpsyt.2025.1584719 PMID: 40766924

Fried, E. I., Flake, J. K., & Robinaugh, D. J. (2022). Revisiting the theoretical and methodological foundations of depression measurement. *Nature Reviews Psychology*, *1*(6), 358–368. DOI: 10.1038/s44159-022-00050-2

Fu, C. H., Erus, G., Fan, Y., Antoniades, M., Arnone, D., Arnott, S. R., & Davatzikos, C. (2023). AI-based dimensional neuroimaging system for characterizing heterogeneity in brain structure and function in major depressive disorder: COORDINATE-MDD consortium design and rationale. *BMC Psychiatry*, *23*(1), 59.

Fujita, J., Yano, Y., Shinoda, S., Sho, N., Otsuki, M., Suda, A., Takayama, M., Moroga, T., Yamaguchi, H., Ishii, M., & Miyazaki, T. (2025). Challenges in Implementing a Mobile AI Chatbot Intervention for Depression Among Youth on Psychiatric Waiting Lists: Randomized Controlled Study Termination Report. *JMIRx Med*, *6*, e70960–e70960. DOI: 10.2196/70960 PMID: 41055096

Fulmer, R., Joerin, A., Gentile, B., Lakerink, L., & Rauws, M. (2018). Using psychological artificial intelligence (Tess) to relieve symptoms of depression and anxiety: Randomized controlled trial. *JMIR Mental Health*, *5*(4), e64. DOI: 10.2196/mental.9782

Fusaroli, R., Lambrechts, A., Bang, D., Bowler, D. M., & Gaigg, S. B. (2016). *"Is Voice A Marker for Autism Spectrum Disorder? A Systematic Review And Meta-Analysis"*. https://doi.org/DOI: 10.1101/046565

Gamble, A. (2020). Artificial intelligence and mobile apps for mental healthcare: A social informatics perspective. *Aslib Journal of Information Management*, *72*(4), 509–523. DOI: 10.1108/AJIM-11-2019-0316

Garbin, C., Marques, N., & Marques, O. (2023). Machine learning for predicting opioid use disorder from healthcare data: A systematic review. *Computer Methods and Programs in Biomedicine*, *236*, 107573. DOI: 10.1016/j.cmpb.2023.107573

Garg, A., Reza, S. M., & Babinski, D. (2025, March). Enhancing ADHD Diagnostic Assessments with Virtual Reality integrated with Biofeedback and Artificial Intelligence. In *2025 8th International Conference on Information and Computer Technologies (ICICT)* (pp. 442-447). IEEE.

Garriga, R., Mas, J., Abraha, S., Hofer, M., Yang, H., Haller, D. M., Gonzalez-Huerta, J. M., Echarri, O., Sintes, R., Montalvo, I., Duran-Sindreu, C., Molinuevo, J. L., Ros, E., Mestre, A., Miguel, J. C., Subirana, I., Perera-Lluna, A., Vieta, E., Bulbena, A., & García-Altés, A. (2022). Machine learning model to predict mental health crises from electronic health records. *Nature Medicine*, *28*(6), 1240–1248. DOI: 10.1038/s41591-022-01811-5

Gautam, P., & Singh, P. (2020). A machine learning approach to identify socio-economic factors responsible for patients dropping out of substance abuse treatment. *American Journal of Public Health Research*, *8*(5), 140–146. DOI: 10.12691/ajphr-8-5-1

Ghaffar Nia, N., Kaplanoglu, E., & Nasab, A. (2023). Evaluation of artificial intelligence techniques in disease diagnosis and prediction. *Discover Artificial Intelligence*, *3*(1), 5. Advance online publication. DOI: 10.1007/s44163-023-00049-5

Giorgi, S., & Curtis, B. (2024). Leveraging AI to predict substance use disorder treatment outcomes. *Neuropsychopharmacology : Official Publication of the American College of Neuropsychopharmacology*, *49*, 335–333. DOI: 10.1038/s41386-023-01700-6

Giovanola, B., & Tiribelli, S. (2023). Beyond bias and discrimination: Redefining the AI ethics principle of fairness in healthcare machine-learning algorithms. *AI & Society*, *38*(2), 549–563. DOI: 10.1007/s00146-022-01455-6 PMID: 35615443

Goldberg, S. B., Rowe, G., Malte, C. A., Ruan, H., Owen, J. J., & Miller, S. D. (2020). Routine monitoring of therapeutic alliance to predict treatment engagement in a Veterans Affairs substance use disorders clinic. *Psychological Services*, *17*(3), 291–299. DOI: 10.1037/ser0000337

Gooding, P., & Kariotis, T. (2021). Ethics and Law in Research on Algorithmic and Data-Driven Technology in Mental Health Care: Scoping Review. *JMIR Mental Health*, *8*(6), e24668. DOI: 10.2196/24668 PMID: 34110297

Goodwin, N. L., Choong, J. J., Hwang, S., Pitts, K., Bloom, L., Islam, A., & Golden, S. A. (2024). Simple Behavioral Analysis (SimBA) as a platform for explainable machine learning in behavioral neuroscience. *Nature Neuroscience*, *27*(7), 1411–1424.

Gopinath, N. (2023). Artificial intelligence and neuroscience: An update on fascinating relationships. *Process Biochemistry*, *125*, 113–120.

Graff, F. S., Morgan, T. J., Epstein, E. E., McCrady, B. S., Cook, S. M., Jensen, N. K., & Kelly, S. (2009). Engagement and retention in outpatient alcoholism treatment for women. *The American Journal on Addictions*, *18*(4), 277–288. DOI: 10.1080/10550490902925540

Grant, B. F., Stinson, F. S., Dawson, D. A., Chou, S. P., Dufour, M. C., Compton, W., Pickering, R. P., & Kaplan, K. (2004). Prevalence and co-occurrence of substance use disorders and independent mood and anxiety disorders. *Archives of General Psychiatry*, *61*(8), 807–816.

Grecucci, A., Lapomarda, G., Messina, I., Monachesi, B., Sorella, S., & Siugzdaite, R. (2022). Structural Features Related to Affective Instability Correctly Classify Patients With Borderline Personality Disorder. A Supervised Machine Learning Approach. *Frontiers in Psychiatry*, *13*. Advance online publication. DOI: 10.3389/fpsyt.2022.804440

Grootendorst-van Mil, N., Chang, C. K., Chandran, D., Schirmbeck, F., van Beveren, N., Shetty, H., & Hayes, R. D. (2025). Obsessive-compulsive symptoms relating to psychosocial functioning for people with schizophrenia, schizoaffective disorder, or bipolar disorder. *Acta Neuropsychiatrica*, *37*, e45.

Groppa, S., Gonzalez-Escamilla, G., Tinkhauser, G., Baqapuri, H. I., Sajonz, B., Wiest, C., Pereira, J., Herz, D. M., Dold, M. R., Bange, M., Ciolac, D., Almeida, V., Neuber, J., Mirzac, D., Martín-Rodríguez, J. F., Dresel, C., Muthuraman, M., Adarmes Gomez, A. D., Navas, M., & Coenen, V. A. (2024). Perspectives of Implementation of Closed-Loop Deep Brain Stimulation: From Neurological to Psychiatric Disorders. *Stereotactic and Functional Neurosurgery*, *102*(1), 40–54. DOI: 10.1159/000535114

Grosshans, M., Paul, T., Fischer, S. K., Lotzmann, N., List, H., Haag, C., & Mutschler, J. (2024). Conversation-based AI for anxiety disorders might lower the threshold for traditional medical assistance: A case report. *Frontiers in Public Health*, *12*, 1399702. DOI: 10.3389/fpubh.2024.1399702

Guglielmucci, F., & Di Basilio, D. (2025). Predicting Engagement With Conversational Agents in Mental Health Therapy by Examining the Role of Epistemic Trust, Personality, and Fear of Intimacy: Cross-Sectional Web-Based Survey Study. *JMIR Human Factors*, *12*, e70698–e70698. DOI: 10.2196/70698 PMID: 40737594

Gupta, A., Kumar Maurya, M., Dhere, K., & Kumar Chaurasiya, V. (2024). Privacy-Preserving Hybrid Federated Learning Framework for Mental Healthcare Applications: Clustered and Quantum Approaches. *IEEE Access : Practical Innovations, Open Solutions*, *12*, 145054–145068. DOI: 10.1109/ACCESS.2024.3464240

Gupta, N. V., Murugan, M. D., & Shanbhag, S. J. (2025). AI/ML-driven nanocarriers for the management of neurodegeneration. In *The neurodegeneration revolution* (pp. 361–372). Academic Press.

Haider, R., Megha, W. A., Juba, J. T., Alamgir, A., & Ahmad, L. (2025). The conversational revolution in health promotion: Investigating chatbot impact on healthcare marketing, patient engagement, and service reach. *International Journal of Science and Research Archive*, *15*(3), 1585–1592.

Halkiopoulos, C., Gkintoni, E., Aroutzidis, A., & Antonopoulou, H. (2025). Advances in Neuroimaging and Deep Learning for Emotion Detection: A Systematic Review of Cognitive Neuroscience and Algorithmic Innovations. *Diagnostics (Basel)*, *15*(4), 456. DOI: 10.3390/diagnostics15040456

Hamdoun, S., Monteleone, R., Bookman, T., & Michael, K. (2023). AI-Based and Digital Mental Health Apps: Balancing Need and Risk. *IEEE Technology and Society Magazine*, *42*(1), 25–36. DOI: 10.1109/MTS.2023.3241309

Hamideh, D., & Nebeker, C. (2020). The digital health landscape in addiction and substance use research: Will digital health exacerbate or mitigate health inequities in vulnerable populations? *Current Addiction Reports*, *7*(3), 317–332. DOI: 10.1007/s40429-020-00325-9

Hanauer, M., Sielbeck-Mathes, K., Banks, B., Mitori, J., & Reuveny, A. (2021). Demographic predictors of dropping out of treatment (DOT) in substance use disorder treatment. *Substance Use & Misuse*, *56*(8), 1155–1160. DOI: 10.1080/10826084.2021.1913805

Hasan, M. E., Hossain, M. S., Mamun, M. A., Al-Mamun, F., Roy, N., & Almerab, M. M. (2025). Predicting substance use behaviors among students taking university entrance test: A cross-sectional study with machine learning techniques. *Current Psychology (New Brunswick, N.J.)*, *44*, 8015–8031. DOI: 10.1007/s12144-024-06934-1

Hasan, M. M., Young, G. J., Patel, M. R., Modestino, A. S., Sanchez, L. D., & Noor-E-Alam, M. (2021). A machine learning framework to predict the risk of opioid use disorder. *Machine Learning with Applications*, *6*, 100144. DOI: 10.1016/j.mlwa.2021.100144

Hassabis, D., Kumaran, D., Summerfield, C., & Botvinick, M. (2017). Neuroscience-Inspired Artificial Intelligence. *Neuron*, *95*(2), 245–258.

Hassan, S. A., Kareem, M., Sammany, M., & Banoon, S. R. (2024). Artificial intelligence as a predictive tool in drug addiction: A comprehensive review. *Journal of Misan Researches.*

Hassan, Y. M., Wanas, A., Ali, A. A., & El-Sayed, W. M. (2025). Integrating artificial intelligence with nanodiagnostics for early detection and precision management of neurodegenerative diseases. *Journal of Nanobiotechnology*, *23*(1), 668.

Hastings, J. (2024). Preventing harm from non-conscious bias in medical generative AI. *The Lancet. Digital Health*, *6*(1), e2–e3. DOI: 10.1016/S2589-7500(23)00246-7 PMID: 38123253

Heberle, B. A., Kluwe-Schiavon, B., Bicca, C., Rothmann, L. M., Grassi-Oliveira, R., & Viola, T. W. (2024). Examining predictors of cocaine withdrawal syndrome at the end of detoxification treatment in women with cocaine use disorder. *Journal of Psychiatric Research*, *169*, 247–256. DOI: 10.1016/j.jpsychres.2023.11.043

Heilig, M., MacKillop, J., Martinez, D., Rehm, J., Leggio, L., & Vanderschuren, L. J. (2021). Addiction as a brain disease revised: Why it still matters, and the need for consilience. *Neuropsychopharmacology : Official Publication of the American College of Neuropsychopharmacology*, *46*(10), 1715–1723. DOI: 10.1038/s41386-021-01045-1

Heinz, M. V., Bhattacharya, S., Trudeau, B., Quist, R., Song, S. H., Lee, C. M., & Jacobson, N. C. (2023). Testing domain knowledge and risk of bias of a large-scale general artificial intelligence model in mental health. *Digital Health*, *9*. Advance online publication. DOI: 10.1177/20552076231170499 PMID: 37101589

Heinz, M. V., Mackin, D. M., Trudeau, B. M., Bhattacharya, S., Wang, Y., Banta, H. A., Jewett, A. D., Salzhauer, A. J., Griffin, T. Z., & Jacobson, N. C. (2025). Randomized trial of a generative AI chatbot for mental health treatment. *NEJM AI, 2*(4). Advance online publication. DOI: 10.1056/aioa2400802

He, J., & Ji, F. (2025). Artificial Intelligence and Social Media for the Detection of Eating Disorders. *International Journal of Eating Disorders.*

He, Y., Yang, L., Qian, C., Li, T., Su, Z., Zhang, Q., & Hou, X. (2023). Conversational Agent Interventions for Mental Health Problems: Systematic Review and Meta-analysis of Randomized Controlled Trials. *Journal of Medical Internet Research, 25*, e43862. DOI: 10.2196/43862 PMID: 37115595

Higgins, O., & Wilson, R. L. (2025). Integrating Artificial Intelligence (<scp>AI</scp>) With Workforce Solutions for Sustainable Care: A Follow Up to Artificial Intelligence and Machine Learning (<scp>ML</scp>) Based Decision Support Systems in Mental Health. *International Journal of Mental Health Nursing*, *34*(2). Advance online publication. DOI: 10.1111/inm.70019

Higgins, O., Wilson, R. L., & Chalup, S. K. (2024). Using machine learning to assist decision making in the assessment of mental health patients presenting to emergency departments. *Digital Health, 10.* Advance online publication. DOI: 10.1177/20552076241287364 PMID: 39534524

Hirschfeld, R. M. A. (2001). The comorbidity of major depression and anxiety disorders: Recognition and management in primary care. *Primary Care Companion to the Journal of Clinical Psychiatry*, *3*(6), 244–254.

Hoggatt, K. J., Harris, A. H., Hayes, C. J., Washington, D., & Williams, E. C. (2025). Improving diagnosis-based quality measures: An application of machine learning to the prediction of substance use disorder among outpatients. *BMJ Open Quality, 14*(1). Advance online publication. DOI: 10.1136/bmjoq-2024-003929

Hong, S., Walton, B., Kim, H. W., & Lipsey, A. D. (2024). Improving treatment completion for young adults with substance use disorder: Machine learning-based prediction algorithms. *Journal of Psychiatric Research, 178*, 41–49. DOI: 10.1016/j.jpsychres.2024.04.007

Hoose, S., & Králiková, K. (2024). Artificial Intelligence in Mental Health Care: Management Implications, Ethical Challenges, and Policy Considerations. *Administrative Sciences*, *14*(9), 227. DOI: 10.3390/admsci14090227

Hornstein, S., Forman-Hoffman, V., Nazander, A., Ranta, K., & Hilbert, K. (2021). Predicting therapy outcome in a digital mental health intervention for depression and anxiety: A machine learning approach. *Digital Health, 7*. Advance online publication. DOI: 10.1177/20552076211060659 PMID: 34868624

Horwitz, A. G., Mills, E. D., Sen, S., & Bohnert, A. S. B. (2024). Comparative Effectiveness of Three Digital Interventions for Adults Seeking Psychiatric Services. *JAMA Network Open*, *7*(7), e2422115. DOI: 10.1001/jamanetworkopen.2024.22115

Hossain, S., Hossain, S., Ahmed, F., Islam, R., Sikder, T., & Rahman, A. (2017). Prevalence of tobacco smoking and factors associated with the initiation of smoking among university students in Dhaka, Bangladesh. *Central Asian Journal of Global Health*, *6*(1), 244. DOI: 10.5195/cajgh.2017.244

Hosseini Tabaghdehi, S. A., & Ayaz, Ö. (2025). AI ethics in action: A circular model for transparency, accountability and inclusivity. *Journal of Managerial Psychology*. Advance online publication. DOI: 10.1108/JMP-03-2024-0177

Hosseinpoor, A. R., Parker, L. A., d'Espaignet, T. E., & Chatterji, S. (2011). Social determinants of smoking in low- and middle-income countries: Results from the World Health Survey. *PLoS One*, *6*(5), e20331. DOI: 10.1371/journal.pone.0020331

Houghton, D. C., Spratt, H. M., Keyser-Marcus, L., Bjork, J. M., Neigh, G. N., Cunningham, K. A., & Moeller, F. G. (2023). Behavioral and neurocognitive factors distinguishing post-traumatic stress comorbidity in substance use disorders. *Translational Psychiatry*, *13*(1), 296. DOI: 10.1038/s41398-023-02591-3

Hou, J., & Wang, L. L. (2025). Explainable AI for Clinical Outcome Prediction: A Survey of Clinician Perceptions and Preferences. *AMIA Joint Summits on Translational Science Proceedings. AMIA Joint Summits on Translational Science*, *2025*, 215–224. PMID: 40502256

Houssein, E. H., Hammad, A., & Ali, A. A. (2022). Human emotion recognition from EEG-based brain–computer interface using machine learning: A comprehensive review. *Neural Computing & Applications*, *34*(15), 12527–12557.

Hsu, F. M., Chen, H. C., Wang, K. C., Ling, W. L., & Chen, N. C. (2024). Application of time series analysis in predicting postpartum depression: Integrating data from the hospitalization period and early postpartum weeks. *Archives of Women's Mental Health*. Advance online publication. DOI: 10.1007/s00737-024-01521-6 PMID: 39367991

Huang, J., Galal, G., Etemadi, M., & Vaidyanathan, M. (2022). Evaluation and Mitigation of Racial Bias in Clinical Machine Learning Models: Scoping Review. *JMIR Medical Informatics*, *10*(5), e36388. DOI: 10.2196/36388

Hua, Y., Beam, A., Chibnik, L. B., & Torous, J. (2025). From statistics to deep learning: Using large language models in psychiatric research. *International Journal of Methods in Psychiatric Research*, *34*(1). Advance online publication. DOI: 10.1002/mpr.70007 PMID: 39777756

Huhn, A. S., Hobelmann, J. G., Ramirez, A., Strain, E. C., & Oyler, G. A. (2019). Trends in first-time treatment admissions for older adults with alcohol use disorder: Availability of medical and specialty clinical services in hospital, residential, and outpatient facilities. *Drug and Alcohol Dependence*, *205*, 107694. DOI: 10.1016/j.drugalcdep.2019.107694

Huhn, A. S., Hobelmann, J. G., Strickland, J. C., Oyler, G. A., Bergeria, C. L., Umbricht, A., & Dunn, K. E. (2020). Differences in availability and use of medications for opioid use disorder in residential treatment settings in the United States. *JAMA Network Open*, *3*(2), e1920843. DOI: 10.1001/jamanetworkopen.2019.20843

Hu, J., Zhao, C., Shi, C., Zhao, Z., & Ren, Z. (2024). Speech-based recognition and estimating severity of PTSD using machine learning. *Journal of Affective Disorders*, *362*, 859–868.

Husain, L., Greenhalgh, T., Hughes, G., Finlay, T., & Wherton, J. (2022). Desperately seeking intersectionality in digital health disparity research: Narrative review to inform a richer theorization of multiple disadvantage. *Journal of Medical Internet Research*, *24*(12), e42358. DOI: 10.2196/42358

Husnain, N. A., Ahmad, N. A., Saeed, N. A., & Din, N. S. M. U. (2024). Harnessing AI in depression therapy: Integrating technology with traditional approaches. *International Journal of Science and Research Archive*, *12*(2), 2585–2590. DOI: 10.30574/ijsra.2024.12.2.1512

Huys, Q. J., Pizzagalli, D. A., Bogdan, R., & Dayan, P. (2013). Mapping anhedonia onto reinforcement learning: A behavioural meta-analysis. *Biology of Mood & Anxiety Disorders*, *3*(1), 12.

Ibrahim, H., Liu, X., Zariffa, N., Morris, A. D., & Denniston, A. K. (2021). Health data poverty: An assailable barrier to equitable digital health care. *The Lancet. Digital Health*, *3*(4), e260–e265. DOI: 10.1016/S2589-7500(20)30317-4 PMID: 33678589

Idowu, O. F., & Idowu, S. (2025). Artificial Intelligence Applications in Mental Health Crisis Prediction: Navigating Privacy, Consent, and Fairness in Clinical Decision-Making. *International Journal of Computer Applications Technology and Research*. https://doi.org/DOI: 10.7753/IJCATR1408.1009

Ienca, M., & Ignatiadis, K. (2020). A JOB Neuroscience Artificial Intelligence in Clinical Neuroscience. *Methodological and Ethical Challenges*, *11*(2), 77–87.

Ilgen, M. A., Jain, A., Lucas, E., & Moos, R. H. (2007). Substance use-disorder treatment and a decline in attempted suicide during and after treatment. *Journal of Studies on Alcohol and Drugs*, *68*(4), 503–509. DOI: 10.15288/jsad.2007.68.503

Ilyas, C. M. A., Nunes, R., Nasrollahi, K., Rehm, M., & Moeslund, T. B. (2021, February). Deep emotion recognition through upper body movements and facial expression. In *VISIGRAPP* (Vol. 5, pp. 669–679). VISAPP.

Iniesta, R., Stahl, D., & McGuffin, P. (2016). Machine learning, statistical learning and the future of biological research in psychiatry. *Psychological Medicine*, *46*(12), 2455–2465. DOI: 10.1017/S0033291716001367

Inkster, B., Sarda, S., & Subramanian, V. (2018). An empathy-driven, conversational artificial intelligence agent (Wysa) for digital mental well-being: Real-world data evaluation mixed-methods study. *JMIR mHealth and uHealth*, *6*(11), e12106. PMID: 30470676

Insel, T. R. (2017). Digital phenotyping: Technology for a new science of behavior. *Journal of the American Medical Association*, *318*(13), 1215–1216.

Insel, T., Cuthbert, B., Garvey, M., Heinssen, R., Pine, D. S., Quinn, K., Sanislow, C., & Wang, P. (2010). Research Domain Criteria (RDoC): Toward a New Classification Framework for Research on Mental Disorders. *The American Journal of Psychiatry*, *167*(7), 748–751. DOI: 10.1176/appi.ajp.2010.09091379

Islam, A. B. M. R., Khan, K. M., Scarbrough, A., Zimpfer, M. J., Makkena, N., Omogunwa, A., & Ahamed, S. I. (2023). An artificial intelligence–based smartphone app for assessing the risk of opioid misuse in working populations using synthetic data: Pilot development study. *JMIR Formative Research*, *7*, e45434. DOI: 10.2196/45434

Islam, S. U., Ahmed, M. B., Ahsan, H., & Lee, Y. S. (2022). Role of biomarkers in personalized medicine. In Shehzad, A. (Ed.), *Cancer biomarkers in diagnosis and therapeutics* (pp. 249–275). Springer., DOI: 10.1007/978-981-16-5759-7_11

Iwaya, L. H.. (2023). On the privacy of mental health apps: An empirical investigation and its implications for app development. *Empirical Software Engineering*, *28*(1), 2. DOI: 10.1007/s10664-022-10236-0 PMID: 36407814

Iyortsuun, N. K., Kim, S. H., Jhon, M., Yang, H. J., & Pant, S. (2023). A review of machine learning and deep learning approaches on mental health diagnosis. *Health Care, 11*(3), 285. DOI: 10.3390/healthcare11030285

Izquierdo, A., Aguirre, C., Hart, E. E., & Stolyarova, A. (2019). Rodent models of adaptive value learning and decision-making. In *Psychiatric Disorders: Methods and Protocols* (pp. 105–119). Springer New York.

Jacobson, N. C., Bentley, K. H., Walton, A., Wang, S. B., Fortgang, R. G., Millner, A. J., Coombs, G., Rodman, A. M., & Coppersmith, D. D. L. (2020). Ethical dilemmas posed by mobile health and machine learning in psychiatry research. *Bulletin of the World Health Organization, 98*(4), 270–276. DOI: 10.2471/BLT.19.237107 PMID: 32284651

Jacobson, N. C., & Bhattacharya, S. (2022). Digital biomarkers of anxiety disorder symptom changes: Personalized deep learning models using smartphone sensors accurately predict anxiety symptoms from ecological momentary assessments. *Behaviour Research and Therapy, 149*, 104013. DOI: 10.1016/j.brat.2021.104013 PMID: 35030442

Jacobson, N. C., & Feng, B. (2022). Digital phenotyping of generalized anxiety disorder: Using artificial intelligence to accurately predict symptom severity using wearable sensors in daily life. *Translational Psychiatry, 12*(1), 336. DOI: 10.1038/s41398-022-02038-1

Jacobson, N. C., Lekkas, D., Huang, R., & Thomas, N. (2020). Deep learning paired with wearable passive sensing data predicts deterioration in anxiety disorder symptoms across 17-18 years. *Journal of Affective Disorders, 282*(1). Advance online publication. DOI: 10.1016/j.jad.2020.12.086

Jain, A., Brooks, J. R., Alford, C. C., Chang, C. S., Mueller, N. M., Umscheid, C. A., & Bierman, A. S. (2023). Awareness of Racial and Ethnic Bias and Potential Solutions to Address Bias With Use of Health Care Algorithms. *JAMA Health Forum, 4*(6), e231197. DOI: 10.1001/jamahealthforum.2023.1197 PMID: 37266959

Jain, D. (2023). Regulation of Digital Healthcare in India: Ethical and Legal Challenges. *Health Care, 11*(6), 911. DOI: 10.3390/healthcare11060911

Jaques, N., Taylor, S., Sano, A., & Picard, R. (2017, September). Predicting tomorrow's mood, health, and stress level using personalized multitask learning and domain adaptation. In *IJCAI 2017 Workshop on artificial intelligence in affective computing* (pp. 17-33). PMLR.

Javanbakht, A., Hinchey, L., Gorski, K., Ballard, A., Ritchie, L., & Amirsadri, A. (2024). Unreal that feels real: Artificial intelligence-enhanced augmented reality for treating social and occupational dysfunction in post-traumatic stress disorder and anxiety disorders. *European Journal of Psychotraumatology*, *15*(1), 2418248.

Jayatilake, S., & Ganegoda, G. (2021). Involvement of machine learning tools in healthcare decision making. *Journal of Healthcare Engineering*, *6679512*. Advance online publication. DOI: 10.1155/2021/6679512

Jeyakumar, T., Younus, S., Zhang, M., Clare, M., Charow, R., Karsan, I., Dhalla, A., Al-Mouaswas, D., Scandiffio, J., Aling, J., Salhia, M., Lalani, N., Overholt, S., & Wiljer, D. (2023). Preparing for an Artificial Intelligence–Enabled Future: Patient Perspectives on Engagement and Health Care Professional Training for Adopting Artificial Intelligence Technologies in Health Care Settings. *JMIR AI*, *2*, e40973. DOI: 10.2196/40973

Jiang, S., Jia, Q., Peng, Z., Zhou, Q., An, Z., Chen, J., & Yi, Q. (2025). Can artificial intelligence be the future solution to the enormous challenges and suffering caused by Schizophrenia? *Schizophrenia*, *11*(1), 32.

Jiao, Y., Zhao, K., Wei, X., Carlisle, N. B., Keller, C. J., Oathes, D. J., Fonzo, G. A., & Zhang, Y. (2025). Deep graph learning of multimodal brain networks defines treatment-predictive signatures in major depression. *Molecular Psychiatry*, *30*(9), 3963–3974.

Jing, Y., Hu, Z., & Fan, P.. (2020). Analysis of substance use and its outcomes by machine learning I. Childhood evaluation of liability to substance use disorder. *Drug and Alcohol Dependence*, *206*, 107605. DOI: 10.1016/j.drugalcdep.2019.107605

Jirsaraie, R. (2025). *Applying Machine Learning to Developmental Psychopathology* (Doctoral dissertation, Washington University in St. Louis).

Joerin, A., Rauws, M., Fulmer, R., & Black, V. (2020). Ethical artificial intelligence for digital health organizations. *Cureus*, *12*(3).

Johnstone, S. J., Roodenrys, S., Blackman, R., Johnston, E., Loveday, K., Mantz, S., & Barratt, M. F. (2012). Neurocognitive training for children with and without AD/HD. *Attention Deficit and Hyperactivity Disorders*, *4*, 11–23.

Joshi, M. L., & Kanoongo, N. (2022). Depression detection using emotional artificial intelligence and machine learning: A closer review. *Materials Today: Proceedings*, *58*, 217–226.

Joyce, D. W., Kormilitzin, A., Smith, K. A., & Cipriani, A. (2023). Explainable artificial intelligence for mental health through transparency and interpretability for understandability. *NPJ Digital Medicine*, *6*, 6. DOI: 10.1038/s41746-023-00751-9 PMID: 36653524

Jungmann, S. M., Klan, T., Kuhn, S., & Jungmann, F. (2019). Accuracy of a Chatbot (Ada) in the Diagnosis of Mental Disorders: Comparative Case Study With Lay and Expert Users. *JMIR Formative Research*, *3*(4), e13863. DOI: 10.2196/13863

Kaack, L. H., Donti, P. L., Strubell, E., Kamiya, G., Creutzig, F., & Rolnick, D. (2022). Aligning artificial intelligence with climate change mitigation. *Nature Climate Change*, *12*(6), 518–527.

Kaczmarek-Majer, K., Dominiak, M., Antosik, A. Z., Hryniewicz, O., Kamińska, O., Opara, K., Owsiński, J., Radziszewska, W., Sochacka, M., & Święcicki, Ł. (2025). Acoustic features from speech as markers of depressive and manic symptoms in bipolar disorder: A prospective study. *Acta Psychiatrica Scandinavica*, *151*(3), 358–374. DOI: 10.1111/acps.13735 PMID: 39118422

Kaiser Family Foundation. (2023). Mental Health Care Health Professional Shortage Areas (HPSAs). https://www.kff.org/other/state-indicator/mental-health-care-health-professional-shortage-areas-hpsas/

Kaldo, V., Isacsson, N., Forsell, E., Bjurner, P., Abdesslem, F. B., & Boman, M. (2021). AI-driven adaptive treatment strategies in internet-delivered CBT. *European Psychiatry : the Journal of the Association of European Psychiatrists*, *64*(S1), S20. DOI: 10.1192/j.eurpsy.2021.75

Kalin, N. H. (2020). The critical relationship between anxiety and depression. *The American Journal of Psychiatry*, *177*(5), 365–367.

Kambeitz-Ilankovic, L., Meisenzahl, E. M., Cabral, C., von Saldern, S., Kambeitz, J., Falkai, P., & Koutsouleris, N. (2016). Prediction of outcome in the psychosis prodrome using neuroanatomical pattern classification. *Schizophrenia Research*, *173*(3), 159–165.

Kamel Rahimi, A., Pienaar, O., Ghadimi, M., Canfell, O. J., Pole, J. D., Shrapnel, S., van der Vegt, A. H., & Sullivan, C. (2024). Implementing AI in Hospitals to Achieve a Learning Health System: Systematic Review of Current Enablers and Barriers. *Journal of Medical Internet Research*, *26*, e49655. DOI: 10.2196/49655

Kameyama, J., Kodera, S., & Inoue, Y. (2024). Ethical, legal, and social issues (ELSI) and reporting guidelines of AI research in healthcare. *PLOS Digital Health*, *3*(9), e0000607. DOI: 10.1371/journal.pdig.0000607

Kam, H., & Jeong, H. (2020). Pharmacogenomic Biomarkers and Their Applications in Psychiatry. *Genes*, *11*(12), 1445. DOI: 10.3390/genes11121445

Kamra, V., Kumar, P., & Mohammadian, M. (2020). Machine Learning Based Psychological Disease Support Model Assisting Psychoanalysts and Individuals in Clinical Decision Ministration. *International Journal of Computing and Digital Systems*, *9*(4), 665–675. DOI: 10.12785/ijcds/090414

Kang, T., Zhang, Y., Zhao, J., Li, X., Jiang, H., Niu, X., & Yuan, T.-F. (2022). Characterizing impulsivity in individuals with heroin use disorder. *International Journal of Mental Health and Addiction*. Advance online publication. DOI: 10.1007/s11469-022-00941-8

Kanjo, E., Younis, E. M., & Ang, C. S. (2019). Deep learning analysis of mobile physiological, environmental and location sensor data for emotion detection. *Information Fusion*, *49*, 46–56.

Karimian, G., Petelos, E., & Evers, S. M. A. A. (2022). The ethical issues of the application of artificial intelligence in healthcare: A systematic scoping review. *AI and Ethics*, *2*(4), 539–551. DOI: 10.1007/s43681-021-00131-7

Karthik, S., & Sudha, M. (2021). Predicting bipolar disorder and schizophrenia based on non-overlapping genetic phenotypes using deep neural network. *Evolutionary Intelligence*, *14*(2), 619–634.

Kawa, S., & Giordano, J. (2012). A brief historicity of the Diagnostic and Statistical Manual of Mental Disorders: Issues and implications for the future of psychiatric canon and practice. *Philosophy, Ethics, and Humanities in Medicine; PEHM*, *7*, 2. DOI: 10.1186/1747-5341-7-2

Khawaja, Z., & Bélisle-Pipon, J.-C. (2023). Your robot therapist is not your therapist: Understanding the role of AI-powered mental health chatbots. *Frontiers in Digital Health*, *5*. Advance online publication. DOI: 10.3389/fdgth.2023.1278186 PMID: 38026836

Khazaneha, M., Bakhshinejad, B., Mehrabani, M., Sabahi, A., Khaksari, M., Shafiee, M., & Mehrbani, M. (2024). Machine learning in obsessive-compulsive disorder medications. *Heliyon*, *10*(21).

Khera, R., Haimovich, J., Hurley, N. C., McNamara, R., Spertus, J. A., Desai, N., & Krumholz, H. M. (2021). Use of machine learning models to predict death after acute myocardial infarction. *JAMA Cardiology*, *6*(6), 633–641. DOI: 10.1001/jamacardio.2021.0197

Khodayari-Rostamabad, A., Reilly, J. P., Hasey, G., Debruin, H., & MacCrimmon, D. (2010, August). Diagnosis of psychiatric disorders using EEG data and employing a statistical decision model. In *2010 Annual International Conference of the IEEE Engineering in Medicine and Biology* (pp. 4006-4009). IEEE.

Kibria, M. G., Kucirka, L., & Mostafa, J. (2025). Assessing AI Explainability: A Usability Study Using a Novel Framework Involving Clinicians. *2025 IEEE 13th International Conference on Healthcare Informatics (ICHI)*, 553–564. https://doi.org/DOI: 10.1109/ICHI64645.2025.00069

Kilts, C. D., Schweitzer, J. B., Quinn, C. K., Gross, R. E., Faber, T. L., Muhammad, F., & Drexler, K. P. (2001). Neural activity related to drug craving in cocaine addiction. *Archives of General Psychiatry*, *58*(4), 334–341. DOI: 10.1001/archpsyc.58.4.334

Kim, E. S., Berkovits, L. D., Bernier, E. P., Leyzberg, D., Shic, F., Paul, R., & Scassellati, B. (2013). Social robots as embedded reinforcers of social behavior in children with autism. *Journal of Autism and Developmental Disorders*, *43*, 1038–1049.

Kim, J. (2023). *Data brokers and the sale of Americans' mental health data*. Duke Sanford School of Public Policy.

Kim, J., Pacheco, J. P. G., Golden, A., Aboujaoude, E., van Roessel, P., Gandhi, A., & Rodriguez, C. I. (2025). Artificial Intelligence in Obsessive-Compulsive Disorder: A Systematic Review. *Current Treatment Options in Psychiatry*, *12*(1), 23.

Kim, S., Kim, H., Kim, S., Lee, H., Hammoodi, A., Choi, Y., Kim, H. J., Smith, L., Kim, M. S., Fond, G., Boyer, L., Baik, S. W., Lee, H., Park, J., Kwon, R., Woo, S., & Yon, D. K. (2025). Machine learning–based prediction of substance use in adolescents in three independent worldwide cohorts: Algorithm development and validation study. *Journal of Medical Internet Research*, *27*, e62805. DOI: 10.2196/62805

Kintsugi. (2022). Kintsugi Health. https://www.kintsugihealth.com/

Kline, A. C., Cooper, A. A., Rytwinski, N. K., & Feeny, N. C. (2018). Long-term efficacy of psychotherapy for posttraumatic stress disorder: A meta-analysis of randomized controlled trials. *Clinical Psychology Review*, *59*, 30–40. DOI: 10.1016/j.cpr.2017.10.009

Klingberg, T., Fernell, E., Olesen, P. J., Johnson, M., Gustafsson, P., Dahlström, K., & Westerberg, H. (2005). Computerized training of working memory in children with ADHD-a randomized, controlled trial. *Journal of the American Academy of Child and Adolescent Psychiatry*, *44*(2), 177–186.

Klinkman, M. S., Coyne, J. C., Gallo, S., & Schwenk, T. L. (1998). False positives, false negatives, and the validity of the diagnosis of major depression in primary care. *Archives of Family Medicine*, *7*(5), 451. PMID: 9755738

Knowles, B., Richards, J. T., & Kroeger, F. (2022). *The Many Facets of Trust in AI: Formalizing the Relation Between Trust and Fairness.* Accountability, and Transparency.

Kollins, S. H., DeLoss, D. J., Cañadas, E., Lutz, J., Findling, R. L., Keefe, R. S., & Faraone, S. V. (2020). A novel digital intervention for actively reducing severity of paediatric ADHD (STARS-ADHD): A randomised controlled trial. *The Lancet. Digital Health*, *2*(4), e168–e178.

Koob, G. F., & Volkow, N. D. (2016). Neurobiology of addiction: A neurocircuitry analysis. *The Lancet. Psychiatry*, *3*(8), 760–773. DOI: 10.1016/S2215-0366(16)00104-8

Koops, S., Brederoo, S. G., de Boer, J. N., Nadema, F. G., Voppel, A. E., & Sommer, I. E. (2023). Speech as a Biomarker for Depression. *CNS & Neurological Disorders - Drug Targets*, *22*(2), 152–160. DOI: 10.2174/1871527320666211213125847 PMID: 34961469

Kostick-Quenet, K. M., Cohen, I. G., Gerke, S., Lo, B., Antaki, J., Movahedi, F., Njah, H., Schoen, L., Estep, J. E., & Blumenthal-Barby, J. S. (2022). Mitigating Racial Bias in Machine Learning. *The Journal of Law, Medicine & Ethics*, *50*(1), 92–100. DOI: 10.1017/jme.2022.13 PMID: 35243993

Kothgassner, O. D., Goreis, A., Kafka, J. X., Van Eickels, R. L., Plener, P. L., & Felnhofer, A. (2019). Virtual reality exposure therapy for posttraumatic stress disorder (PTSD): A meta-analysis. *European Journal of Psychotraumatology*, *10*(1), 1654782. Advance online publication. DOI: 10.1080/20008198.2019.1654782

Koutsouleris, N., Hauser, T. U., Skvortsova, V., & De Choudhury, M. (2022). From promise to practice: Towards the realisation of AI-informed mental health care. *The Lancet. Digital Health*, *4*(1), e829–e840. DOI: 10.1016/s2589-7500(22)00153-4

Koutsouleris, N., Kambeitz-Ilankovic, L., Ruhrmann, S., Rosen, M., Ruef, A., & Dwyer, D. B.PRONIA Consortium. (2018). Prediction models of functional outcomes for individuals in the clinical high-risk state for psychosis or with recent-onset depression: A multimodal, multisite machine learning analysis. *JAMA Psychiatry*, *75*(11), 1156–1172.

Krueger, R. F., & Eaton, N. R. (2015). Transdiagnostic factors of mental disorders. *World Psychiatry; Official Journal of the World Psychiatric Association (WPA)*, *14*(1), 27–29. DOI: 10.1002/wps.20175 PMID: 25655146

Kuhail, M. A., Alturki, N., Alramlawi, S., & Alhejori, K. (2023). Interacting with educational chatbots: A systematic review. *Education and Information Technologies*, *28*(1), 973–1018.

Kumar, V., Ntoutsi, E., Rajawat, P. S., Medda, G., & Recupero, D. R. (2024). *Unlocking LLMs: Addressing Scarce Data and Bias Challenges in Mental Health.*

Kumar, Y., Koul, A., Singla, R., & Ijaz, M. F. (2022). Artificial intelligence in disease diagnosis: A systematic literature review, synthesizing framework and future research agenda. *Journal of Ambient Intelligence and Humanized Computing*, *14*(7), 8459–8486. DOI: 10.1007/s12652-021-03612-z

Kuncel, N. R., Wee, S., Serafin, L., & Hezlett, S. A. (2010). The validity of the Graduate Record Examination for master's and doctoral programs: A meta-analytic investigation. *Educational and Psychological Measurement*, *70*(2), 340–352. DOI: 10.1177/0013164409344508

Kung, T. H., Cheatham, M., Medenilla, A., Sillos, C., De Leon, L., Elepaño, C., Madriaga, M., Aggabao, R., Diaz-Candido, G., Maningo, J., & Tseng, V. (2023). Performance of ChatGPT on USMLE: Potential for AI-assisted medical education using large language models. *PLOS Digital Health*, *2*(2), e0000198. DOI: 10.1371/journal.pdig.0000198 PMID: 36812645

Kuziemsky, C., Maeder, A. J., John, O., Gogia, S., Basu, A., Meher, S., & Ho, K. (2019). Role of artificial intelligence within the telehealth domain. *Yearbook of Medical Informatics*, *28*(1), 35–40. DOI: 10.1055/s-0039-1677897

Lappan, S. N., Brown, A. W., & Hendricks, P. S. (2020). Dropout rates of in-person psychosocial substance use disorder treatments: A systematic review and meta-analysis. *Addiction (Abingdon, England)*, *115*(2), 201–217. DOI: 10.1111/add.14885

Le Glaz, A., Haralambous, Y., Kim-Dufor, D. H., Lenca, P., Billot, R., Ryan, T. C., & Lemey, C. (2021). Machine learning and natural language processing in mental health: Systematic review. *Journal of Medical Internet Research*, *23*(5), e15708.

Leaning, I. E., Ikani, N., Savage, H. S., Leow, A., Beckmann, C., Ruhé, H. G., & Marquand, A. F. (2024). From smartphone data to clinically relevant predictions: A systematic review of digital phenotyping methods in depression. *Neuroscience and Biobehavioral Reviews*, *158*, 105541. DOI: 10.1016/j.neubiorev.2024.105541 PMID: 38215802

Leavy, S. (2018). Gender bias in artificial intelligence. *Proceedings of the 1st International Workshop on Gender Equality in Software Engineering*, 14–16. https://doi.org/DOI: 10.1145/3195570.3195580

Lebedeva, A. K., Westman, E., Borza, T., Beyer, M. K., Engedal, K., Aarsland, D., Selbaek, G., & Haberg, A. K. (2017). MRI-based classification models in prediction of mild cognitive impairment and dementia in late-life depression. *Frontiers in Aging Neuroscience*, *9*(FEB), 1–11.

Lee, D., & Yoon, S. N. (2021). Application of artificial intelligence-based technologies in the healthcare industry: Opportunities and challenges. *International Journal of Environmental Research and Public Health*, *18*, 271. DOI: 10.3390/ijerph18010271

Lee, E. E., Torous, J., De Choudhury, M., Depp, C. A., Graham, S. A., Kim, H. C., Paulus, M. P., Krystal, J. H., & Jeste, D. V. (2021). Artificial Intelligence for Mental Health Care: Clinical Applications, Barriers, Facilitators, and Artificial Wisdom. *Biological Psychiatry: Cognitive Neuroscience and Neuroimaging*, *6*(9), 856–864.

Lee, M., & Passarotti, A. M. (2022). Editorial: Addressing the challenges in the diagnosis of depressive disorder in children and adolescents. *Frontiers in Psychiatry*, *13*. Advance online publication. DOI: 10.3389/fpsyt.2022.1011301

Le, J. T., Mahoney, A. E. J., Court, J. L., & Shiner, C. T. (2025). Barriers and Facilitators of Digital Mental Health Use in Regional, Rural, and Remote Australia: A Comparison of Clinician and Consumer Perspectives. *The Australian Journal of Rural Health*, *33*(2). Advance online publication. DOI: 10.1111/ajr.70011

Lekadir, K., Frangi, A. F., Porras, A. R., Glocker, B., Cintas, C., Langlotz, C. P., Weicken, E., Asselbergs, F. W., Prior, F., Collins, G. S., Kaissis, G., Tsakou, G., Buvat, I., Kalpathy-Cramer, J., Mongan, J., Schnabel, J. A., Kushibar, K., Riklund, K., Marias, K., & Starmans, M. P. A. (2025). FUTURE-AI: International consensus guideline for trustworthy and deployable artificial intelligence in healthcare. *BMJ (Clinical Research Ed.)*, *081554*. Advance online publication. DOI: 10.1136/bmj-2024-081554

Lekkas, D., & Jacobson, N. C. (2021). Using artificial intelligence and longitudinal location data to differentiate persons who develop posttraumatic stress disorder following childhood trauma. *Scientific Reports*, *11*(1), 10303.

Lenton-Brym, A. P., Collins, A., Lane, J., Busso, C., Ouyang, J., Fitzpatrick, S., Kuo, J. R., & Monson, C. M. (2025). Using machine learning to increase access to and engagement with trauma-focused interventions for posttraumatic stress disorder. *British Journal of Clinical Psychology*, *64*(1), 125–136. DOI: 10.1111/bjc.12468

Leo, A. J., Schuelke, M. J., Hunt, D. M., Metzler, J. P., Miller, J. P., Areán, P. A., Armbrecht, M. A., & Cheng, A. L. (2022). A Digital Mental Health Intervention in an Orthopedic Setting for Patients With Symptoms of Depression and/or Anxiety: Feasibility Prospective Cohort Study. *JMIR Formative Research*, *6*(2), e34889. DOI: 10.2196/34889

Leung, C., Pei, J., Hudec, K., Shams, F., Munthali, R., & Vigo, D. (2022). The Effects of Nonclinician Guidance on Effectiveness and Process Outcomes in Digital Mental Health Interventions: Systematic Review and Meta-analysis. *Journal of Medical Internet Research*, *24*(6), e36004. DOI: 10.2196/36004 PMID: 35511463

Lever, J., Barbarino, J. M., Gong, L., Huddart, R., Sangkuhl, K., Whaley, R., Whirl-Carrillo, M., Woon, M., Klein, T. E., & Altman, R. B. (2020). PGxMine: Text mining for curation of PharmGKB. *Pacific Symposium on Biocomputing. Pacific Symposium on Biocomputing*, *25*, 611–622.

Levkovich, I. (2025). Is Artificial Intelligence the Next Co-Pilot for Primary Care in Diagnosing and Recommending Treatments for Depression? *Medical Science*, *13*(1), 8. DOI: 10.3390/medsci13010008

Levola, J., Aranko, A., & Pitkänen, T. (2021). Psychosocial difficulties and treatment retention in inpatient detoxification programmes. *Nordisk Alkohol- & Narkotikatidskrift : NAT*, *38*(5), 434–449. DOI: 10.1177/14550725211021263

Leza, L., Haro, B., López-Goñi, J. J., & Fernández-Montalvo, J. (2024). Substance use disorder and lifetime suicidal behaviour: A scoping review. *Psychiatry Research*, *334*, 115830. DOI: 10.1016/j.psychres.2024.115830

Liang, H., Tsui, B. Y., Ni, H., Valentim, C. C., Baxter, S. L., Liu, G., & Xia, H. (2019). Evaluation and accurate diagnoses of pediatric diseases using artificial intelligence. *Nature Medicine*, *25*(3), 433–438.

Liang, S., Deng, W., Li, X., Greenshaw, A. J., Wang, Q., Li, M., & Li, T. (2020). Biotypes of major depressive disorder: Neuroimaging evidence from resting-state default mode network patterns. *NeuroImage. Clinical*, *28*, 102514.

Liao, C., & Kwan, A. C. (2021). Applying reinforcement learning to rodent stress research. *Chronic Stress (Thousand Oaks, Calif.)*, *5*, 2470547020984732.

Liebenow, B., Jones, R., DiMarco, E., Trattner, J. D., Humphries, J., Sands, L. P., & Kishida, K. T. (2022). Computational reinforcement learning, reward (and punishment), and dopamine in psychiatric disorders. *Frontiers in Psychiatry*, *13*, 886297.

Li, J., & Washington, P. (2024). A Comparison of Personalized and Generalized Approaches to Emotion Recognition Using Consumer Wearable Devices: Machine Learning Study. *JMIR AI, 3*, e52171. DOI: 10.2196/52171 PMID: 38875573

Lim, C. C., Sun, T., Leung, J., Chung, J. Y., Gartner, C., Connor, J., & Chan, G. C. (2022). Prevalence of adolescent cannabis vaping: A systematic review and meta-analysis of US and Canadian studies. *JAMA Pediatrics*, *176*(1), 42–51. DOI: 10.1001/jamapediatrics.2021.4360

Lin, B., Bouneffouf, D., Cecchi, G., & Varshney, K. (2024). Towards Healthy AI: Large Language Models Need Therapists Too. Cornell University, 61–70. https://doi.org/DOI: 10.18653/v1/2024.trustnlp-1.6

Linardon, J., & Torous, J. (2025). Integrating artificial intelligence and smartphone technology to enhance personalized assessment and treatment for eating disorders. *International Journal of Eating Disorders*, *58*(8), 1415–1424.

Lind, B. K., McCarty, D., Gu, Y., Baker, R., & McConnell, J. K. (2019). Predictors of substance use treatment initiation and engagement among adult and adolescent Medicaid recipients. *Substance Abuse*, *40*(3), 285–291. DOI: 10.1080/08897077.2018.1550467

Lin, E., Lin, C. H., & Lane, H. Y. (2020). Precision psychiatry applications with pharmacogenomics: Artificial intelligence and machine learning approaches. *International Journal of Molecular Sciences*, *21*(3).

Lin, E., Lin, C.-H., & Lane, H.-Y. (2020). Precision Psychiatry Applications with Pharmacogenomics: Artificial Intelligence and Machine Learning Approaches. *International Journal of Molecular Sciences*, *21*(3), 969. DOI: 10.3390/ijms21030969 PMID: 32024055

Lin, E., Lin, C.-H., & Lane, H.-Y. (2021). Machine Learning and Deep Learning for the Pharmacogenomics of Antidepressant Treatments. *Clinical Psychopharmacology and Neuroscience : the Official Scientific Journal of the Korean College of Neuropsychopharmacology*, *19*(4), 577–588. DOI: 10.9758/cpn.2021.19.4.577

Lipschitz, J. M., Lin, S., Saghafian, S., Pike, C. K., & Burdick, K. E. (2025). Digital phenotyping in bipolar disorder: Using longitudinal Fitbit data and personalized machine learning to predict mood symptomatology. *Acta Psychiatrica Scandinavica*, *151*(3), 434–447. DOI: 10.1111/acps.13765 PMID: 39397313

Liu, H., & Lang, B. (2019). Machine learning and deep learning methods for intrusion detection systems: A survey. *applied sciences, 9*(20), 4396.

Liu, S., Wang, R., Zhang, L., Zhu, X., Yang, R., Zhou, X., Wu, F., Yang, Z., Jin, C., & Wang, G. (2025). *PsychBench: A comprehensive and professional benchmark for evaluating the performance of LLM-assisted psychiatric clinical practice.*

Liu, H., Peng, H., Song, X., Xu, C., & Zhang, M. (2022). Using AI chatbots to provide self-help depression interventions for university students: A randomized trial of effectiveness. *Internet Interventions : the Application of Information Technology in Mental and Behavioural Health, 27*, 100495. DOI: 10.1016/j.invent.2022.100495

Liu, J. C., Goetz, J., Sen, S., & Tewari, A. (2021). Learning From Others Without Sacrificing Privacy: Simulation Comparing Centralized and Federated Machine Learning on Mobile Health Data. *JMIR mHealth and uHealth, 9*(3), e23728. DOI: 10.2196/23728 PMID: 33783362

Liu, L., Edland, S., Myers, M. G., Hofstetter, C. R., & Al-Delaimy, W. K. (2016). Smoking prevalence in urban and rural populations: Findings from California between 2001 and 2012. *The American Journal of Drug and Alcohol Abuse, 42*(2), 152–161. DOI: 10.3109/00952990.2015.1125494

Liu, Q., He, H., Yang, J., Feng, X., Zhao, F., & Lyu, J. (2019). Changes in the global burden of depression from 1990 to 2017: Findings from the Global Burden of Disease study. *Journal of Psychiatric Research, 126*, 134–140. DOI: 10.1016/j.jpsychires.2019.08.002

Liu, T., Giorgi, S., Yadeta, K., Schwartz, H. A., Ungar, L. H., & Curtis, B. (2022). Linguistic predictors from Facebook postings of substance use disorder treatment retention versus discontinuation. *The American Journal of Drug and Alcohol Abuse, 48*(5), 573–585. DOI: 10.1080/00952990.2022.2091450

Liu, X., Cruz Rivera, S., Moher, D., Calvert, M. J., Denniston, A. K., Ashrafian, H., Beam, A. L., Chan, A.-W., Collins, G. S., Deeks, A. D. J., ElZarrad, M. K., Espinoza, C., Esteva, A., Faes, L., Ferrante di Ruffano, L., Fletcher, J., Golub, R., Harvey, H., Haug, C., & Yau, C. (2020). Reporting guidelines for clinical trial reports for interventions involving artificial intelligence: The CONSORT-AI extension. *The Lancet. Digital Health, 2*(10), e537–e548. DOI: 10.1016/S2589-7500(20)30218-1 PMID: 33328048

Liu, Y., Liu, Y., Tang, Y., Jiang, D., & Yu, H. (2021). A closed-loop healthcare processing approach based on deep reinforcement learning. *Multimedia Tools and Applications, 80*(12), 18691–18708. DOI: 10.1007/s11042-020-08896-5

Livingston, M. (2020). Preventing Racial Bias in Federal AI. *Journal of Science Policy & Governance, 16*(02). Advance online publication. DOI: 10.38126/JSPG160205

Livingston, M., Raninen, J., Pennay, A., & Callinan, S. (2023). The relationship between age at first drink and later risk behaviours during a period of youth drinking decline. *Addiction (Abingdon, England)*, *118*(2), 256–264. DOI: 10.1111/add.16036

Lloyd, K. (2018). *Bias Amplification in Artificial Intelligence Systems.*

Logothetis, N. K. (2002). The neural basis of the blood-oxygen-level-dependent functional magnetic resonance imaging signal. *Philosophical Transactions of the Royal Society of London. Series B, Biological Sciences*, *357*(1424), 1003–1037. DOI: 10.1098/rstb.2002.1114

Lorenzoni, G., Tavares, C., Nascimento, N., Alencar, P., & Cowan, D. (2025). Assessing ML classification algorithms and NLP techniques for depression detection: An experimental case study. *PLoS One*, *20*(5), e0322299. DOI: 10.1371/journal.pone.0322299

Lucas, G. M., Gratch, J., King, A., & Morency, L. P. (2014). It's only a computer: Virtual humans increase willingness to disclose. *Computers in Human Behavior*, *37*, 94–100.

Luo, N., Shi, W., Yang, Z., Song, M., & Jiang, T. (2024). Multimodal Fusion of Brain Imaging Data: Methods and Applications. *Machine Intelligence Research*, *21*(1), 136–152.

Lu, Z., Xie, C., Liu, N., Xie, Y., & Lu, H. (2023). Can we predict aggression? Determining the predictors of aggression among individuals with substance use disorder in China undergoing enforced detoxification through machine learning. *Journal of Affective Disorders*, *320*, 628–637. DOI: 10.1016/j.jad.2022.12.050

Maas, L. C., Lukas, S. E., Kaufman, M. J., Weiss, R. D., Daniels, S. L., Rogers, V. W., & Renshaw, P. F. (1998). Functional magnetic resonance imaging of human brain activation during cue-induced cocaine craving. *The American Journal of Psychiatry*, *155*(1), 124–126. DOI: 10.1176/ajp.155.1.124

Machado, H., Silva, S., & Neiva, L. (2025). Publics' views on ethical challenges of artificial intelligence: A scoping review. *AI and Ethics*, *5*(1), 139–167. DOI: 10.1007/s43681-023-00299-6

Maia, T. V., & Frank, M. J. (2017). An integrative perspective on the role of dopamine in schizophrenia. *Biological Psychiatry*, *81*(1), 52–66.

Mak, K. K., Lee, K., & Park, C. (2019). Applications of machine learning in addiction studies: A systematic review. *Psychiatry Research*, *275*, 53–60. DOI: 10.1016/j.psychres.2019.03.001

Mak, W. W. S., Ng, S. M., & Leung, F. H. T. (2023). A Web-Based Stratified Stepped Care Platform for Mental Well-being (TourHeart+): User-Centered Research and Design. *JMIR Formative Research, 7*, e38504. DOI: 10.2196/38504 PMID: 36947112

Malgaroli, M., Hull, T. D., Zech, J. M., & Althoff, T. (2023). Natural language processing for mental health interventions: A systematic review and research framework. *Translational Psychiatry, 13*(1), 309.

Malouin-Lachance, A., Capolupo, J., Laplante, C., & Hudon, A. (2025). Does the Digital Therapeutic Alliance Exist? Integrative Review. *JMIR Mental Health, 12*, e69294–e69294. DOI: 10.2196/69294 PMID: 39924298

Mandal, A., Chakraborty, T., & Gurevych, I. (2025). *Towards Privacy-aware Mental Health AI Models: Advances*. Challenges, and Opportunities.

Manning, K. Y., Llera, A., & Lebel, C. (2025). Reliable Multimodal Brain Signatures Predict Mental Health Outcomes in Children. *Biological Psychiatry: Cognitive Neuroscience and Neuroimaging*, •••, 1–13.

Mansoor, M. A., & Ansari, K. H. (2024). Early detection of mental health crises through artificial-intelligence-powered social media analysis: A prospective observational study. *Journal of Personalized Medicine, 14*(9), 958. DOI: 10.3390/jpm14090958 PMID: 39338211

Marcovitz, D. E., McHugh, R. K., Volpe, J., Votaw, V., & Connery, H. S. (2016). Predictors of early dropout in outpatient buprenorphine/naloxone treatment. *The American Journal on Addictions, 25*(6), 472–477. DOI: 10.1111/ajad.12414

Marlatt, G. A., & Witkiewitz, K. (2005). Relapse prevention for alcohol and drug problems. In Marlatt, G. A., & Donovan, D. M. (Eds.), *Relapse prevention: Maintenance strategies in the treatment of addictive behaviors* (2nd ed., pp. 1–44). Guilford Press.

Marmar, C. R., Brown, A. D., Qian, M., Laska, E., Siegel, C., Li, M., Abu-Amara, D., Tsiartas, A., Richey, C., Smith, J., Knoth, B., & Vergyri, D. (2019). Speech-based markers for posttraumatic stress disorder in US veterans. *Depression and Anxiety, 36*(7), 607–616. DOI: 10.1002/da.22890 PMID: 31006959

Marques, L., Valentine, S. E., Kaysen, D., Mackintosh, M. A., Dixon De Silva, L. E., Ahles, E. M., Young, S. J., Shtasel, D. L., Simon, N. M., & Wiltsey-Stirman, S. (2019). Provider fidelity and modifications to cognitive processing therapy in a diverse community health clinic: Associations with clinical change. *Journal of Consulting and Clinical Psychology, 87*(4), 357–369. DOI: 10.1037/ccp0000384

Martinez-Martin, N. (2022). Minding the AI: Ethical challenges and practice for AI mental health care tools. In *Artificial intelligence in brain and mental health: Philosophical, ethical & policy issues* (pp. 111–125). Springer International Publishing.

Martinez-Martin, N., Greely, H. T., & Cho, M. K. (2021). Ethical Development of Digital Phenotyping Tools for Mental Health Applications: Delphi Study. *JMIR mHealth and uHealth*, *9*(7), e27343. DOI: 10.2196/27343

Martinez-Martin, N., Insel, T. R., Dagum, P., Greely, H. T., & Cho, M. K. (2018). Data mining for health: Staking out the ethical territory of digital phenotyping. *NPJ Digital Medicine*, *1*(1), 68. DOI: 10.1038/s41746-018-0075-8 PMID: 31211249

Martinez-Martin, N., Luo, Z., Kaushal, A., Adeli, E., Haque, A., Kelly, S. S., Wieten, S., Cho, M. K., Magnus, D., Fei-Fei, L., Schulman, K., & Milstein, A. (2021). Ethical issues in using ambient intelligence in health-care settings. *The Lancet. Digital Health*, *3*(2), e115–e123. DOI: 10.1016/S2589-7500(20)30275-2 PMID: 33358138

Martz, M. E., Hart, T., Heitzeg, M. M., & Peltier, S. J. (2020). Neuromodulation of brain activation associated with addiction: A review of real-time fMRI neurofeedback studies. *NeuroImage. Clinical*, *27*, 102350. DOI: 10.1016/j.nicl.2020.102350

Marzi, S. J., Schilder, B. M., Nott, A., Frigerio, C. S., Willaime-Morawek, S., Bucholc, M., & Llewellyn, D. J. (2023). Artificial intelligence for neurodegenerative experimental models. *Alzheimer's & Dementia*, *19*(12), 5970–5987.

Maslach, C., & Leiter, M. P. (2016). Burnout. In Stress: Concepts, cognition, emotion, and behavior (pp. 351-357). Academic Press.

Maslej, M. M., Kloiber, S., Ghassemi, M., Yu, J., & Hill, S. L. (2023). Out with AI, in with the psychiatrist: A preference for human-derived clinical decision support in depression care. *Translational Psychiatry*, *13*(1), 210. DOI: 10.1038/s41398-023-02509-z PMID: 37328465

Maté, G. (2008). *In the Realm of Hungry Ghosts: Close Encounters with Addiction.* North Atlantic Books.

Mattos, B. P., Mattjie, C., Barros, R. C., & Grassi-Oliveira, R. (2024). Craving for a robust methodology: A systematic review of machine learning algorithms on substance-use disorders treatment outcomes. *International Journal of Mental Health and Addiction.* Advance online publication. DOI: 10.1007/s11469-024-01403-z

MBDesk. (2024, October 25). Infiheal launches AI Therapist Healo at star-studded Mumbai event. MediaBrief. https://mediabrief.com/infiheal-ai-therapist-healo/

McCoy, T. H., & Perlis, R. H. (2024). Characterizing research domain criteria symptoms among psychiatric inpatients using large language models. *Journal of Mood and Anxiety Disorders*, *8*, 100079. DOI: 10.1016/j.xjmad.2024.100079 PMID: 40655912

McCradden, M. D., Baba, A., Saha, A., Ahmad, S., Boparai, K., Fadaiefard, P., & Cusimano, M. D. (2020). Ethical concerns around use of artificial intelligence in health care research from the perspective of patients with meningioma, caregivers and health care providers: A qualitative study. *CMAJ Open*, *8*(1), E90–E95. DOI: 10.9778/cmajo.20190151 PMID: 32071143

Mccradden, M., Hui, K., & Buchman, D. Z. (2023). Evidence, ethics and the promise of artificial intelligence in psychiatry. *Journal of Medical Ethics*, *49*, 573–579.

McGorry, P. D., Hartmann, J. A., Spooner, R., & Nelson, B. (2018). Beyond the "at risk mental state" concept: Transitioning to transdiagnostic psychiatry. *World Psychiatry; Official Journal of the World Psychiatric Association (WPA)*, *17*(2), 133–142. DOI: 10.1002/wps.20514 PMID: 29856558

McHugh, R. K., Murray, H. W., Hearon, B. A., Pratt, E. M., Pollack, M. H., Safren, S. A., & Otto, M. W. (2013). Predictors of dropout from psychosocial treatment in opioid-dependent outpatients. *The American Journal on Addictions*, *22*(1), 18–22. DOI: 10.1111/j.1521-0391.2013.00322.x

McKellar, J., Harris, A. H., & Moos, R. H. (2006). Predictors of outcome for patients with substance-use disorders five years after treatment dropout. *Journal of Studies on Alcohol and Drugs*, *67*(5), 685–693. DOI: 10.15288/jsa.2006.67.685

McLellan, A. T., Lewis, D. C., O'Brien, C. P., & Kleber, H. D. (2000). Drug dependence, a chronic medical illness: Implications for treatment, insurance, and outcomes evaluation. *Journal of the American Medical Association*, *284*(13), 1689–1695. DOI: 10.1001/jama.284.13.1689

Meadi, M. R., Sillekens, T., Metselaar, S., van Balkom, A., Bernstein, J., & Batelaan, N. (2025). Exploring the ethical challenges of conversational AI in mental health care: Scoping review. *JMIR Mental Health*, *12*(1), e60432.

Mehltretter, J., Rollins, C., Benrimoh, D., Fratila, R., Perlman, K., Israel, S., Miresco, M., Wakid, M., & Turecki, G. (2020). Analysis of Features Selected by a Deep Learning Model for Differential Treatment Selection in Depression. *Frontiers in Artificial Intelligence*, *2*. Advance online publication. DOI: 10.3389/frai.2019.00031

Mehrabi, N., Morstatter, F., Saxena, N., Lerman, K., & Galstyan, A. (2022). A survey on bias and fairness in machine learning. *ACM Computing Surveys*, *55*(6), 1–35. DOI: 10.1145/3457607

Mehta, A., Niles, A. N., Vargas, J. H., Marafon, T., Couto, D. D., & Gross, J. J. (2021). Acceptability and effectiveness of artificial intelligence therapy for anxiety and depression (Youper): Longitudinal observational study. *Journal of Medical Internet Research*, *23*(6), e26771. PMID: 34155984

Mendes, J. P. M., Moura, I. R., Van de Ven, P., Viana, D., Silva, F. J. S., Coutinho, L. R., Teixeira, S., Rodrigues, J. J. P. C., & Teles, A. S. (2022). Sensing Apps and Public Data Sets for Digital Phenotyping of Mental Health: Systematic Review. *Journal of Medical Internet Research*, *24*(2), e28735. DOI: 10.2196/28735 PMID: 35175202

Menon, S., Swathi, J., Anit, S. K., Nair, A. P., & Sarath, S. (2019). Driver face recognition and sober–drunk classification using thermal images. In *2019 International Conference on Communication and Signal Processing (ICCSP)* (pp. 400–404). IEEE. https://doi.org/DOI: 10.1109/ICCSP.2019.8697908

Merikangas, K. R., & Avenevoli, S. (2000). Implications of genetic epidemiology for the prevention of substance use disorders. *Addictive Behaviors*, *25*(6), 807–820. DOI: 10.1016/S0306-4603(00)00129-5

Merikangas, K. R., & McClair, V. L. (2012). Epidemiology of substance use disorders. *Human Genetics*, *131*(6), 779–789. DOI: 10.1007/s00439-012-1168-0

Miloff, A., Lindner, P., Hamilton, W., Reuterskiöld, L., Andersson, G., & Carlbring, P. (2016). Single-session gamified virtual reality exposure therapy for spider phobia vs. traditional exposure therapy: Study protocol for a randomized controlled non-inferiority trial. *Trials*, *17*(1), 60. Advance online publication. DOI: 10.1186/s13063-016-1191-6

Miner, A. S., Milstein, A., & Hancock, J. T. (2017). Talking to machines about personal mental health problems. *Journal of the American Medical Association*, *318*(13), 1217–1218.

Minerva, F., & Giubilini, A. (2023). Is AI the future of mental healthcare? *Topoi*, *42*(3), 809–817. DOI: 10.1007/s11245-023-09932-3

Mitsala, A., Tsalikidis, C., Pitiakoudis, M., Simopoulos, C., & Tsaroucha, A. K. (2021). Artificial Intelligence in Colorectal Cancer Screening, Diagnosis and Treatment. A New Era. *Current Oncology (Toronto, Ont.)*, *28*(3), 1581–1607. DOI: 10.3390/curroncol28030149 PMID: 33922402

Moghadasi, M. N., Zhuang, Y., & Gellban, H. (2020, July). Robo: A counselor chatbot for opioid-addicted patients. In *Proceedings of the 2020 2nd Symposium on Signal Processing Systems* (pp. 91–95). ACM. https://doi.org/DOI: 10.1145/3410352.3410359

Monaco, F., Vignapiano, A., Piacente, M., Pagano, C., Mancuso, C., Steardo, L.Jr, & Corrivetti, G. (2024). An advanced artificial intelligence platform for a personalised treatment of eating disorders. *Frontiers in Psychiatry*, *15*, 1414439.

Moningka, H., Lichenstein, S., Worhunsky, P. D., DeVito, E. E., Scheinost, D., & Yip, S. W. (2019). Can neuroimaging help combat the opioid epidemic? A systematic review of clinical and pharmacological challenge fMRI studies with recommendations for future research. *Neuropsychopharmacology : Official Publication of the American College of Neuropsychopharmacology*, *44*(2), 259–273. DOI: 10.1038/s41386-018-0232-4

Monroy-Fraustro, D., Maldonado-Castellanos, I., Aboites-Molina, M., Rodríguez, S., Sueiras, P., Altamirano-Bustamante, N. F., De Hoyos-Bermea, A., & Altamirano-Bustamante, M. M. (2021). Bibliotherapy as a Non-pharmaceutical Intervention to Enhance Mental Health in Response to the COVID-19 Pandemic: A Mixed-Methods Systematic Review and Bioethical Meta-Analysis. *Frontiers in Public Health*, *9*. Advance online publication. DOI: 10.3389/fpubh.2021.629872

Monson, C. M., Shields, N., Suvak, M. K., Lane, J. E. M., Shnaider, P., Landy, M. S. H., Wagner, A. C., Sijercic, I., Masina, T., Wanklyn, S. G., & Stirman, S. W. (2018). A randomized controlled effectiveness trial of training strategies in cognitive processing therapy for posttraumatic stress disorder: Impact on patient outcomes. *Behaviour Research and Therapy*, *110*, 31–40. DOI: 10.1016/j.brat.2018.08.007

Monteith, S., Glenn, T., Geddes, J., Whybrow, P. C., Achtyes, E., & Bauer, M. (2022). Expectations for Artificial Intelligence (AI) in Psychiatry. *Current Psychiatry Reports*, *24*(11), 709–721.

Moonajilin, M. S., Kamal, M. K. I., Mamun, F. A., Safiq, M. B., Hosen, I., Manzar, M. D., & Mamun, M. A. (2021). Substance use behavior and its lifestyle-related risk factors in Bangladeshi high school-going adolescents: An exploratory study. *PLoS One*, *16*(7), e0254926. DOI: 10.1371/journal.pone.0254926

Mörch, C.-M., Gupta, A., & Mishara, B. L. (2020). Canada protocol: An ethical checklist for the use of artificial Intelligence in suicide prevention and mental health. *Artificial Intelligence in Medicine*, *108*, 101934. DOI: 10.1016/j.artmed.2020.101934 PMID: 32972663

Morel, T., Cornet, V., & Nguyen, T. (2020). Predicting hospital readmissions among patients with substance use and mental health disorders using machine learning. *International Journal of Medical Informatics*, *141*, 104225. DOI: 10.1016/j.ijmedinf.2020.104225

Moreno-Agostino, D., Wu, Y., Daskalopoulou, C., Hasan, M. T., Huisman, M., & Prina, M. (2020). Global trends in the prevalence and incidence of depression:a systematic review and meta-analysis. *Journal of Affective Disorders*, *281*, 235–243. DOI: 10.1016/j.jad.2020.12.035

Moreno, H. R., & Plant, R. T. (1993). A prototype decision support system for differential diagnosis of psychotic, mood, and organic mental disorders. *Medical Decision Making*, *13*(1), 43–48. DOI: 10.1177/0272989X9301300106

Moriarty, A. S., Meader, N., Snell, K. I. E., Riley, R. D., Paton, L. W., Dawson, S., Hendon, J., Chew-Graham, C. A., Gilbody, S., Churchill, R., Phillips, R. S., Ali, S., & McMillan, D. (2022). Predicting relapse or recurrence of depression: Systematic review of prognostic models. *The British Journal of Psychiatry*, *221*(2), 448–458. DOI: 10.1192/bjp.2021.218 PMID: 35048843

Mullerpattan, G. S., Pearala, N., Shetty, T., Hegde, P. R., Patley, R., Manjunatha, N., Math, S. B., & Kumar, C. N. (2025). Trainers' Perspectives Towards Digital Mental Health Training for Primary Care Providers: Insights from Focused Group Discussion. *Indian Journal of Psychological Medicine*. Advance online publication. DOI: 10.1177/02537176251360938

Murphy, D., & Busuttil, W. (2014). PTSD, stigma and barriers to help-seeking within the UK Armed Forces. *Journal of the Royal Army Medical Corps*, *161*(4), 322–326. DOI: 10.1136/jramc-2014-000344

Murphy, K. P. (2012). *Machine learning: A probabilistic perspective*. MIT Press.

Na, H., Hua, Y., Wang, Z., Shen, T., Yu, B., Wang, L., Wang, W., Torous, J., & Chen, L. (2025). *A Survey of Large Language Models in Psychotherapy: Current Landscape and Future Directions*.

Nadeem, A., Abedin, B., & Marjanovic, O. (2020). Gender bias in AI: A review of contributing factors and mitigating strategies. *ACIS 2020 Proceedings*. 27.

Naeger, S., Mutter, R., Ali, M. M., Mark, T., & Hughey, L. (2016). Post-discharge treatment engagement among patients with an opioid-use disorder. *Journal of Substance Abuse Treatment*, *69*, 64–71. DOI: 10.1016/j.jsat.2016.07.004

Nahum-Shani, I., Smith, S. N., Spring, B. J., Collins, L. M., Witkiewitz, K., Tewari, A., & Murphy, S. A. (2018). Just-in-Time Adaptive Interventions (JITAIs) in Mobile Health: Key Components and Design Principles for Ongoing Health Behavior Support. *Annals of Behavioral Medicine*, *52*(6), 446–462. DOI: 10.1007/s12160-016-9830-8 PMID: 27663578

Nasir, M., Summerfield, N. S., Oztekin, A., Knight, M., Ackerson, L. K., & Carreiro, S. (2021). Machine learning–based outcome prediction and novel hypotheses generation for substance use disorder treatment. *Journal of the American Medical Informatics Association : JAMIA*, *28*(6), 1216–1224. DOI: 10.1093/jamia/ocab008

Naslund, J. A., Aschbrenner, K. A., Kim, S. J., McHugo, G. J., Unützer, J., Bartels, S. J., & Marsch, L. A. (2017). Health behavior models for informing digital technology interventions for individuals with mental illness. *Psychiatric Rehabilitation Journal*, *40*(3), 325.

Nasrallah, H. A. (2021). Re-Inventing the Dsm as A Transdiagnostic Model: Psychiatric Disorders Are Extensively Interconnected. *Annals of Clinical Psychiatry*, *33*(3), 148–150. DOI: 10.12788/acp.0037 PMID: 34398730

National Academies of Sciences, Engineering, and Medicine. (2019). The Promise of Adolescence: Realizing Opportunity for All Youth. Washington, DC: The National Academies Press. https://doi.org/DOI: 10.17226/25388

National Institute on Drug Abuse. (2018). Principles of drug addiction treatment: A research-based guide (3rd ed.). https://nida.nih.gov/publications/principles-drug-addiction-treatment-research-based-guide-third-edition

National Institute on Drug Abuse. (2020). Drugs, brains, and behavior: The science of addiction. https://nida.nih.gov/publications/drugs-brains-behavior-science-addiction

National Institute on Drug Abuse. (2023). Monitoring the Future Survey: Trends in Prevalence of Various Drugs. https://nida.nih.gov/drug-topics/trends-statistics/monitoring-future

National Institute on Drug Abuse. (2023). *Substance use disorder: Clinical and public health approaches.* National Institutes of Health. https://nida.nih.gov/publications

Nazari, S., Pourmand, S. M., Makki, S. M., Brand, S., & Vousooghi, N. (2022). Potential biomarkers of addiction identified by real-time PCR in human peripheral blood lymphocytes: A narrative review. *Biomarkers in Medicine*, *16*(9), 739–758. DOI: 10.2217/bmm-2021-0291

Nemesure, M. D., Heinz, M. V., Huang, R., & Jacobson, N. C. (2021). Predictive modeling of depression and anxiety using electronic health records and a novel machine learning approach with artificial intelligence. *Scientific Reports*, *11*(1), 1980. DOI: 10.1038/s41598-021-81368-4

Nickson, D., Meyer, C., Walasek, L., & Toro, C. (2023). Prediction and diagnosis of depression using machine learning with electronic health records data: A systematic review. *BMC Medical Informatics and Decision Making*, *23*(1), 271. DOI: 10.1186/s12911-023-02341-x

Nicol, G., Wang, R., Graham, S., Dodd, S., & Garbutt, J. (2022). Chatbot-Delivered Cognitive Behavioral Therapy in Adolescents With Depression and Anxiety During the COVID-19 Pandemic: Feasibility and Acceptability Study. *JMIR Formative Research*, *6*(11), e40242. DOI: 10.2196/40242

Nilsen, P., Svedberg, P., Nygren, J., Frideros, M., Johansson, J., & Schueller, S. (2022). Accelerating the impact of artificial intelligence in mental healthcare through implementation science. *Implementation Research and Practice*, *3*, 26334895221112033. Advance online publication. DOI: 10.1177/26334895221112033

Nochaiwong, S., Ruengorn, C., Thavorn, K., Hutton, B., Awiphan, R., Phosuya, C., Ruanta, Y., Wongpakaran, N., & Wongpakaran, T. (2021). Global prevalence of mental health issues among the general population during the coronavirus disease-2019 pandemic: A systematic review and meta-analysis. *Scientific Reports*, *11*(1), 1–18.

Norcross, J. C., & Lambert, M. J. (2019). What works in the psychotherapy relationship: Results, conclusions, and practices.

Nordheim, K., Walderhaug, E., Alstadius, S., Kern-Godal, A., Arnevik, E., & Duckert, F. (2018). Young adults' reasons for dropout from residential substance use disorder treatment. *Qualitative Social Work: Research and Practice*, *17*(1), 24–40. DOI: 10.1177/1473325016654559

Norman, S. B., Tate, S. R., Anderson, K. G., & Brown, S. A. (2007). Do trauma history and PTSD symptoms influence addiction relapse context? *Drug and Alcohol Dependence*, *90*(1), 89–96. DOI: 10.1016/j.drugalcdep.2007.03.002

Norori, N., Hu, Q., Aellen, F. M., Faraci, F. D., & Tzovara, A. (2021). Addressing bias in big data and AI for health care: A call for open science. *Patterns (New York, N.Y.)*, *2*(10), 100347. DOI: 10.1016/j.patter.2021.100347 PMID: 34693373

O'Connor, S., & Liu, H. (2024). Gender bias perpetuation and mitigation in AI technologies: Challenges and opportunities. *AI & Society*, *39*(4), 2045–2057. DOI: 10.1007/s00146-023-01675-4

O'Leary, A., Lahey, T., Lovato, J., Loftness, B., Douglas, A., Skelton, J., Cohen, J. G., Copeland, W. E., McGinnis, R. S., & McGinnis, E. W. (2024). Using Wearable Digital Devices to Screen Children for Mental Health Conditions: Ethical Promises and Challenges. *Sensors (Basel), 24*(10), 3214. DOI: 10.3390/s24103214 PMID: 38794067

Ogbo, F. A., Mathsyaraja, S., Koti, R. K., Perz, J., & Page, A. (2018). The burden of depressive disorders in South Asia, 1990–2016: Findings from the global burden of disease study. *BMC Psychiatry, 18*(1). Advance online publication. DOI: 10.1186/s12888-018-1918-1

Ogilvie, L., Prescott, J., & Carson, J. (2022). The use of chatbots as supportive agents for people seeking help with substance use disorder: A systematic review. *European Addiction Research, 28*(6), 405–418. DOI: 10.1159/000525460

Ogilvie, L., Prescott, J., & Carson, J. (2025). An overview of the applied use of chatbots for substance use disorder: Past, present and future. *Counselling & Psychotherapy Research, 25*, e12786. DOI: 10.1002/capr.12786

Oh, S., Joung, Y. S., Chung, T. M., Lee, J., Seok, B. J., Kim, N., & Son, H. M. (2024). Diagnosis of ADHD using virtual reality and artificial intelligence: An exploratory study of clinical applications. *Frontiers in Psychiatry, 15*, 1383547.

Okpete, U. E., & Byeon, H. (2024). Challenges and prospects in bridging precision medicine and artificial intelligence in genomic psychiatric treatment. *World Journal of Psychiatry, 14*(8), 1148–1164. DOI: 10.5498/wjp.v14.i8.1148

Olah, J., Diederen, K., Gibbs-Dean, T., Kempton, M. J., Dobson, R., Spencer, T., & Cummins, N. (2023). Online speech assessment of the psychotic spectrum: Exploring the relationship between overlapping acoustic markers of schizotypy, depression and anxiety. *Schizophrenia Research, 259*, 11–19. DOI: 10.1016/j.schres.2023.03.044 PMID: 37080802

Olah, J., Spencer, T., Cummins, N., & Diederen, K. (2024). Automated analysis of speech as a marker of sub-clinical psychotic experiences. *Frontiers in Psychiatry, 14*. Advance online publication. DOI: 10.3389/fpsyt.2023.1265880 PMID: 38361830

Olawade, D. B., Wada, O. Z., Odetayo, A., David-Olawade, A. C., Asaolu, F., & Eberhardt, J. (2024). Enhancing mental health with artificial intelligence: Current trends and future prospects. *Journal of Medicine, Surgery, and Public Health, 3*, 100099. DOI: 10.1016/j.glmedi.2024.100099

Oliver, R., Pérez-Sabater, J., Paz-Arbaizar, L., Herrero-Quevedo, D., Artés-Rodríguez, A., Lancho, A., & Olmos, P. M. (2025). *A Vector-Quantized Foundation Model for Patient Behavior Monitoring*.

Omarov, B., Zhumanov, Z., Gumar, A., & Kuntunova, L. (2023). Artificial intelligence enabled mobile chatbot psychologist using AIML and cognitive behavioral therapy. *International Journal of Advanced Computer Science and Applications*, *14*(6), 137–146. DOI: 10.14569/ijacsa.2023.0140616

Onnela, J. P., & Rauch, S. L. (2016). Harnessing smartphone-based digital phenotyping to enhance behavioral and mental health. *Neuropsychopharmacology : Official Publication of the American College of Neuropsychopharmacology*, *41*(7), 1691–1696.

Onnela, J.-P., & Rauch, S. L. (2016). Harnessing Smartphone-Based Digital Phenotyping to Enhance Behavioral and Mental Health. *Neuropsychopharmacology : Official Publication of the American College of Neuropsychopharmacology*, *41*(7), 1691–1696. DOI: 10.1038/npp.2016.7

Orji, R., & Moffatt, K. (2018). Persuasive technology for health and wellness: State-of-the-art and emerging trends. *Health Informatics Journal*, *24*(1), 66–91.

Ostojic, D., Lalousis, P. A., Donohoe, G., & Morris, D. W. (2024). The challenges of using machine learning models in psychiatric research and clinical practice. *European Neuropsychopharmacology*, *88*(January), 53–65.

Ouimette, P., Coolhart, D., Funderburk, J. S., Wade, M., & Brown, P. J. (2007). Precipitants of first substance use in recently abstinent substance use disorder patients with PTSD. *Addictive Behaviors*, *32*(8), 1719–1727. DOI: 10.1016/j.addbeh.2006.11.020

Pandi, M.-T., Koromina, M., Tsafaridis, I., Patsilinakos, S., Christoforou, E., van der Spek, P. J., & Patrinos, G. P. (2021). A novel machine learning-based approach for the computational functional assessment of pharmacogenomic variants. *Human Genomics*, *15*(1), 51. DOI: 10.1186/s40246-021-00352-1

Panlilio, L., Stull, S., Bertz, J., Burgess-Hull, A., Kowalczyk, W., Phillips, K., & Preston, K. (2020). Beyond abstinence and relapse: Cluster analysis of drug-use patterns during treatment as an outcome measure for clinical trials. *Psychopharmacology*, *237*(11), 3369–3381. DOI: 10.1007/s00213-020-05618-5

Pan, Y., Feaster, D. J., Odom, G., Brandt, L., Hu, M. C., Weiss, R. D., & Balise, R. R. (2022). Specific polysubstance use patterns predict relapse among patients entering opioid use disorder treatment. *Drug and Alcohol Dependence Reports*, *5*, 100128. DOI: 10.1016/j.dadr.2022.100128

Papamalis, F. E., Kalyva, E., Teare, M. D., & Meier, P. S. (2020). The role of personality functioning in drug misuse treatment engagement. *Addiction (Abingdon, England)*, *115*(4), 726–739. DOI: 10.1111/add.14872

Paraschiv, E. A., Băjenaru, L., Petrache, C., Bica, O., & Nicolau, D. N. (2024). AI-driven neuro-monitoring: Advancing schizophrenia detection and management through deep learning and EEG analysis. *Future Internet*, *16*(11), 424.

Pardiñas, A. F., Owen, M. J., & Walters, J. T. R. (2021). Pharmacogenomics: A road ahead for precision medicine in psychiatry. *Neuron*, *109*(24), 3914–3929. DOI: 10.1016/j.neuron.2021.09.011

Park, J., Arunachalam, R., Silenzio, V., & Singh, V. K. (2022). Fairness in Mobile Phone–Based Mental Health Assessment Algorithms: Exploratory Study. *JMIR Formative Research*, *6*(6), e34366. DOI: 10.2196/34366 PMID: 35699997

Park, S.-C., & Kim, Y.-K. (2020). *Anxiety Disorders in the DSM-5: Changes*. Controversies, and Future Directions., DOI: 10.1007/978-981-32-9705-0_12

Parra, F., Benezeth, Y., & Yang, F. (2022). Automatic Assessment of Emotion Dysregulation in American, French, and Tunisian Adults and New Developments in Deep Multimodal Fusion: Cross-sectional Study. *JMIR Mental Health*, *9*(1), e34333. DOI: 10.2196/34333

Patel, V.. (2018). The Lancet Commission on Global Mental Health and Sustainable Development. *Lancet*, *392*(10157), 1553–1598. DOI: 10.1016/S0140-6736(18)31612-X

Pavez, J., & Allende, H. (2024). A Hybrid System Based on Bayesian Networks and Deep Learning for Explainable Mental Health Diagnosis. *Applied Sciences (Basel, Switzerland)*, *14*(18), 8283. DOI: 10.3390/app14188283

Pavlopoulos, A., Rachiotis, T., & Maglogiannis, I. (2024). An Overview of Tools and Technologies for Anxiety and Depression Management Using AI. *Applied Sciences (Basel, Switzerland)*, *14*(19), 9068. DOI: 10.3390/app14199068

Pearson, R., Pisner, D., Meyer, B., Shumake, J., & Beevers, C. G. (2019). A machine learning ensemble to predict treatment outcomes following an Internet intervention for depression. *Psychological Medicine*, *49*(14), 2330–2341. DOI: 10.1017/S003329171800315X

Pelham, W. E.Jr, Fabiano, G. A., & Massetti, G. M. (2005). Evidence-based assessment of attention deficit hyperactivity disorder in children and adolescents. *Journal of Clinical Child and Adolescent Psychology*, *34*(3), 449–476.

Penedo, J. M. G., Rubel, J., Meglio, M., Bornhauser, L., Krieger, T., Babl, A., Muiños, R., Roussos, A., Delgadillo, J., Flückiger, C., Berger, T., Lutz, W., & Grosse Holtforth, M. (2023). Using machine learning algorithms to predict the effects of change processes in psychotherapy: Toward process-level treatment personalization. *Psychotherapy (Chicago, Ill.)*, *60*(4), 536–547. DOI: 10.1037/pst0000507

Pennebaker, J. W., & Chung, C. K. (2013). 18 Expressive writing: Connections physical and mental health to. The Oxford handbook of health psychology, 417.

Perlis, R. H. (2016). Abandoning personalization to get to precision in the pharmacotherapy of depression. *World Psychiatry; Official Journal of the World Psychiatric Association (WPA)*, *15*(3), 228–235. DOI: 10.1002/wps.20345

Perlis, R. H., Goldberg, J. F., Ostacher, M. J., & Schneck, C. D. (2024). Clinical decision support for bipolar depression using large language models. *Neuropsychopharmacology : Official Publication of the American College of Neuropsychopharmacology*, *49*(9), 1412–1416. DOI: 10.1038/s41386-024-01841-2

Perlis, R. H., Verhaak, P. F., Goldberg, J., Cusin, C., Ostacher, M., Malhi, G. S., Zarate, C. A., Shelton, R. C., Iosifescu, D. V., Tohen, M., Jha, M. K., Sajatovic, M., & Berk, M. (2025). Clinical decision support for pharmacologic management of treatment-resistant depression with augmented large language models. *Journal of Mood and Anxiety Disorders*, *12*, 100142. DOI: 10.1016/j.xjmad.2025.100142

Pesapane, F., Bracchi, D. A., Mulligan, J. F., Linnikov, A., Maslennikov, O., Lanzavecchia, M. B., Tantrige, P., Stasolla, A., Biondetti, P., Giuggioli, P. F., Cassano, E., & Carrafiello, G. (2021). Legal and Regulatory Framework for AI Solutions in Healthcare in EU, US, China, and Russia: New Scenarios after a Pandemic. *Radiation*, *1*(4), 261–276. DOI: 10.3390/radiation1040022

Peterson, L. E. (2009). K-nearest neighbor. *Scholarpedia*, *4*(2), 1883. DOI: 10.4249/scholarpedia.1883

Pham, H., Zhou, Y., Mahmood, Z., & Radev, D. (2024). A fully generative motivational interviewing counsellor chatbot. arXiv preprint arXiv:2401.10075.

Pham, T., Tran, T., Luo, W., & Venkatesh, S. (2020). Deepcare: A deep dynamic memory model for predictive medicine. *arXiv*. https://arxiv.org/abs/2007.02064

Piette, J. D., Newman, S., Krein, S. L., Marinec, N., Chen, J., Williams, D. A., Edmond, S. N., Driscoll, M., LaChappelle, K. M., Kerns, R. D., Maly, M., Kim, H. M., Farris, K. B., Higgins, D. M., Buta, E., & Heapy, A. A. (2022). Patient-Centered Pain Care Using Artificial Intelligence and Mobile Health Tools. *JAMA Internal Medicine*, *182*(9), 975. DOI: 10.1001/jamainternmed.2022.3178

Pirro, V., Oliveri, P., Sciutteri, B., Salvo, R., Salomone, A., Lanteri, S., & Vincenti, M. (2013). Multivariate strategies for screening evaluation of harmful drinking. *Bioanalysis*, *5*(6), 687–699. DOI: 10.4155/bio.13.12

Plitta, M., Barnes, K. A., Wallace, G. L., Kenworthy, L., & Martin, A. (2015). Resting-state functional connectivity predicts longitudinal change in autistic traits and adaptive functioning in autism. *Proceedings of the National Academy of Sciences of the United States of America*, *112*(48), E6699–E6706.

Polcin, D. L., & Korcha, R. (2017). Housing status, psychiatric symptoms, and substance abuse outcomes among sober living house residents over 18 months. *Addictive Disorders & Their Treatment*, *16*(3), 138–150. DOI: 10.1097/ADT.0000000000000105

Popat, R., & Ive, J. (2023). Embracing the uncertainty in human-machine collaboration to support clinical decision-making for mental health conditions. *Frontiers in Digital Health*, *5*, 1188338. DOI: 10.3389/fdgth.2023.1188338 PMID: 37731823

Poudel, U., Jakhar, S., Mohan, P., & Nepal, A. (2025). AI in Mental Health: A Review of Technological Advancements and Ethical Issues in Psychiatry. *Issues in Mental Health Nursing*, •••, 1–9.

Prochaska, J. J., Vogel, E. A., Chieng, A., Kendra, M., Baiocchi, M., Pajarito, S., & Robinson, A. (2021). A therapeutic relational agent for reducing problematic substance use (Woebot): Development and usability study. *Journal of Medical Internet Research*, *23*(3), e24850. PMID: 33755028

Prochaska, J., Vogel, E., Chieng, A., Kendra, M., Baiocchi, M., & Malalang, D.. (2021). A randomized controlled trial of a therapeutic relational agent for reducing substance misuse during the COVID-19 pandemic. *Drug and Alcohol Dependence*, *227*, 108986. DOI: 10.1016/j.drugalcdep.2021.108986

Prokhorenkova, L., Gusev, G., Vorobev, A., Dorogush, A. V., & Gulin, A. (2018). CatBoost: Unbiased boosting with categorical features. *Advances in Neural Information Processing Systems*, *31*, 6638–6648.

Purgato, M., Tedeschi, F., Turrini, G., Cadorin, C., Compri, B., Muriago, G., Ostuzzi, G., Pinucci, I., Prina, E., Serra, R., Tarsitani, L., Witteveen, A. B., Roversi, A., Melchior, M., McDaid, D., Park, A., Petri-Romão, P., Kalisch, R., Underhill, J., & Barbui, C. (2025). Effectiveness of a stepped-care programme of WHO psychological interventions in a population of migrants: Results from the RESPOND randomized controlled trial. *World Psychiatry; Official Journal of the World Psychiatric Association (WPA), 24*(1), 120–130. DOI: 10.1002/wps.21281 PMID: 39810692

Purificato, E., Boratto, L., & De Luca, E. W. (2024). User modeling and user profiling: A comprehensive survey. *arXiv*. https://doi.org//arXiv.2402.09660DOI: 10.48550

Putica, A., Khanna, R., Bosl, W., Saraf, S., & Edgcomb, J. (2025). Ethical decision-making for AI in mental health: The Integrated Ethical Approach for Computational Psychiatry (IEACP) framework. *Psychological Medicine, 55*, e213. DOI: 10.1017/S0033291725101311 PMID: 40702980

Quaak, M., Van De Mortel, L., Thomas, R. M., & Van Wingen, G. (2021). Deep learning applications for the classification of psychiatric disorders using neuroimaging data: Systematic review and meta-analysis. *NeuroImage. Clinical, 30*, 102584.

Quintanilla, M. E., Morales, P., Santapau, D., Ávila, A., Ponce, C., Berrios-Cárcamo, P., & Ezquer, F. (2023). Chronic voluntary morphine intake is associated with changes in brain structures involved in drug dependence in a rat model of polydrug use. *International Journal of Molecular Sciences, 24*(23), 17081. DOI: 10.3390/ijms242317081

Rabinowitz, J. A., Wells, J. L., Strickland, J. C., Hochheimer, M., Kahn, G., Ellis, J. D., & Huhn, A. S. (2025). Predictors of treatment attrition among individuals in substance use disorder treatment: A machine learning approach. *Addictive Behaviors, 163*, 108265. DOI: 10.1016/j.addbeh.2024.107865

Radanliev, P. (2025). Ethical methodologies for digital identity privacy in AI-driven dance movement therapy as a preventative mental health mechanism in the extended reality. *Frontiers in Virtual Reality, 6*. Advance online publication. DOI: 10.3389/frvir.2025.1589744

Rahsepar Meadi, M., Sillekens, T., Metselaar, S., van Balkom, A., Bernstein, J., & Batelaan, N. (2025). Exploring the Ethical Challenges of Conversational AI in Mental Health Care: Scoping Review. *JMIR Mental Health, 12*, e60432. DOI: 10.2196/60432 PMID: 39983102

Rajapaksha, R. M. D. S., Filbey, F., Biswas, S., & Choudhary, P. (2022). A Bayesian learning model to predict the risk for cannabis use disorder. *Drug and Alcohol Dependence, 236*, 109476. DOI: 10.1016/j.drugalcdep.2022.109476

Rajkomar, A., Dean, J., & Kohane, I. (2019). Machine learning in medicine. *The New England Journal of Medicine, 380*(14), 1347–1359. DOI: 10.1056/NEJMra1814259

Rasheed, S. (2021). A review of the role of machine learning techniques towards brain–computer interface applications. *Machine Learning and Knowledge Extraction, 3*(4), 835–862.

Ray, A., Bhardwaj, A., Malik, Y. K., Singh, S., & Gupta, R. (2022). Artificial intelligence and Psychiatry: An overview. *Asian Journal of Psychiatry, 70*, 103021.

Rector, A., Minor, K., Minor, K., McCormack, J., Breeden, B., Nowers, R., & Dorris, J. (2025). *Validating Pharmacogenomics Generative Artificial Intelligence Query Prompts Using Retrieval-Augmented Generation*. RAG.

Reece, A. G., Reagan, A. J., Lix, K. L. M., Dodds, P. S., Danforth, C. M., & Langer, E. J. (2016). *Forecasting the onset and course of mental illness with Twitter data*. arXiv. https://arxiv.org/abs/1608.07740

Regier, D. A., Narrow, W. E., Clarke, D. E., Kraemer, H. C., Kuramoto, S. J., Kuhl, E. A., & Kupfer, D. J. (2013). DSM-5 Field Trials in the United States and Canada, Part II: Test-Retest Reliability of Selected Categorical Diagnoses. *The American Journal of Psychiatry, 170*(1), 59–70. DOI: 10.1176/appi.ajp.2012.12070999

Richter, L., Pugh, B. S., & Ball, S. A. (2017). Assessing the risk of marijuana use disorder among adolescents and adults who use marijuana. *The American Journal of Drug and Alcohol Abuse, 43*(3), 247–260. DOI: 10.1080/00952990.2016.1263640

Richter, T., Fishbain, B., Richter-Levin, G., & Okon-Singer, H. (2021). Machine Learning-Based Behavioral Diagnostic Tools for Depression: Advances, challenges, and future directions. *Journal of Personalized Medicine, 11*(10), 957. DOI: 10.3390/jpm11100957

Rizzo, A. S., & Shilling, R. (2017). Clinical virtual reality tools to advance the prevention, assessment, and treatment of PTSD. European Journal of Psychotraumatology, 8(sup5). *Article, 1414560*. Advance online publication. DOI: 10.1080/20008198.2017.1414560

Roberts, W., Zhao, Y., Verplaetse, T., Moore, K., Peltier, M., Burke, C., & McKee, S. (2022). Using machine learning to predict heavy drinking during outpatient alcohol treatment. *Alcohol, Clinical and Experimental Research, 46*(4), 657–666. DOI: 10.1111/acer.14802

Rodríguez-Martínez, A., Amezcua-Aguilar, T., Cortés-Moreno, J., & Jiménez-Delgado, J. J. (2023). Qualitative analysis of conversational chatbots to alleviate loneliness in older adults as a strategy for emotional health. *Healthcare (Basel, Switzerland), 12*(1), 62. DOI: 10.3390/healthcare12010062

Roepke, A. M., Jaffee, S. R., Riffle, O. M., McGonigal, J., Broome, R., & Maxwell, B. (2015). Randomized controlled trial of SuperBetter, a smartphone-based/internet-based self-help tool to reduce depressive symptoms. *Games for Health Journal, 4*(3), 235–246. DOI: 10.1089/g4h.2014.0046

Roesler, D., Johnny, S., Conway, M., & Chen, A. T. (2024). A theory-informed deep learning approach to extracting and characterizing substance use related stigma in social media. *BMC Digital Health, 2*, 60. DOI: 10.1186/s44247-024-00065-0

Rogan, J., Bucci, S., & Firth, J. (2024). Health Care Professionals' Views on the Use of Passive Sensing, AI, and Machine Learning in Mental Health Care: Systematic Review With Meta-Synthesis. *JMIR Mental Health, 11*, e49577. DOI: 10.2196/49577

Rooksby, J., Morrison, A., & Murray-Rust, D. (2019). Student Perspectives on Digital Phenotyping. *Proceedings of the 2019 CHI Conference on Human Factors in Computing Systems*, 1–14. https://doi.org/DOI: 10.1145/3290605.3300655

Royal College of Psychiatrists. (2022). Two-thirds of vacant children's mental health roles unfilled. https://www.rcpsych.ac.uk/news-and-features/latest-news/detail/2022/01/07/two-thirds-of-vacant-children-s-mental-health-roles-unfilled

Ruan, F. Y., Zhang, A., Oh, J. Y., Jin, S., & Jacobson, N. C. (2025). *Foundation Models for Wearable Movement Data in Mental Health Research.*

Ruan, Z., Seger, C. A., Yang, Q., Kim, D., Lee, S. W., Chen, Q., & Peng, Z. (2023). Impairment of arbitration between model-based and model-free reinforcement learning in obsessive–compulsive disorder. *Frontiers in Psychiatry, 14*, 1162800.

Rubel, J. A., Zilcha-Mano, S., Giesemann, J., Prinz, J., & Lutz, W. (2020). Predicting personalized process–outcome associations in psychotherapy using machine learning approaches—A demonstration. *Psychotherapy Research, 30*(3), 300–309. DOI: 10.1080/10503307.2019.1597994

Rucker, D. C., & Webster, R. J.III. (2011). Statics and dynamics of continuum robots with general tendon routing and external loading. *IEEE Transactions on Robotics, 27*(6), 1033–1044.

Rush, A. J., Trivedi, M. H., Wisniewski, S. R., Nierenberg, A. A., Stewart, J. W., Warden, D., Niederehe, G., Thase, M. E., Lavori, P. W., Lebowitz, B. D., McGrath, P. J., Rosenbaum, J. F., Sackeim, H. A., Kupfer, D. J., Luther, J., & Fava, M. (2006). Acute and Longer-Term Outcomes in Depressed Outpatients Requiring One or Several Treatment Steps: A STAR*D Report. *The American Journal of Psychiatry, 163*(11), 1905–1917. DOI: 10.1176/ajp.2006.163.11.1905

Rutledge, R. B., Chekroud, A. M., & Huys, Q. J. (2019). Machine learning and big data in psychiatry: Toward clinical applications. *Current Opinion in Neurobiology, 55*, 152–159. DOI: 10.1016/j.conb.2019.02.006 PMID: 30999271

Rządeczka, M., Sterna, A., Stolińska, J., Kaczyńska, P., & Moskalewicz, M. (2024). The efficacy of conversational artificial intelligence in rectifying the theory of mind and autonomy biases: Comparative analysis. *arXiv preprint arXiv:2406.13813*. https://arxiv.org/abs/2406.13813

Sabry, F., Eltaras, T., Labda, W., Alzoubi, K., & Malluhi, Q. (2022). Machine learning for healthcare wearable devices: The big picture. *Journal of Healthcare Engineering, 2022*, 4653923. Advance online publication. DOI: 10.1155/2022/4653923

Sadeghi, M., Richer, R., Egger, B., Schindler-Gmelch, L., Rupp, L. H., Rahimi, F., ... & Eskofier, B. M. (2024). Harnessing multimodal approaches for depression detection using large language models and facial expressions. *npj Mental Health Research, 3*(1), 66.

Saeidnia, H. R., Hashemi Fotami, S. G., Lund, B., & Ghiasi, N. (2024). Ethical Considerations in Artificial Intelligence Interventions for Mental Health and Well-Being: Ensuring Responsible Implementation and Impact. *Social Sciences, 13*(7), 381.

Saeidnia, H. R., Hashemi Fotami, S. G., Lund, B., & Ghiasi, N. (2024). Ethical considerations in artificial intelligence interventions for mental health and well-being: Ensuring responsible implementation and impact. *Social Sciences, 13*(7), 381. DOI: 10.3390/socsci13070381

Sallam, M. (2023). ChatGPT utility in health care education, research, and practice: Systematic review on the promising perspectives and valid concerns. *Health Care, 11*(6), 887. DOI: 10.3390/healthcare11060887 PMID: 36981544

Salyers, A. J., Bull, S., Silvasstar, J., Howell, K., Wright, T., & Banaei-Kashani, F. (2025). Building and beta-testing Be Well Buddy Chatbot, a secure, credible and trustworthy AI chatbot that will not misinform, hallucinate or stigmatize substance use disorder: Development and usability study. *JMIR Human Factors, 12*, e69144. DOI: 10.2196/69144

Santomauro, D. F.. (2021). Global prevalence and burden of depressive and anxiety disorders in 204 countries and territories in 2020 due to the COVID-19 pandemic. *Lancet*, *398*(10312), 1700–1712. DOI: 10.1016/S0140-6736(21)02143-7

Sasikala, D. B., & Sachan, S. (2024). Decoding Decision-making: Embracing Explainable AI for Trust and Transparency. In *Exploring the Frontiers of Artificial Intelligence and Machine Learning Technologies*. San International Scientific Publications. https://doi.org/DOI: 10.59646/efaimltC3/133

Scassellati, B., Admoni, H., & Matarić, M. (2012). Robots for use in autism research. *Annual Review of Biomedical Engineering*, *14*(1), 275–294.

Scassellati, B., Boccanfuso, L., Huang, C. M., Mademtzi, M., Qin, M., Salomons, N., & Shic, F. (2018). Improving social skills in children with ASD using a long-term, in-home social robot. *Science Robotics*, *3*(21), eaat7544.

Schacht, J. P., Anton, R. F., & Myrick, H. (2013). Functional neuroimaging studies of alcohol cue reactivity: A quantitative meta-analysis and systematic review. *Addiction Biology*, *18*(1), 121–133. DOI: 10.1111/j.1369-1600.2012.00464

Schmidt, P., Biessmann, F., & Teubner, T. (2020). Transparency and trust in artificial intelligence systems. *Journal of Decision Systems*, *29*(4), 260–278. DOI: 10.1080/12460125.2020.1819094

Schultebraucks, K., Yadav, V., Shalev, A. Y., Bonanno, G. A., & Galatzer-Levy, I. R. (2022). Deep learning-based classification of posttraumatic stress disorder and depression following trauma utilizing visual and auditory markers of arousal and mood. *Psychological Medicine*, *52*(5), 957–967. DOI: 10.1017/S0033291720002718 PMID: 32744201

Sedlakova, J., & Trachsel, M. (2022). Conversational artificial intelligence in psychotherapy: A new therapeutic tool or agent? *The American Journal of Bioethics*, *23*(5), 4–13. DOI: 10.1080/15265161.2022.2048739

Sentinella-Jerbić, F. (2024). *EXPLAINABILITY OF MACHINE LEARNING MODELS IN PREDICTION OF AFFECTIVEDISORDERS* (Doctoral dissertation, Fakultet elektrotehnike i računarstva). https://repozitorij.fer.unizg.hr/en/islandora/object/fer%3A12717/datastream/PDF/view

Seo, D., Lacadie, C. M., Tuit, K., Hong, K. I., Constable, R. T., & Sinha, R. (2013). Disrupted ventromedial prefrontal function, alcohol craving, and subsequent relapse risk. *JAMA Psychiatry*, *70*(7), 727–739. DOI: 10.1001/jamapsychiatry.2013.762

Sethuraman, D., Ananya, E., Jeffrey, J. J., Thangavel, S. K., Rangasami, P., & Somasundaram, K. (2025). Framework for drug user analysis and prediction. In *Proceedings of the Fourth International Conference on Sentiment Analysis and Deep Learning (ICSADL-2025)*. IEEE. https://doi.org/DOI: 10.1109/ICSADL.2025.1234567

Shabankareh, M., Khamoushi Sahne, S. S., Nazarian, A., & Foroudi, P. (2025). The impact of AI perceived transparency on trust in AI recommendations in healthcare applications. *Asia-Pacific Journal of Business Administration*. Advance online publication. DOI: 10.1108/APJBA-12-2024-0690

Shah, S. T. H., Shah, S. A. H., Panagiotopoulos, K., Pigueiras-del-Real, J., Qayyum, K., Shah, S. B. H., & Deriu, M. A. (2025). Artificial intelligence coupled with the Internet of Things targeting neurodevelopmental challenges in preterm neonates. *Journal of Multiscale Neuroscience*, *4*(1).

Shaik, T., Tao, X., Higgins, N., Gururajan, R., Li, Y., Zhou, X., & Acharya, U. R. (2022). *FedStack: Personalized activity monitoring using stacked federated learning*. https://doi.org/DOI: 10.1016/j.knosys.2022.109929

Sharew, N. T., Clark, S. R., Schubert, K. O., & Amare, A. T. (2024). Pharmacogenomic scores in psychiatry: Systematic review of current evidence. *Translational Psychiatry*, *14*(1), 322. DOI: 10.1038/s41398-024-02998-6

Sharifani, K., & Amini, M. (2023). Machine Learning and Deep Learning: A Review of Methods and Applications. *World Information Technology and Engineering Journal*, *10*(07), 3897–3904.

Sharma, A., Lin, I. W., Miner, A. S., Atkins, D. C., & Althoff, T. (2023). Human–AI collaboration enables more empathic conversations in text-based peer-to-peer mental health support. *Nature Machine Intelligence*, *5*(1), 46–57. DOI: 10.1038/s42256-022-00593-2

Sharma, A., & Verbeke, W. J. M. I. (2020). Improving Diagnosis of Depression With XGBOOST Machine Learning Model and a Large Biomarkers Dutch Dataset (n = 11,081). *Frontiers in Big Data*, *3*. Advance online publication. DOI: 10.3389/fdata.2020.00015

Sharma, A., & Verbeke, W. J. M. I. (2021). Understanding importance of clinical biomarkers for diagnosis of anxiety disorders using machine learning models. *PLoS One*, *16*(5), e0251365. DOI: 10.1371/journal.pone.0251365

Sheth, S. A., Bijanki, K. R., Metzger, B., Allawala, A., Pirtle, V., Adkinson, J. A., Myers, J., Mathura, R. K., Oswalt, D., Tsolaki, E., Xiao, J., Noecker, A., Strutt, A. M., Cohn, J. F., McIntyre, C. C., Mathew, S. J., Borton, D., Goodman, W., & Pouratian, N. (2022). Deep Brain Stimulation for Depression Informed by Intracranial Recordings. *Biological Psychiatry*, *92*(3), 246–251. DOI: 10.1016/j.biopsych.2021.11.007

Shiffman, S., Stone, A. A., & Hufford, M. R. (2008). Ecological momentary assessment. *Annual Review of Clinical Psychology*, *4*, 1–32. DOI: 10.1146/annurev.clinpsy.3.022806.091415 PMID: 18509902

Shin, J., Yoon, H., Lee, S., Park, S., Liu, Y., Choi, J. D., & Lee, S.-J. (2023). *FedTherapist: Mental Health Monitoring with User-Generated Linguistic Expressions on Smartphones via Federated Learning.*

Shipp, S., & Aeon, B. (2019). Temporal focus and recovery: How time perspective predicts substance use treatment outcomes. *Addiction Research and Theory*, *27*(3), 189–198. DOI: 10.1080/16066359.2018.1519422

Shivaprasad, S., Chadaga, K., Dias, C. C., Sampathila, N., & Prabhu, S. (2024). An interpretable schizophrenia diagnosis framework using machine learning and explainable artificial intelligence. *Systems Science & Control Engineering*, *12*(1), 2364033.

Shokri, R., & Shmatikov, V. (2015, October). Privacy-preserving deep learning. In *Proceedings of the 22nd ACM SIGSAC Conference on Computer and Communications Security* (pp. 1310–1321). ACM. https://doi.org/DOI: 10.1145/2810103.2813687

Shrestha, S., Stapp, J., Taylor, M., Leach, R., Carreiro, S., & Indic, P. (2023). Towards device agnostic detection of stress and craving in patients with substance use disorder. In *Proceedings of the Annual Hawaii International Conference on System Sciences* (pp. 3156–3163). IEEE. https://doi.org/DOI: 10.24251/HICSS.2023.383

Siddals, S., Torous, J., & Coxon, A. (2024). "It happened to be the perfect thing": Experiences of generative AI chatbots for mental health. *Npj Mental Health Research*, *3*(1). Advance online publication. DOI: 10.1038/s44184-024-00097-4

Singhal, A., Neveditsin, N., Tanveer, H., & Mago, V. (2024). Toward Fairness, Accountability, Transparency, and Ethics in AI for Social Media and Health Care: Scoping Review. *JMIR Medical Informatics*, *12*, e50048. DOI: 10.2196/50048

Skorburg, J. A., O'Doherty, K., & Friesen, P. (2024). Persons or data points? Ethics, artificial intelligence, and the participatory turn in mental health research. *The American Psychologist*, *79*(1), 137–149. DOI: 10.1037/amp0001168 PMID: 38236221

Smith, K. (2014). Mental health: A world of depression. *Nature*, *515*, 180–181. DOI: 10.1038/515180a

Solaiman, B., Malik, A., & Ghuloum, S. (2023). Monitoring Mental Health: Legal and Ethical Considerations of Using Artificial Intelligence in Psychiatric Wards. *American Journal of Law & Medicine*, *49*(2–3), 250–266. DOI: 10.1017/amj.2023.30

Solans Noguero, D., Ramírez-Cifuentes, D., Ríssola, E. A., & Freire, A. (2023). Gender bias when using artificial intelligence to assess anorexia nervosa on social media: Data-driven study. *Journal of Medical Internet Research*, *25*, e45184.

Son, Y., Clouston, S. A. P., Kotov, R., Eichstaedt, J. C., Bromet, E. J., Luft, B. J., & Schwartz, H. A. (2020). World Trade Center responders in their own words: Predicting PTSD symptom trajectories with AI-based language analyses of interviews. arXiv preprint arXiv:2011.06457. https://arxiv.org/abs/2011.06457

Squarcina, L., Villa, F. M., Nobile, M., Grisan, E., & Brambilla, P. (2021). Deep learning for the prediction of treatment response in depression. *Journal of Affective Disorders*, *281*, 618–622. DOI: 10.1016/j.jad.2020.11.104

Squires, M., Tao, X., Elangovan, S., Gururajan, R., Zhou, X., Li, Y., & Acharya, U. R. (2023). Identifying predictive biomarkers for repetitive transcranial magnetic stimulation response in depression patients with explainability. *Computer Methods and Programs in Biomedicine*, *242*, 107771. DOI: 10.1016/j.cmpb.2023.107771

Sreeramareddy, C. T., Pradhan, P. M. S., Mir, I. A., & Sin, S. (2014). Smoking and smokeless tobacco use in nine South and Southeast Asian countries: Prevalence estimates and social determinants from Demographic and Health Surveys. *Population Health Metrics*, *12*(1), 22. DOI: 10.1186/s12963-014-0022-0

Srinivasan, S. M., Park, I. K., Neelly, L. B., & Bhat, A. N. (2015). A comparison of the effects of rhythm and robotic interventions on repetitive behaviors and affective states of children with Autism Spectrum Disorder (ASD). *Research in Autism Spectrum Disorders*, *18*, 51–63.

Sripada, R. K., Ready, D. J., Ganoczy, D., Astin, M. C., & Rauch, S. A. (2020). When to change the treatment plan: An analysis of diminishing returns in VA patients undergoing prolonged exposure and cognitive processing therapy. *Behavior Therapy*, *51*(1), 85–98. DOI: 10.1016/j.beth.2019.05.003

Stade, E. C., Stirman, S. W., Ungar, L. H., Boland, C. L., Schwartz, H. A., Yaden, D. B., Sedoc, J., DeRubeis, R. J., Willer, R., & Eichstaedt, J. C. (2024). Large language models could change the future of behavioral healthcare: A proposal for responsible development and evaluation. *Npj Mental Health Research, 3*(1). Advance online publication. DOI: 10.1038/s44184-024-00056-z

Stasolla, F., Curcio, E., Zullo, A., Passaro, A., & Gioia, M. D. (2024). Integrating Artificial Intelligence-Based Programs into Autism Therapy: Innovations for Personalized Rehabilitation. *Sci. Intell. Syst, 41*, 169–176.

Staszak, M., Staszak, K., Wieszczycka, K., Bajek, A., Roszkowski, K., & Tylkowski, B. (2022). Machine learning in drug design: Use of artificial intelligence to explore the chemical structure–biological activity relationship. *Wiley Interdisciplinary Reviews. Computational Molecular Science, 12*(2), e1568. DOI: 10.1002/wcms.1568

Stawarz, K., Preist, C., & Coyle, D. (2019). Use of smartphone apps, social media, and web-based resources to support mental health and well-being: Online survey. *JMIR Mental Health, 6*(7), e12546. DOI: 10.2196/12546

Stein, A. (2025, April 22). Are therapy chatbots effective for depression and anxiety? A critical comparative review. https://apsa.org/are-therapy-chatbots-effective-for-depression-and-anxiety/

Sun, C., van Soest, J., & Dumontier, M. (2023). Generating synthetic personal health data using conditional generative adversarial networks combining with differential privacy. *Journal of Biomedical Informatics, 143*, 104404. DOI: 10.1016/j.jbi.2023.104404 PMID: 37268168

Sun, H., Chen, Y., Huang, Q., Lui, S., Huang, X., Shi, Y., & Gong, Q. (2018). Psychoradiologic utility of MR imaging for diagnosis of attention deficit hyperactivity disorder: A radiomics analysis. *Radiology, 287*(2), 620–630.

Sun, J., Dong, Q. X., Wang, S. W., Zheng, Y. B., Liu, X. X., Lu, T. S., & Han, Y. (2023). Artificial intelligence in psychiatry research, diagnosis, and therapy. *Asian Journal of Psychiatry, 87*, 103705.

Sun, J., Lu, T., Shao, X., Han, Y., Xia, Y., Zheng, Y., & Lu, L. (2025). Practical AI application in psychiatry: Historical review and future directions. *Molecular Psychiatry*, •••, 1–10.

Sutton, R. S., & Barto, A. G. (2018). *Reinforcement Learning: An Introduction* (2nd ed.). MIT Press., https://www.andrew.cmu.edu/course/10-703/textbook/BartoSutton.pdf

Suva, M., & Bhatia, G. (2024). Artificial intelligence in addiction: Challenges and opportunities. *Indian Journal of Psychological Medicine*, *46*(3), 213–220. DOI: 10.1177/02537176241234567

Swift, J. K., & Callahan, J. L. (2009). The impact of client preferences on treatment engagement and dropout. *Journal of Clinical Psychology*, *65*(2), 147–155. DOI: 10.1002/jclp.20543

Symons, M., Feeney, G. F. X., Gallagher, M. R., Young, R. M., Connor, J. P., Mc, D., & Young, R. (2019). Machine learning vs addiction therapists: A pilot study predicting alcohol dependence treatment outcome from patient data in behavior therapy with adjunctive medication. *Journal of Substance Abuse Treatment*, *99*, 156–162. DOI: 10.1016/j.jsat.2019.01.002

Taha Jijo, B., & Mohsin Abdulazeez, A. (2021). Classification based on decision tree algorithm for machine learning. *Journal of Applied Science and Technology Trends*, *2*(1), 20–28. DOI: 10.38094/jastt20109

Tahir, W. Bin, Khalid, S., Alshahrani, S., Alharbi, S. S., & Alhasson, H. F. (2025). ContextVecNet: A Context-Driven Multimodal Learning Framework for Depression Detection. *IEEE Journal of Biomedical and Health Informatics*, •••, 1–12. DOI: 10.1109/JBHI.2025.3602719 PMID: 40864577

Takizawa, R., Fukuda, M., Kawasaki, S., Kasai, K., Mimura, M., & Pu, S.Joint Project for Psychiatric Application of Near-Infrared Spectroscopy (JPSY-NIRS) Group. (2014). Neuroimaging-aided differential diagnosis of the depressive state. *NeuroImage*, *85*, 498–507.

Talati, D. V. (2025). Machine Learning for Personalized Brain Stimulation: AI-Optimized Neuromodulation Treatments. *International Journal of Science and Research Archive*, *14*(3), 331–338. DOI: 10.30574/ijsra.2025.14.3.0607

Talkspace. (2018). Online therapy, counseling online, marriage counseling. https://www.talkspace.com/

Tanguay-Sela, M., Benrimoh, D., Popescu, C., Perez, T., Rollins, C., Snook, E., Lundrigan, E., Armstrong, C., Perlman, K., Fratila, R., Mehltretter, J., Israel, S., Champagne, M., Williams, J., Simard, J., Parikh, S. V., Karp, J. F., Heller, K., Lin-naranta, O., & Margolese, H. (2021). *Evaluating the Perceived Utility of an Artificial Intelligence-Powered Clinical Decision Support System for Depression Treatment Using a Simulation Centre*. https://doi.org/DOI: 10.1101/2021.04.21.21255899

Tassinari, D. L., Pedro, M. O. P., Pedro, M. P., Negrão, A. B., Amaral, R. A., Malbergier, A., Crispim, D. H., & Castaldelli-Maia, J. M. (2025). Artificial intelligence-driven and technological innovations in the diagnosis and management of substance use disorders. *International Review of Psychiatry (Abingdon, England)*, *37*(1), 52–58. DOI: 10.1080/09540261.2024.2432369

Thenral, M., & Annamalai, A. (2020). Telepsychiatry and the Role of Artificial Intelligence in Mental Health in Post-COVID-19 India: A Scoping Review on Opportunities. *Indian Journal of Psychological Medicine*, *42*(5), 428–434. DOI: 10.1177/0253717620952160

Thompson, P. M., Stein, J. L., Medland, S. E., Hibar, D. P., Vasquez, A. A., Renteria, M. E., & Le Hellard, S. (2014). The ENIGMA Consortium: Large-scale collaborative analyses of neuroimaging and genetic data. *Brain Imaging and Behavior*, *8*(2), 153–182.

Timmons, A. C., Duong, J. B., Simo Fiallo, N., Lee, T., Vo, H. P. Q., Ahle, M. W., Comer, J. S., Brewer, L. C., Frazier, S. L., & Chaspari, T. (2023). A Call to Action on Assessing and Mitigating Bias in Artificial Intelligence Applications for Mental Health. *Perspectives on Psychological Science*, *18*(5), 1062–1096. DOI: 10.1177/17456916221134490 PMID: 36490369

Tomičić, A., & Gjorgjioska, M. A. (2024). Epistemic inequality in the digital era: Unpacking biases in digital mental health. *Theory & Psychology*, *34*(6), 777–797. DOI: 10.1177/09593543241279131

Tong, J., Xu, D. J., Yan, A., & Li, Z. (2024). Leveraging Artificial Intelligence to Address the Paradox of Judgment and Accountability in Depression Treatment.

Topol, E. J. (2019). High-performance medicine: The convergence of human and artificial intelligence. *Nature Medicine*, *25*(1), 44–56.

Torous, J.. (2021). Digital mental health and COVID-19: Using technology today to accelerate the curve on access and quality tomorrow. *JMIR Mental Health*, *7*(3), e18848. DOI: 10.2196/18848

Torous, J., Linardon, J., Goldberg, S. B., Sun, S., Bell, I., Nicholas, J., Hassan, L., Hua, Y., Milton, A., & Firth, J. (2025). The evolving field of digital mental health: Current evidence and implementation issues for smartphone apps, generative artificial intelligence, and virtual reality. *World Psychiatry; Official Journal of the World Psychiatric Association (WPA)*, *24*(2), 156–174. DOI: 10.1002/wps.21299 PMID: 40371757

Torous, J., Lipschitz, J., Ng, M., & Firth, J. (2019). The potential of digital phenotyping to advance the contributions of nutritional psychiatry. *Nutrition (Burbank, Los Angeles County, Calif.), 66*, 110554. DOI: 10.1016/j.outlook.2020.03.007

Tran, T., Luo, W., Phung, D., Harvey, R., Berk, M., Kennedy, R. L., & Venkatesh, S. (2014). Risk stratification using data from electronic medical records better predicts suicide risks than clinician assessments. *BMC Psychiatry, 14*(1), 1–9.

Tremain, H., McEnery, C., Fletcher, K., & Murray, G. (2020). The Therapeutic Alliance in Digital Mental Health Interventions for Serious Mental Illnesses: Narrative Review. *JMIR Mental Health, 7*(8), e17204. DOI: 10.2196/17204 PMID: 32763881

Tsoi, E. W. S., Mak, W. W. S., Ho, C. Y. Y., & Yeung, G. T. Y. (2022). A Web-Based Stratified Stepped Care Mental Health Platform (TourHeart): Semistructured Interviews With Stakeholders. *JMIR Human Factors, 9*(2), e35057. DOI: 10.2196/35057 PMID: 35560109

Tucmeanu, E. R., & Tucmeanu, A. I. (2025). Cognitive Neuroscience Breakthroughs Exploring Brain Mechanisms With Ai To Advance Learning Memory Disorder Treatments In Modern Science. *AI-Neurosciencescape, 1*(1), 16–29.

Turner Lee, N. (2018). Detecting racial bias in algorithms and machine learning. *Journal of Information. Communication and Ethics in Society, 16*(3), 252–260. DOI: 10.1108/JICES-06-2018-0056

Tzirakis, P., Trigeorgis, G., Nicolaou, M. A., Schuller, B. W., & Zafeiriou, S. (2017). End-to-end multimodal emotion recognition using deep neural networks. *IEEE Journal of Selected Topics in Signal Processing, 11*(8), 1301–1309.

U.S. Department of Health and Human Services, Substance Abuse and Mental Health Services Administration, Center for Behavioral Health Statistics and Quality. (2017). *National Survey of Substance Abuse Treatment Services (N-SSATS) 2016: Data on substance abuse treatment facilities*. Author. https://www.samhsa.gov/data/sites/default/files/2016_NSSATS.pdf

Uban, A. S., Chulvi, B., & Rosso, P. (2021). An emotion and cognitive based analysis of mental health disorders from social media data. *Future Generation Computer Systems, 123*, 480–494. DOI: 10.1016/j.future.2021.05.032

Uban, A. S., Chulvi, B., & Rosso, P. (2021). *On the Explainability of Automatic Predictions of Mental Disorders from Social Media Data.*, DOI: 10.1007/978-3-030-80599-9_27

Uddin, M., Wang, Y., & Woodbury-Smith, M. (2019). Artificial intelligence for precision medicine in neurodevelopmental disorders. *NPJ Digital Medicine, 2*(1), 112.

Uhlhaas, P., & Torous, J. (2019). Digital tools for youth mental health. *NPJ Digital Medicine*, *2*(1), 104.

Ullman, S. (2019). Using neuroscience to develop artificial intelligence. [). American Association for the Advancement of Science.]. *Science*, *363*(6428), 692–693.

Ullrich, H. E. (2019). Culture, Empathy, and the Therapeutic Alliance. *Psychodynamic Psychiatry*, *47*(4), 425–440. DOI: 10.1521/pdps.2019.47.4.425 PMID: 31913784

Uludag, K. (2023b). *ChatGPT can distinguish grandiose delusional thoughts from non-grandiose thoughts* (SSRN Scholarly Paper No. 4392582). SSRN Electronic Journal. https://doi.org/DOI: 10.2139/ssrn.4392582

Uludag, K. (2023a). *The use of AI-supported chatbot in psychology. SSRN.* https://doi.org/DOI: 10.2139/ssrn.4331367

Uludag, K. (2024). Exploring the association between textual parameters and psychological and cognitive factors. *Psychology Research and Behavior Management*, *17*, 1139–1150. https://pubmed.ncbi.nlm.nih.gov/38505355/ PMID: 38505355

UNICEF. (2021). The State of the World's Children 2021: On My Mind – Promoting, protecting and caring for children's mental health. https://www.unicef.org/reports/state-worlds-children-2021

University of Colorado. (2023). *DTOX project summary: Enhancing real-time craving tracking and therapist feedback.* Department of Psychiatry Research Briefs.

Ünlü, A., Hakkarainen, P., Karjalainen, K., Tammi, T., & Subasi, A. (2025). Identifying risk factors of substance use in Finland: A machine learning approach. *Substance Use & Misuse*. Advance online publication. DOI: 10.1080/10826084.2025.2516738

Vafaie, N., & Kober, H. (2022). Association of drug cues and craving with drug use and relapse: A systematic review and meta-analysis. *JAMA Psychiatry*, *79*(7), 641–650. DOI: 10.1001/jamapsychiatry.2022.0937

Valentine, L., D'Alfonso, S., & Lederman, R. (2023). Recommender systems for mental health apps: Advantages and ethical challenges. *AI & Society*, *38*(4), 1627–1638. DOI: 10.1007/s00146-021-01322-w PMID: 35068708

Van Genugten, C., Thong, M. S. Y., van Ballegooijen, W., Kleiboer, A., Spruijt-Metz, D., Smit, J. H., Sprangers, M. A. G., Terhorst, Y., & Riper, H. (2025). Beyond the current state of just-in-time adaptive interventions in mental health: A systematic review. *Frontiers in Digital Health*, *7*, 1460167. DOI: 10.3389/fdgth.2025.1460167 PMID: 39935463 van Melle, W. (1978). MYCIN: A knowledge-based consultation program for infectious disease diagnosis. *International Journal of Man-Machine Studies, 10*(3), 313–322. DOI: 10.1016/S0020-7373(78)80049-2

van Straten, C. L., Peter, J., & Kühne, R. (2024). "You" versus "children": A repeated-measures experiment on the effects of social robots' use of (im) personal address forms when talking to children. *International Journal of Child-Computer Interaction, 42*, 100682.

Vaquerizo-Villar, F., Gutiérrez-Tobal, G. C., Calvo, E., Álvarez, D., Kheirandish-Gozal, L., Del Campo, F., & Hornero, R. (2023). An explainable deep-learning model to stage sleep states in children and propose novel EEG-related patterns in sleep apnea. *Computers in Biology and Medicine, 165*, 107419.

Vayena, E., Blasimme, A., & Cohen, I. G. (2018). Machine learning in medicine: Addressing ethical challenges. *PLoS Medicine, 15*(11), e1002689. DOI: 10.1371/journal.pmed.1002689

Vedanta, S. P., & Rao, M. (2024). PsychSynth: Advancing Mental Health AI Through Synthetic Data Generation and Curriculum Training. *2024 9th International Conference on Computer Science and Engineering (UBMK)*, 1–6. https://doi.org/DOI: 10.1109/UBMK63289.2024.10773545

Venniro, M., Banks, M. L., Heilig, M., Epstein, D. H., & Shaham, Y. (2020). Improving translation of animal models of addiction and relapse by reverse translation. *Nature Reviews. Neuroscience, 21*(11), 625–643. DOI: 10.1038/s41583-020-0369-z

Verma, M., Chanthar, K. M. M. V., & Beg, M. J. (2025). *Ethical Considerations Surrounding the Use of AI-Interventions in Application of Mental Healthcare.*, DOI: 10.4018/979-8-3693-3112-5.ch009

Verma, M., Chanthar, K. M., & Beg, M. J. (2025). Ethical Considerations Surrounding the Use of AI-Interventions in Application of Mental Healthcare. In Uludag, K., & Ahmad, N. (Eds.), *Chatbots and Mental Healthcare in Psychology and Psychiatry* (pp. 193–222). IGI Global Scientific Publishing.,

Veterans Administration/Department of Defense Clinical Practice Guideline Working Group. (2023). *Management of post-traumatic stress and acute stress disorder.* Office of Quality and Performance.

Vieira, S., Gong, Q. Y., Pinaya, W. H., Scarpazza, C., Tognin, S., Crespo-Facorro, B., & Mechelli, A. (2020). Using machine learning and structural neuroimaging to detect first episode psychosis: Reconsidering the evidence. *Schizophrenia Bulletin, 46*(1), 17–26.

Vindigni, G. (2023). Exploring digital therapeutics: game-based and ehealth interventions in mental health care: potential, challenges, and policy implications. *British Journal of Healthcare and Medical Research-Vol, 10*(3).

Volkow, N. D. (2023). Public remarks during the National Drug & Alcohol Facts Week. National Institute on Drug Abuse. https://nida.nih.gov/news-events/national-drug-alcohol-facts-week

Volkow, N. D., & Blanco, C. (2023). Substance use disorders: A comprehensive update of classification, epidemiology, neurobiology, clinical aspects, treatment and prevention. *World Psychiatry; Official Journal of the World Psychiatric Association (WPA)*, *22*(2), 203–229. DOI: 10.1002/wps.21045

Volkow, N. D., Han, B., Compton, W. M., & Blanco, C. (2021). Cannabis use and risk of psychosis and suicidal thoughts among teens and young adults. *JAMA Psychiatry*, *78*(2), 123–134.

Vredenburgh, K. (2024). Transparency and Explainability for Public Policy. *LSE Public Policy Review*, *3*(3).

Waite, M. R., Heslin, K., Cook, J., Kim, A., & Simpson, M. (2023). Predicting substance use disorder treatment follow-ups and relapse across the continuum of care at a single behavioral health center. *Journal of Substance Abuse Treatment*, *147*, 208933. DOI: 10.1016/j.jsat.2022.208933

Wakefield, J. C. (2016). Diagnostic Issues and Controversies in DSM-5: Return of the False Positives Problem. *Annual Review of Clinical Psychology*, *12*(1), 105–132. DOI: 10.1146/annurev-clinpsy-032814-112800 PMID: 26772207

Waldman, S. A., & Terzic, A. (2019). Healthcare evolves from reactive to proactive. *Clinical Pharmacology and Therapeutics*, *105*(1), 10. PMID: 30597564

Wallert, J., Boberg, J., Kaldo, V., Mataix-Cols, D., Flygare, O., Crowley, J. J., Halvorsen, M., Ben Abdesslem, F., Boman, M., Andersson, E., Hentati Isacsson, N., Ivanova, E., & Rück, C. (2022). Predicting remission after internet-delivered psychotherapy in patients with depression using machine learning and multi-modal data. *Translational Psychiatry*, *12*(1), 357. DOI: 10.1038/s41398-022-02133-3

Walsh, C. G., Chaudhry, B., Dua, P., Goodman, K. W., Kaplan, B., Kavuluru, R., Solomonides, A., & Subbian, V. (2020). Stigma, biomarkers, and algorithmic bias: Recommendations for precision behavioral health with artificial intelligence. *JAMIA Open*, *3*(1), 9–15. DOI: 10.1093/jamiaopen/ooz054

Wampold, B. E. (2015). How important are the common factors in psychotherapy? An update. *World Psychiatry; Official Journal of the World Psychiatric Association (WPA), 14*(3), 270–277.

Wang, C., Jiang, Y., Peng, Z., Li, C., Bang, C., Zhao, L., Lv, J., Sepulcre, J., Yang, C., He, L., Liu, T., Barron, D., Li, Q., Hirschtick, R., Kim, B.-H., Li, X., & Yuan, Y. (2025). *Towards a general-purpose foundation model for fMRI analysis.*

Wang, A., & Sun, J. (2025). Personalized EEG-guided brain stimulation targeting in major depression via network controllability and multi-objective optimization. *BMC Psychiatry, 25*(1), 723. DOI: 10.1186/s12888-025-07171-x

Wang, E., Chang, W.-L., Shen, J., Bian, Q., Huang, P. L., & Lai, X. (2022). Effect of artificial intelligence on one-to-one emotional regulation and psychological intervention system of middle school students. *The International Journal of Neuropsychopharmacology, 25*(Suppl 1), A62–A63. DOI: 10.1093/ijnp/pyac032.086

Wang, J., & Fan, W. (2025). The effect of ChatGPT on students' learning performance, learning perception, and higher-order thinking: Insights from a meta-analysis. *Humanities & Social Sciences Communications, 12*(1), 1–21. DOI: 10.1057/s41599-025-1234-9

Wang, Q., Wang, M., Yang, Y., & Zhang, X. (2022). Multi-modal emotion recognition using EEG and speech signals. *Computers in Biology and Medicine, 149*, 105907.

Wang, T.-F., Huang, R.-C., Yang, S.-C., Chou, C., & Chen, L.-C. (2020). Evaluating the Effects of a Mobile Health App on Reducing Patient Care Needs and Improving Quality of Life After Oral Cancer Surgery: Quasiexperimental Study. *JMIR mHealth and uHealth, 8*(7), e18132. DOI: 10.2196/18132 PMID: 32716303

Wang, Z., Meng, Z., & Chen, C. (2022). Screening of potential biomarkers in peripheral blood of patients with depression based on weighted gene co-expression network analysis and machine learning algorithms. *Frontiers in Psychiatry, 13*. Advance online publication. DOI: 10.3389/fpsyt.2022.1009911

Wara, T. U., Fahad, A. H., Das, A. S., & Shawon, M. M. H. (2025). A systematic review on sleep stage classification and sleep disorder detection using artificial intelligence. *Heliyon, 11*(12).

Ware, O. D., Manuel, J. I., & Huhn, A. S. (2021). Adults with opioid and methamphetamine co-use have lower odds of completing short-term residential treatment than other opioid co-use groups: A retrospective health services study. *Frontiers in Psychiatry, 12*, 784229. DOI: 10.3389/fpsyt.2021.784229

Warrier, U., Warrier, A., & Khandelwal, K. (2023). Ethical considerations in the use of artificial intelligence in mental health. *The Egyptian Journal of Neurology, Psychiatry and Neurosurgery*, *59*(1), 139.

Weinberger, A. H., Kashan, R. S., Shpigel, D. M., Esan, H., Taha, F., Lee, C. J., Funk, A. P., & Goodwin, R. D. (2017). Depression and cigarette smoking behavior: A critical review of population-based studies. *The American Journal of Drug and Alcohol Abuse*, *43*(4), 416–431. DOI: 10.3109/00952990.2016.1141915

Weinstein, Z. M., Kim, H. W., Cheng, D. M., Quinn, E., Hui, D., Labelle, C. T., & Samet, J. H. (2017). Long-term retention in office-based opioid treatment with buprenorphine. *Journal of Substance Abuse Treatment*, *74*, 65–70. DOI: 10.1016/j.jsat.2016.12.010

Weizenbaum, J. (1966). ELIZA—A computer program for the study of natural language communication between man and machine. *Communications of the ACM*, *9*(1), 36–45. DOI: 10.1145/365153.365168

Welch, V., Wy, T. J., Ligezka, A., Hassett, L. C., Croarkin, P. E., Athreya, A. P., & Romanowicz, M. (2022). Use of mobile and wearable artificial intelligence in child and adolescent psychiatry: Scoping review. *Journal of Medical Internet Research*, *24*(3), e33560.

Widge, A. S. (2023). Closed-Loop Deep Brain Stimulation for Psychiatric Disorders. *Harvard Review of Psychiatry*, *31*(3), 162–171. DOI: 10.1097/HRP.0000000000000367

Wiebe, A., Selaskowski, B., Paskin, M., Asché, L., Pakos, J., Aslan, B., & Braun, N. (2024). Virtual reality-assisted prediction of adult ADHD based on eye tracking, EEG, actigraphy and behavioral indices: A machine learning analysis of independent training and test samples. *Translational Psychiatry*, *14*(1), 508.

Wies, B., Landers, C., & Ienca, M. (2021). Digital Mental Health for Young People: A Scoping Review of Ethical Promises and Challenges. *Frontiers in Digital Health*, *3*. Advance online publication. DOI: 10.3389/fdgth.2021.697072

Williams, C. M., Chaturvedi, R., Urman, R. D., Waterman, R. S., & Gabriel, R. A. (2021). Artificial intelligence and a pandemic: An analysis of the potential uses and drawbacks. *Journal of Medical Systems*, *45*, 1–3.

Williams, D., Hornung, H., Nadimpalli, A., & Peery, A. (2021). Deep learning and its application for healthcare delivery in low- and middle-income countries. *Frontiers in Artificial Intelligence*, *4*, 553987. DOI: 10.3389/frai.2021.553987

Williamson, S. M., & Prybutok, V. (2024). Balancing privacy and progress: A review of privacy challenges, systemic oversight, and patient perceptions in AI-driven healthcare. *Applied Sciences (Basel, Switzerland)*, *14*(2), 675. DOI: 10.3390/app14020675

Williams, S. D., & Williams, J. (2020). Posttraumatic stress in organizations: Types, antecedents, and consequences. *Business and Society Review*, *125*(1), 23–40. DOI: 10.1111/basr.12192

Wilson, J. (2015). Mental health matters. *Clinical Communication in Medicine*, (January), 151–155.

Wilton, R., & Deverteuil, G. (2006). Spaces of sobriety/sites of power: Examining social model alcohol recovery programs as therapeutic landscapes. *Social Science & Medicine*, *63*(3), 649–661. DOI: 10.1016/j.socscimed.2006.01.022

Winter, N. R., Blanke, J., Leenings, R., Ernsting, J., Fisch, L., Sarink, K., Barkhau, C., Emden, D., Thiel, K., Flinkenflügel, K., Winter, A., Goltermann, J., Meinert, S., Dohm, K., Repple, J., Gruber, M., Leehr, E. J., Opel, N., Grotegerd, D., & Hahn, T. (2024). A Systematic Evaluation of Machine Learning–Based Biomarkers for Major Depressive Disorder. *JAMA Psychiatry*, *81*(4), 386.

Wolfers, T., Buitelaar, J. K., Beckmann, C. F., Franke, B., & Marquand, A. F. (2015). From estimating activation locality to predicting disorder: A review of pattern recognition for neuroimaging-based psychiatric diagnostics. *Neuroscience and Biobehavioral Reviews*, *57*, 328–349.

World Economic Forum. (2011). The Global Economic Burden of Non-Communicable Diseases. https://www.weforum.org/reports/global-economic-burden-non-communicable-diseases

World Health Organization (WHO). (2014). Preventing suicide: A global imperative. https://www.who.int/publications/i/item/9789241564779

World Health Organization (WHO). (2020). The impact of COVID-19 on mental, neurological and substance use services: results of a rapid assessment. https://www.who.int/publications/i/item/9789240124554

World Health Organization (WHO). (2021). Mental Health Atlas 2020. https://www.who.int/publications/i/item/9789240036703

World Health Organization (WHO). (2022). World Mental Health Report: Transforming mental health for all. https://www.who.int/publications/i/item/9789240049338

World Health Organization. (2018). *Global status report on alcohol and health 2018*. World Health Organization. https://www.who.int/publications/i/item/9789241565639

World Health Organization. (2019). WHO guideline: recommendations on digital interventions for health system strengthening.

World Health Organization. (2023). Global status report on alcohol and health 2023. https://www.who.int/publications/i/item/9789240063875

World Health Organization. WHO & World Health Organization: WHO. (2023, March 31). Depressive disorder (depression). https://www.who.int/news-room/fact-sheets/detail/depression

Wright, T., Salyers, A., Howell, K., Harrison, J., Silvasstar, J., & Bull, S. (2025). A pilot study of an AI chatbot for the screening of substance use disorder in a health-care setting. *AI*, *6*(6), 113. DOI: 10.3390/ai6060113

Wu, S., Ell, K., Jin, H., Vidyanti, I., Chou, C.-P., Lee, P.-J., Gross-Schulman, S., Sklaroff, L. M., Belson, D., Nezu, A. M., Hay, J., Wang, C.-J., Scheib, G., Di Capua, P., Hawkins, C., Liu, P., Ramirez, M., Wu, B. W., Richman, M., & Guterman, J. (2018). Comparative Effectiveness of a Technology-Facilitated Depression Care Management Model in Safety-Net Primary Care Patients With Type 2 Diabetes: 6-Month Outcomes of a Large Clinical Trial. *Journal of Medical Internet Research*, *20*(4), e147. DOI: 10.2196/jmir.7692

Wu, Z., Yue, Q., Zhao, Z., Wen, J., Tang, L., Zhong, Z., Yang, J., Yuan, Y., & Zhang, X. (2023). A cross-sectional study of smoking and depression among US adults: NHANES (2005–2018). *Frontiers in Public Health*, *11*, 1134234. DOI: 10.3389/fpubh.2023.1134234

Wysa. (2023). Everyday mental health. https://www.talkspace.com/

Xu, X., Peng, H., Sun, L., Bhuiyan, M. Z. A., Liu, L., & He, L. (2021). *FedMood: Federated Learning on Mobile Health Data for Mood Detection*. https://doi.org/DOI: 10.1109/TII.2021.3113708

Xu, Y., Hübener, I., Seipp, A. K., Ohly, S., & David, K. (2017, March). From the lab to the real-world: An investigation on the influence of human movement on Emotion Recognition using physiological signals. In *2017 IEEE international conference on pervasive computing and communications workshops (PerCom Workshops)* (pp. 345-350). IEEE.

Xu, J., Li, X., Liang, X., Zhang, X., Ying, G., & Liu, J. (2025). The risk factors for relapse behavior in individuals with substance use disorders: An interpretable machine learning study. *Journal of Affective Disorders*, *387*, 119520. DOI: 10.1016/j.jad.2024.12.056

Yadav, N., Pandey, S., Gupta, A., Dudani, P., Gupta, S., & Rangarajan, K. (2023). Data Privacy in Healthcare: In the Era of Artificial Intelligence. *Indian Dermatology Online Journal*, *14*(6), 788–792. DOI: 10.4103/idoj.idoj_543_23 PMID: 38099022

Yang, J., Dung, N. T., Thach, P. N., Phong, N. T., & Dinh, V. (2023a). Generalizability assessment of AI models across hospitals: A comparative study in low-middle income and high-income countries. *medRxiv*. https://doi.org/DOI: 10.1101/2023.11.06.12345

Yang, J., & Giummarra, M. J. (2021). Compulsory and voluntary drug treatment models in China: A need for improved evidence-based policy and practice to reduce the loaded burden of substance use disorders. *The International Journal on Drug Policy*, *92*, 103063. DOI: 10.1016/j.drugpo.2020.103063

Yang, J., Soltan, A. A. S., Eyre, D. W., & Clifton, D. A. (2023). Algorithmic fairness and bias mitigation for clinical machine learning with deep reinforcement learning. *Nature Machine Intelligence*, *5*(8), 884–894. DOI: 10.1038/s42256-023-00697-3 PMID: 37615031

Yang, L., Du, Y., Yang, W., & Liu, J. (2023b). Machine learning with neuroimaging biomarkers: Application in the diagnosis and prediction of drug addiction. *Addiction Biology*, *28*(2), e13267. DOI: 10.1111/adb.13267

Yang, S. W., Lee, K. S., Heo, J. S., Choi, E. S., Kim, K., Lee, S., & Ahn, K. H. (2024). Machine learning analysis with population data for prepregnancy and perinatal risk factors for the neurodevelopmental delay of offspring. *Scientific Reports*, *14*(1), 13993.

Yeh, S. C., Lin, S. Y., Wu, E. H. K., Zhang, K. F., Xiu, X., Rizzo, A., & Chung, C. R. (2020). A virtual-reality system integrated with neuro-behavior sensing for attention-deficit/hyperactivity disorder intelligent assessment. *IEEE Transactions on Neural Systems and Rehabilitation Engineering*, *28*(9), 1899–1907.

Yoo, J. H., Kang, C., Lim, J. S., Wang, B., Choi, C. H., Hwang, H., & Kim, J. W. (2024). Development of an innovative approach using portable eye tracking to assist ADHD screening: A machine learning study. *Frontiers in Psychiatry*, *15*, 1337595.

Young, G. (2013). Breaking Bad: DSM-5 Description, Criticisms, and Recommendations. *Psychological Injury and Law*, *6*(4), 345–348. DOI: 10.1007/s12207-013-9181-8

Younis, E. M., Mohsen, S., Houssein, E. H., & Ibrahim, O. A. S. (2024). Machine learning for human emotion recognition: A comprehensive review. *Neural Computing & Applications*, *36*(16), 8901–8947.

Yu, D., & Fang, J. H. (2024). Using artificial intelligence methods to study the effectiveness of exercise in patients with ADHD. *Frontiers in Neuroscience*, *18*, 1380886.

Zafar, F., Alam, L. F., Vivas, R. R., Wang, J., Whei, S. J., Mehmood, S., & Nazir, Z. (2024). The role of artificial intelligence in identifying depression and anxiety: A comprehensive literature review. *Cureus*, *16*(3), e56472.

Zaremba, D., Dohm, K., Redlich, R., Grotegerd, D., Strojny, R., Meinert, S., & Dannlowski, U. (2018). Association of brain cortical changes with relapse in patients with major depressive disorder. *JAMA Psychiatry*, *75*(5), 484–492.

Zavlis, O., Story, G., Friedrich, C., Fonagy, P., & Moutoussis, M. (2025). A systematic review of computational modeling of interpersonal dynamics in psychopathology. *Nature Mental Health*, •••, 1–11.

Zhang-James, Y., Chen, Q., Kuja-Halkola, R., Lichtenstein, P., Larsson, H., & Faraone, S. V. (2020). Machine-learning prediction of comorbid substance use disorders in ADHD youth using Swedish registry data. *Journal of Child Psychology and Psychiatry, and Allied Disciplines*, *61*(12), 1370–1379. DOI: 10.1111/jcpp.13234

Zhang, L., Zhang, S., Zhang, X., & Zhao, Y. (2025). A Multimodal Artificial Intelligence Model for Depression Severity Detection Based on Audio and Video Signals. *Electronics (Basel)*, *14*(7), 1464.

Zhang, M., Yang, Y., Zhao, Y., Sui, C., Sui, Y., Jiang, Y., & Huang, M. (2024). The application of integrating electroencephalograph-based emotion recognition technology into brain–computer interface systems for the treatment of depression: A narrative review. *Advanced Technology in Neuroscience*, *1*(2), 188–200.

Zhang, T., Sun, L., Yin, X., Chen, H., Yang, L., & Yang, X. (2024). Burden of drug use disorders in the United States from 1990 to 2021 and its projection until 2035: Results from the GBD study. *BMC Public Health*, *24*(1), 1639. DOI: 10.1186/s12889-024-19142-0

Zhang, W., Mao, K., & Chen, J. (2024). A Multimodal approach for detection and assessment of depression using text, audio and video. *Phenomics*, *4*(3), 234–249.

Zhao, C., Xu, Y., Li, R., Li, H., & Zhang, M. (2025). Artificial intelligence in ADHD assessment: A comprehensive review of research progress from early screening to precise differential diagnosis. *Frontiers in Artificial Intelligence*, *8*, 1624485.

Zheng, A., & Casari, A. (2018). *Feature engineering for machine learning: Principles and techniques for data scientists*. O'Reilly Media.

Zheng, J., Wei, X., Wang, J., Lin, H., Pan, H., & Shi, Y. (2021). Diagnosis of Schizophrenia Based on Deep Learning Using fMRI. *Computational and Mathematical Methods in Medicine*, •••, 2021.

Zhong, R., Wu, X., Chen, J., & Fang, Y. (2025). Using Digital Phenotyping to Discriminate Unipolar Depression and Bipolar Disorder: Systematic Review. *Journal of Medical Internet Research*, *27*, e72229.

Zhong, W., Luo, J., & Zhang, H. (2024). The therapeutic effectiveness of artificial intelligence-based chatbots in alleviation of depressive and anxiety symptoms in short-course treatments: A systematic review and meta-analysis. *Journal of Affective Disorders*, *356*, 459–469.

Zhou, Y., Pham, H., & Radev, D. (2019). Addict Free: Mobile support for location-based relapse prevention. In *Proceedings of the Conference on Human Factors in Computing Systems (CHI)*.

Zidaru, T., Morrow, E. M., & Stockley, R. (2021). Ensuring patient and public involvement in the transition to AI-assisted mental health care: A systematic scoping review and agenda for design justice. *Health Expectations*, *24*(4), 1072–1124. DOI: 10.1111/hex.13299 PMID: 34118185

Zlatintsi, A., Filntisis, P. P., Garoufis, C., Efthymiou, N., Maragos, P., Menychtas, A., Maglogiannis, I., Tsanakas, P., Sounapoglou, T., Kalisperakis, E., Karantinos, T., Lazaridi, M., Garyfalli, V., Mantas, A., Mantonakis, L., & Smyrnis, N. (2022). E-Prevention: Advanced Support System for Monitoring and Relapse Prevention in Patients with Psychotic Disorders Analyzing Long-Term Multimodal Data from Wearables and Video Captures. *Sensors (Basel)*, *22*(19), 7544. DOI: 10.3390/s22197544 PMID: 36236643

Zogan, H., Razzak, I., Wang, X., Jameel, S., & Xu, G. (2022). Explainable depression detection with multi-aspect features using a hybrid deep learning model on social media. *World Wide Web (Bussum)*, *25*(1), 281–304.

Zou, Y. M. (2024). Digital Mental Health in the Corporate Sphere: Evaluating Trends, Tools, and Impacts on Organizational Dynamics (Doctoral dissertation, Massachusetts Institute of Technology). [Original source: https://studycrumb.com/alphabetizer]

About the Contributors

Gorkem Derin is a dedicated researcher specializing in trauma research, committed to unraveling the complexities of traumatic experiences and their impact on mental health. With a relentless pursuit of knowledge and a deep empathy for those affected by trauma, Gorkem has emerged as a prominent figure in the field of trauma studies. He is currently employed as a researcher at Istanbul University-Cerrahpaşa.

Kadir Uludag, Ph.D., is an accomplished researcher in the field of Applied Psychology, with expertise in areas such as schizophrenia research, drug addiction, machine learning, and educational psychology. He completed his Ph.D. at the Chinese Academy of Sciences and is currently engaged in a postdoctoral research position at Shanghai Jiao Tong University. In addition to his academic pursuits, Kadir is actively involved in knowledge dissemination and community engagement.

***

Hariz Aftab is a doctoral researcher at Lovely Professional University (LPU), Phagwara, Punjab, India. He is currently engaged in research and contributes actively to academic discourse through his scholarly pursuits.

Mirza Jahanzeb Beg, PhD is a psychologist, researcher, and author specializing in clinical psychology, psychotherapy, and the application of artificial intelligence (AI) in mental health. He holds a PhD in Psychology with a focus on clinical psychology and AI in mental health. He serves as the Head of the Centre for Advanced Behavioural Policy, Innovation and Leadership (CABPIL), which works at the intersection of behavioural science, technology, and policy, addressing themes such as digital inequality, AI ethics, and the psychology of the digital divide. He is also an Assistant Professor of Psychology with expertise in psychopathology, psychotherapy, research methods, and human behavioural disorders. Dr. Beg has published more than a dozen scientific articles and editorials, authored two books, and contributed to national and international journals, magazines, and newspapers. His perspectives on AI and psychotherapy were recently featured on Deutschlandradio (Radio Germany), a national public broadcaster with over 35 million listeners annually, alongside leading scientists from the USA, UK, and Europe. He has worked with researchers ranked among the world's top 2% in mental health at Stanford University and has collaborated with premier Indian institutions such as JIPMER, AIIMS, and NIMHANS. A recipient of a Gold Medal in Clinical Psychology, Dr. Beg also holds advanced training in Diplomacy, International Law, and United Nations procedures from the University of New South Wales, Sydney, and has been mentored by Nobel Peace Prize laureate and President of Timor-Leste, Dr. José Ramos-Horta. Recognized as a thought leader at the intersection of behavioural science, technology, and governance, he has participated in numerous international dialogues and conferences bridging academia, industry, and policy. His national and global engagements include invited lectures, expert panels, and collaborative initiatives on AI, mental health innovation, and societal well-being. Beyond academia, his interests span technology, policy, geopolitics, philosophy, mysticism, music, and poetry.

Kübra Celik holds a BSc in Psychology and completed both her MSc and PhD in Neuroscience, where she conducted translational research to investigate the mechanisms of prenatal stress, epilepsy, Parkinson's disease, and hypoxia. Alongside her laboratory work, she has led and contributed to neuropsychological studies, integrating translational neuroscience with cognitive and behavioral assessment. She is currently working at the Department of Psychology in Fenerbahce University.

Samet Çelik is an Assistant Professor of Experimental Psychology at Bartın University, with a PhD in Neuroscience completed in 2023. His research focuses on the neurobiological effects of environmental factors on brain health, using advanced neuroimaging and electrophysiological methods such as EEG, fMRI, fNIRS, eye-tracking, and cortical thickness analysis.

Eity Maheshwari received her Master's degree in Psychology from Panjab University in 2022, following a Bachelor's in Psychology from the University of Delhi in 2020. She has experience working as a counselling psychologist in a clinical setting and currently serves as a psychologist at Infiheal, a mental health startup based in Mumbai, India.

Aashi Saraiya is an undergraduate psychology student at Mithibai College of Arts in India. At the same time, she is also working as a psychology intern at Infiheal, which is a Healthtech company.

Srishti Srivastava is an entrepreneur and health technologist who holds a B.Tech and M.Tech degree in Chemical Engineering from IIT Bombay (2014) and an Executive MBA from Cornell University (Cornell Maha60 2023–2024). Her journey into psychology began after personal struggles with anxiety following her appearance on TV Quiz Show India's Child Genius, fueling her dedication to mental health. In the public sector, Ms. Srivastava served as a Chief Minister's Fellow in Maharashtra, launching state wide government scheme "MahaTribes" to support tribal artisans. Her private sector experience includes roles as a financial risk consultant at KPMG and leading clinical data analysis at Krixi Corporation, a US-based health tech startup. In 2022, she founded Infiheal to provide accessible, stigma-free mental healthcare, which was applauded for its AI-based scalable approach by Prime Minister Narendra Modi in his 108th national Address. Ms. Srivastava has since contributed to public policy, speaking at the World Bank Roundtable in 2023, presenting her research on digital mental health to 10 US Senate offices in 2024, and advising the Government of Maharashtra on entrepreneurship and skill development. Ms. Srivastava's expertise and commitment to mental health and policy reform continue to drive meaningful, transformative impact.

Sruthi Suresh works as a Psychology Educator and TOK Coordinator at the Knowledgeum Academy in Bengaluru. In 2018, she completed her M.Sc. in Counselling Psychology and worked as an IB DP Psychology Faculty for the next two years. As part of her Ph.D. program at CHRIST University from 2020 to 2025, she has been an active scholar, engaging with the department as a Research Assistant, Teaching Assistant, Impact Assessment Research Team Lead, and Department Magazine Editor. She writes and presents widely on issues related to child and adolescent mental health, teacher education, and social emotional learning.

Kashvi Tuli is a Dance Movement Therapy Facilitator, registered under Creative Movement Therapy Association of India, which is a member of American Dance Therapy Association. She has received her BA Psychology Honors from Indraprastha College for Women, University of Delhi, New Delhi in 2024. Currently, she is also pursuing a Post Graduate Diploma in Guidance and Counseling from Jamia Milia Islamia University, New Delhi.

Anushka Varma received her MSc in Counselling Studies from the University of Edinburgh in 2022, after earning her B.A. (Honours) in Psychology from the University of Delhi in 2021. She worked in crisis intervention at the Edinburgh Crisis Centre for two years before transitioning to her current role as a psychologist at Infiheal, a mental health startup based in Mumbai, India. Her primary research interests include AI and mental health, crisis intervention, and chronic mental health conditions.

Index

A

C

D

E

F

G

I

M

N

P

R

S

T

V

W

www.ingramcontent.com/pod-product-compliance
Lightning Source LLC
LaVergne TN
LVHW081531300926
849161LV00006B/1377